New Science Library presents traditional topics from a modern perspective, particularly those associated with the hard sciences—physics, biology, and medicine—and those of the human sciences—psychology, sociology, and philosophy.

The aim of this series is the enrichment of both the scientific and spiritual view of the world through their mutual dialogue and exchange.

New Science Library is an imprint of Shambhala Publications.

General Editor       Ken Wilber
Consulting Editors   Jeremy W. Hayward
                     Francisco Varela

# THE INFOMEDICAL MODEL

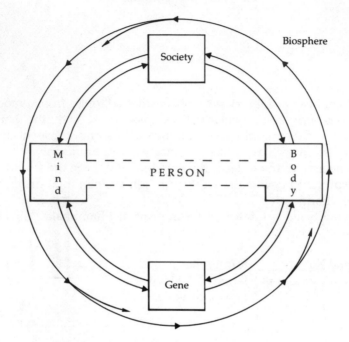

# The Second Medical Revolution

## From Biomedicine to Infomedicine

Laurence Foss and Kenneth Rothenberg

Foreword by George L. Engel, M.D.

New Science Library
SHAMBHALA
Boston & London
1987

*This book is dedicated to*
*Elmer Thomas F. and Madeleine Booth F.*
*Bernard R. and Freda Shuman R.*

New Science Library
An imprint of Shambhala Publications, Inc.
314 Dartmouth Street
Boston, Massachusetts 02116

9 8 7 6 5 4 3 2 1

FIRST EDITION

PRINTED IN THE UNITED STATES OF AMERICA

Distributed in the United States by Random House and in Canada by
Random House of Canada Ltd.

**Library of Congress Cataloging-in-Publication Data**

Foss, Laurence.
  The second medical revolution.

  Bibliography: p.
  1. Medicine—Philosophy. 2. Holistic medicine.
I. Rothenberg, Kenneth. II. Title. III. Title:
Infomedicine.
R723.F67  1987      610'.1      86-29652
ISBN 0-87773-394-5

# Contents

# Foreword

In this seminal volume Laurence Foss and Kenneth Rothenberg have taken it upon themselves to tackle one of the most important and one of the most difficult tasks of this century, that is, to make a solid case for the need to supersede the classical paradigm upon which biomedicine is founded. As such, their *infomedical model* provides a formula which not only builds on but goes considerably beyond what others have so far proposed. In the Kuhnian sense it does truly demarcate a medical revolution.[1]

Who are these revolutionaries who would man the barricades in behalf of a second medical revolution? I first became acquainted with Laurence Foss through a letter dated October 20, 1982, along with a bulky manuscript bearing the forbidding title "The Search for Medical Foundations," by him and Kenneth Rothenberg. By way of identifying himself, he wrote only: "My field of interest is philosophy of science. I have become particularly interested in the area of philosophy of medicine. Six years ago I had the opportunity to participate in the formulation of a rationale statement for instituting a graduate school of nursing. That prospect evolved for me into an evaluation of the field of medicine itself. The results are the enclosed manuscript." He inquired whether I could help to guide this study to a wider audience. I had no clue as to the authors' credentials to undertake so formidable a task.

In my response a month or so later, I chided Foss for telling me so little about himself and his co-author, not even a degree or academic status beyond his use of the stationery of Wayne County Community College. Nonetheless, I went on to say, "I must tell you I was immediately impressed with the clarity of your presentation and the scholarship with which the issues are addressed. . . . Certainly if the work maintains the standard and pace set in the first few chapters, it warrants serious consideration for publication." In due course I did establish that Foss had earned a Ph.D. in philosophy from the University of Notre Dame in 1968 and Rothenberg a doctorate in education from Wayne State University, and that both were instructors in Interdisciplinary Studies at Wayne County Community College in Detroit.

1. T. S. Kuhn, *The Structure of Scientific Revolutions*, 2nd ed. (Chicago: University of Chicago Press, 1970).

Eventually I finished reading the manuscript. Then I reread it, increasingly intrigued not just with the writers' grasp of the problems but also with the originality of their approach. Though obviously medically unsophisticated, they nonetheless achieved unexpectedly high standards even in that area. And best of all, though an early draft, it was eminently readable, not just in its command of the language but in its organization. I realized by then that I had to meet Foss and Rothenberg face to face before I could go any further.

And so we did; for three full days in June 1983, we sat in my study at home and talked. I knew then, beyond any question, that a seminal work was in process and must come to fruition. Not insignificant in that judgment were two considerations. First was their willingness and ability to grapple with and master medical and biomedical concepts at levels of understanding considerably beyond what one ordinarily expects from colleagues not trained in medical disciplines. In that realm I knew I could be of help, at least by calling to their attention salient literature which they would otherwise be unlikely to have access to or knowledge of. And second, which became increasingly clear with the passage of time, was their evident capacity for sustained growth. With each revision they moved beyond what had already seemed reasonably complete and encompassing formulations to make more connections and achieve further integration. Their infomedical model, as it finally appears in the present text, evolved and matured even in the face of no little resistance from me. But they never compromised their professional and intellectual autonomy or integrity. When I found in successive versions that they were still persisting in bracketing the biopsychosocial model with other perspectives that they had characterized as seeking only détente with biomedicine, I naturally enough objected. Their term *détente* referred to medical movements such as holistic medicine, environmental medicine, and behavioral medicine which attempt to complement biomedicine by extending the range of medical focus to include extrasomatic factors but fail to recognize the foundations contradiction such an additive strategy entails. But as step by step they established the philosophical and scientific foundations of their infomedical model, I could not but concede that their analysis of the place of the biopsychosocial model (and of general systems theory in its formulation) in the medical revolution was not without merit. *Biopsychosocial* as a term by which to convey postmodern scientific thinking is clearly inadequate for medicine. As Foss and Rothenberg convincingly argue, *bio, psycho-*, and *socio-* do not by themselves convey anything that is necessarily uniquely human; and what is more exquisitely human than medicine? Further, those prefixes do not even reference the ecosystem. The very word *biopsychosocial*, as though linking three entities, all too readily pulls one back toward the classical Newtonian-Cartesian position, a tripartite dualist re-edition of *psychosomatic* or *psychophysiological*. Unfortunately, too many present-day proponents of the biopsychosocial model are using the term in just this fashion. *Infomedical model*, as a term, makes for a better counterpart to *biomedical* if for no other reason than that it not only stands on its own, but it links information from multiple levels of organization (mind, culture, body), surely a distinctive feature of post-modern science.

In Foss and Rothenberg's hands, the infomedical model clearly articulates for medicine a scientific revolution, in the Kuhnian sense. This revolution is premised on the postmodern scientific and philo-sophic foundations ascribable to such sciences as quantum mechanics, irreversible thermodynamics, and information theory. Essentially it involves a conceptual shift from a biological systems infrastructure to a self-organizing systems infrastructure.

What distinguishes this effort from earlier treatments is the rigor with which they trace historically the implications and the soundness of the scientific and philosophical commitments imposed on medicine, depending on whether they derive from such modern sciences as classical mechanics and statistical thermodynamics which underlie biomedicine, the first medical revolution; or from the postmodern sciences which underlie the infomedical model, the second medical revolution. With penetrating logic they document the inadequacy of the various ecumenical efforts that try to compensate for the deficiencies of biomedicine and still leave the biomedical edifice intact, as holistic medicine, behavioral medicine, and environmental medicine have es-sayed to do. Such compromise solutions cannot overcome the impasse. Only a genuine scientific revolution can do so, one fully founded on the postmodern sciences, as they subsume their predecessors as special cases. For medicine, Foss and Rothenberg remind us, where the issues literally are a matter of life and death, a revolutionary revision is overdue. Merely the irreconcilability of the biomedical model with anything human in itself justifies such a position.

Biomedicine has always relied heavily on the logical-possibility argument. This argument commits the scientist to continue the search for ultimately single-level physical explanations of all phenomena be-cause, although the task may seem difficult, there are no logical barriers to achieving such understanding. But, as the authors develop, such a defense of biomedicine's single-level reductionist agenda fails not so much because it is impossible in principle but because it is impossible in fact. Once postmodern principles of interactionism, emergence, loop structure, mutual causality, and self-organization are in place, neither what is human nor what is ecological can any longer be ignored or excluded by being deemed reducible to something else.

Max Planck once wrote: "A new scientific truth does not triumph by convincing its opponents and making them see the light, but rather because its opponents eventually die, and a new generation grows up that is familiar with it."[2] It remains to be seen how much longer it will be before a generation emerges for whom the worldview engendered by postmodern science is common knowledge. This book should hasten that day.

George L. Engel, M.D., Sc.D. (Hon.)
Professor Emeritus of Psychiatry
Professor Emeritus of Medicine
University of Rochester
School of Medicine

March 1, 1987
Rochester, New York

2. M. Planck, in M. B. Strauss (ed.), *Familiar Medical Quotations* (Boston: Little, Brown, 1968), p. 521.

# *Preface*

At its headwaters the world of rational inquiry is formed of limiting
questions. These are foundations questions, questions reaching out to
the very boundaries of rational intelligibility, to Kant's *Grenze der
Vernunft*. Normally, their answers "go without saying." That is, in our
workaday disciplinary lives, answers to these questions represent, in
Stephen Toulmin's words, "at most, the 'constitutive tautologies' of that
entire disciplinary activity, or scientific 'form of life'—questions that
could apparently be pressed only from intellectual confusion, or else in a
spirit of machine breaking." To raise these questions neither out of
intellectual confusion nor in a spirit of machine breaking is to take the
foundations initiative. One can respond to the calling; it remains for
others to judge whether the initiative has, in actuality, been taken.

# Acknowledgments

We wish to acknowledge the continuing encouragement and editorial comment of George L. Engel, M.D., University of Rochester, whose seminal career work helped inspire this book. We wish also to acknowledge the encouragement of Joan Mersch, C.C.U. Coordinator, Stanford University, and in particular her contribution to Chapter 11. We thank Larry Dossey for seeing promise in this work and assistance in getting it to the editor's desk. To Dr. Margo E. King, Oakland University, we extend our thanks for her ongoing and discerning editorial judgments. To Harry A. Carson for his warm colleagueship, which kept alive the "conversation" over the years. To Janet Goldwasser, not just for her typing skills but for her quiet editorial assistance. And to our late brother in spirit, Hugh Whipple, we acknowledge a debt for a sense of the universe as a self-organizing community.

The authors thank the following publishers for permission to reprint material copyrighted or controlled by them: Academic Press, Inc., for permission to reprint figures from R. L. Blum in *Computers and Biomedical Research* 15, © 1982, and for permission to reprint figures from A. Cunningham and from S. M. Plaut and S. B. Friedman in Ader and Cohen (eds.), *Psychoneuroimmunology,* © 1981; The Lancet Ltd. for permission to reprint figures from S. Greer, T. Morris, and K. W. Pettingale in *The Lancet* 2 (Oct. 13, 1979), © 1979; and *TIME* for permission to reprint the diagram "Tracking the Chemistry of Stress," from *Time Magazine,* June 6, 1983. Copyright © 1983 Time Inc. All rights reserved.

Whereupon are the foundations thereof fastened?
Or who laid the cornerstone thereof?

—Job 38:6

So the second scientific revolution has abandoned the hidden
tenets of the first. Its model of nature no longer assumes that
she must be causal, continuous, and independent. These
assumptions were idealized from everyday experience, and
they were right, and splendidly successful, during two centuries when physics worked and measured on the everyday
scale. They have turned out to be false on the small scale of the
atom and on the large scale of the nebulas, and at least inappropriate to studies of the living.

—Jacob Bronowski
*A Sense of the Future*

Our orthodox models in medicine have come to the same fate
as the models of the first scientific revolution: they are . . .
inappropriate to studies of the living. Just as the older physical
models of the universe wrongly attributed causal and independent qualities to the universe, the current medical models
impart the same qualities to man. And just as the clockwork
picture of the universe that was dictated by these attributes
was abandoned in the onslaught of new data, our mechanistic
views of health and illness will give way to new models which,
too, will be more consistent with the true face of the universe.
. . . A feature of such a new model will be its ability to span the
heretofore unbridgeable chasm separating a humanistic medicine and a reductionistic bioscience. . . . No future prospect for
medicine could be headier than the potential resolution of this
ageless debate.

—Larry Dossey
*Space, Time and Medicine*

# Introduction

Ideas are the spectacles through which we look at events in
order to see information.

—Edward DeBono,
*Po: Beyond Yes and No*

Medicine was at the beginning of civilization the mother of
sciences and played a large role in the integration of early
cultures. Then it constituted for a long time the bridge over
which science and humanism maintained some contact. Today
it has once more the opportunity of becoming a catalytic force
in civilization by pointing to the need, and providing the lead-
ership, for the development of a science of man. The continued
growth of technological civilization, indeed its very survival,
requires an enlargement of our understanding of man's nature.
. . . In its highest form, medicine remains potentially the richest expression of science because it is concerned with all the
various aspects of man's humanness.

—René Dubos,
"Hippocrates in Modern Dress"

In the widest sense, the inspiration for this book is the pursuit of a
postmodern worldview for science, cosmology, and ethics. In this spirit,
we have proceeded in medicine. We find the field of medicine the most
interesting avenue for exploring these areas. Medicine stands out as the
one research enterprise where the soundness of its scientific and philosophical commitments are literally a matter of life and death.

*The Second Medical Revolution* argues for paradigm change in medicine and attempts to construct the matrix for such a change. Our aim is

to explore the loop-structured connections between the individual hu-
manself ("a new way of being an animal in the world") and its roots in
the biological, psychological, and wider cultural milieu and beyond. Our
objective is to identify a fully defined postmodern medical strategy that
treats the individual patient in the context of his or her mutually
interacting "biocultural" identity.

The twentieth century has witnessed a revolution in science.
Stephen Toulmin chronicles this revolution as the passage from a
modern to a postmodern era: "The 'modern' science that developed
during 250 years from A.D. 1650 on has begun, in the course of the
twentieth century, to be superseded by 'post-modern' science; and in
certain crucial respects, as a result, scientists have broken through
bounds and restrictions that were placed on the scientific enterprise by
its original founders" (1981, 70). This book addresses the implications of
this revolution for the scientific and philosophical foundations upon
which the practice of medicine is based. Its thesis is that the foundations
upon which biomedicine is based have been superseded.

Biomedicine is defined as today's scientific medicine. It achieves
medical advances by means of an increased understanding of the
biological mechanisms of the body. The argument follows two fronts. At
the pragmatic level, we examine the difficulties that are encountered
when the premises of biomedicine attempt to explain psychosocial
factors in disease causation. In this way, we see the difficulties inherent
in an enterprise whose premises are, in principle if not always in
practice, reductionistic and dualistic. The significance of these difficulties is heightened as psychosocial factors increasingly emerge as factors
in today's disease burden ("afflictions of civilization"). At the conceptual
level, we examine the transition from modern sciences upon which the
biomedical strategy is based to postmodern sciences upon which a
successor infomedical strategy is based. Here we examine the transition
from such sciences as classical mechanics and statistical thermodynamics to such sciences as quantum mechanics, irreversible thermodynamics, and information theory. Postmodern foundations not only supersede modern foundations, but prove to explain more advantageously a
comprehensive array of factors, including biological, psychological,
sociological, and ecological factors, in disease causation.

Our method is to identify the firmly established philosophical and
scientific foundations of modern medicine. These foundations have
their origins in the seventeenth-century conceptual revolution spearheaded by Newton and Descartes. Today they culminate in Western
medicine's biotechnic successes. We examine these foundations with
respect to both medical events that fall outside their explanatory range,
and their conceptual limitation with respect to the frontiers of postmo-

dern science. Finally, we offer a successor medical model founded on postmodern scientific foundations.

Our contribution, we feel, is twofold. First, this effort underscores the importance of the foundations of medicine as a discipline in its own right. As such, our analysis supports the idea that the premises of medicine should be subject to sustained examination to ensure the best fit of premises to contemporary health care needs. Second, we offer the matrix for a biocultural medicine ("the second medical revolution") constructed upon postmodern scientific foundations.

We conclude that the nature of today's disease burden exacts a change in the premises of the contemporary medical field; the implications of this, when spelled out, are dramatic. Further, findings in twentieth-century postmodern sciences mandate such a revolutionary change in premises. Briefly, such a change can be described as a shift from engineering to cybernetics; otherwise phrased, from a biological systems infrastructure to a self-organizing systems infrastructure—from a biomedical to an "infomedical" model.

## Background

The emergence of modern scientific medicine marked the beginning of today's firmly established medical foundations. Its appearance represented a dramatic change from all that had come before. Prescientific medicine was for the most part based on folk wisdom, *ad hoc* procedures, and subjective explanations. Scientific medicine, on the other hand, introduced the orderly search for the physical causes and cures of disease: medical education today emphasizes both the hard sciences and their derivative reductionist life sciences as the best preparation for medical practice. That this course relies almost exclusively on a physical approach to disease is testimony to the widespread acceptance and influence of the modern scientific revolution.

So successful has this revolution been that it may seem surprising that this book chooses to refer to it as the *first* revolution of medicine. Surely, one might respond, the rise of scientific medicine has been *the* revolution; we need not number it. The medical community, so the astonished observer might argue, has been pointed in the correct direction by embracing scientific rationality. All that is necessary is that the requisite commitment of time, money, and effort be mobilized to build on past successes. Certainly we can anticipate continued success, the achievement of greater understanding and hence the increased ability to control and cure disease by sticking with the strategy that has taken us this far. Lewis Thomas takes just such a position:

Now, new information is coming in cascades, and is filled with meaning and astonishment for all of us. And it should not need mentioning that the greatest part of this information has come from laboratories engaged in the fundamental biological sciences—from the fields of immunology, bacteriophage and microbial genetics, cell biology, membrane structure and physiology, neurophysiology, and molecular biology. (1977, 119)

The fields that Thomas points to have yielded important information and promise to continue to do so in the future. They serve as a checklist of reductionist sciences, the signature of modern scientific medicine. Their centrality to the contemporary medical community is the mark of the first medical revolution.

We use the term *revolution* in the Kuhnian sense of a change in paradigm. A reigning paradigm is the conceptual framework that determines in what manner we approach the world in general and a specific area of interest in particular. Thomas Kuhn states that "paradigm changes do cause scientists to see the world of their research-engagement differently. In so far as their only recourse to that world is through what they see and do, we may want to say that after a revolution scientists are responding to a different world" (1970, 111). We will argue that certain events that are currently perceived as "crisis" issues in medicine cannot be dealt with adequately by continuing with medicine as usual. Certain issues facing the medical community can best be understood as signs pointing to the need for a new formulation of such touchstone concepts as those of disease, patient, health, and therapy. Such a reconceptualization is consistent with the emerging understanding of one of the leading concepts of postmodern science, self-organizing systems.

We begin with medicine's current "predicament." From one perspective, the medical enterprise is flourishing. The dollar value of activity generated has grown exponentially over the past decade. Research budgets since World War II have soared. Dramatic breakthroughs as well as the discussion of impending discoveries are a routine part of news reporting. Biotechnology is a contemporary catchphrase on the lips of everyone from medical professionals to investors. Infusing today's medical enterprise is a sense of optimism. John Knowles's claim that "we have developed the finest biomedical research effort in the world, and our medical technology is second to none" (1977, 7) reflects this underlying optimism. A commonly held view is that medical science is on the right track ("it is biological science that most of us in medicine are betting on for the future" [Thomas 1977, 111])—hence, dramatic breakthroughs are a matter of time and effort.

From another perspective, the medical enterprise is in a state of crisis. Critics have surfaced both outside and within the medical community. Books and articles routinely appear that question the present and future status of medicine—some with such ominous titles as "The End of Medicine," "Medical Nemesis," "Doing Better and Feeling Worse," "The Unkindest Cut," "The Post-Physician Era." These sources of criticism are, of course, related. On the external front, the medical enterprise is attacked on grounds such as these:

- The growing concern that medicine's range of significant etiological factors is limited. Too much that pertains to our general sense of health falls outside the domain of medicine per se.
- Medicine's failure to achieve the same successes in the cure of chronic diseases as it has with infectious diseases. The disappointing results to date from the expensive war on cancer serve as an example.
- Medicine's guidance by principles that fail to acknowledge the human role in creating social conditions (overcrowding, crime, pollution, etc.) that themselves are agents in promoting disease.
- The dissatisfaction resulting from the depersonalization of the doctor-patient relationship—an index of which is the increased numbers in the medical ranks who provide specialized as opposed to primary care.

These issues and others are examined throughout this book. We argue that cumulatively they add up to the need to make a choice: Do our current spectacles enable us to see today's health needs and administer wisely to them? Or is an examination called for to ensure that the last prescription, so effective over the past century (the first revolution), continues to provide the kind of binocular vision useful for seeing the full range of these needs? The objective of this study is to show that such an examination is in order and that in making it—gauging the continued suitability of our premises—we will discover that a second medical revolution is both necessary and in some sense under way. Briefly sketched, our argument proceeds along the following four steps:

1. The firmly established foundations of modern scientific medicine are identified. It is the scientific and philosophical commitment to the natural science paradigm that provides the foundations for the biomedical model.
2. Critics of biomedicine present their case. Here medical countermovements are identified. The strengths of their arguments as well as their failure to restructure medical foundations are examined. Nevertheless, their efforts are recognized as a prelude to change.
3. Here the critique of modern medicine is aimed at the foundations level. The scientific and philosophical argument for paradigm succession is offered. Postmodern scientific findings are used to argue in favor of a revolutionary shift from a biological systems infrastruc-

ture to a self-organizing systems infrastructure, or from a biomedical to an "infomedical" model.

4. The revolutionary implications of the self-organizing systems foundations are explored. In particular, with respect to today's leading diseases, diagnoses and therapies of biomedical pathophysiology are contrasted with those of infomedical pathopsychosociophysiology.

A more detailed look at these steps follows.


# The Argument

*Part One.* The first goal of this book is to offer a framework in which today's state of medical affairs is made intelligible. This involves presenting the biomedical model. Such a presentation will provide the reader with today's story of medicine—the broad sweep of ideas, major premises, images, and influences on Western medical thought. Together they represent the influence of medicine's first revolution—the rise of Enlightenment Age science and its impact on medicine. As such, the biomedical model is based on the dominant natural science paradigm, which in turn guides the research and practice activities of the medical enterprise. Invoking Kuhn's definition, a paradigm is based on "accepted examples of actual scientific practice—examples which include law, theory, application, and instrumentation together—[and] provide models from which spring particular coherent traditions of scientific research." The generally accepted paradigm becomes the basis for "normal science," which is "research firmly based upon one or more past scientific achievements, achievements that some particular scientific community acknowledges for a time as supplying the foundation for its further practice" (1970, 10). In rendering the biomedical model, we see that it is founded upon a generally accepted tradition that has all the important characteristics of a reigning paradigm, and that medical researchers and self-conscious practitioners are engaged in the activity of normal science based on this tradition.

At the foundation of the biomedical model is the assumption that the principles and methodology of natural science permit a scientific approach to the genesis and cure of disease. General acceptance of modern scientific explanatory assumptions serves as a methodological directive in the conduct of inquiry for the contemporary medical enterprise. Such assumptions exercise great influence over most of today's medical research and clinical practice agenda. Among the presuppositions animating these modern sciences are a methodological reductionism and operational dualism. These imbue, in turn, medical science. For example, modern scientific medicine, three centuries after Descartes, is still based, in George Engel's words, on "the notion of the body as a machine, of disease as a consequence of breakdown of the machine, and of the doctor's task as repair of the machine" (1977, 131). Even so humanistically oriented a physician and researcher as Lewis Thomas firmly adheres to the doctrine of specific disease causation (exemplified in the nineteenth-century triumph of the germ theory of disease), whereby disease is caused often by a single factor, sometimes by a cluster of factors—but invariably physical factors. Says Thomas: "For every disease there is a single key mechanism that dominates all others. If one can find it, and then think one's way around it, one can control the disorder. . . . In short, I believe that the major diseases of human beings have become approachable biological puzzles, ultimately solvable" (1979, 168). Because human patients are presupposed to be complex biological organisms, medical problems are reducible to physiological and ultimately cellular and molecular phenomena with the aim of finding a mechanism that is central to the problem.

The basis for the natural science strategy choice can be traced to the dramatic successes of modern science ("the scientific revolution") over the past three centuries. Thus, biomedical proponents argue that emulating this strategy provides the soundest methodological policy for the medical community and, in fact, many successes in medicine serve as instances of the wisdom of this choice. The decline of infectious diseases, a legacy of medicine's first revolution, serves as an exemplar of the applications of modern scientific principles to both disease understanding and cure. The foundational significance of the natural science strategy on the biomedical model suggests the need to fully elaborate the presuppositions upon which it is founded and the medical paradigm it entails.

The scope of biomedical research and practice is identified and referred to as "biomedical reductionism." Biomedical reductionism has evolved such that it may itself be distinguished according to either the classic "one disease, one cause" approach or a more complex "disease as a symptom of systemic disorder" approach. Here the system referred to is a bodily system in that the diagnostic laws invoked are predominantly those of pathophysiology. It is generally acknowledged that most research and practice carried on in the medical enterprise are either mechanically or, more often, systemically oriented in this latter somatic sense.

In the course of formally spelling out the biomedical model, particular attention is focused on its implications with respect to three significant concepts: disease, patient, and range of appropriate therapies. The definitions given to these concepts are an artifact of the espoused underlying paradigm. Kuhn argues that the paradigm guiding the enterprise determines what problems warrant research, which observations serve as data, how the scientist responds to and anticipates the world—literally, "a paradigm is prerequisite to perception itself" (1970, 113). This study, in discussing the biomedical model or any potential successor, will pay particular attention to how the guiding paradigm encourages the medical researcher or practitioner to define or "see" disease, patient, and therapy. Briefly, the natural science paradigm encourages the medical community to see or conceptualize the nature of disease as a process accounted for by deviations from the norm of measurable biological (somatic) parameters caused by an intrinsically damaging physical change agent or too much or too little of some critical factor. This agent or factor may determine the time of onset, the severity, and the course of a disease. The human patient is conceptualized as a biological organism such that, in Descartes's phrase, "were there no mind in it at all, it [the body] would not cease to have the same functions." And appropriate treatment is conceptualized as a physical intervention (chemical, electrical, or surgical) that will counteract the pathogenic agent and neutralize it or supplement a deficiency.

According to the concepts above, the biomedical model/paradigm encourages the view that disease can in principle be explained by means of the language of the life sciences, such as pathophysiology, bacteriology, and histology. These disciplines, in turn, are explained (their cognitive content is reduced) by means of the language of the biophysical and physical sciences. This interplay of explanatory levels (medical disciplines ultimately reducible to the language of chemistry and physics) constitutes a significant strength of the biomedical model. Embracing the natural science strategy commits the medical researcher to pursue a reductionist strategy—termed the "hard science turn"—that has achieved stunning successes in the natural sciences. Endorsed with confidence, it is a strategy that can lead to the kind of results sought by the medical community. And proponents would argue that medicine needs only to stay the course. The first revolution is *the* revolution.

*Part Two.* In Part Two, the charge is made that the biomedical model is pathology-inducing in its own right by virtue of its systematic exclusion of extrasomatic etiological factors in its disease equation. Critics of biomedicine claim that such practice places an overemphasis on the *diseased body* and fails to administer adequately to the needs of the *sick person*. Herein lies the debate in the contemporary medical foundations arena: the biomedical reductionists versus a group of several countermovements ("the insurgents") promoting such alternatives as holistic, behavioral, and environmental medicine.

It appears that the countermovements taken together offer the medical community a choice between fundamentally different orientations. Accordingly, it seems that the controversy between the biomedical establishment and the insurgents would lead the medical community into a thoroughgoing debate over foundation issues. It is a contention of this study that this is *not* the case. Importantly, it can be shown that the controversy shows no promise of being resolved so that the medical enterprise adopts a more adequate alternative medical model (and underlying paradigm). The reason is that the countermovements fail to offer distinct laws and premises both grounded scientifically and entailing an approach to disease that encompasses all significant etiological factors. To overcome the shortcomings of biomedicine would require such a dramatic reconceptualization of medicine's foundational premises as to signal the emergence of medicine's second revolution.

One reason proponents of medical countermovements do not follow through with a sustained attack on foundational principles is because of the profound influence of the biomedical legacy on their own thinking. The very vocabulary of contemporary medicine—which the insurgents accept and use—secretes the classical science worldview on which biomedicine rests. So pervasive is this influence that even reform-minded elements in the medical community are circumvented from successfully proposing radical (nonbiomedical) approaches by virtue of biomedical presuppositions reflected in such content terms as *disease, cure, system,* and *cause.* No wonder conceptual revolutions are so rare: they must overcome the objections of the experts who have gained status via the reigning paradigm, and they must overcome the embedded bias of the language, which also reflects the reigning paradigm.

*Part Three.* To this point, we have argued that the natural science paradigm and the biomedical model it entails is flawed—it does not provide an adequate image that allows us to "see" the (medical) world in a way that encompasses the full range of significant etiological variables. The task now is to address the central issue facing the contemporary medical enterprise—that is, the choice of an appropriate scientific paradigm on which to base research, practice, and education. The primary goals of Part Three are to ferret out this alternative and show how it can serve both to chart future research directions and to make comprehensible a number of events in contemporary medicine not rationalized by "scientific medicine." Achieving this goal mandates medicine's second revolution.

Two steps are required for an alternative model/paradigm to be taken seriously. The first is to overcome what will be termed the "logical possibility argument." This is the ultimate defense of the principles of the first revolution. It is offered by the natural science advocate and derivatively the biomedical proponent. Their argument, which favors physicochemical reductionism, goes like this:

Like so many other fields of inquiry, the premises underlying biomedicine are adapted from and emulate the premises underlying the conduct of inquiry found in the natural sciences. This is in recognition of the generally accepted view that the premises and research directives of the natural sciences offer the best strategy for any discipline which seeks to have its findings taken seriously. To accept these premises is to accept the promissory note that all phenomena will eventually yield to reductionist explanations. Thus, when an apparent anomaly appears—e.g., placebo phenomena, a seeming mind-body event—the logical possibility argument dictates treating this as a phenomenon that will eventually be reducible to a body-body event. Why? Because there is no logical contradiction in assuming so. In this way the premises underlying medicine's first revolution remain intact. There is no warrant to the assertion that such apparent psychobiological events are in principle irreducible to physical laws. In other words, seemingly anomalous events are construed as events that have yet to be explained in physicochemical terms. They constitute outstanding problems on the research agenda, not challenges to the premises of the paradigm. Calling them anomalies is to commit what Ernest Nagel terms "an elementary blunder." It is to confuse what has yet to be explained with what cannot be explained.[1]

The logical possibility argument is a serious obstacle to overcome for any advocate of an alternative paradigm. To effectively critique the biomedical model must now be viewed as a challenge to the strategy shaping the approach adopted in the basic sciences on which the principles of biomedicine, an applied science, rest. To offer only clinical successes, even under strict experimental conditions, does not ground a revolution in thought or practice. One must also show that these successes can be grounded on basic sciences which themselves provide an explanatory framework that includes premises and research directives—in other words, an intact scientific paradigm on which any serious alternative model must rest. As noted, such a paradigm must include "law, theory, application, and instrumentation together" (Kuhn). The failure of the insurgents to offer such a program (and hence overcome the logical possibility argument) will help explain why in the face of some very exciting clinical results, the medical community often responds with skepticism. The biomedical proponent assumes there are no grounds for giving up his or her paradigm, for it may very well come to explain the same event reductionistically. That this has many times been the case only serves to bolster the reductionist argument.

The second step is to present the successor candidate, that is,

1. The logical possibility argument is in large part derived from the counterarguments Ernest Nagel presents in *The Structure of Science* as he defends the natural science explanatory framework against alternatives which challenge its general applicability.

establish the framework for medicine's second revolution. Here a three-tiered model is required. In this way, the successor model can offer a framework that rivals the existing biomedical model that can boast of such a multileveled approach. In this sense, the components of any serious paradigm would look like Figure I-1.

This three-tiered approach illustrates the complex considerations involved in the choice of a paradigm as well as the demanding requirements imposed on a revolutionary alternative. Considered together, one sees the strong incentive for staying with an existing paradigm even in the face of seeming anomalies. To embrace a paradigm is to accept a whole package of interrelated premises, presuppositions, and commitments—in a word, an integrated worldview. The appearance of seeming anomalies or clinical successes based on alternative premises is not alone sufficient for one to reject the tradition of one's professional preparation. Years of study are spent coming to appreciate the community's prior successes which have been a product of this paradigm or worldview. Involved are "particular coherent traditions of scientific research," in Kuhn's phrase.

Figure I-1 provides a sketch of the components of such a worldview with the characteristics of the biomedical paradigm highlighted. Tier 1—the explanatory strategy—is the most fundamental level. It is at this level that we can identify metaphysical presuppositions or operational

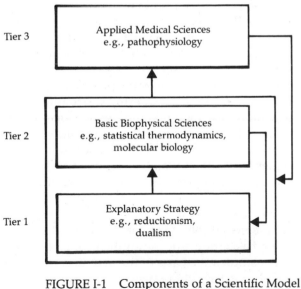

FIGURE I-1    Components of a Scientific Model
for an Applied Science
(A Biomedical Approach)

directives that dictate how the scientist approaches the subject of inquiry. These directives—reductionism, dualism, and others in the case of the biomedical model—shape the methodological approach, define the problems, and determine meaningful data. The nature of these directives is both determined by the basic biophysical sciences (tier 2) and an influence on them (hence the bottom upward arrow). Largely defining the conduct of inquiry of those sciences, these directives influence the direction of their research and so help shape the nature of their findings; and, conversely, explanatory successes of the sciences reinforce confidence in the directives. These sciences—statistical thermodynamics, molecular biology, and others in the case of the biomedical model—provide the "hard science" foundation that theoretically underwrites the principles of the applied science (tier 3). Again, explanatory successes in the applied sciences inspire further confidence in the soundness of their combined base (hence the top downward arrow). Together these three levels provide an integrated framework for a professional community to go about the business (normal science) of pushing outward on its frontiers. They constitute its paradigm, "supplying the foundation for its further practice" (Kuhn). Successes at the tier 2 level provide further reinforcement for the explanatory strategy (tier 1) as well as increased confidence that tier 3 research should continue to reflect a commitment to the overall worldview expressed at the tier 1 level. The logical possibility argument further bolsters confidence in the natural science paradigm. Anomalies, rather than suggesting abandonment of the reigning paradigm, lead to the issuing of a promissory note. This note recommits the researcher to the premises of the paradigm.

The objective of Part Three is to meet the two stated conditions for a conceptual revolution (successor model) in medicine—countering the logical possibility argument and offering a three-tiered alternative model. This study contends that the principles, findings, and methodology of certain postmodern sciences permit a scientific approach to the genesis and cure of disease based on the premise that the patient is at a minimum a biopsychosocial system or, in information theory terms, an information-processing system. Strictly physicalist premises (e.g., regarding the patient simply as a biological organism) are rejected. Endorsed is a concept of comprehensive health care that recognizes the interactive nature of what heretofore has been differentiated into disease cure (biomedicine), patient care (holistic "medicine"), and social "cure" (environmental medicine). Now the three, mutualistically, are seen to define in part the basis for a truly scientific medicine. The adoption of this viewpoint constitutes the basis of the second medical revolution.

The second medical revolution involves a shift in scientific paradigms from a unidirectional (cause-and-effect), "atomic" paradigm, in which a given stimulus has a predictable response, to a mutual causal, "genetic" paradigm. Here a given response is not a direct result of the stimulus; rather it is the result of rule-governed processes that define the stimulated system. As such, the final state of the system is not determined and reducible. This paradigm informs such postmodern sciences as information theory, quantum mechanics, and irreversible thermodynamics. The term *self-organizing systems* is taken from the last-mentioned discipline. A self-organizing systems medical model incorporates mutual causal processes that are characteristic of complex systems whose states are determined by negative and positive feedback. It recognizes that the biomedical model/paradigm based on unidirectional causality cannot be reconciled with what many findings in the medical literature suggest and the insurgents' critique asserts—that is, the patient is at a minimum a biopsychosocial system. And the authenticated scientific grounds for saying so exclude the option of invoking the logical possibility argument.

The contours of a self-organizing systems medical model are offered. Basic conditions necessary for self-organizing systems include an openness toward the environment that involves energy exchange and a system state far from equilibrium. The latter condition is consistent with the ecological insight that systems are in dynamic balance (steady state) rather than an equilibrium state. Self-organizing systems can only be understood based on interactive principles, thereby rejecting reductionist and dualist premises. It is argued that the revised premises embodied in the self-organizing systems model point to a solution to medicine's crisis: the provision of a framework at once scientific and capable of dealing with those extrasomatic aspects of disease inaccessible to biomedical treatment. In particular, the patient can be formally conceptualized as a mind-body unity in an open-system energy and information exchange with the physical and social environment.

At first glance, a position that recognizes the interactive influence of mental-emotional states and physiological states might be dismissed as philosophically naive, an instance of offering a purportedly scientific medical model based on Cartesian interactionism. However, such is not the case. Cartesian interactionism posits that physical events can causally interact with both other physical events and mental events, and that mental events can causally interact with both other mental events and physical events. This position fails because of the puzzling issue of psychophysical causality—how something nonphysical (*res cogitans*) can causally interact with something physical (*res extensa*). This study does not embrace such a position. Rather, the position taken is that of "cybernetic interactionism." This position is "cybernetic" to distinguish it from psychophysical dualism and "interactionist" to distinguish it from a single-level, reductionist explanatory model.

Cybernetic interactionism asserts that complex (self-organizing) systems are irreducible—their primitive unit is the loop structure of which the governing influence and the governed series of orderly processes are logically derivative. As an instance of cybernetic interactionism, we can now view the human patient, passing from morbidity to health through, for example, clinical biofeedback treatment, as a special case of a complex system displaying self-organizing behavior.

The major contention of this study is that self-organizing systems concepts offer the basis for a successor paradigm that can underwrite a more adequate scientific medical model. Graphically, this complex inter-relationship among (1) the explanatory strategy or methodological direc-tives animating the development of a body of science, (2) the basic biophysical sciences themselves, and (3) derivative sciences such as those characterizing an applied discipline like medicine or engineering, can again be delineated in the following triple-tiered fashion. Here the same scheme used to present the biomedical version (Figure I-1) of the necessary components for a scientific model is used to offer a self-organizing systems version. The point to be emphasized is that both versions, though resting on qualitatively different premises, can claim scientific standing.

Both models (Figures I-1 and I-2) claim internal consistency and scientific integrity. However, the self-organizing systems advocates

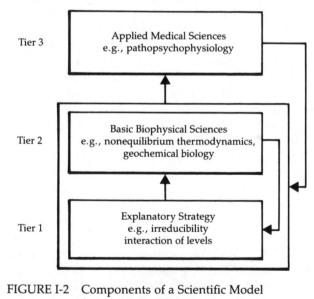

FIGURE I-2   Components of a Scientific Model
for an Applied Science
(A Self-organizing Systems Medical Approach)

bolster their position by claiming that postmodern scientific findings call into question the scientific acceptability of biomedical premises. Here it can be pointed out that there is a body of knowledge (quantum physics and nonequilibrium thermodynamics) by reference to which the implied biomedical ideal of an exclusively physicochemical or single-level description can be shown incapable of realization, not in principle but in fact. Such a body of knowledge underwrites a successor, interaction-of-levels ideal, called here an infomedical model.

*Part Four.* The revolutionary potential of the infomedical model is the focus of the final section of this book. As a first step, two medical strategies are illustrated. The first is an engineering strategy based on natural science foundations. The second is a cybernetic strategy based on self-organizing systems foundations. The dramatic differences between the two crystallize over the interactive levels of organization evident in the latter strategy. Here the critical issue between the biomedical and infomedical paradigms surfaces: can mental events cause disease? An examination of this question through proponents and opponents of such a connection is revealing. Resolution invites examining perhaps the most significant issue facing the medical enterprise: the choice between a reductionist and an interactionist medical strategy. Scientific and philosophical foundations are at stake.

A characteristic of both the self-organizing systems paradigm and the medical landscape that it tries to make intelligible is its evolutionary as well as revolutionary nature. We can see this as the postmodern disease equation takes on added dimensions when the significant interactive levels of organization are factored in. In particular, as the human species has evolved, the nature of the critical imbalances that can be disruptive has evolved. With the emergence of mind, a medically significant "psycho-active" factor joins the somatic component in the disease equation. In this way, members of the human community are subject to diseases that do not threaten members of other biotic communities. With the emergence of qualitatively more complex social structures, a "socio-active" series of factors (sedentary lifestyles, unnatural working environments, deadlines) enters the disease equation. This can be accounted for, in part, by the fact that natural responses (the results of species evolution) no longer dovetail with the heightened pace of social change. The emergence of the world-reshaping impact of collective decision-making as embodied in today's technologies further extends the list of etiologically emergent elements in the disease equation to include "eco-active" factors. Here it is recognized that humans, in the course of cultural development, can impact and have dramatically impacted (i.e., qualitatively changed) the environment in which they must adapt to maintain their health.

This study views medicine in its widest and most fundamental sense. As we examine the major currents of thought that have established modern medicine, certain issues begin to emerge, some radical in nature. These issues, rich in theoretical and philosophical controversy, go to the very foundations of modern medicine. They have for the most part been neglected by the medical community. As we raise them, a picture begins to form. What is born out of the excesses of a strict biomedical (scientific) approach to medicine matures into splintered countermovements that seem to offer polar balance. Yet the persuasiveness and perseverance of biomedicine, with the full weight of early modern science supporting it, provides a framework so ingrained in the vocabulary and thought of the medical enterprise that it diminishes both the attractiveness and the impact of any alternative thesis. We see as a result that the medical community is generally not interested in expending its energy and resources on theoretical or experimental alternatives. Rather, the medical enterprise has understandably concentrated its research efforts (normal science) on projects reflecting the generally accepted biomedical science premises. Challenging the wisdom of continuing to pursue this course of action—the foundations initiative—is the concluding focus of Part Four.

A final comment before proceeding to the body of this study. The medical models (biological and self-organizing systems) discussed are in sharp contrast with each other. The mechanism-systems antithesis draws lines rigidly—e.g., dualist and interactionist. We could, as a qualification, point to a *conceptual evolution* means of expressing the anachronism of pursuing a biomedical approach in a self-organizing universe. Namely, in the course of investigating biological organisms (systems) since Descartes' and Newton's times, our understanding of the properties of (human) organisms has evolved and enlarged: organisms can metabolize but they can also feel, compute, empathize, reflect, socialize, and so on. Hence any basic explanatory strategy must satisfy a number of conditions. To quote Stephen Toulmin:

> First and foremost, it must set aside all the absolute distinctions that were by-products of seventeenth century theory (mind and matter, physical and psychical, etc.), since these represent false and needless antitheses. . . . This means posing all problems having to do directly with intellectual and perceptual capacities in terms of the total relationship between our sensory systems, our brains, and the environment with which we have to deal—which includes the conceptual patterns we inherit or acquire.
>
> We may call the resulting explanation mechanistic [or physicalistic or reductionist . . . ] if we please, but this no longer matters. Once the Cartesian [and Newtonian] antitheses have been cleared away, we achieve nothing by asserting that our systems are material, physical, or mechanical—for these adjectives no longer have any opposites, and their use in no

way alters the fact that we have chosen to study mental activities in the first place. (1967, 831)

Thus the "infomedical" claim made in this book for the emergence of the successive psycho-active, socio-active, and eco-active components of the disease equation just reflects our enlarging understanding of the capabilities of the (human) organism—that it is a complex homeodynamic system embedded in an expanding webwork of cybernetic circularities. The webwork expands over time (natural—and cultural—evolution) as well as our understanding of its full dimensions (conceptual evolution). And the medical researcher ever plays theory catch-up, striving to narrow the gap between the inherited conceptual structure and the new knowledge coming in, often nudging the categories on which the structure is built: a "rebuilding the ship while at sea" activity. So the expression *biological organism* simply receives a more and more comprehensive meaning until, lo, it's our "bionoospheric" superentity with all the properties and interconnections this concept entails!

> . . . the growth of our discriminatory capacities interlocks with the development of our linguistic equipment . . . conceptual phylogeny . . . (Toulmin 1967, 831)

# PART ONE

---

# The First Revolution

Nature, and Nature's Laws lay hid in Night.
God said, *Let Newton be!* and All was *Light*.

—Alexander Pope
"Epitaph Intended for Sir Isaac Newton"

We now view the disease-specific schemes of psychosomatic
medicine as an outdated response to the unknown physiology
of the disease. We have, indeed, reverted to purely organic
hypotheses of its pathogenesis, and these have been confirmed
for us by recent triumphs in the areas of immunology, immunogenetics, and pharmacology.

—Gerald Weissmann
"Proust in Khaki"

Viewed from the perspective of science, the present period of
medicine is an era of great achievement and even greater
promise.

—Donald Seldin
*Beyond Tomorrow*

# INTRODUCTION TO PART ONE

The growth of modern medicine since the seventeenth century parallels the story of many fields of thought and practice. That is, fields have taken on their contemporary characteristics as a result of the influence of modern science. The rise of science signaled a new age, a new worldview, and new foundations upon which to proceed. Among the products was medicine's first revolution. Scientific medicine has emerged as one of humankind's major achievements. Many infectious and parasitic diseases, for example, have now yielded to the increased understanding of the mechanisms of the body. At no other time in history has there been so much optimism regarding the prospects for health care as since the rise of the New Science.

In Part One we examine the emergence of scientific medicine. Doing so, we develop a historical perspective from which to view competing (prescientific and scientific) concepts of health, disease, and appropriate therapeutic care. Of particular interest is how the ideas of progress and reason, so central to the Enlightenment period, came to influence the field of medicine.

We offer the biomedical model as a way of characterizing the dominant premises that guide modern medicine. Derived in part from Newtonian physics and Cartesian dualism, its underlying premises assume that the body can be considered separately from the mind and that understanding the body can proceed from knowledge of its parts and how they interrelate. Biochemical explanations in physiology, for example, offer an illustration of this hierarchy.

In the course of formally spelling out the biomedical model, we will give particular attention to certain concepts. These include the biomedical definition of disease, patient, and therapy. These concepts are central to any discussion of medical theory. They serve to help define the scope of physician responsibility as well as the nature of the curriculum that best prepares one for medical practice. The identification and examination of the biomedical model isolates a theme that will be returned to at other times in this study—the mutuality of philosophy, methodology, and clinical practice.

In Part One we begin with a historical view of the emergence of modern medicine and continue by giving definition to the resulting biomedical model—medicine's first revolution. Next we identify the philosophical foundations of biomedicine. We accomplish this, in part, by examining the natural science worldview and what it assumes, followed by examining the impact this worldview has on a more narrowly conceived medical worldview. Finally, we view as a mutually reinforced, circular process the link between the generally accepted foundations of the contemporary medical enterprise and both the shape of research and the grounds for assessing its success. Briefly, in Part One we will argue that the generally accepted foundations of medicine determine the question to be asked, what methods are used to answer the question, what counts as an answer and, finally, whether the question-and-answer session was a success.

# 1

## The Making of Modern Medicine

The myths of Hygieia and Asclepius symbolize the never-ending oscillation between two different points of view in medicine. For the worshippers of Hygieia, health is the natural order of things, a positive attribute to which men are entitled if they govern their lives wisely. According to them, the most important function of medicine is to discover and teach the natural laws which will ensure a man a healthy mind in a healthy body. More sceptical, or wiser in the ways of the world, the followers of Asclepius believe that the chief role of the physician is to treat disease, to restore health by correcting any imperfections caused by the accidents of birth or life.
                                                            —René Dubos
                                                        *Mirage of Health*

## Historical Roots

Conventionally, medicine's genealogical tree is traced to Hippocrates, the father of Western medicine, from whose writings a holistic concept of disease may be inferred. Typical of fragments that survive is his celebrated description of health: "Health depends upon a state of equilibrium among the various internal factors which govern the operations of the body and the mind; the equilibrium in turn is reached only when man lives in harmony with his external environment" (Dubos 1959, 114). Health is a function of mind-body/nature equilibrium, a psychophysiological-environmental balance or harmony. By implication, disease is a state of mind-body/nature disequilibrium. Whatever serves directly to preserve this equilibrium pertains to health care; whatever serves to restore it pertains to curative medicine. Similar passages can be found throughout the writings of Hippocrates. Consistent with them is Galen's observation in the second century A.D. that depressed women were more likely to get cancer than happy women, so associating personality types with particular diseases. Diagnosing behavioral and biological factors interactively, this suggests ongoing concern for a holistic or biobehavioral approach to medicine. Hence we do not say that we are ill and are made well, but rather that we are well and are made ill. This approach mirrors the Hygieian strain in the evolution of health concepts to which Dubos refers. Health is preserved by way of life and not, as in the Asclepian strain, by treatment of disease: "Health is the natural order of things to which men are entitled if they govern their lives wisely."

Crucial to the reversal from a preservative to a restorative approach were two seventeenth-century events that had a decisive influence on scientific thought to the end of the nineteenth century. These mark the beginning of a conceptual change that was to underwrite medicine's first revolution. One, initiated by Descartes in his *Traité de l'homme*, posited a fundamental division of reality into two separate, independent realms, that of mind, *res cogitans*, and that of body or matter, *res extensa*. The body is a machine, said Descartes, "so built up and composed of nerves, muscles, veins, blood and skin, that though there were no mind in it at all, it would not cease to have the same [functions]." A human being consists of a mind plus a body, much as a unit of transportation might be thought to consist of a driver plus a machine. The nature of their interaction thereafter became the focus of debate. Converging with this bold disjunction of mind and matter was a novel conception of the universe stemming from Newton's *Mathematical Principles of the Natural World*. That work licensed belief in the universe as a great harmonious and materially ordered machine based on the traffic of interchangeable particles moving in a random, disorderly manner and giving rise by their multiplicity to statistical order and regularity, as in classical physics and gas laws. By the eighteenth century the conceptual lens through which reality was viewed had been significantly shaped by these two works. The Cartesian model of two separate and independent realms, thought and matter, encouraged scientists to view matter as inert and entirely separate from themselves, a view fostered by the Newtonian model. Humans, as objective observers, could regard nature as something independent from them and unaffected by the act of observation. Large-scale events unfolded in characteristic, regular ways, following Newton's equations in mechanics and, later, Maxwell's equations in electromagnetics. These processes moved inexorably, independently of the scientist, who was simply a detached observer.

The influence of this physical paradigm on the life sciences was decisive. The natural world, a complex material whole, was composed of assembled atomic parts which, when interacting with sufficient complexity, could form biological systems as complex as human beings. Newtonian mechanics sanctioned the idea of organized complexity, such as found in biological systems, as in principle reducible to the interaction of its physical parts. (From these revolutionary beginnings,

Darwin, two centuries later, was to offer a mechanism—natural selection operating on random mutations—for rationalizing this reducibility.) Cartesian dualism sanctioned the idea of the body as a machine that could be analyzed independently of the mind, much as an automobile engine can be analyzed separately from the driver. Scientific advances made by applying the methodology incorporating these dualistic and reductionist premises undercut the holistic ties to the Greek and Roman approach to health and disease. The body came to be viewed as a machine, independent of psychological and environmental factors. As such, disease, like malfunctioning in a machine, suggested the need for repair.

Thus, the influential ideas that gave birth to the Age of Enlightenment had a revolutionary impact on medical thinking. One result was that the emerging notion of scientific thinking tipped the balance in favor of curative over preservative medicine. This was the beginning of a shift in thinking whose momentum is a contemporary fact in medical disciplines as well as in other areas of contemporary thought. Next, we will examine the considerable influence on medical thinking of the two premises that form the Enlightenment legacy, those concerning progress and reason.

## The Enlightenment Legacy: The Elements of the First Revolution

The "Enlightenment legacy" describes the contemporary influence of ideas having their origins in the Enlightenment Age. This was a period of vast intellectual change. Two historical premises have their roots in this period. Both are offered as significant influences on contemporary medical practice. The first recognizes the emergence of the idea of progress, which encouraged the view that humans are capable, through reason, of improving conditions in human affairs. Joined to this capability, expectations surfaced that the evolving scientific paradigm would be an important vehicle in achieving this promised advance in the human condition. Continuous with this is the second premise, which recognizes that the foundation of reason lies in the application of scientific method. The strategy thought most suitable to the human sciences in order to meet these growing social expectations was the emulation of the methods of the natural sciences. This strategy was generating considerable enthusiasm since it had yielded such impressive results in explaining natural phenomena.

Elucidating the above premises offers a perspective in which to conceptualize contemporary medical science and the practice it entails. This perspective pertains to a tradition that evolved as the modern era of philosophy and science developed. It is referred to as the basis of medicine's first revolution because it encompassed a worldview that heretofore had not been embraced.

Charles Beard says that "among the ideas which have held sway in public and private affairs for the last two hundred years, none is more significant or likely to exert more influence in the future than the concept of progress" (1932, ix–xi). Here progress refers to the idea that civilization has moved, is moving, and will move in a desirable direction. It is surprising how recent is this faith in human progress. John Herman Randall notes that the ancient world had no concept of progress. As late as the Renaissance, humans still looked back at the Golden Age of antiquity as an unreachable peak. "Only with the growth of science in the seventeenth century could men dare to cherish such an overweening ambition" (1940, 382). Two defining characteristics of this period have had an ongoing influence to the present time, particularly on the medical sciences. These are a faith in science and a belief in the human ability to exercise control over that which is understood scientifically. Both notions derive from the idea of progress. Both were revolutionary for their day.

The universe, as the eighteenth century viewed it through Newton's eyes, was a great harmonious and materially ordered machine. All events happening within the universe could be explained by mechanical principles. Newton's influence was a factor in creating an interest in scientific method and the formation of a coherent body of beliefs. Method, a key ingredient of reason, is the critical link between Newton and the emerging diverse fields of inquiry. Reason came to be seen as a force that humans possess to allow them to penetrate appearances. Thus, an understanding of nature provides humankind with the power to shape events. Reason was seen as a power that "does not let us transcend the empirical world, rather to feel at home in it" (Cassirer 1951, 13).

This method, seen as so successful in the investigation of nature, was accepted as appropriate for investigating the social and biological nature of humans as well. The notion of biophysics began to take concrete shape. Thus the emerging medical disciplines were spawned in the shadow of the natural sciences. Ernst Cassirer notes the dramatic spread of Newtonian analysis. He states that "A new field of knowledge of highest importance became accessible to reason as soon as reason learned to subject this field to the special methods of reduction and synthesis" (1951, 11).

The Newtonian worldview, which had an almost immediate impact on scientific investigation, led to a dramatically new conception of the universe in general. Newton's universe was a great clock. It could be reduced to matter in motion and therefore understood according to mechanical principles. In medical studies, these premises seemed to find early confirmation in the development of modern physiology. Thomas McKeown notes Kepler's description of the dioptric mechanism by which the eye produces the retinal image. "A little later," he adds, "there was an even more dramatic demonstration of the validity of the mechanistic approach in Harvey's discovery of the circulation of the blood, which Descartes, needless to say, warmly welcomed" (1979, 4). By the end of the nineteenth century, with the development of the sciences of physiology, cellular pathology, and bacteriology, the preeminence of a biochemical and physiomaterial approach to disease was consolidated. The major elements of the first revolution were in place. The body was recognized as a physiological mechanism, the patient as a biological entity whose protection from disease depended on internal intervention. The highest level of organization studied was the individual organism. Patients were considered independently of the psychosocial and environmental forces to which, in a contrasting (prerevolutionary) Hygieian view of disease, they must adapt in order to maintain health.

Thus, the Enlightenment Age can be seen as an intellectual movement of mass scope. This intellectual transformation heralded a new era in humankind's conceptual approach to the world. "The structure of the cosmos is no longer to be looked at, but to be penetrated" (Cassirer 1951, 11). The age of analysis was born. The human mind came to be seen as an analytic tool capable of penetrating nature, not on the basis of innate certainty, but through the application of reason to objects of experience. The reductionist spirit sought to discover the laws that eighteenth-century intellectuals were confident existed within the grasp of the inquiring mind. As a result, the human role now was one of an active agent fashioning the social world as a result of scientifically gained knowledge.

The idea of progress has at its root the belief that knowledge as embodied in theory is the most fruitful means for enlightened action. Organized scientific inquiry, says J. B. Bury, "was a sign that an age of intellectual optimism had begun, in which the science of nature would play a leading role" (1932, 97). The application of such principles revolutionized medicine and formed the basis for its present state. This bridge, connecting the methods of physical science as the basis for inquiry in diverse areas of human interest, might be one of the most significant results of the eighteenth century. It defines the modern intellectual patrimony. For Randall it is in the construction of a "science of man" or, rather, in the vision of its possibility that the eighteenth century has its soundest claim to important achievement.

We see the significance of the Enlightenment legacy today in the momentum that was generated in this period and the resulting commitments that it has encouraged. The momentum can be attributed to the impressive explanatory and predictive advances that were occurring in the natural sciences. These achievements soon translated into a commitment to focus considerable human energies in applying these same methodological principles to all fields of inquiry. As this is done, so the conviction goes, humans will have the requisite knowledge with which to master their environment and exercise control over their destinies. Here the dynamic relationship of reason, defined in terms of method, and the idea of progress come together to influence human activities. The result was nothing short of a revolution in human affairs in general, and among other areas, medicine in particular. How this momentum, commitment, and resulting conviction have shaped contemporary medical thinking is the subject of the next chapter.

# 2

## The Biomedical Model

Embracing the natural science paradigm provided the foundation for the rise of biomedicine. This led to advances that would come to distinguish the first revolution. Chapter 2 will serve to formally spell out the biomedical model. Interest will focus on identifying three defining concepts of any medical model—disease, patient, and therapy—and in particular how the biomedical model defines them. Also to be discussed is the rise of the objective physician—a dramatic byproduct of the biomedical commitment.

## The Biomedical Model: Matter over Mind

By the mid-nineteenth century medicine was fully integrating first-revolution premises into medical practice. Medicine was infused by a physicalist approach. Most notable during this period was the recognition that certain organic entities (e.g., bacteria) caused certain diseases and that their pathogenic effect could be avoided or reversed by certain substances (e.g., antitoxins and vaccines). As Lester S. King chronicles, a "revolution in attitude" was launched. Most notable was Koch's discovery of the tubercle bacillus. "A new vista was opening up. If the cause of tuberculosis were found, the prospects were truly bright for future discoveries. Theory and laboratory experimentation acquired greater esteem" (King 1983, 796). The medical community as well as the general population gained faith that, as offending pathogens were discovered, the appropriate vaccine would be developed. In the ensuing three-quarters of a century much has been achieved to vindicate this belief. Lewis Thomas notes, "We use the hybrid term 'biomedical' science as shorthand to describe the whole inquiry that underlies modern medicine," adding, "it is biological science that most of us in medicine are betting on for the future, and it therefore seems natural to attach the words biology and medicine together to name the enterprise" (1977, 111).

George Engel describes the biomedical approach as having "a firm base in the biological sciences, enormous technologic resources at its command, and a record of astonishing achievement in elucidating mechanisms of disease and devising new techniques" (1977, 129). Yet, in his view, this approach has brought medicine to a state of crisis. The expression of that crisis highlights a major orientation of biomedicine: "Medicine's crisis stems from the logical inference that since 'disease' is defined in terms of somatic parameters, physicians need not be concerned with psychosocial issues that lie outside medicine's responsibilities and authority." For the moment, whether they should or should not is not at issue. For present purposes, clarifying the nature of this alleged crisis provides an opportunity to see how members of the medical profession define the scope of their field and the limits of their responsibility. The concepts that are at the foundation of the biomedical model surface as arguments concerning what is medically relevant. For example, Engel cites a comment by one authority at a Rockefeller Foundation seminar on the concept of health who urged that medicine "concentrate on the 'real' diseases and not get lost in the psychosociological underbrush." Another participant is said to have called for "a disentanglement of the organic elements of disease from the psychosocial elements of human malfunctions," arguing that medicine should deal only with the former. The implication is that since medicine wisely restricts itself to those elements of disease which can be explained in the language of physiology, biology, and ultimately biochemistry and physics, physicians are well advised to steer clear of problems that cannot be placed on the same secure, scientific footing. These problems include those that the first quoted participant said have "arisen from the abdication of the theologian and the philosopher" and, conceivably, the psychologist, the sociologist, and the anthropologist.

Such views serve to define the range of concerns for which doctors hold themselves responsible. Accordingly, there is scientific medicine, and this deals systematically with a certain range of health problems. That there is a still wider range of problems, arising from "the psychosocial elements of human malfunctions," should not automatically mean that they fall within the physician's responsibility. They might fall within the range of psychosomatic medicine, public health care, medical anthropology, or some other allied health field external to "scientific medicine" and the physician role per se. By the mid-twentieth century these fields had become more extramedical specialties than dimensions of medicine itself. Here we see the implications of the reductive hierarchy in medical education—a legacy of the Flexner Report. As such, medicine "must by definition become dissociated from concerns of a social nature, the solution of which lie outside [medicine's] boundaries" (Seldin 1977, 34).

By the middle of this century a medical strategy was firmly in place.

It mandated a "keen sense of the biologic basis of disease" (Evans 1978, 256). Medicine's first revolution was an accomplished fact. Its underlying premises were that the body can be separately considered from the mind (dualism) and that understanding the body can proceed from knowledge of its parts and how they interrelate (reductionism). Physiology and cellular pathology (but not, for example, historical demography or medical ecology) became primary disciplines of study. Their principles were subsumed—in theory at least—under laws governing the sciences of molecular biology, biochemistry, and physics. Biochemical explanations in physiology offer an illustration of this hierarchy. Clinical practice is based on the principles of physiology. Physiological processes themselves largely fall within the scope of the same physicochemical laws governing similar processes in inorganic systems. Concerned with organs, tissues, and cells, the theoretical focus of physiology is subsequently trained on molecules, leading to today's molecular theory of disease causation. At any given stage, of course, promissory notes have to be issued. The situation in physiology today exemplifies the somewhat incomplete character of the life sciences relative to the tacit program of establishing continuity with the laws of chemistry and physics.

By the turn of the century, the psychosocial dynamics attending illness had in large part been relegated to the side effects of pathology. Research was guided by the "one diagnosis to a patient" strategy animating Koch's celebrated postulates. "No physician can properly think out a process of disease unless he is able to fix for it a place in the body," proclaimed Rudolf Virchow toward the close of the nineteenth century. From this time onward, medical thinking concentrated more and more on causal mechanisms affecting organs, tissues, and cells to the relative exclusion of psychosocial and econoetic variables. The development of biomedical technologies accelerated this orientation. As the twentieth century began, the microscope—like the stethoscope earlier and the x-ray later—had, says Stanley Reiser, "encouraged a physical separation of the doctor from his patient in the diagnosis of illness." As biomedical technologies proliferated, this separation was to widen: "To some clinicians this separation did not appear to endanger accurate diagnosis, for they believed that the signs of disease elicited at the patient's bedside were secondary in importance—mere indications of more fundamental alterations in tissues that diagnostic technology such as the microscope could detect" (1978a, 90). In effect if not in intention, medical theory and clinical practice came to rest on a disease concept based on a methodological commitment to the independence of observer (physician) and observed (patient), and a philosophical commitment to the separation both of mind and body and of accidental and environmentally induced way-of-life factors.

The medical definition of disease, courses basic to the medical school curriculum, and the range of treatment therapies for which physicians held themselves responsible—all were consistent with Descartes' conception of the person (patient) according to which "though there were no mind in it at all, [the body] would not cease to have the same functions." This separation of the organic elements of disease from other elements of human malfunction underlies what is commonly regarded as scientific medicine. The body of knowledge underwriting it is double-tiered. At bottom are the sciences forming today's pre-med curriculum. Stemming from this body of knowledge and shaping clinical practice are the sciences constituting the medical school curriculum. The basic sciences are physics, chemistry, and biology, which underpin the specifically medical focus of disciplines that are concerned with bodily structure, function, and disease processes.

In method and orientation these two tiers of science, basic and applied, reflect a concept of disease roughly circumscribed by the following definition:

> Disease: (Fr. *des* from + *aise* ease) a definite morbid process having a characteristic train of symptoms: it may affect *the whole body or any of its parts*, and its etiology, pathology and prognosis may be known or unknown.
> —*Dorland's Illustrated Medical Dictionary* (1974) [italics added]

The locus of disease is the body; the human patient is denoted by the phrase "the whole body."

Now, the body may be viewed strictly on the model of a machine, a physiological mechanism, with disease as the result of a defective part. Or the body may be viewed on the model of an organism, with disease as a failure in the growth, development, or adjustment of the biological organism as a whole rather than any of its parts taken in isolation. Although Cartesian in implying a separation of mind and body, this view recognizes body systems, organs, and functions, not as separate entities or processes, but as dynamically interrelated. While disease may affect one particular organ or system, the manifestations and consequences of disease affect the entire body of the individual; the parts of the organism are capable of nonsummative behavior. This interpretation best describes the biomedical approach. We may represent this mathematically according to the following system of simultaneous differential equations:

$$\frac{dQ1}{dt} = f(Q_1, Q_2, \ldots Q_n) \quad \text{(nervous system)}$$

$$\frac{dQ2}{dt} = f(Q_1, Q_2, \ldots Q_n) \quad \text{(endocrine system)}$$

$$\frac{dQ3}{dt} = f(Q_1, Q_2, \ldots Q_n) \quad \text{(immune system)}$$

.

.

.

———————

$$\frac{dQn}{dt} = f(Q_1, Q_2, \ldots Q_n) \quad \text{(biological organism)}$$

where $Q_1$ stands for any of the interrelated body systems, organs, or functions.

A number of assumptions govern the source of pathogenicity and hence the treatment based on this concept of the patient. Some of them are:

PATHOGENICITY

*Too much.* Examples are ultraviolet light, cholesterol, water, carbon dioxide, growth hormones, insulin.

*Too little.* Examples are protein, water, vitamins, insulin, growth hormones.

*Intrinsically damaging.* Examples are microbial agents, radiation, chemicals.

TREATMENT

Counteract the above influences by reducing, replacing, neutralizing.

In the above scheme, it should be noted that present-day biomedical theory no longer places all physical change agents in the environment; some are internal, at least within their ahistorical perspective, e.g., autoimmunity, genetic (molecular) defects, and insulin deficiency.

We are now in a position to state three premises of the biomedical model:

PREMISE 1: DISEASE

Disease is conceptualized as a process accounted for by deviations from the norm of measurable biological (somatic) parameters. The causes include the presence of too much or too little of a critical substance, or an intrinsically harmful change agent.

PREMISE 2: PATIENT

The human subject of disease is conceptualized as a biological organism ("whole body") such that, in Descartes's phrase, "were there no mind in it at all, it [the body] would not cease to have the same functions."

Premise 3: Therapy

Appropriate treatment is conceptualized as a physical intervention (chemical, electrical, or surgical) that will compensate for the surplus or deficiency or neutralize the pathogenic agent.

According to this premise set, disease can in principle be explained by means of the language of the life sciences, such as pathophysiology, bacteriology, and histology. These disciplines in turn are explained (their cognitive content is reduced) by means of the language of the biophysical and physical sciences. These include molecular biology, biological chemistry, and ultimately physics.

The above premises and their underlying explanatory vehicles permeate any characterization of the biomedical model. In fact, the best way to understand the contemporary medical enterprise is to view it as the interrelationship of metaphysics, science, and practice. This important interplay can be illustrated in Table 2.1.

This biomedical model has been identified by means of its broad historical development and the ensuing mutual influence of the three

TABLE 2.1   The Biomedical Model

| PHILOSOPHY | DISCIPLINARY MATRIX | PRACTICE |
|---|---|---|
| *Concepts by Which to Approach the World* | *Scientific Disciplines of Medical Science* | *Medical Strategy* |
| Reductionism | Life Sciences: | 1. Treat disease as a deviation from the norm of measurable biological parameters. |
| Mechanism | Pathophysiology | |
| Causality | Bacteriology | |
| Determinism | Histology | |
| Dualism | etc. | |
| *Concepts by Which to Approach Inquiry* | (These are in turn explained by) | 2. Treat the patient as a biological organism. |
| Objectivity | | 3. Appropriate treatments include compensating for or replacing critical substances and neutralizing intrinsically damaging agents. |
| Ahistoricity | Physical Sciences: | |
| Aculturicity | Molecular biology | |
| Impersonality | Biochemistry | |
| Universality | Physics | |
| Self-correctiveness | | |
| Convergence | | |

categories, philosophy, disciplinary matrix, and practice. As suggested by the graphic in Table 2.1, the metaphysical presuppositions—concepts by which to approach the (medical) world—underwrite the methodologies of the life sciences and the physical sciences. The successes in these disciplines, particularly those in the physical sciences from the seventeenth century forward, provide further grounds for accepting the metaphysical presuppositions upon which they are based. Together they represent a significant first-revolution impact on medical theory and practice.

Historically speaking, the idea that disease is an effect of a diagnosable physical condition—too much, too little, or intrinsically damaging—and that treatment consists of reversing this physical condition offered an economical explanation for a number of remarkable cures. Here, for example, patients suffering from cholera or syphilis or tuberculosis benefited from the pharmacological action of the drug prescribed; vitamin-deficient patients benefited by vitamin supply; lead-poisoning patients benefited from removal or detoxification. Successes like these provided support for the presuppositions and disciplines that contributed to this practice. Further, they lend support to the idea that metaphysical conceptions and methodological mandates have influenced the practice of modern Western medicine.

Nowhere is the interrelationship of philosophy and practice more clearly evident than in the research directives of biomedicine. For example, Attallah Kappas's definition of clinical research reemphasizes its natural science foundations. We can recognize in his statement elements of the Enlightenment legacy—materialism, optimism, and scientific rationality. Observing first that the term "clinical research" encompasses a broad range of medical and scientific activities "whose ultimate purpose is to understand the normal physiology of man and to make discoveries concerning the mechanisms and treatment of human diseases," Kappas further specifies: "But a more specific definition . . . focuses . . . at the closest interface between medicine and science, and therefore as an endeavor that has the potential for generating new knowledge, which can flow both toward the practice of medicine and toward the biological and chemical sciences on which the rational practice of medicine can be based" (1977, 54).

According to G. L. Spaeth and G. W. Barber, "A major determinant of our conception of disease is our epistemology, our understanding of how we know. As our epistemology changes, so do our concepts of disease and health." As an example, these authors cite "Occam's razor," the tenet that simplicity is a virtue and if hypothetical entities can be avoided in an explanation, they should be. They state: "As medical students we were taught this fundamental principle in the form of 'one diagnosis to a patient.' The optimism and the methodology generated by those beliefs, and the application of this 'experiential simplification,' led to the remarkable scientific discoveries that have become a hallmark of the last 300 years of mankind's development" (1980, 11). Here we see how epistemological considerations (in this case a single cause having a single effect) influence the thrust of medical diagnostic efforts—the focal point of medical practice.

Ian McWhinney states that "a constant theme is the tendency for medicine to be dominated by the mechanistic values of objectivity, precision, and standardization. This dominance of mechanistic over other values has not only affected our actions but also our concept of medical knowledge. . . . Medical education has become concerned overwhelmingly with objective knowledge. The episteme of technology has become the episteme of medicine" (1978, 299).

Doubtless much of the success accruing to a strategy based on the biomedical approach stems from the compactness of its conceptual base, which enables diagnosis to isolate variables highly tractable to idealization and measurement. Bertrand Russell aptly remarks, "Scientific progress has been made by analysis and artificial isolation. It is therefore in any case prudent to adopt the mechanistic view as a working hypothesis, to be abandoned only when there is clear evidence against it" (1948). Historically, the Cartesian identification of "real" diseases with the organic elements of disease reflects metaphysical assumptions about the nature of the human being.[1] However, the modern adoption of this identification doubtless owes as much to methodological considerations and the availability of new diagnostic techniques and disciplines as to metaphysical preconceptions. Below, we argue that the complex interplay of these forces has given rise to today's dominant medical strategy and the biomedical model on which it rests.

We are now in a position to offer two biomedical laws:

Biomedical Law 1: Human diseases reflect the outcome of an interaction among measurable physiologic variables. Prevalence, cause, and outcome of disease are a function of the physicochemical laws governing the human organism.

Biomedical Law 2: Change in the state of one physiological variable mutually activates an appropriate change in another.

A consistent theme throughout any discussion of the biomedical model is the philosophical commitment to the separation of mind and

1. Richard Carter (1983) argues that Descartes's philosophic works, no less than his works in physics and mathematics, were "vastly elaborated foundations for his medicine"; that "the unique goal of Descartes' thought was an improvised medical therapy, and even his philosophy is a medical philosophy." He adds: ". . . modern thought starts from questions posed by Descartes' medical research and theory into questions concerned with such matters as the definition of life, the neuro-anatomical base of perception and thinking, and the relation between mind and body."

body and the methodological commitment to the idea that all bodily events have determinate causes. A testimony to this commitment is echoed in an editorial statement in the *New England Journal of Medicine:* "It is time to acknowledge that our belief in disease as a direct reflection of mental state is largely folklore" (Angell 1985*a*, 1572). The assumption is clear that extraphysical agents indicate the need for further scientific investigation. They are invoked until the "relatively simple" physical causes are eventually identified.

In the next section we examine a dramatic by-product of the commitment to the biomedical model. It is the rise of the objective physician. Here the relationship of science and technology is viewed in a medical context, with emphasis on their interrelationship and their combined impact on practice.

## Scientific Medicine and the Objective Physician

Out of medicine's first revolution arose today's concept of objective diagnosis and rational treatment—the two pillars of biomedical practice. To appreciate the intellectual revolution that this represents, it is useful to recall the state of the art of medicine as late as the nineteenth century. Therapeutics were still entirely empirical and largely directed toward the relief of symptoms. "Scientific medicine, which it ought to be my duty to teach," wrote Claude Bernard in 1848, "does not exist." Throughout the seventeenth and eighteenth centuries the dominant clinical view was epitomized by the relative indifference shown by physicians to the collateral ideas that microorganisms could generate disease and that the microscope (which was readily available as early as the seventeenth century) could be used in advancing that idea. Such ideas bore no relation to still prevalent humoral theories of disease. This indifference is exemplified in the attitude of the illustrious seventeenth-century physician Thomas Sydenham and his philosopher-physician friend John Locke. Both scorned the use of the microscope on grounds that it diverted physicians from interest in bedside observations. According to Reiser, they and their colleagues regarded as hopeless any efforts to investigate events inaccessible to the unaided senses, believing "that Nature's inner structure was too recondite to master." Locke further argued, "Even if physicians could describe the minute composition of matter, no logical relationship existed between the macroscopic and microscopic worlds, so that no predictions about the one could be made from the knowledge of the other" (Reiser 1978*a*, 73).

Not until the latter part of the nineteenth century, says J. E. Stark, (1975, 278), did advances in experimental pathology and pharmacology begin to establish medicine on a rational basis, largely as a result of the work of giants like Bernard, Virchow, Pasteur, Lister, and others. Reiser speaks of this period as marking the rise of the "objective physician." The progression from the bedside-manner physician approach characteristic of pre-nineteenth-century medicine to today's objective physician mirrors the development and use of a series of diagnostic techniques for more accurately identifying and measuring changes in disease symptoms. It also mirrors a subtle shift in what count as disease symptoms and diagnostic criteria. The ready availability of new and accurate diagnostic methods for detecting somatic signposts can be shown to have wielded an enabling influence on the prevailing concept of disease. Variables measured by the new fact-gathering techniques by that very fact acquired etiological prominence. The ability to secure precise numerical measures of physiological processes—like heart sounds, blood and respiratory rates, body temperature—affected the physician's perception of the nature of disease. Detection of pathology came increasingly to consist in translation of physiological events into the quantifiable language of machines. Success of treatment based on the quantitatively more accurate information available fortified the physician's growing conviction of disease as a somatic phenomenon, a conviction by degrees institutionalized through increasing reliance on this information. Technological innovation (itself propelled by this growing methodological orientation) made possible new diagnostic methods. And these methods, in turn, implicitly subserved a particular medical strategy. Criteria of medical objectivity (medical practice based on accurately measured somatic symptoms) and definition of medical goals followed as a matter of course.

This interplay of the artifacts of medicine's first revolution—the availability of diagnostic technologies, a new concept of disease, and norms of medical objectivity—is illustrated by Reiser. He chronicles a series of dramatic events starting with René Laennec's 1823 invention of the stethoscope. The stethoscope, he says, afforded a new way of measuring bodily sounds. By degrees, sounds heard through the stethoscope came to be regarded as among the most reliable signs of disease. Over the next century and a half the idea of the detection of pathology by bodily signs was generalized and widely applied. Through the discovery of a succession of fact-gathering techniques—the x-ray, the electrocardiograph, the introduction of chemical theory into diagnostic theory—there evolved a new standard of diagnostic objectivity. Reiser notes that, prior to the mid-nineteenth century, the physician relied chiefly on three diagnostic techniques to determine the nature of illness. One was the clinical dialogue consisting of the patient's narrative of his symptoms, partly guided by the physician's questions. Another was the physician's direct observations of the outward appearance of the patient's body. And a third was the physician's manual examination of the body, taking the pulse rate, probing the tissues beneath the skin, and the like. Chief among these was the clinical dialogue. Reiser describes it in these terms:

> Illness stirs introspection and curiosity in people about the circumstances which might have influenced its genesis, the sensations felt which led to suspicions that a problem existed, the decision to seek help (was it too late or in time for therapy to be effective?), the possible length of therapy, the cost, the pain, the likely outcome. Transformed by passage through the patient's mind, such impressions can yield a uniquely personal statement of the meaning of the illness to the patient and provide crucial information about its causes, when harvested by the physician through dialogue. (1978*b*, 305)

Until the nineteenth century, clinical dialogue had been the chief means of learning about an illness. The meaning to the patient of the illness, patient attitudes, and expectations concerning its outcome were, like pulse rate and blood count, deemed important diagnostic variables. Gradually, first-revolution thinking eroded the importance attached to clinical dialogue. By the early nineteenth century, physicians were growing acutely aware of the unreliability of memory and the inadequacies of ordinary language to describe the effects of illness. Turning away from using the patients' descriptions of their illness, physicians sought greater use of the physical examination, using manual techniques and the simple instruments available. But in time, says Reiser, "the word descriptions of the doctor were challenged just as the word descriptions of the patient had been." Gradually there grew "a distrust of the accuracy with which sense impressions gained at the bedside were engraved on the memory of the doctor, a distrust of his ability to accurately describe and recall these impressions, and to attain full insight into the facts that he had acquired" (1978*a*, 228).

Stepping into this vacuum were the increasingly accurate instruments of the sort whose prototype was Laennec's stethoscope. These enabled the translation of physiological processes into the quantifiable language of machines. Clinical dialogue, once a staple of Western medicine, whose relative effectiveness was never seriously questioned, came to be abandoned. It was abandoned because its effectiveness could not be rationalized by the emerging explanatory norms. It fell into disuse owing to the purported unreliability of the physician's memory in accurately recording the patient's word description of the effects of illness and the inadequacies of an ordinary vocabulary to describe those effects. Reiser compares the effects of the introduction of the stethoscope near the start of the nineteenth century and the reign of technology in medicine it precipitated with the effects of printing in Western culture. Books brought with them detachment and a critical attitude not possible in an oral tradition.

> Similarly, auscultation helped to create the objective physician, who could move away from involvement with the patient's experiences and sensations, to a more detached relation, less with the patient but more with the sounds from within the body. Undistracted by the motives and beliefs of the patient, the auscultator could make a diagnosis from sounds that he alone heard emanating from body organs, sounds that he believed to be objective bias-free representations of the disease process. (1978a, 38)

Ushering in the era of pathology detection by internal body signs, the stethoscope helped to create the objective physician. Commenting on this development, Sandra Harding remarks, "Choice of a new fact-gathering technique often produces new conceptions of 'normal biology' and its causes and thus a different conception of health and disease." Exemplifying this process, she observes that "an anatomical perspective on disease began to replace the ancient 'humors' perspective only when physicians began dissecting dead bodies and manipulating live ones in physical examinations. Later, with the introduction of the microscope and techniques of chemical analysis, pathology came to refer not to anatomical lesions but to alterations in the elementary physical and chemical constituents of tissues" (1978, 348). Involvement with the patient's experiences and sensations, motives and beliefs, was a casualty of the shift to a new diagnostic technique. Through nonattention to them, they became, by implication, diagnostically irrelevant. A new conception of pathology came to the fore. The "problems of illness hatched from beliefs, illusions, values, and other facets of cultural and mental life," offered by Reiser as diagnostically significant, were shunned in favor of technology-produced evidence. In place of those problems, technologically produced signs of the sort made accessible through the stethoscope and its descendants held sway.

Prized are devices by which subjective sensory events can be converted into numbers, pictures, and graphs whose objectivity, or at least intersubjectivity, is beyond question. This conversion of physiological signals into graphs and numbers "allowed physicians to obtain clear and accurate records, to preserve these signals so that changes in pattern could be studied over time; to free these signals from the limitations of private analysis . . . and open them to group inquiry; to make them objective and to invest them with unambiguous meanings that were evident to all physicians" (Reiser 1978a, 121). This was a remarkable development and, when generalized, characterizes the legacy of the industrial revolution. In medicine, one of its spinoffs was an evolution in diagnostic method: from reliance on the patient's verbal evidence (clinical dialogue) to reliance on the physician's manual examination (physical examination) and, finally, to reliance on technical experts in subjects such as biological chemistry and reliance on machines such as x-ray machines. This evolution has been decisive for shaping the course of Western medicine. It gave rise to the eighteenth-century "birth of the clinic,"—*la clinique*, in Michel Foucault's phrase, a place where citizens could literally take their bodily problems, unfettered by their natural social surroundings (Foucault 1972). Its harvest has been today's imposing diagnostic armamentarium, which has, according to Reiser, turned the physician away from the therapeutic use of, say, the doctor-patient relationship: "The numbers generated by the thermometer, the graphs drawn by the electrocardiograph, the pictures created by the x-ray machine, the images captured by the microscope, the diagnostic judgments rendered by the computer—all are generally assumed to be free of the flaws and biases that admittedly distort facts gathered by human beings through their natural senses. Such evidence, it is further assumed, is therefore the most valuable in diagnosing and treating disease" (1978a, 229). Here we see the critical interrelationship of philosophy (metaphysical presuppositions) and medical practice; for only against the premise of disease as an exclusively somatic phenomenon, a condition accounted for by deviations from the norm of biological parameters, is such an assumption warranted.

In view of the growth in complexity and sophistication of latter-day biotechnologies, this premise, admittedly, is increasingly attractive. To this growth may be added today's organized application to medical practice, through clinical pathology, of complicated chemical, microscopical, and bacteriological techniques associated with laboratory analysis. Now the premise, and the biomedical strategy it harbors, becomes still more attractive. The distinction between objective and "merely subjective" diagnostic evidence becomes embedded in clinical practice. Relevant evidence means evidence that can be measured by the diagnostic techniques in use. "Sounds heard emanating from body organs" rather than "motives and beliefs of the patient" are today's "objective, bias-free representations of the disease process." Evidence gathered by auscultation is of course more objective than that gathered by clinical dialogue. But observe that the inference that they are "objective representations of the disease process" follows only upon adoption of the premise that disease is a deviation from biological norms alone.

In sum, the prerevolutionary assumption that the meaning to the patient of the illness could itself be a diagnostic tool was submerged in the growing technical debate over how best to achieve objective accuracy in the description of physical disease symptoms. The abovementioned methodological concepts by which to approach inquiry (Table 2.1), so crucial to advancement of the physical sciences, had the operational effect, when combined with the Cartesian concept of dualism, of converting the patient into a physical object. Accordingly, the physician sought to be objective toward the patient—not, however, for example, as a psychophysiological unity but as a complex biological system. Through this unspoken turn from what type of information is vital for diagnosis to how most accurately to record physical diagnostic information (the type of information the new technologies could process), pathogenesis came increasingly to be conceptualized as an exclusively physical process. Pathogenic signs sought were physical in nature, and disease agencies came to be recognized as physical agencies. By indirection, the meaning of the illness to the patient, a psychophysiological or biobehavioral agency, could have little or no relevance to objective disease analysis. Out of this unselfconscious mating, today's rational medicine was born. The capabilities of medical technologies, initially designed as aids in achieving physician goals, came to guide standards of relevance and so reshape these goals. Our premises, or in this case our tools, are the spectacles through which we look at events to see information.

The purpose of this section has been to show how use of the stethoscope and its progeny, by making possible detachment and a critical attitude, has helped create the objective physician. Doing so, it has encouraged the adoption of a particular concept of disease and the medical strategy that accompanies it. According to Reiser, "Modern medicine has now evolved to a point where diagnostic judgments based on 'subjective' evidence—the patient's sensations and the physician's own observations of the patient—are being supplanted by judgments based on 'objective' evidence, provided by laboratory procedures and by mechanical and electronic devices" (1978a, ix). That diagnostic method is an artifact of the concept of disease, that the concept of disease is in turn an artifact of the concept of the patient, and that each is mutually reinforcing can be graphically displayed. Diagnostic method, disease concept, and patient concept are mutually related. This interrelation—a product of the first revolution—shapes medical strategy.

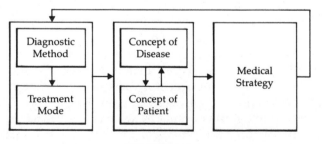

FIGURE 2.1

We have contended that the legacy of a body of narrowly accurate diagnostic techniques constitutes an internal constraint on the strategy espoused. At the same time, the dominant scientific paradigm within which the strategy is pursued—here the Newtonian paradigm—may be said to constitute an external constraint. Both constraints are incorporated in the Figure 2.2, a historical embodiment of Figure 2.1 and the source of today's concept of scientific medicine. With Figure 2.2 we come full circle to the mutuality of philosophy, methodology, and clinical practice. Espousal of a philosophical framework shapes the direction of medical research and comes to define norms of success. Success in practice reinforces belief in the framework, assuring further application of the techniques used for carrying out the practice.

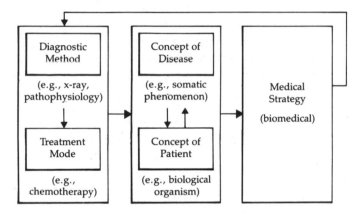

FIGURE 2.2    The Impact on Medicine of the Newtonian
Physical Paradigm

# 3

## The Philosophical Foundations
## of Biomedicine

In anticipation of what will be a challenge to the dominant standing of
the biomedical model in Parts Two and Three, this chapter examines the
philosophical commitment involved in the general acceptance of
biomedical premises. In so doing, the foundation premises and assumptions underlying biomedicine are specified. Particular interest is directed
toward the manner in which these premises entail a commitment to
assumed properties regarding the nature of the world we live in. It will
be seen that to accept the biomedical perspective is to accept a package
of premises and assumptions concerning the nature of the world and
the best approach by which to come to understand it.

## Natural Science Foundations

Like so many other diverse fields of inquiry, the premises underlying
biomedicine are adopted from and thus emulate the premises underlying the conduct of inquiry found in the natural sciences. To examine
these natural science foundations is to elucidate just what is implied by
the methods shaping modern theoretical science.

The roots of the seventeenth-century scientific revolution sprang
from intellectual soil nurtured by Cartesian dualism and Democritean
atomism. Acceptance of Cartesian dualism, which dichotomized the
material and immaterial worlds, permitted the scientist to concentrate
on aspects of nature more readily subject to experimentation and quanti-
fication *(res extensa)*. Acceptance of Democritean atomism permitted the
scientist conceptually to break down complex wholes into ever-simpler
parts. Inner dynamisms could be analyzed by reference to a glossary of
terms ideally containing reference only to particles and their motions.
This coupling of dualism and atomism produced a climate congenial to
directing scientific inquiry away from the more deductive and rationalistic approach of neo-Aristotelian physics and toward a more hypothetico-

deductive and empiricist approach. Limiting essential variables to readily measurable ones led to a gain in precision and economy of expression. An increasingly definable process of inquiry was emerging. This logic of method can be characterized by its approach to the subject of inquiry as being determined and capable of reductionistic explanations. Further, the methodological stance of the inquirer was seen to be most effective when tempered by standards of objectivity, ahistoricity, aculturicity, and impersonality.

Over the next two and a half centuries, so successful was the outcome of applying this logic that proceeding in accord with it came to be identified with proceeding in accord with the precepts of rational (descriptive) inquiry in general and theoretical science in particular. The empirical basis for this growing identification was the fact that applying these directives produced as a matter of historical record an unprecedented series of predictive-explanatory successes in those seventeenth-through nineteenth-century physical sciences which grew out of, in terms of their subject matter, and displaced, in terms of their methodological directives, their neo-Aristotelian predecessors. The analytic and reductionist temperament gained increasing influence.

As these sciences matured, by the close of the nineteenth century, physics presented a very ordered and comprehensive picture of the world. Events unfolded in characteristic ways, following Newton's equations in mechanics, Clausius' in thermodynamics, and Maxwell's in electromagnetics. Moving inexorably, independently of the scientist, who was simply a discerning spectator, these processes presented a picture that was tempting to regard as essentially complete. Newton's "single vision," William Blake called it. The greater the explanatory successes, the more reason to be disposed toward the adequacy of the directives by application of which the successes were wrought. It is difficult not to read these methodological directives into the frameworks described by Newton's, Clausius', and Maxwell's equations. There is a mutuality between the world posited by the scientific framework described by the equations and the methodological assumptions informing the inquiry by which the framework was established.

As these sciences acquired preeminence in the physical domain, commanding all they surveyed, their influence spread to other domains as well. By the nineteenth century the life sciences were impelled toward the analytical clarity provided by the subsumption of more and more data under a maximally economical number of general principles, ultimately the first principles of physics. Illustrating the extent of this transition, a representative of the mid-nineteenth-century European school of physiologists, Emil Du Bois-Reymond, wrote in the introduction to an 1848 book on animal electricity that "if our methods only were sufficient, an analytical mechanics [Newtonian physics] of general life processes would be possible and fundamentally would reach even to the problem of the freedom of the will." Here we see early evidence of the directive urging reductionism, in this case the reduction of life processes to the language and processes of physics—laws regarding elementary particles in motion.

At about the same time, beginning with the early Darwinians and their contemporaries working in physiological psychology, the mind sciences came to pattern their methods on the life sciences. Harold Morowitz points to the impetus for this shift. He notes that "the stress evolutionists placed on our 'apeness' made us subject to biological study by methods appropriate to nonhuman primates and, by extension, to other animals. The Pavlovian school reinforced that theme, and it became a cornerstone of many behavioral theories. While no general agreement has emerged among psychologists as to how far reductionism should be carried, most will readily concede that our actions have hormonal, neurological, and physiological components" (1980,12). Thus grew a general tradition of reductionism and mechanism in psychology exemplified in its radical form by the viewpoint expressed by Carl Sagan in his best-selling book *The Dragons of Eden*: "My fundamental premise about the brain is that its workings—what we sometimes call 'mind'— are a consequence of its anatomy and physiology and nothing more" (in Morowitz 1980, 12).

At the time that various schools of psychology were attempting to reduce their science to the principles of the life sciences, schools of biology were also looking for more basic levels of explanation in the physical sciences. Morowitz characterizes the contemporary expression of their outlook. He cites the co-discoverer of the genetic code, the molecular biologist Francis Crick, who states in his book *Of Molecules and Men* that "The ultimate aim of the modern movement in biology is in fact to explain *all* biology in terms of physics and chemistry" (1980, 15). Morowitz adds: "He [Crick] goes on to say that by physics and chemistry he refers to the atomic level, where our knowledge is secure. By use of the italicized *all*, he expresses the viewpoint among an entire generation of biochemists and molecular biologists." Morton Beckner describes a prevalent orientation in biology:

> Probably most biologists think that the facts of physiology, genetics, morphogenesis, and such are, in an obvious sense, nothing more than complex physicochemical facts. . . . The situation is this: Biologists admit that their science is, in practice, to some extent autonomous; but they are also inclined to believe that any autonomous principle, such as Mendel's laws, are only provisionally autonomous and that, if we only knew enough, they could be shown to be consequences of nonbiological theory. (1972, 311)

David Hull writes: "A type of explanation that originated in the study of purely physical phenomena has been extended to biological and social phenomena. All events are explained in terms of antecedent events organized in causal chains and networks, characterizable in terms of universal laws which make no reference to the causal efficaciousness of future events or higher levels of organization" (1974, 6). Inquiry in virtually all sciences was conducted in compliance with the directives of "scientific method," such that doing science came to mean proceeding in accord with those directives. Those directives included the principles of reductionism, unidirectional causality, and determinism, which together dictate a certain stance between the inquirer and the subject of inquiry.

Among the recurring foundations issues is the applicability of natural science premises to the life sciences. At stake is what constitutes the proper methodological stance the medical scientist assumes toward the subject of his or her inquiry—the human patient. Regarding the effort to reduce the life sciences to the language of the natural sciences, Carl Hempel attempts to put this issue in perspective. He differentiates between the belief that sciences like biology, physiology, and psychology will eventually be reduced to physics and chemistry and the fact that they have not yet been so reduced. This difference enables him to identify directives like those identified above as procedural in intent, not substantive. Embracing a mechanistic approach, for example, does not embody an inductive generalization about the structure of the world— or, in the present instance, about the nature of the human patient. It is, says Hempel, "perhaps best construed, not as a specific thesis or theory . . . but as a heuristic maxim, as a principle for the guidance of research. Thus understood, it enjoins the scientist to persist in the search for basic physico-chemical theories of biological [and psychological] phenomena rather than resign himself to the view that the concepts and principles of physics and chemistry are powerless to give an adequate account of the phenomena of life [and mind]" (1966, 106).

Ernest Nagel makes the same point with respect to the principle of efficient causality. He dispenses with the idea that the principle states an empirical truth and assigns to it the role of a generally accepted presupposition in the contemporary practice of science: "[It] is a directive instructing us to search for explanations possessing certain broadly delimited features; and even repeated failure to find such explanations for any given domain of events is no logical bar to further search" (1961, 322).

For Hempel, Nagel, and others the very notion of science requires the acceptance of principles like mechanism, reductionism, and causality so construed. It is the perspective with which one comes to the process of inquiry if one wishes to engage in the scientific effort. Whether the world is or is not in reality a "machine," or the human patient a physiological mechanism, and whether the behavior of the machine's or the mechanism's units is determined by the behavior of its constituent parts is not the central issue. While these concepts may be artifacts of a given method, the major issue is in what manner the search should proceed. This is described by Stephen Toulmin as the strategy of methodological determinism:

> It is suggested that the physicist does not need to assert that the world is a machine, i.e., that the behavior of any system he chooses to study will prove to be as mechanical as the movements of, say, a steam engine; but that he needs only to assume, for professional purposes, that everything in the particular field he is studying is determined and mechanical. This latter, tentative assumption is spoken of as methodological determinism, and contrasted with the more general and dogmatic, metaphysical determinism. (1953, 166)

Two interrelated dimensions can now be identified that are crucial to any logic of method. The first pertains to the philosophy of science. For the natural science paradigm this involves the interplay of methodological and metaphysical issues such as reductionism, determinism, and efficient causality. The second dimension pertains to the activity of science itself—the search for laws that explain.

Important to the present inquiry is recognition that the two activities coexist in fruitful tension and are mutually reinforcing components of the overall scientific enterprise. In this sense science is conducted in a multiple-tiered language. There is a patently scientific tier in which the search for scientific generalizations, like those of classical (or relativistic) physics (e.g., laws of motion), is conducted. This is the substantive side of science. It has its procedural counterpart. Hence, there is also an infrascientific tier consisting of the application of certain methodological directives for guiding the search which characterizes activity at the former tier. Since this procedural tier underlies the substantive tier, we shall call it tier 1 and its substantive counterpart tier 2. This procedural tier (tier 1) comprises the heuristic maxims (e.g., reductionism) that make up the logic of scientific method at the time the search (tier 2) is undertaken. The effort to ascertain whether there are certain directives or ideals that are necessary to a logic of scientific method can only be regarded as an ongoing "conversation" in philosophy of science.

Nagel, like Hempel, specifies general ideals or goals toward which scientific inquiry in general and lawlike explanation in particular should be directed. These ideals include reductionism, determinism, and causality. Speaking to one of these ideals, causality, Nagel states:

> Acceptance of the principle of causality as a maxim of inquiry . . . is an *analytical consequence* of what is commonly meant by "theoretical science." . . . it is difficult to understand how it would be possible for modern theoretical science to surrender the general ideal expressed by the principle

without becoming thereby transformed into something incomparably different from what the enterprise actually is. (1961, 324)

It is unquestionably true that the general ideal expressed by the principle of causality, like the other ideals noted, is inseparable from the enterprise of theoretical science as embodied in sciences formulated during the period dating from the middle of the seventeenth century to almost the time when Nagel is writing, the mid-twentieth century. If we characterize this as the period of "modern theoretical science," it is indeed "difficult to understand how it would be possible for modern theoretical science to surrender the general ideal expressed by [these] principle[s] without becoming thereby transformed into something incomparably different from what the enterprise actually is."

Other features of scientific method are well known and often written about. Jay Rosenberg describes key features that characterize the method of science as "interpersonal, a-cultural, a-temporal, impersonal, of universal scope, self-corrective, and convergent" (1974, 89). These features tell the scientist how to approach the act of inquiry. They define the proper relationship between the inquirer and that which is the subject of inquiry. They restrain the inquirer from attaching meanings and interpretations to the data separate from the data themselves. These are to be distinguished from the earlier principles (reductionism, mechanism, etc.) which dictate the relationship between the inquirer and the presumed nature of the world being inquired into.

We are now in a position to give concrete form to the central features of the logic of method which is at the foundation of the contemporary biomedical model. These consensus features of scientific method may be brought together and divided into two groups, directives by which to approach the world and directives by which to approach inquiry (see Table 3.1).

It is important to note that the basis for adopting these ideals or

TABLE 3.1   Logic of the Scientific Method

| DIRECTIVES BY WHICH TO APPROACH THE WORLD | DIRECTIVES BY WHICH TO APPROACH INQUIRY |
| --- | --- |
| Reductionism | Objectivity |
| Mechanism | Ahistoricity |
| Causality | Aculturicity |
| Determinism | Impersonality |
| Dualism | Universality |
| | Self-correctiveness |
| | Convergence |

directives was in the first instance pragmatic and utilitarian: sciences based on them seemed to promise and assuredly delivered more than their neo-Aristotelian predecessors, based on alternative directives. Therefore a particular methodological strategy, forged historically in the crucible of seventeenth- through early-twentieth-century scientific practice, was by the mid-twentieth century enshrined as *the* scientific method. Responding to those who would "dethrone" reductionism and mechanism, Gerald Edelman states that "to agree with this view is to support the forces of mysticism and anti-intellectualism" (1977, 7–8).

Thus far, this chapter has sought to identify concepts which some influential writers in philosophy of science generally accept as necessary for the conduct of theoretical science. The directives of methodological determinism, reductionism, and efficient causality were singled out. Though they start out as tentative assumptions, there seems to be a point after which they become, as for Hempel, Nagel, Edelman, and others, the very perspective with which one comes to the process of inquiry if one wishes to engage in the scientific effort. For Hempel they are an integral part of the only option available for achieving genuine explanation. For Nagel they are an analytical consequence of the practice of theoretical science. For Edelman they are defining features of intellectualism. For all three they possess or have achieved the status of necessary conditions of empirical inquiry. In the next section, our task will be to define certain world properties that these concepts presuppose.

## The Natural Science Worldview: Two World Properties

The defining characteristics of Table 3.1 say something more about the scientific enterprise than just its preference for a physicalist and empirical approach to the pursuit of truth. Rather, they point to underlying presuppositions that together form the basis for a worldview that the natural science paradigm advocate (and derivatively the biomedical advocate) is philosophically committed to. Involved are a number of assumptions, two of which have been briefly discussed. First is the assumption embodied in the explanatory concepts of the left-hand column, that there is ideally a unified, physicalist language in whose vocabulary all events, physical, biological, and mental, are ultimately expressible. This is evidenced by the contemporary preference for reductionism. In other words, the behavior of nature's organized systems, whether physical, biological, or psychological, is understood by coming to understand the principles that account for the arrangement of their constituent elements; and these arrangements in turn are finally explainable by reference to the physical sciences. Hence, Hempel's ultimatum: either persist in the search for basic physicochemical theories of all phenomena or despair at the prospect of explanation. This ultimatum, insists Hempel, is to be construed as reflecting not an inductive generalization about the structure of the world but "a principle for the guidance of research."

This assumption that levels of organization do not involve ontologically new entities beyond the elements of which it is comprised, and that in the fullness of time a fundamental-level language will reflect this proposition, underwrites a methodological policy that proceeds in a reductionist manner. As such it countenances conferring primary status to matter and the material world and secondary or epiphenomenal status to the biological and mental worlds. In this way, we come to understand what is out there by recognizing that life and mind are essentially a struggle against the laws of physics, chance products in a world governed by the laws of mechanics and thermodynamics. Thus, operationally speaking, modern science proceeds on the premise that life, the human being, and culture are, in the last analysis, transient events, by-products of physical organization. And interacting material particles represent the natural order of things; they are the ultimate stuff of the universe. In a forceful expression of this thesis, Hull states, "Today, both scientists and philosophers take ontological reduction for granted. Vitalism is dead. Organisms are 'nothing but' atoms, and that is that" (1981, 126).

Thus Nagel's preference for theories, even biological theories, to be stated in a form consistent with that forged in the physical sciences. Expressing confidence that the methods of the physical sciences are adequate for the study of biological systems, Nagel suggests "that eventually the whole of biology would become simply a chapter of physics and chemistry" (1961, 398). Consistent with this viewpoint he declares that "The claim that there are emergent properties in the sense of emergent evolution is entirely compatible with the belief in the universality of the causal principle, at any rate in the form that there are determinate conditions for the occurrence of all events" (1961, 377). This conforms to the view that all explanations might ultimately prove to be determinate explanations. At the heart of the methodology in question is the desire to explain organismic and mentalistic phenomena in a way that is consistent with these same deterministic notions. Endorsement of such principles or analytical consequences of what is (and must be) meant by "theoretical science" carries with it far-reaching implications.

In particular, proceeding methodologically in a manner that is reductionistic, mechanistic, and deterministic implies the following world property:

1. *Fundamental-Level World Property*

The worldview implied by the prevailing logic of inquiry presupposes a single fundamental material level of reality. Levels of organization do not involve ontologically new entities beyond the fundamental level elements of which the given entity is comprised. There is a unified physicalist language in whose vocabulary all phenomena subject to scientific inquiry—psychological, biological and physical—can in principle be described.

It is this assumption of a world that is radically continuous or symmetrical (nonemergent) that is consistent with a methodological policy that is reductionistic, mechanistic, and deterministic.

A second assumption embraced by the scientific enterprise, this one indicated by the right-hand column of Table 3.1, is that the by-product of the pursuit of knowledge—that is, ideas—do not themselves have a material impact on that which is to be known. This assumption that there is an "external permanency" upon which our ideas have no effect underwrites a methodological policy that proceeds in an ahistorical, acultural, and impersonal manner. As such it countenances a separation of knower from the known, subject from object and, generally speaking, the view that the pursuit of knowledge proceeds in a detached manner such that ideas themselves are not a "material force." In this way, we come to understand what is out there by creating the necessary distance by which to see more clearly. The link between this assumption and the rise of the objective physician chronicled in the last chapter is transparent. Thus, modern science operates on the premise that the person, as subject or observer, is separate from nature or the external world, which is the object. Edmund Leach formulates this in the premise that "all true science must aim at objective truth, and that means that the human observer must never allow himself to get emotionally mixed up with his subject matter. . . . Detachment is obligatory" (1973, 8). Eric and Mary Josephson add, "To understand and control nature—the goals of modern science and technology—men first had to separate or alienate themselves from it. As Whitehead puts it, 'Nature, in scientific thought . . . had its laws formulated without any reference to dependence on individual observers' " (1962, 36). Hence, with reference to the content and methods of modern science, humans are twice alienated, as it were: alienated by the workings of nature (the second law of thermodynamics), and alienated by a permanent spectator status in the process of coming to understand these workings ("external permanency").

Proceeding methodologically in such a manner implies a second world property:

## 2. External-Permanency World Property

The worldview implied by the prevailing logic of method presupposes a world in which ideas do not have a material impact on the structural lines of reality. There is an "external permanency" upon which thinking can have no effect.

It is this assumption of a world in which ideas have no material impact that is consistent with a methodological policy that is acultural, ahistorical, and impersonal.

These two world properties are cited because they represent commitments entailed by the general acceptance of the natural science paradigm. They are products of this acceptance. Nothing in the New Science is inconsistent with either world property. To the contrary, the basic laws of the early modern sciences—paradigmatically those of mechanics and thermodynamics—appear to support these properties. While a unified language of science has not as yet been achieved, there is no compelling scientific reason, nor logical bar, precluding its eventual formulation. The tacit, if not overt, thrust of modern science has rather been toward subsuming the principles of the life sciences and even the mind sciences under those of the physical sciences: tacit because the argument in favor of the ultimate reduction of biological and psychological concepts to the language of physics and chemistry is often conducted on philosophical grounds removed from the typical forums that occupy members of the scientific community, who seldom work in more than one of these areas. While not expressly affirmed in tier 2 language, then, world properties 1 and 2 are implicitly promoted by virtue of persistent and unselfconscious application of explanatory concepts like those of Table 3.1. Procedural and substantive tiers may therefore be advanced as sustaining the mutually reinforcing and complementary relationship illustrated in Figure 3.1.

The world has the properties attributed to it by world properties 1 and 2 (tier 1) to the extent that, first, the predictive–explanatorily successful natural sciences proceed as if it has these properties; and, second, the

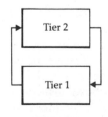

FIGURE 3.1

findings of these sciences (tier 2) are not inconsistent with the world's having these properties.

The objective of the next section is to view the broad patterns of thought associated with the New Science as they relate to currents in medical thought. It will be seen that these world properties yield a counterpart set of specifically medical world properties. These are identified and examined. In the process, the threads of metaphysics, science, and practice will be woven together into a fabric of views concerning the contemporary medical enterprise.

## The Natural Science Worldview: Two Medical World Properties

Hull notes the dramatic transition from pre-Enlightenment thinking to the contemporary scientific view:

> During the early years of science, certain modes of explanation, which are most appropriate to biological phenomena in general and human behavior in particular, were read into all of nature. Just as a man might strive to be virtuous and a species might strive to reproduce itself, a rock falling to the earth was interpreted as striving to attain its natural place. The opposite tack has become increasingly popular since the time of Galileo and Newton. A type of explanation that originated in the study of purely physical phenomena has been extended to biological and social phenomena. All events are explained in terms of antecedent events organized in causal chains and networks, characterizable in terms of universal laws which make no reference to the causal efficaciousness of future events or higher levels of organization. (1974, 6)

Hull's comment serves to underline the broad change that has taken place in scientific thinking as the primacy of final causality gave way to efficient causality.

The issue of biology and medicine as autonomous disciplines that employ *sui generis* modes of explanation provides an opportunity to examine just what attitudes, commitments, and convictions dominate these fields. One view is that physiological facts will prove, in the fullness of time, to be "nothing more than complex physicochemical facts." According to this view, if we "knew enough," medical and biological concepts would be fully explicable in physicochemical terms. The argument in favor of the ultimate reduction of biological or medical concepts to the language of physics and chemistry is one of those issues usually argued on philosophical grounds removed from the typical forums that occupy members of the medical community. However, how this issue is resolved is important and exerts considerable influence in terms of attitudes regarding the respectability and scientific standing of findings in medicine. It is pivotal to the foundations of medicine agenda. According to Marx Wartofsky, medical scientists and medical practitioners find themselves "in a certain posture of standing in the shadow of the sciences as aspirants to some more perfect kind of knowledge which the natural sciences in particular represent" (1978, 267). It is the stature and respectability of the established physical science paradigm that explain why "contemporary medical reasoning borrows its causal concepts from other ('theoretical') parts of science in accordance with currently accepted explanatory goals" (Maull 1981, 179). Ronald Munson writes that "medicine prefers to have its rules of diagnosis, treatment, and prevention grounded in scientific knowledge of causal mechanisms" (1981, 194). He describes the goal of scientific medicine as the reduction of normal functioning, disease processes, and therapeutic procedures in terms of biological theories.

The question whether medicine itself is a science or whether only the concepts used in medicine are based on related fields of scientific inquiry (biology, in particular) is an openly debated question in philosophy-of-medicine journals. What is clear from the comments above is that at the foundations level the enterprise of medicine relies on the canons of the natural science paradigm and has incorporated this paradigm's conduct of inquiry into its dominant goal-seeking strategy. Acknowledging the many vital processes that have been successfully explained in physicochemical terms, Ernest Nagel states that many outstanding biologists are "confident that eventually the whole of biology would become simply a chapter of physics and chemistry" (1961, 398). And consider Edelman's enthusiastic endorsement, made almost a generation later: "Modern biology has shown quite convincingly that, so far, there is no limit to methodological reductionism and to mechanism" (1977, 8). More pointedly, Munson states, "What is true of physics is also true of medicine. . . . Biological explanations of 'real' [physical] diseases . . . are both in principle possible and are avidly sought by medical researchers" (1981, 202).

The implied world properties that are entailed by the commitment to the canons of theoretical science permeate the foundations of contemporary medical thought by way of their extension into the domain of biological inquiry. In other words, the commitment to certain presuppositions about the pervasive structure of reality can be regarded as influential in the narrower domains of biology and medicine. The identification of these derivative medical (world) properties and the sort of world to which this strategy choice commits the medical science community are examined. The considerable extent that medicine reduces its cognitive content to biology and its subdisciplines is a measure of the importance of the presuppositions accepted in the life sciences.

In order to identify the implied properties of the medical domain, writers in the field of philosophy of science and philosophy of medicine as well as methodologically self-conscious medical practitioners will be referenced. The implied world properties consistent with the canons of theoretical science are matched by a medical worldview with a similarly consistent set of implied world properties.

The adoption of the natural science methodological strategy by the medical science enterprise means attaching the same importance to the principles of causality, reductionism, determinism, and prediction that have already been identified as part of the commitment to the natural science conduct of inquiry. This suggests offering the following implied medical world property as a derivative of the first implied world property of the Enlightenment worldview:

1. *The Mechanisms of Disease: Medical World Property*
   The medical community presupposes a world in which the "fundamental-level" world property can be extended to pathogenesis. This is actualized by treating disease as a function of an eradicable physical condition. In the practice of medicine, any putative extrasomatic pathogenic factor is redescribed in terms of its concomitant somatic process that is its biological substrate and is treated accordingly.

The above-stated medical world property embodies two foundational properties that were seen to be central to the Enlightenment worldview. First, there is the optimism reflected in the idea of progress. Here knowledge serves to aid in the achievement of goals held in common by the members of the enterprise. In this case, it is the desire to cure human illness. Spaeth and Barber characterize this medical attitude in these terms: "The optimism and the methodology generated by these beliefs [confidence in the scientific method] . . . led to the remarkable scientific discoveries that have become a hallmark of the last 300 years of mankind's development. Included in this is what might be called the Oslerian concept of the medical profession: 'There seems to be no limit to the possibilities of scientific medicine' " (1980, 11). And second, because the methodology presupposes a world in which there are determinant conditions for all events, there is inherent predictability. This provides the practitioner with the ability to predict both disease processes and the consequences of alternative actions (therapies). Thus, the doctor can (or someday will) exercise the kind of control needed to overcome disease. Kenneth Schaffner offers the following argument for accepting biomedical theories: they "admit of all the important features of theories in physics and chemistry: . . . [they] are testable and have excess empirical content, they organize knowledge in inductive and sometimes even deductive ways, they change and are accepted and replaced in accordance with rational canons, and they are applicable for prediction and control in crucially important areas such as . . . health-care delivery" (1980, 88). Emphasizing the same point, Munson states, "In seeking to promote health, medicine can be described as a quest for *control* over factors affecting health. Knowledge or understanding of biological processes is important to medicine, because it leads to control" (1981, 194).

Reductionism, the view that complex entities are best understood by reference to fundamental or building-block entities, is an essential feature of the natural science strategy. It is through a reductionistic research strategy that the medical enterprise anticipates breakthroughs in attaining a mechanistic understanding of disease processes. According to Arthur Zucker, "there is a philosophy of science for medicine . . . [and] a more subtle part of it . . . requires biochemical understanding. Medical science strives to find mechanisms to help explain and predict medical problems and solutions. . . . [For example,] it was a reductionistic breakthrough that created a mechanistic understanding for some genetic diseases" (1981, 146).

Such comments support the contention that the contemporary medical enterprise has been built upon foundations established by the intellectual transformation that characterized the rise of the scientific worldview. Here it can be seen that the commitment to the natural science paradigm further commits the medical community to a view of its relevant domain of inquiry as one that is deterministic, reductionistic, and characterized by causal mechanisms. Further, this commitment presupposes that we live in a world in which we can exercise control through understanding the inherently predictable outcome of various actions.

In addition to the above considerations, the adoption of the natural science methodological strategy means attaching the same importance to conducting inquiry in a manner that is acultural, atemporal, and impersonal in medicine as in physics and chemistry. This is consistent with C. S. Pierce's characterization of the scientific method, that "it is necessary that a method should be found by which our beliefs may be caused by nothing human, but by some external permanency—by something upon which our thinking has no effect" (1960). This suggests offering the following implied medical world property:

## 2. *The Physical Nature of Disease: Medical World Property*

The medical community presupposes a world in which the "external permanency" world property can be extended to the patient. This is actualized by the separation of the wider society and the mind from the sick body. In the practice of medicine, the locus of disease is the sick body, upon which the nature of the social organization and the thoughts of the patient (and the doctor) have no causal impact.

The above-stated medical world property is an important foundational principle because it bears so directly on the central aim of the medical enterprise; that is, curing disease. To the extent that disease is strictly interpreted in physical terms, so then are research energies focused in this direction. That this is the case is a function of the methodological strategy choice. Little wonder that "there is a common view that the proper study of the physician is biochemistry" (Murphy 1978, 276). This conception of the domain of medical inquiry is a natural extension of the commitment to the presuppositions of the physical sciences. According to Hull, "Today, both scientists and philosophers take ontological reduction for granted" (1981, 126). The force with which this view is held is a measure of the intensity by which this second implied medical property is applicable to efforts of the medical enterprise. To the extent that the presuppositions determine what is considered "real" and therefore the object of research interest, this natural extension is significant.

# The Reductionist Argument

Crucial to embracing both the first and second medical world properties is acceptance of the reductionist argument that levels of organization do not involve ontologically new entities beyond the elements of which it is comprised. The success of this argument provides support for what has emerged as biomedicine's core foundational principles.

Hull, a defender of the reductionist program, has examined this argument and will be quoted at length. Essential to his argument is narrowing the distinctions between animate and inanimate entities and the reducibility of mind to material organization. He states:

> There are not many trends discernable in science, but one of them seems to be the shifting of key scientific concepts from the category of things and substances to the category of properties, especially relational and organizational properties. Life is no more a thing than is time, space, gravity, or magnetism. One might well add mind to this list. If life is viewed as an organizational property of certain material systems, then we do not have to worry about where life came from when the first living creatures arose from inanimate substances. (1974, 131)

Here potentially distinctive or emergent properties such as life and mind are defined in terms of properties of material systems. The emphasis is on nonemergence and the continuity of physical structures rather than viewing them in metaphysically alternative ways.

Addressing the issue of ontological levels of organization and to what extent, if any, the existence of these (qualitatively different or emergent) entities require alternative modes of explanation, Hull states:

> The *degree* to which biologists must pay attention to organization in the explanation of even the simplest vital processes may be greater than that necessary for physicists in explaining purely physical systems. The *extent* to which records of the past history of living organisms are retained in their organization, especially at the level of individual organisms and their genomes, may be greater than that to be found for inanimate objects. The *amount* of contingency involved in the explanations of biological phenomena may be greater than is characteristic of certain very restricted kinds of physical phenomena. But these differences are matters of degree and not kind. If one examines actual physical theories, and not the usual textbook examples, one discovers that the differences between biological and purely physical phenomena do not look so great. Biologists do not have a corner on organization. Graphite and diamond are extremely different gross substances. Yet they are both made out of one and the same element— carbon—and nothing else. All their gross differences stem solely from differences in the organization of their constituent molecules. (1974, 133)

Hull's argument in defense of reductionism rests on the blurring of lines that antireductionists believe to be crucial. This, as well as other arguments that lead to the same conclusion, is accepted by those who agree that the natural science paradigm offers the most attractive methodological strategy for achieving the disease-cure goals of the medical enterprise. As such the focus of attention is on the "avid" search for understanding of disease in causal-mechanical terms. According to this strategy, it is not necessary to assume the existence of nonreductive entities. In this way the methodological continuity can be maintained as the biological sciences adopt and emulate the natural science conduct of inquiry. Hull's reductionist argument is one instance among others in which natural science foundations are defended. Their applicability to medical disciplines for the most part goes unquestioned.

Two implied properties of the domain of medicine have been identified and placed in both a historical and a contemporary context. Though they have been discussed separately, they are interrelated since they are both derived from a single, internally consistent worldview. They interrelate to the degree that inherently predictable, causal mechanisms complement entities that are (physically) reducible and do not themselves evolve into or give rise to stochastically transformative levels of complexity. This can be seen in Zucker's description of reductionism as a strategy in medicine:

> As a scientific strategy, reducing medicine to physiology means only that, where possible, research should take a certain bent toward molecular mechanisms. The presupposition of reduction in medicine is that all disease

is physiology gone astray. Where there is truly no physiological problem, there is no disease. . . . The ideal goal of reductionistic medicine would be diagnostics [and treatment] accomplished by a biochemical-biophysical survey of the patient's body. Ideally, psychological problems would be captured by this technique. It is part of the assumptions of reductionistic medicine that, at the very least, mental states have clinically useful physical correlates. (1981, 149–150)

Proponents of a naturalistic strategy for the medical enterprise do not belabor the point that the achievement of theories that can be reduced to biochemistry and ultimately physics is not only difficult but in fact may very well never be accomplished. In the face of what seem to be insurmountable obstacles to the attainment of the very aims of research, it is interesting to examine the nature of the arguments upon which the continued efforts are based. It can be seen that a defense of the strategy entails a commitment to the implied medical world properties.

In succession, Nagel examines and counters organismic attacks on the viability of the mechanistic program. Organismic critiques offered involved such claims as the following:

1. The activity of the whole cannot be fully explained in terms of the activities of the parts isolated by analysis.
2. No part of any living entity and no single process of any complex organic unity can be fully understood in isolation from the structure and activities of the organism as a whole.
3. Living bodies are characterized by "hierarchical organization" and processes. As such, an animate body is not a system of homogeneous parts, but rather parts that must be distinguished according to different levels. Critics deny that processes found at higher levels of a hierarchy are "caused" by, or are fully explicable in terms of, lower-level properties.

Nagel defends against the claim that the mechanistic approach is generally inadequate to biological subject matter. Reaching the same conclusion as Hull, cited above, he argues that areas that some consider to be distinctive of biology with respect to the physical sciences in actuality reflect differences of degree, not kind. With respect to the distinguishing feature of hierarchical organization, Nagel argues "that various forms of hierarchical organization are exhibited by the materials of physics and chemistry, and not only those of biology" (1961, 436). Here again lines of distinction are blurred.

While proponents of the natural science methodological strategy do not claim to make dogmatic judgments about the structure of reality, their methodological presuppositions address reality "as if" it had certain properties. As this discussion has tried to show, the medical enterprise addresses its domain of inquiry as if the two medical properties referred to above characterize the world of its inquiry. This approach is consistent with Toulmin's position that physicists need not assert that the world is a machine; rather they need only assume that what is being studied is determined and mechanical.

The extent to which proponents of a naturalistic scientific foundation for the medical/biological sciences defend against critics of this strategy provides support for the notion that the world properties identified above are actually generally embraced assumptions about the world. In other words, a defense of the method entails a defense of the implied world properties.

This discussion has touched on several of the most often stated difficulties that antireductionists claim. The attacks were fended off by reiterating the theme that, though the obstacles may be serious, they do not prove that a naturalistic-based biological science could not overcome them and hence produce a body of fully formulated biological theory. For the purpose of this study, what is of particular interest is that the above arguments made by Nagel and Hull support the claim that the methodological strategy being examined does purport to apply to a world in which there is no logical obstacle in treating it as inherently continuous, deterministic, and hence predictable. It is but one step to go on from there and claim that the yet to be achieved ability to predict will then provide the ability to control. According to Jacob Bronowski, "Man masters nature not by force but by understanding. . . . we control [nature] only by understanding her laws. . . . We must be content that power is the byproduct of understanding" (1965, 10).

We are now in a position to tie together the philosophical commitments entailed by biomedicine's acceptance of the natural science foundations and the three premises (disease, patient, and therapy) of the biomedical model identified in Chapter 2. It will be recalled that the biomedical model's concept of disease is a variation from the norm of biological parameters. Disease so understood conforms nicely to the canons of inquiry dictated by the natural science paradigm. Biological parameters can be judged objectively, their identification determined by the result of empirical investigation and free from the bias of the observer (physician). Disease as such is located in the body. It exists as a physically identifiable variation locatable in space. The patient, conceptualized as a biological organism, can be diagnosed in a context-free environment. Since disease is "biology gone awry" and the biological organism is best understood by focusing on and thereby understanding its constituent parts, there is little need to delve further than searching for the mechanism of disease—the somatic root. Therapy is conceptualized as a physical agent that counters the biological problems of too much, too little, or intrinsically damaging. Treatment is therefore focused within the body. It seeks to restore the organism to within the range of acceptable biological parameters. By understanding the patient at the level of its fundamental constituent parts, the mechanisms of disease are more effectively grasped and the appropriate response more effectively determined. Thus, we see these important biomedical concepts closely linked to the medical world properties identified. Disease, patient, and therapy are physical in nature, and we gain understanding and control when the assumptions, insights, and methods appropriate to natural science are employed.

Regarding the "logic of scientific method," illustrated in Table 3.1, we can offer a derivative "logic of biomedical scientific method" as in Table 3.2.

We have seen that acceptance of the natural science logic of method implies the acceptance of a particular worldview. In turn this has had an impact on research and practice of the contemporary medical enterprise. In the next section, we will show how the natural science commitment determines the medical research agenda termed here the "hard science turn."

## The Hard Science Turn

The hard science turn highlights the practical consequences of a commitment to the medical world properties. It illustrates how potentially controversial areas are dealt with by making them fit the "puzzle form" as defined by these properties. These properties derive from the natural science commitment:

> The basic tactic of natural science is analysis: fragment a phenomenon into its components, analyze each part and process in isolation, and thereby derive an understanding of the subject. In physics, chemistry, even biology, this tactic has worked splendidly. (Sinsheimer, 1978, 27)

TABLE 3.2    Logic of the Biomedical Scientific Method

| DIRECTIVES BY WHICH TO APPROACH THE PATIENT | DIRECTIVES BY WHICH TO APPROACH DIAGNOSIS |
| --- | --- |
| Reductionism | Objectivity |
| Mechanism | Ahistoricity |
| Causality | Aculturicity |
| Determinism | Impersonality |
| Dualism | Universality |
|  | Self-correctiveness |
|  | Convergence |

It will be seen how this strategy influences the questions asked and the solutions sought.

The hard science turn inclines us to see all data through the lens of a reductionist analysis, reflecting the values of objectivity, precision, and standardization. To see this turn at work, it is instructive to observe how members of the medical and scientific communities respond when confronted with potentially controversial experimental findings. One such area seeks to show the therapeutic efficacy of subjective states in the mitigation of organic symptoms. It will be seen how, in conformity with foundational premises, investigators routinely turn toward the search for the concomitant physical process and then reinterpret those states in a way that fits the reductionist directive. That is, they designate the correlative neurochemical process as the clinically useful component of the subjective state. In equation form this turn may be expressed as follows:

$$\text{APPARENT MIND-BODY EVENT} \longrightarrow \left( \begin{array}{c} \text{CONCOMITANT} \\ \text{NEUROCHEMICAL} \\ \text{PROCESS} \end{array} + \begin{array}{c} \text{REDUCTIONIST} \\ \text{DIRECTIVE} \end{array} \right) = \begin{array}{c} \text{BRAIN-BODY} \\ \text{EVENT} \end{array}$$

The Hard Science Turn

In what follows, this formula will be referred to as the hard science turn. It offers clues to the way foundational premises influence experimental design procedures and so weave the mesh of the perceptual net of medical researchers.

Adam Smith's response to Norman Cousins's claim for the therapeutic efficacy of laughter exemplifies the influence of this turn. Cousins's celebrated "Anatomy of an Illness" first appeared in the *New England Journal of Medicine* and subsequently was the subject of widespread discussion in and out of the professional medical community. Cousins chronicled his successful, unconventional cure of an illness tentatively diagnosed as collagen disease. (Smith's earlier mention of Cousin's cure in his *Powers of Mind* had spurred Cousins to tell his own story in more detail.) In what follows it will be shown how the momentum of the biomedical framework and its implicit premises carries Smith to his interpretation of the significance of Cousins's experience. The validity of Cousins's contention is not at issue here.

Smith subtitles his article, "Can a Change of Attitude Cure Dread Diseases?" Viewed within the vocabulary of biomedical premises, the question appears to cross categories. "Change of attitude" and "cure of disease" inhabit different logical spaces; how can mind (*res cogitans*) act on matter (*res extensa*)? Events that evoke such a question are likely to be regarded as surprising (anomalous) unless the referent of "change of attitude" is translated into a language compatible with "cure of disease," namely the language of physical events. At the risk of defaulting one's premises, it may be anticipated that proposed answers will eventually be of a form to reaffirm the framework that the events seem to challenge. Smith's response is indicative in this regard.

In Smith's retelling, Cousins, taking responsibility for his own cure, "checked out of the hospital and into a hotel. He had read up on stress and vitamin C, and he took massive doses of that vitamin. And he laughed. He sent for and screened The Marx Brothers movies and tapes of *Candid Camera*. . . . his symptoms disappeared and he returned to work." (1980, 11). Of interest is the number of behavioral change agents this account touches on—a manifest concern for health setting, active patient acquisition of medical information, mobilization of patient attitudes toward the illness, heightened expectations toward its outcome, and a will to recover. Besides this there is use of a prospective "holistic" change agent, laughter—"internal jogging," Cousins calls it—plus the use of a somewhat controversial physical change agent, ascorbic acid. Which of these, if any, were responsible for the cure? "I've been over and over my own case," says Cousins:

> Did the ascorbic acid help collagen formation? I certainly think so. What about the laughter? Well, oxygen deprivation is a common characteristic of every illness. So, if you want to be hard nosed, you can say that laughter enhances respiration, oxygenates the blood, combats the levels of carbon dioxide—like internal jogging. (in Smith 1980, 11–12)

This reference to being hard-nosed leads Cousins to distinguish between the art and science of medicine. While medical school students are well trained, they are not well educated, Cousins is quoted as saying: "They [know] the science of medicine but not the art of medicine." "I agree with Cousins," says Smith. As will be seen, this belief is qualified. Practicing the so-called art of medicine turns out to be, for Smith, a holding action, until the science of medicine arrives to displace the ground expeditiously held by the art. Smith further quotes Cousins, who raises the sixty-four-thousand-dollar question:

> We've all grown up with externalization. An illness is what happens after you bump into a germ. The germ comes from outside. Then you take something from a bottle to fix it. But other people bump into germs and nothing happens. Their defenses work. *Why do some defenses work when others don't?* (in Smith 1980, 12; italics added)

The premises at hand ordain the direction of the response. Thus, Smith notes first that the specific sites in brain cells upon which morphine and other opiates act have been identified by brain researchers; that the brain contains its own opiatelike substances, such as enkephalin and endorphin, which are speculated to stem not only physical pain but psychological stress as well. This discovery "spurred brain mappers to look for other natural substances in the receptor sites of brain cells." This sets the stage for Smith's estimate of the probable direction of medical research and the overall implication of Cousins's experience of laughter as a possible therapeutic agent. Because Smith's reaction is typical of the biomedical reaction, it throws light on residual thought patterns within the medical community:

> My speculation is that the brain researchers will go on cataloging the body's own apothecary and why it does what it does and why it can resist some conditions yet surrender to others. In ten or fifteen years, the neuro-scientists will have come up with some reasons why laughter and attitude have an effect, and these researchers will have dutifully assigned the appropriate natural substances to the appropriate parts of the brain and body. They will consider Norman's insights and experiences curious, antiquated, and charming, effective in a cumbersome way, just as historians of science consider the old researchers into combustion, who thought, before the isolation of oxygen, that a combustible released a substance called phlogiston when it burned. (1980, 12)

Several features of this response are noteworthy. One is the expression "the body's own apothecary." That the body is the ultimate referent of analysis is foreshadowed in the supposition that a reason has to be found why laughter and attitude have an organic effect. (Ordinarily a reason wouldn't be sought for why organic health had an effect on a person's attitude.) To the neuroscientists and biomedical researchers such reasons would be expected to take the general form of responses to the question: What neurochemical events are activated by bodily processes concomitant with laughter and attitudinal change? Thus, the neuroscientist might seek to explain a nonmaterial measure (like change of attitude) by translating it into the vocabulary of its physicochemical correlate. Consistent with dualist premises, the locus of attention is not the person (mind-body unity) who adopts an attitude, but the body (biological organism) in which resides the physiological process concomitant with the adopted attitude.

This means that the nonmaterial event can be effective (therapeutic or pathogenic) *because of* but not *in addition to* or to the exclusion of its correlative neurochemical event. In Smith's hands this seems to be the form the argument takes:

laughter  : natural   :: phlogiston : oxygen
(attitude    substance
in mind)    (in brain)

That is, the release of a natural substance in the brain explains the therapeutic efficacy of laughter in that it dispenses with the need to prescribe laughter, just as the oxygen concept dispenses with the need to posit phlogiston. Historically, phlogiston was a proxy (metaphysical) concept awaiting, as it were, a legitimate physical explanation. Retrospectively its application can be seen as a holding action, serving to cover the fact that no explanation for combustible behavior in the vocabulary of chemistry was yet available. Phlogiston is not explained; rather it is explained away by the concept of oxygen. After the discovery of oxidation, the need for the phlogiston concept was eliminated.

Here we see the assimilation of persons and subjective behavior (choosing to manipulate one's physiological state through altering one's attitude—inducing laughter, for example) to combustibles and chemical behavior. This assimilation indicates how methodological directives shape the form of answers sought. Hence, the reasonableness of Smith's proportionality and the unreasonableness of its mind-over-matter counterpart:

| behavioral agent (laughter) interacting with chemical agent (ascorbic acid) | : | mitigation of collagen disease | :: | mean kinetic energy of molecules | : | temperature of gas |
|---|---|---|---|---|---|---|

Consistent with the physical theory of disease causation, mental-emotional states, like attitudes or purposively induced laughter, are explained away in favor of the neurophysiological processes of which they are the precipitate.

## The Psychodynamics of Neurochemical Analgesia

We have suggested that the manner in which our sixty-four-thousand-dollar question is permitted to be framed preordains the direction of solution. In ten or fifteen years, neuroscientists can only offer reasons for body behavior of the sort Smith anticipates, not because of the way the world is but because of the world properties embraced. These properties dictate constraints within which reasons can be framed. If the ultimate referent is the body, the ultimate solution can be framed only in the language of the body—pathophysiology, neurochemistry, and so forth. The reason behind the apparent therapeutic efficacy of "phlogiston" (laughter) can only be sought, and found, among chemical (neurochemical) phenomena. Hence the thrust of Smith's proportionality. In fact, Smith's prediction is already being borne out. To the question "Can free will be reduced to the interplay of brain chemicals?" neuroscientist Solomon Snyder answers in a way that indicates he accepts the question as making good sense. "We don't know the answer," he replies. Elaborating, he demurs from the suggestion that because we can intend to create certain emotional states, like a relaxed attitude, and succeed, we therefore possess a faculty of mind with some leverage over the brain. The grounds of his demurral reveal the drawing power of the hard science turn. It might mean this, he says, "except that the mind itself is spun from the brain." He goes on to speculate, "Maybe the mind is a particular type of electrical field that arises from the operation of the brain, I don't know" (in Goleman, 1980, 76).

This use of "electrical field" is not inconsistent with prebehavioralistic-era uses of *mind* ("soul field") or the biofeedback theorist's use of *mind-brain*. However, we must be cautious here, for such an expression can be readily misunderstood. The concept of an electrical field either is or is not of a different logical type from that of the brain operations from which it arises. If it is of a different type, it functions as the biofeedback theorist's mind-brain concept and is subject to the same nonreductionist analysis. But if it is not—that is, if it is an electrical field consistent with traditional engineering principles—then it would seem incapable of the explanatory role ascribed to it, namely exhibiting free-will behavior. Of course, the notion of "different logical type" comes under scrutiny here, and this leads back to the meaning given to Snyder's terms "arises from" or "spun from." Is the mind "spun from" the brain as the brain and other animate matter are "spun from" inanimate matter?

The question of the appropriate meaning to be given to expressions like "spun from" and "arises from," in other words, is derivative upon a prior commitment to certain world properties. Is the universe composed of radical discontinuities or continuities?: do matter, life, mind . . . represent mutually irreducible ontological levels (nonreductionism) or not (reductionism)? The fundamental-level world property dictates the latter answer: they do not. This is sound first-revolution thinking. In this way the issue of appropriate research directions derives from our foundational premises.

Arguing not from the data of neuroscience but from twentieth-century findings in metamathematics, Douglas Hofstadter proposes a solution to the question addressed by Snyder. The answer is instructive in showing how pervasive are the premises on which the methodological strategy in question rests. Invoking the analogy of the way the Gödelian sentence achieves its meaning via one level mirroring its metalevel, Hofstadter offers the basis for a solution:

> The explanations of "emergent" phenomena in our brains—for instance . . . consciousness and free will—are based on . . . an interaction between levels in which the top level reaches back down toward the bottom level and influences it, while at the same time being itself determined by the bottom level. In other words, a self-reinforcing "resonance" between different levels. (1980, 709)

This apparent "interactionist" violation of the fundamental-level world property prompts Hofstadter to caution. "This should not be taken as an antireductionist position. It just implies that a reductionist explanation of a mind, *in order to be comprehensible,* must bring in 'soft' concepts such as levels, mappings, and meanings. In principle, I have no doubt that a totally reductionist but incomprehensible explanation of the brain exists . . ." (1980, 709).

The earlier distinction between different tiers of analysis illuminates Snyder's and Hofstadter's responses and their use of expressions like "spun from," "arises from," and "based on." The meaning given to these expressions draws on the methodological directives and explanatory presuppositions (tier 1) guiding the sciences underwriting biomedicine, which includes neurochemistry and molecular biology (tier 2). Our present interest is how the meaning implied in the use of these expressions reflects the influence of the hard science turn. In Snyder's case, this is surprising only in the sense that he is working at the frontiers of the interface between mind and brain (Snyder is trained in both psychiatry and pharmacology). It might be thought therefore that he would hold in abeyance, pending results of further studies like his own, the status of any methodological directives that prejudice the issue in favor of the ultimacy of either brain (matter) or mind. Instead, Snyder's remarks imply that the status of such directives, in particular the one favoring the ultimacy of matter (reductionism), is beyond question; that is, it is immune to future experimental findings like his own. That the mind is "spun from" the brain is a logical bar to the idea of a faculty of mind having leverage over the brain only by holding invariant the fundamental-level world property—or, in the language of method, the commitment to reductionism. Still, data alluded to in the questions put to Snyder—data of the sort uncovered by researchers in the use of behavioral and placebo therapies—appear to be of a sort capable of mounting a challenge to these premises, or commitments. Here, however, we are led back to the multiple-tiered and mutually reinforcing nature of grounds for adopting methodological commitments and infrascientific premises. Methods cohere to the world in proportion as sciences employing them reveal such a world. Only in the event and to the extent that they do not are the methods subject to reexamination.

A final illustration reinforces the notion that hazy areas that can be potentially controversial are dealt with by making them fit prior commitments. Interpretation of a recent placebo-effect experiment shows how such commitments serve not only to guide research policy but to steer scientists away from areas not accessible to the tools at hand.

Concerning an experiment on the mechanism of placebo analgesia, Snyder notes that the experimenters "asked if placebos relieve pain by triggering enkephalin." According to Snyder, they found that "a psychological influence on pain was due to the action of a specific neuro-transmitter" (Goleman, 1980, 76). As with its predecessors, "arises from" and "spun from," the expression "due to" is used in a way that raises as many issues as it is meant to allay. For the direction of the cause-effect relation seems not to be inherent in the experimental results; rather it is given by the presuppositions with which those results are approached. Thus, it would make no less sense to reverse the cause-effect implication. We might state that the action of a specific neurotrans-mitter in influencing pain (by acting on opiatelike receptor sites in brain cells) was *due to* a psychological influence (like expectancies regarding treatment outcome). In this event, we could with equal plausibility speak not of "The Mechanism of Placebo Analgesia"—the title of the *Lancet* article in question—but instead "The Psychodynamics of Neuro-chemical Analgesia."

Now, a similar experiment might be designed to establish the nature of these dynamics. That is, an agent might be administered (call it behavioral "nalaxone"—a positive-expectation antagonist, e.g., a willful switch from positive to negative expectations) designed to inhibit the flow of enkephalin to neural receptor sites. The possibility of achieving this outcome measures the warrant for concluding that the action of a specific neurotransmitter is *due to* a psychological influence, or, return-ing to the previous question put to Snyder, that the interplay of brain chemicals can be *reduced to* free-will activity.

J. D. Levine, N. D. Gordon, and H. L. Fields, the investigators of the experiment Snyder refers to, draw an inference similar to Snyder's:

> This study supports the hypothesis that endorphin activity *accounts for* placebo analgesia, first because nalaxone causes a significantly greater increase in pain ratings in placebo responders than in non-responders, and second because prior administration of nalaxone reduces the probability of a positive placebo response.

And:

> If, as the present study suggests, the analgesic effect of placebo is *based on* the action of endorphins, future research can proceed with an analysis of variables affecting endorphin activity rather than simply recording behav-ioral manifestations of placebo effects. (1978, 656, 657; italics added)

These italicized variants on the phrase "based on" would seem tacitly to import with their use the reductionist presupposition. Consider the inference made by Howard Fields, one of the team members of this experiment. Reviewing its import, he says:

> We could completely reverse placebo analgesia by a chemical manipulation. Since nalaxone is a pure narcotic antagonist, the tentative conclusion from

the study is that the placebo effect is based on the release of endorphins. (1978, 172)

But what if for Fields's first sentence we substitute its converse. Thus: "we could completely reverse chemical analgesia by placebo manipulation." According to the results of our imagined experiment, now the final sentence would read: "the chemical effect is *based on* the release of (negative) expectations" (placebo manipulation).

Of course the imagined experiment would warrant this conclusion only upon adoption of different world properties, in particular a fundamental-level world property that dictated a fundamental idealist rather than materialist level of reality. And it bears repeating that the experimental evidence itself confirms neither directive. For while it is true that the effect of placebo pain medication can be blocked by the prior administration of nalaxone, a substance that is known to inhibit the action of the endorphins, it is equally true that the release of endorphins can itself be blocked at its source by the administration of a behavioral "nalaxone"—for example, a willful switch to a negative expectation concerning pain outcome. And this behavioral "nalaxone" might likewise be regarded as a "substance" (attitude) known to inhibit the action of the flow of endorphins (Miller, 1970).

This brings us back to the question of what our vocabulary (world properties, methodological tools) permits. This was our motivating question: "Why do the defenses of some *patients* work when the defenses of others do not?" The italicized word stands for "the hosts or loci of disease," here the persons as distinct from the biological organisms. The interactive mix that makes up the defenses of the patient (and thereby for which the researcher can search) can extend only so far as the limits of the researcher's tools and vocabulary. And we have seen that the range of biomedical tools extends only over "the sick body upon which the nature of . . . the thoughts of the patient and doctor have no causal impact," to quote from the second medical world property. Defenses can be sought only within the body or, when discovered outside the body (e.g., doctor-patient relationship, a laughing attitude), must be translated into a single-level, physicalist vocabulary. And this is an exclusively body vocabulary.

We have come full circle. To interpret the experimental results as offering a basis for showing the neurochemical mechanism of placebo analgesia is to endorse the vocabulary provided by biomedical premises. To interpret these results as offering a basis for showing the psychodynamics of neurochemical analgesia would require endorsement of a radically different set of premises, an "other explanation." Depending on the vocabulary inherited, medical research will tend to be guided and experimental results interpreted accordingly. The net result of this convertibility argument (the neurochemistry of placebo analgesia or the psychodynamics of neurochemical analgesia) is that the findings of medical research are an integral but insufficient base for determining a prudent medical strategy.

Thus far in this section we have contended that areas of potential controversy ("crises") are difficult to recognize because explanatory frameworks, not individual findings, are minimum units of meaning. In the absence of a fully developed successor framework, there is nothing by means of which to distinguish threats to one's framework from research challenges within one's framework. Individual findings, however surprising, rather than calling for reevaluation of premises, in the absence of a successor framework remain simply outstanding problems on our research agenda. They call at most for what Kuhn calls "ad hoc modifications of theory." But just as the notion of crisis is framework-dependent, so also is its mirror notion, success in achieving stated framework goals. For goals, too, can be stated only within the compass of the framework's vocabulary. To claim that something possibly achievable within a yet to be articulated framework (reaching the moon by climbing a tall-enough tree) has not been achieved is to speak nonsense. In this way the question concerning an appropriate research policy is closely linked to the question of an appropriate method for gauging research success. The question "To what extent do foundational premises, by influencing the choice of puzzle forms, color our selection of research directions?" is a sister question to "To what extent do foundational premises, by influencing the choice of puzzle forms, color our estimate of the success of our research effort?"

# PART TWO

# Prelude to Revolt

. . . May God us keep
From single Vision and Newton's sleep.
                    —William Blake

[Medical students'] ideas reflect the predominant notions in
society about the work of the doctor: that he is concerned with
the diagnosis and treatment of disease in individual patients,
that most patients are cured by treatment and that it is on
medical intervention that health primarily depends. It is like a
slap in the face for a student to be told at the outset of his
training that at least on the second and third points these ideas
need revision: that health is not determined mainly by medical
intervention and that the needs of patients extend far beyond
what can be achieved by investigation and active treatment.
                    —Thomas McKeown
                    *The Role of Medicine*

A merry heart doeth good like a medicine: but a broken spirit
drieth the bones.
                    —Proverbs 17:23

# INTRODUCTION TO PART TWO

P art Two examines the medical landscape from a foundations perspective. Here various medical specialties, disciplines, interest groups, and countermovements—termed insurgents—are viewed as responses to biomedical orthodoxy. The main thesis of Part Two is that the insurgents fail to accomplish what they seem to be attempting. That is, they do not provide the medical enterprise with an alternative to the biomedical model. When the common features of the insurgents are unpacked, what becomes clear is that the philosophical and scientific foundations of contemporary (bio)medicine go unchallenged. The insurgents, in spite of some rather pointed criticisms, seek only to build upon the biomedical edifice. Their position can be stated briefly as détente—the joining together of "biomedical cure" and "holistic care" to achieve a comprehensive health care strategy. Part Two argues that this strategy fails. As attractive and seemingly uncomplicated as détente appears to be, it contains conceptual problems of its own that deflect research and practice from significant etiological factors. *It will be shown that the insurgents do not follow the implications of their arguments to their logical conclusion. For if they did, they would provide the basis for alternative medical foundations—medicine's second revolution.*

# 4

## The Medical Landscape:
## Response to the Limitations
## of Biomedicine

Biomedicine is based on physicalist premises. This approach is underscored by the positivist conviction that "the whole of biology would become simply a chapter of physics and chemistry." There is no doubt that acceptance of such a position has led to increased understanding of the mechanisms of disease, which has in turn led to breakthroughs in disease management. In this view, it is not difficult to see why Western medicine is often referred to as one of humankind's most outstanding contemporary achievements—"the envy of the world," as John Knowles called it. However, in the midst of the success, there is the unsettling sense of "crisis." Critics both within and without the medical community have expressed concern that biomedicine is too narrowly focused in its research and practice. They charge that because biomedicine is guided by a logic that requires all meaningful data to be in principle reducible to a single-level physicalist vocabulary, there will always be a part of medicine beyond the grasp of its scientific capabilities. In the present chapter, this charge will be examined.

## The Critique of Biomedicine

The limits of the biomedical model can be seen in the curious way in which the application of certain terms has emerged in medical dialogue. Such terms as "preventive" versus "curative" medicine, "conditions for" versus "causes of" disease, and "acute" versus "chronic" disease all point to a tension that exists between what the biomedical model can include and what it cannot include within its explanatory range. For example, in spite of the experimental efficacy of placebo treatments, placebo is defined as "an inactive substance . . . given to satisfy the patient's symbolic need for drug therapy" (*Dorland's* 1974). It is telling that the vocabulary is phrased to avoid violating the physicalist premises of the biomedical model (though the explanation for "symbolic need" remains unclear). To recognize the placebo effect as being psychoactive as opposed to biochemically active would violate foundation premises that recognize the primacy of the body to the exclusion of mind.

The same consideration applies to the emergence of disease categories like psychosomatic disease or, more recently, diseases called chronic and degenerative—sometimes termed "diseases of civilization." The reason why these diseases, which include cardiovascular disorders, cancer, arthritis, and respiratory diseases, warrant a novel category is not always made clear. Conceivably the category represents the issuing of a promissory note, one that accepts biomedical premises. Implicit is the general acceptance that further research into chronic illness will lead to the same success achieved with acute infectious diseases. In other words, the two categories of illness differ in degree and not in kind.

This tension is nowhere more evident than in the distinctions made between the science of medicine and the art of medicine. From the critic's point of view, the art of medicine starts where the science of medicine begins to show its limitations. According to this view, scientific medicine can explain only a portion of the disease spectrum—that part which comports with somatic premises. Those areas which have been relegated to the category of art of medicine—a euphemistic way of saying their successes cannot be explained in biomedical terms—occupy a secondary status in the medical scheme.

John Powles sees as paradoxical that there should be so much enthusiasm for developments in contemporary medicine when a realistic appraisal suggests that decreasing returns and increasing costs best characterize today's medical story. Even in the category of infectious disease, generally conceded to be the area best exhibiting biomedical prowess, Powles argues that the stunning progress is mostly attributable to the provision of food, sanitary control, and the regulation of births. It was only later that the impressive capacity to intervene in individuals by means of immunization and antibiotics was acquired. Powles's point is to demonstrate "the major importance for health, of man's interactions with his environment—that is, his ecology" (1973, 6).

To help make his case, Powles presents what he considers to be the contemporary disease burden. To do this he posits what he calls a "natural state" of man. He then assesses various disease categories relative to this natural state. It is worthwhile to quote extensively Powles' development of this approach, termed the "baseline argument."

For at least 99 per cent of the duration of their existence on Earth members of the genus *Homo* have lived by hunting and gathering. This way of life was presumably also shared by the preceding pre-hominids. Of the 50,000 odd generations in the last million years of human history, only about 400 have occurred since agriculture was first adopted by one part of the human population. With agriculture came dramatic changes in diet, population density, and patterns of daily life—and the human organism was exposed to stresses that were, in evolutionary terms, novel. It is unlikely that there has been major biological change in man since the Neolithic revolution. Such change is highly improbable with respect to the more recent adoption of urban and advanced industrial patterns of life. The selection pressures associated with hunter-gathering have been predominant in determining man's genetic constitution. It is therefore reasonable to take the functioning of the human organism under such circumstances as a baseline in discussing the impact of civilisation and medical technology on the health of man. (1973, 4)

Powles goes on to examine cardiovascular disease as a major instance of a disease that has increased relative to the posited "natural state" of man. There is a large body of data showing that ischemic heart disease increases with increasing economic development. Such epidemiological evidence supports Powles's claim that "These degenerative processes may be characterised as diseases of maladaptation in the sense that they arise 'because our earlier evolution has left us genetically unsuited for life in an industrialized society.' They constitute a large and growing component of the contemporary disease burden" (1973, 8). Powles reports similar findings with regard to cancer—that "80 per cent of all cancer has its etiology in man's relation to his environment" (1973, 10).

Powles summarizes:

Industrial populations owe their current health standards to a pattern of ecological relationships which serves to reduce their vulnerability to death from infection and to a lesser extent to the capabilities of clinical medicine. Unfortunately this new way of life, because it is so far removed from that to which man is adapted by evolution, has produced its own disease burden. These diseases of maladaptation are, in many cases, increasing. (1973, 12)

Hence, an evolutionary baseline analysis provides insights into both the decline in infectious disease and the increase in chronic disease. And both are diseases of maladaptation.

The above view offers a direct challenge to the biomedical strategy. This strategy, as Powles documents with expenditure figures, is concentrated on short-time hospital care and drugs. For example, Powles views ischemic heart disease as the paradigmatic disease of maladaptation, and the response to it is paradigmatically biomedical—hospital treatment with emphasis on (expensive) intensive cardiac care unit treatment. Such a strategy is based on an engineering approach to medical practice. It is this approach that Powles takes issue with because he sees it as seriously thwarting the medical effort. That is, perceptions of medical problems have been seriously constrained by limits inherent in medical thinking. For example, biomedicine (an engineering approach) focuses on the biology of the individual.[1] As such, "Medicine has deprived itself of the only possible theoretical basis [e.g., evolutionary theory, historical demography, and medical ecology] on which criteria for biological normality in man could rest." Thus, medicine fails to systematically examine "way of life" factors as potential pathological factors. Levels of organization above the individual, such as social structure, are not recognized as significant. "With little understanding of the way of life to which man is biologically adapted, modern medicine is unable to predict the possible harmful consequences of departures from it" (1973, 14).

Arthur Kleinman, Leon Eisenberg, and Byron Good argue that medicine's "crisis" can be (in part) attributed to the failure of biomedicine to distinguish between disease and illness.[2] They argue that

> biomedicine is primarily interested in the recognition and treatment of disease [curing]. So paramount is this orientation that the professional training of doctors tends to disregard illness and its treatment. Biomedicine has increasingly banished the illness experience as a legitimate object of clinical concern. Carried to its extreme, this orientation, so successful in generating technological interventions, leads to a veterinary practice of medicine.
>
> This systematic inattention to illness is in part responsible for patient noncompliance, patient and family dissatisfaction with professional health care, and inadequate clinical care. (1978, 252)

From this point of view, medicine's crisis is a consequence of the range of the physician's responsibility. This range is intimately connected to

1. For a description of this approach, Powles cites A. C. Crombie: "The biology of the individual is more like engineering than physics, in that each type of living organism is a solution to a specific set of engineering problems—problems of intake and conversion of fuel, locomotion, communication, replication and so on which it has to solve to survive. This subject matter has imposed on physiology its characteristic program: to find out how an organism works by taking it to pieces and trying to put it together again from knowledge of the parts" (in Powles 1973, 14). A. C. Crombie, "The Future of Biology: The History of a Program," *Federation Proceedings* 25 (1966): 1448–1453.

2. According to their definition: "That distinction holds that disease in the Western medical paradigm is malfunctioning or maladaptation of biologic and psychophysiologic processes in the individual; whereas illness represents personal, interpersonal, and cultural reactions to disease or discomfort. Illness is shaped by cultural factors governing perception, labeling, explanation, and valuation of the discomforting experience, processes embedded in a complex family, social, and cultural nexus. Because illness experience is an intimate part of social systems of meaning and rules for behavior, it is strongly influenced by culture; it is, as we shall see, culturally constructed" (1978, 258).

the espoused concept of disease, patient, and therapy—all of which are artifacts of the accepted medical model.

John H. Knowles writes, "Chronic and degenerative diseases have replaced acute infectious ones as the primary health problem [and] demand long-term study. They call for an understanding of the interaction between the multiple variables in both causation and the course of a disease, if therapy is to be evaluated effectively" (1977, 5). When contrasted with "acute infectious diseases," this notion of chronic degenerative diseases may be interpreted as a circumspect designation for diseases which it ought to be our responsibility to control but which we cannot, perhaps because of the limitations of our model. On this view, our model theoretically controls acute microbial diseases, while it does not theoretically control chronic nonmicrobial diseases.

How allegations of crisis in medicine are traditionally perceived is exemplified by a self-examination of the field conducted by the Commission on Critical Choices for Americans. Its results were published in the Winter 1977 issue of *Daedalus* under the title "Doing Better and Feeling Worse," with an introduction by Knowles, from which the foregoing quotation is taken. Issues examined range widely, probing the politics, economics, sociology, and ethics of medicine. Conspicuous by its absence is a critical examination of the philosophical, scientific, and methodological premises that underlie contemporary medicine. Not that any single inquiry should be expected to touch all bases; rather what is surprising is the assumption that "a fair appraisal of the 'health system' that now prevails in the United States" (Graubard 1977, 4) comprising "issues that this group found central to any consideration of America's health dilemma" (Knowles 1977, 5) could be conducted independently of an exploration of the conceptual foundations animating that system.

One inference drawn by these panelists is that while curative, or scientific, medicine is effective in the treatment of those diseases for which it was primarily designed, the current dilemma stems from the fact that today's diseases for the most part do not conform to this disease type. They are not infectious. Concludes Aaron Waldovsky: "The Great Equation, Medical Care Equals Health . . . is wrong." It is wrong, he implies, because the medical care system is oriented away from today's critical determinants of health and disease:

> The best estimates are that the medical system (doctors, drugs, hospitals) affects about 10 per cent of the usual indices for measuring health: whether you live at all (infant mortality), how well you live (days lost due to sickness), how long you live (adult mortality). The remaining 90 per cent are determined by factors over which doctors have little or no control, from individual life style (smoking, exercise, worry), to social conditions (income, eating habits, physiological inheritance), to the physical environment

(air and water quality). Most of the bad things that happen to people are at present beyond the reach of medicine. (1977, 105)

A common thread running through the arguments of Powles, Kleinman, and others is that the premises of modern scientific medicine as established in the biomedical model are not adequate to addressing the multifactorial basis for disease. According to Engel, "the biochemical defect constitutes but one factor among many, the complex interaction of which ultimately may culminate in active disease or manifest illness" (1981, 131).

Kazem Sadegh-Zadeh's formal framework for recognizing the interaction of somatic and extrasomatic variables provides further grounds for the restrictiveness of biomedicine. Sadegh-Zadeh's approach is directed not (as above) at examining disease but rather at examining the efficacy of treatments. His initial concern is that one must properly distinguish between *drug* and *treatment*. His point is that a drug is not a treatment but merely one single component of a complex treatment schedule. Here Sadegh-Zadeh offers a parallel critique of biomedicine's narrowly conceived vocabulary for approaching disease and therapy. His use of the term *drug* is synonymous with exemplar biomedical therapies—chemical substances, surgery, and the like. From the biomedical critic's view, Sadegh-Zadeh recognizes the same "complexity" from the treatment perspective that others have argued from the diagnostic perspective.

Sadegh-Zadeh defines a treatment complex as consisting of at least the following eight components:

> (a) species of the treated subject, e.g., dog, human child, adult; (b) his specific diseased state, e.g., acute cystitis; (c) his boundary health conditions, e.g., penicillin allergy; (d) his specific social environment; (e) drug; (f) the image and psychological type of the therapist; (g) his modus therapeuticus placed somewhere between the two extremes "prescribing without further ado" and "being the ideal physician every patient dreams of," and (h) the treatment goal. (1982, 261)

Each component is included specifically because of its impact on controlling the disease state. This suggests that bio-state, psycho-state, and socio-state variables are diagnostically significant for achieving the goal of overall health. The biomedical model does not endorse a diagnostic approach that would include gathering information within each of the above eightfold complex. The implication is that modern medical research is conducted such that approximately three-eighths of the areas calling for research are under active research. The other five-eighths are dealt with, in so far as they are dealt with, under one or other of the following headings:

Prevention

Rehabilitation

Support

Side effects

"Art"

Ad hoc

Not at all (because of the absence of a rationale that would suggest these are areas to be researched as potentially therapeutic)

Thus, the biomedical model must invoke terms outside of its formal vocabulary to fully account for disease and treatment categories. From the critic's perspective, this points to a descriptive inadequacy of the model.

Unless these surplus variables can be shown as either reducible to physical variables or incapable of regimentation, Sadegh-Zadeh's analysis implies a potential scandal in medicine. Biomedicine sanctions "drugs" to counteract pathogenic agents, while there exists no meaningful corresponding vocabulary for describing the remainder of the treatment matrix—no rationale for vigorous and systematic research into the therapeutic potential of extrasomatic factors. One conclusion that may be drawn is that current medical research and practice are half-scientific, half-serendipitous. Money and energies are being misspent not for want of good intentions but for want of a rationale. "It is therefore concluded that the problem of diminishing returns [of modern scientific medicine] is a real one. It results from the nature of the contemporary disease burden and the *limited front* on which medical effort has been concentrated" (Powles 1973, 16; italics added).


# Medical Countermovements

"Medicine's crisis," claims Engel, "stems from the logical inference that since 'disease' is defined in terms of somatic parameters, physicians need not be concerned with psychosocial issues which lie outside medicine's responsibility and authority" (1977, 129). We can identify, as a result, two sources of dissatisfaction that have contributed to a medical landscape that tries to extend biomedicine's narrow focus.

First, major degrees of patients' dissatisfaction became an inescapable consequence of medical practice as soon as the Newtonian-Cartesian worldview became the dominant foundation for what physicians were expected to do with patients. With that the concept of the physician as healer went progressively into decline. As a result, right from the beginning a wide variety of health cults and sects flourished, many of them preferred to regular physicians because treatments were less dangerous and less difficult. These groups included proponents of naturopathy, homeopathy, chiropractic, nutritional medicine, Christian Science, psychic healing, and others, of which the latest version is holistic medicine, which like its predecessors includes some physicians and many who are not physicians. What all of them have in common is an effort to meet the perceived human needs of patients neglected by "scientific medicine." The marketplace has played an enormous part in the rise and fall of popularity of each.

Second, there is dissatisfaction within the medical community. From clinicians to internists, the multicausal basis for disease is widely recognized, yet biomedicine can deal scientifically with only those factors which fit the physically based requirements of the model. For example, Alfred Evans reports that "causation in both infectious and noninfectious disease involves a complex interplay of agents, environmental, and host factors" (1978, 254). Among them he includes socioeconomic level and behavior patterns. For Edmund Pellegrino, the question is "how to maintain the progress we have achieved with scientific medicine while encompassing the many dimensions which are not susceptible to a scientific approach" (private correspondence, 1985).

With these sources of dissatisfaction in mind, we will take a closer look at some elements of the medical landscape that such discontent has given rise to. Our interest will focus on a group of three medical countermovements that will be referred to as the "insurgents." They have been chosen for three reasons. First, each member of this group can boast of a significant following. They are not splinter groups but rather a recognized part of the medical enterprise. Their ideas are routinely published in professional journals, general periodicals, and books in the field of medicine. Second, each member of this group can count among its supporters respected members of the medical community. As such these medical programs receive research funding from nationally recognized sources and argue their case based on empirical findings. And third, each member of this group can be viewed as responding to a perceived limitation of biomedicine. Their effort to avoid the "narrow focus" critique of biomedicine is a common theme to all of them. Specifically, the insurgents chosen are: holistic medicine, environmental medicine, and behavioral medicine.

## HOLISTIC MEDICINE

Proponents of holistic medicine argue that the proper scope of medicine is not just the "diseased body" as biomedical practitioners would propose, but the "sick person." The following definition cited in *Health for the Whole Person* will serve to highlight what is meant by *holistic medicine*—a term which has come to suggest many things.

> First, such an approach involves expanding our focus to include the many personal, familial, social, and environmental factors that promote health, prevent illness, and encourage healing. Second, a holistic approach views the patient as an individual person, not as a symptom-bearing organism. This attitude emphasizes the self-responsibility of the person for his or her health and the importance of mobilizing the person's own health capacities, rather than treating illness only from the outside. Third, the holistic approach tries to make wise use of the many diagnostic, treatment, and health modalities that are available in addition to the standard materia medica. (Hastings 1980, xi)

Proponents of holistic medicine argue that the biomedical model (because of its paradigmatic commitment) requires the researcher and practitioner to focus too narrowly on the somatic nature of disease and thereby exclude proper consideration of the "sick person." Their response is to encourage researchers and practitioners to more vigorously pursue certain alternative clinical avenues—particularly those which involve extrasomatic, caring qualities. In particular, the holistic practitioner encourages the patient to get involved in the healing process. This is consistent with the basic concept of holistic health, which recognizes the impact that attitudes and emotions can have on physiological states. Holistic medicine "holds that the human being is a fully coherent and integrated life-support system with built-in mechanisms of balance and control. In this sense, the mind is regarded not just as a biological switchboard but a center for total management. And it is recognized that the mind must not be bypassed or underestimated in any effort to deal with breakdowns, whether from stress or pathological organisms" (Cousins in Pelletier 1979, xiv). James S. Gordon speaks of the holistic "appreciation of patients as mental and emotional, social and spiritual, as well as physical beings" (1980, 3).

Holistic practitioners view biomedicine as after-the-fact treatment. As such, biomedical practice begins once disease has been found. Holistic practice, on the other hand, sees its role as emphasizing the maintenance of health prior to the appearance of disease. This shift in orientation places the holistic effort in the arena of disease prevention and health maintenance as opposed to the "crisis care of pathology." Following naturally from this is the holistic strategy of preventive medicine, which addresses itself to stress management, diet, exercise, and environmental safeguards. The holistic practitioner thus argues that "health must involve the positive modification of the conditions which lead to disease rather than simple intervention in the mechanism of a disorder after it has occurred" (Pelletier 1979, 5).

## ENVIRONMENTAL MEDICINE

The second medical strategy that warrants examination is environmental medicine. Its proponents maintain that essential to an understanding of the full context of disease is the social and physical environment in which the disease burden of individuals is embedded. Its theoretical grounds are stated by Thomas McKeown, who says:

> During his evolution man, like other living things, was exposed to rigorous natural selection which restricted disease determined irreversibly at fertilization to a low frequency. Most diseases and disabilities are therefore due to environmental influences operating on variable genetic material, and the solution of disease problems depends essentially on the removal or modification of the deleterious agents. (1979, 164)

In order to contrast the respective domains of environmental medicine and biological (bio) medicine, environmental medicine advocates commonly draw a distinction between the mechanisms and the origins of disease. While mainstream medicine investigates disease mechanisms, the focus of environmental medicine is disease origins. Advocates of environmental medicine cite studies in historical demography that identify the underlying reasons for the improvement of health over the past three centuries. It appears that improvement stems mainly not from medical intervention in disease processes but from wider, more general influences. Chief among these are nutritional (provision of food), environmental (removal of hazards), and behavioral (limitations of numbers) influences. Hence, say proponents, "Contrary to what is generally believed, the most fundamental issue confronting medical science is not the solution of one or more of the unsolved biomedical problems: it is evaluation of two approaches to the control of disease, one through an understanding of mechanisms and the other through a knowledge of origins" (McKeown 1979, 166). And: "The most fundamental question in medicine is why disease occurs rather than how it operates after it has occurred; that is to say, conceptually the origins of disease should take precedence over the nature of disease processes" (148).

## BEHAVIORAL MEDICINE

The final counterstrategy chosen for discussion is behavioral medicine. Behavioral medicine incorporates such unusual-sounding disciplines as neuroendocrinology and psychoneuroimmunology. The movement's most basic assumption is that there is an interrelationship among the immune system, the central nervous system, and the endocrine system. Behavioral medicine is "an emerging field which treats mind and body as two ends of the same continuum. The core of basic research in this field is an attempt to locate the specific neurochemical mechanisms by which subjective states—specifically those associated with emotional stress—lead to disease" (Holden 1980, 479). To achieve its goals, behavioral medicine seeks to integrate biological and behavioral knowledge in a multidisciplinary approach.

Proponents of behavioral medicine recognize that the activities of the mind and brain are inseparable. Their approach is to build on the findings that brain activity is linked with body functions. By locating the specific neurochemical mechanisms by which subjective states lead to disease, proponents seek either to develop chemical counteractants to nullify unfavorable reactions or to offer behavioral therapies (biofeedback or other methods of conditioning behavior) that address these reactions. For example, research indicates that the type A personality (hard-driving, impatient, time-conscious) is predictive of coronary trouble as well as is smoking, serum cholesterol, and hypertension. Thus, a goal of behavioral medicine would be to refine just what behaviors are most closely linked with heart attacks and can be demonstrably linked to physical precipitators of heart disease.

Behavioral medicine research is characterized by an intersystemic orientation. For example, findings in neuroendocrinology point to the complex ways in which the central nervous system and endocrine system are connected. By using a systems approach, simple cause-and-effect relationships give way to a more adequate analysis in terms of feedback loops to trace complex interactions.

Behavioral medicine extends the biomedical notion of disease mechanisms to include the mechanisms of subjective states. This accounts for the interest proponents have in the roles that stress, personality, coping styles, and the immune system play in the onset and course of certain diseases. In particular, medical scientists have correlated stress with a dampening or suppression of the immune system. A goal of behavioral medicine is therefore combating the physiological manifestations of stress.

Advocates of behavioral medicine point out that because conditioning can affect immunity, it follows that the brain affects resistance to illness. In surveying the field, Alan Anderson claims that "the evidence of a link between mind and immunity has become difficult to refute. . . . [This interaction] is highlighted by the fact that psychosocial stimuli may sometimes enhance [or suppress] immune activity" (1982, 55). Here we see the basis for the broadening of the biomedical focus—disease understood as the result of a stressful environment suppressing the immune system.

The above treatment of the medical landscape is by no means comprehensive. It serves to illustrate that while biomedical thinking dominates, it has also spawned different orientations that compensate for its excesses. These movements, research agendas, counterstrategies, and so forth, also compete with biomedicine for funding. In some cases the differences with biomedicine are dramatic; in others it is merely an in-house conflict. In any case, there is the appearance that the medical enterprise is involved in active debate over foundation issues. However, this is not the case. The next chapter will argue that the medical landscape is fraught with conceptual confusion, contradictions, and unrecognized dualisms. The debate, to the extent that one exists, leaves medical foundations unchallenged.

# 5

## The Failure of Détente

One gets the sense that the medical landscape—dominated by biomedicine but also including a host of alternative medical modalities that fill in the extrasomatic cracks—is both diverse and comprehensive in its reach. Thus, while "biological models of medicine arbitrarily exclude considerations of emotions, consciousness, and psychosocial variables in order to focus upon specific areas such as the biochemistry of infectious diseases" (Pelletier 1979, 25–26), the counterstrategies include what biomedicine excludes. Hence, the different medical strategies are a response to biomedical "neglect." In the case of holistic medicine, it "has evolved in tandem with the critique of modern biomedicine" (Hastings 1980, 15).

It appears that the additional strategies offer the medical community a choice between fundamentally different orientations. Accordingly, it seems that any controversy between the biomedical establishment and the competing alternatives would lead the medical community into a rigorous debate over foundation issues. It is a contention of this study that this is *not* the case.

This study contends that the extrabiomedical strategies, as attractive and seemingly uncomplicated as they appear to be, actually harbor serious shortcomings of their own. We will argue that the insurgents' thesis—essentially the summative joining together of the strengths of biomedical *cure* and holistic *care*—contains conceptual problems that deflect research and practice from significant etiological factors. The implications of this are so serious that the consequences of accepting this thesis (in any of its forms) are as potentially undermining, both for research and practice, to comprehensive health care as the consequences of accepting its biomedical counterpart.

Basic to any extrabiomedical strategy is a reinterpretation of the health care system so that the biological approach is seen as one part of a more comprehensive program of health care. A complete program will combine the principles of biomedicine and those of preventive medicine. Side by side with a consideration of pathogenic (somatic) factors goes a consideration of extrasomatic factors, the contributing factors of disease. Together these two considerations form a comprehensive health care system. "Each state of health and disease," says Pelletier, "requires a consideration of all contributing factors: psychological, psychosocial, and spiritual" (1979, 31). In what follows it will be argued that this ecumenical solution, bringing under one roof the principles of health care medicine and "crisis intervention" medicine, leads to an impasse. The contours of this impasse can be seen by tracing any of the strategies, central to which is the distinction between preventive medicine on the one hand and curative medicine or medicine per se on the other. Holistic medicine and environmental medicine will be the subject of such an examination.

## The Holistic Option

One classification with wide currency differentiates primary, secondary, and tertiary health care services. According to it, "primary prevention is based upon the diagnosis and treatment of disease in the asymptomatic stage and upon education to promote the avoidance of disease and disability. Secondary prevention is defined as the diagnosis and treatment of disease before serious clinical symptoms have become overtly manifest. A degree of disorder is present, and the concern is to prevent or reduce the development of a more serious disease. Lastly, tertiary care consists of the treatment of severe disorders in order to prevent them from becoming worse or even terminal" (Pelletier 1979, 45). Most of the medical care given today is tertiary care. This is "care which attempts to bring about curative results, alleviate suffering, restore the maximum possible degree of function, and prolong life at any cost" (1979, 45). In what follows, tertiary care will be referred to as curative medicine or medicine per se.

Such a classification has a high degree of plausibility. It permits distinctions between curative or "scientific" medicine (tertiary care) and health care or preventive medicine (primary and secondary care). It is, however, understood that the term *medicine* is accorded to primary and secondary care by metaphorical extension only. For the distinction rests on a basic difference between causes of disease and conditions or side effects of disease. There are etiologic disease agents (pathogens) and there are, in addition, risk factors or triggering agents of disease. Strictly speaking, only the first, pathogens, by virtue of their physical or chemical properties, have the capacity to directly damage cells or other parts of the body. The second, the contributing factors of disease, place a burden on or limit the capacity of an organism or body part. Rather than disease-producing, they are disease-disposing: they render an individual susceptible to etiologic disease agents. While increasing the likelihood of contracting disease, they do not themselves produce disease. Hence the categorical distinction between smoking, a behavior, and carcinogens, a substance. If smoking predisposes one to a particular disease, in this vocabulary it is carcinogens that produce it.

Corresponding to this distinction between pathogenic agents and contributing factors of disease is the distinction between medical interventions and preventive or health maintenance measures. In the language of the holistic option, only the first, physician-directed medical interventions, are aimed at pathologically derived patient symptoms. Preventive measures are aimed rather at providing the individual with ways of maintaining health and avoiding disease. To better understand this division, contrast first, interventions aimed at alleviating ventricular fibrillation (curative), and second, those aimed at modifying certain unhealthy behavior patterns, "type A" behavior, for example (preventive or rehabilitative). Such distinctions, whether or not explicitly acknowledged, are embedded in the institutional role divisions shaping today's health care field. Thus there are physicians, psychological counselors, nurses, physical therapists, public health care officials, and others. While each of these professionals intervenes in typically different ways, it is generally conceded that interventions of only one group are properly medical in the sense of being accredited by professional medical associations and deriving directly from medical science.

Within the framework of such a classification, preventive or holistic health care approaches are not so much an alternative to as an extension and modification of our present medical model. In his book *Holistic Medicine*, Pelletier puts it this way: "Medicine is regarded as one aspect of comprehensive health care. . . . A holistic approach moves from a focus on pathology [tertiary care] to an educational approach that recognizes an individual's ability to use experience for positive change [primary and secondary care]" (1979, 14, 47). Herbert Benson differentiates tertiary-care medicine, today's rigorously scientific approach, and what he terms behavioral medicine. He characterizes behavioral medicine as an interdisciplinary approach to health care incorporating "the principles of medicine, physiology, psychiatry and psychology. It enables you as a patient to be viewed as an entire individual . . . [and] recognizes that your behavior is related to your illness" (1979, 16). Benson issues a call for the peaceful coexistence of scientific and behavioral medicine by integrating older behavioral with more recent scientific successes.

This broadened concept of health care—whether termed behavioral or holistic medicine (here the two can be used interchangeably)— appears to be continuous with, not antithetical to, scientific medicine or biomedicine. James Gordon characterizes holistic medicine as "at least potentially, a corrective to the excesses of biomedicine, a supplement to its deficiencies. . . . It sets our contemporary concern with the cure of diseases in the larger frame of health care, enlarges and enriches the roles of both health care providers and patients, and provides a framework within which many techniques—old and new, Western and non-Western—may be used" (1980, 15). Clearly, holistic medicine seeks détente with biomedicine. Pelletier delineates the boundaries of these two complementary medical approaches: "It would be disastrous to try to force holistic health care into the mold of biomedicine, whose methods are preponderantly surgical or pharmaceutical. The span of holistic medicine is far broader, including prevention, life-style modification, psychological counseling, and supporting the patient as a responsible individual" (1979, 38). All that is necessary is to join holistic care to conventionally prescribed biomedical therapies to create a truly comprehensive health care program. This union forms the holistic option.

This option seems to capture the best of two medical worlds—all bases are covered. But a paradox surfaces. If extrasomatic factors are increasingly recognized as the source of contemporary disorders, then scientific principles underwriting conventional diagnoses cannot be meaningfully invoked—they do not offer reasons for diagnosis and treatment. It is the incidence of such diseases that influential studies document and that Pelletier cites. Thus, the 1975 HEW report, *Forward Plan for Health,* states that lifestyle and the physical and social environments are the dominant influences determining mortality and morbidity in this century. Instead of the infectious diseases that were among the pervasive afflictions of nineteenth- and early-twentieth-century industrial societies (and which played a role in determining biomedically oriented indices of morbidity), the report concludes that the major afflictions of postindustrial societies are not somatic but psychosomatic or psychosociosomatic in origin (HEW 1975). These are diseases that Dubos terms "afflictions of civilization." June Goodfield calls them self-inflicted diseases or "diseases of choice."[1] Hans Selye calls them "stress-related" disorders. They include, besides cardiovascular disease, cancer, arthritis, and respiratory disorders, the pervasive incidence of mental disorders like depression. In an attempt to evaluate the data of the National Center for Health Statistics, a 1973 committee formed for the purpose anticipated this conclusion: "Mortality was a sensitive indicator of health status when the infectious diseases were a major health problem." On the other hand: "Indices sensitive to changes in lifestyle and the quality of life will become increasingly significant" (Hauser et al. 1973, 63, 10). Summing up these findings and others like them, Pelletier concludes: "Most major chronic illnesses in the United States and other

1. "Those which arise from excesses in life-style [characteristic of highly developed technological societies], or the pollution of [their] environment" (1977, 198).

post-industrial nations have environmental and psychosocial components that play important parts in their etiology" (1979, 53).

This conclusion has far-reaching implications for the holistic health movement. Of present interest is its bearing on the continued viability of the holistic option. If treatment prescribed by nonphysician health professionals like practitioners of holistic medicine are designed only for health maintenance and disease prevention (e.g., diet, exercise regimens), then the term *treatment* is applied only in a loose way. If, however, this treatment is prescribed for the purpose of combating components that play vital roles in the etiology of disease, components that may be of a biological *or* nonbiological (behavioral) nature, then federal laws governing clinical practice evidently are at stake. And, on the holistic option, this seems to be the case; a full accounting of the illnesses for which behavioral therapies are prescribed is believed to include deviations from the norm of measurable extrasomatic and somatic variables alike. Fully adequate diagnosis and treatment will therefore have to embrace the prescription of therapies aimed at both sorts of deviation. For example, for some illnesses the prescription of both chemical and stress-reduction therapies may be in order. To the extent to which each sort of therapy is believed to be aimed at pathogenic agents, the greater is its claim to pertaining to medicine per se.

Here we have the critical flaw in the holistic option. Détente—the joining of holistic care and biomedical cure—does not accord with the evidence. If the scope of etiological factors includes "environmental and psychosocial components," then, in fact, an alternative model is being proposed and not just a "more comprehensive" pathology model. What has passed for primary and secondary care is now disease-cure medicine (tertiary care). Etiologic factors are effectively redefined in a way anticipated by Engel. Not only do they include factors that by virtue of their physical and chemical properties have the capacity to damage cells or parts of the body; evidently they also include "factors which . . . place a burden on or limit the capacity of systems concerned with growth, development, or adaptation" (Engel 1960). In effect, advocates of holistic medicine, if unwittingly, propose a new medical model, an interactive medical model.

## The Environmental Option

A close examination of the environmental medicine strategy will provide the grounds for rejecting all forms of détente. We will see the conceptual contradictions in all medical strategies that embrace a "cure plus care" approach. What emerges from such a discussion is the clear-cut need to counter biomedical limitations by embracing a fully articulated alternative that subsumes biomedical premises instead of attempting to build upon them. Fully spelled out, this occasions the second medical revolution.

Examining what the environmental medical advocate means by disease origins is revealing. Sometimes advocates refer to disease origins as "environmental influences on health"; at other times as "the underlying causes of disease." This dual usage can occasion some ambiguity when one is trying to determine whether environmental medicine administers chiefly to the background conditions or the underlying determinants of disease: is it concerned mainly with influences on health or causes of disease? Briefly, it is not always clear whether the "deleterious agents" that environmental medicine addresses are to be regarded as risk factors or etiological factors. Do way-of-life factors associated with cancer of the colon, like removal of dietary fiber, or with ischemic heart disease, like smoking, merely dispose an individual to disease (risk factors)? Or are they central to the production of an individual's disease (etiological factors)? Is environmental medicine essentially preventive medicine, concerned with "social and environmental influences on health," or is it essentially curative medicine, concerned with "the underlying causes of disease"? The question is pivotal, for on its answer turns the foundational question: Is the prevailing concept of disease—a deviation from the norm of an individual's biological parameters—scientifically adequate for reducing the contemporary disease burden?

Plainly, the thrust of environmental medicine is that it is not. Powles finds a theoretical void in mainstream medicine's inability to deal with today's diseases of maladaptation. It stems, he says, from a preoccupation with the biology of the individual at the expense of human population biology: "The resulting inability to deal theoretically (as distinct from statistically) with biological phenomena at levels of organization above a single organism has left medical theory seriously deficient. . . . With little understanding of the way of life to which man is biologically adapted, modern medicine is unable to predict the possible harmful consequences of departures from it" (1973, 14). This would seem to pose a radical challenge to the biomedical concepts of disease—biochemistry gone astray—and patient—a (asocial) biological organism. Notwithstanding, environmental medicine stops short of proposing systematically alternative concepts. While affirming that "disease challenges well-being on three main levels—biological, emotional, and existential," Powles concludes only that the three levels are closely interrelated, not that they are formally interactive: "Thus, the technical mastery of disease [the biological level] is serving to reduce biological malfunctioning. Further, the 'helping to cope' side of medicine is principally serving to reduce the emotional and existential challenge" (1973, 21). The dualism of the biological (curative) and emotional-existential ("helping to cope") sides of medicine would appear to survive the affirmation of their interdependence.

McKeown, reflecting on F. J. Inglefinger's melancholy conclusion that at bottom the findings of environmental medicine should have little bearing on clinical practice,[2] reaches a conclusion consistent with that of Powles. Distinguishing between the role of medicine as an institution and as a practice, he proposes a solution that serves both the technical (biomedical treatment) and nontechnical (psychosocial coping) aspects of medicine. The role of medicine as an institution should, he says, be considered in broadly comprehensive terms. It "should be considered to cover prevention as well as treatment of disease, and to include concern with non-personal as well as personal services." Unless curative treatment is accompanied by preventive care and personal services by nonpersonal services, "medicine would no longer be concerned comprehensively with health matters, and there would be a particularly regrettable division between professions dealing with the prevention and treatment of disease" (McKeown 1979, 192).

This conciliatory solution, whereby the community-oriented, "nonpersonal services" of environmental medicine fall under the general heading of preventive rather than curative medicine, would seem to defuse the charge of a theoretical void in mainstream medicine. In the final analysis, the environmental medicine strategy takes the same additive turn that characterizes the holistic movement generally.[3] And, as before, the biomedical model survives the environment medicine critique.

Ironically, it is the environmentalists' appropriation of a physical theory of disease to which this additive solution may be traced. Such a theory invites joining curative medicine (vanquish the germ) and preventive medicine (eliminate the germ carrier, breeder) as complementary aspects of comprehensive health care. This is ironical, in that proponents of environmental medicine have spearheaded epidemiological studies showing that the decline even of infectious diseases (the primary bulwark of a physical theory of disease) was due more to environmental factors than to medical interventions. Nevertheless, it is

2. In an assessment of the first edition of McKeown's primer on the philosophy of environmental medicine, *The Role of Medicine* (1976), Inglefinger concludes: "The major question is to what extent the assessment of *The Role of Medicine* should change the kind of care that the able and conscientious physician gives his patient. Not very much, I think" (1977, 449).

3. That this is the understanding of the medical community at large is suggested by D.A.K. Black's prediction that, because "the most characteristic function of a doctor lies in the diagnosis and treatment of disease in the individual patient . . . the great majority of doctors will remain concerned with disease and not with 'positive health' or 'community medicine' or 'social medicine.'" *The Logic of Medicine* (London: Oliver and Boyd, 1968); quoted in McKeown (1980, 122).

assimilation of all disease to the infectious disease model that provides environmental medicine with its concept of disease. Or, more accurately, the legacy of that model inhibits medical environmentalists from propounding a disease concept of their own. This reversal—from subsuming infectious disease under a single enviromedical umbrella to advocating two complementary aspects of health care—is telling. For environmental medicine appears to make two ultimately irreconcilable points. First, it wishes to promote the complementarity of environmental medicine (investigation of disease origins) and biological medicine (investigation of causal mechanisms). But second, it wishes to call into question biomedical premises concerning the etiology of disease, in particular infectious diseases, the standard bearer of a physicalist theory. That these dual contentions are irreconcilable is shown by examining the environmentalists' argument for joining the technical and nontechnical aspects of medicine under a single, comprehensive banner. As we will see in Part Four, this argument bears the germ of a genuine revolution.

Biomedical researchers, argues the enviromedicalist, working in the laboratory, can isolate certain microorganisms, e.g., *Plasmodium falciparium*, as causal agents in the production of malignant subtertian malaria. The mechanisms of this disease are elucidated via biochemical processes resulting from the infection of the host organism by these microbes (Fig. 5.1).

Concurrent with these studies, enviromedical researchers can independently isolate carriers of those microorganisms (certain insects) and identify geographical zones and climatological conditions conducive to carrier breeding grounds (tropical marshlands). In this way, conditions increasing the risk of contracting malaria are identified. Now both risk factors (breeding grounds) and etiological factors (micro-organisms) can be isolated. Their mutual relations are shown by means of an enlargement of Figure 5.1, where the dashed arrow signifies risk factor (Fig. 5.2).

Here environmental medicine studies (e.g., epidemiology, historical demography) are seen to have a well-defined, complementary role in comprehensive health care. Isolating contributing factors to the incidence and spread of malarial disease, environmental medicine usefully complements biological medicine as preventive medicine complements curative medicine.

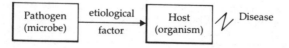

FIGURE 5.1

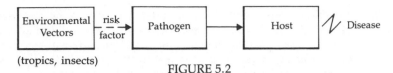

FIGURE 5.2

But even on environmentalist terms this complementary relationship is questionable. Conventionally, infectious diseases have been considered exemplars of the biomedical theory of disease, a function of an eradicable physical condition. Indeed much of the attractiveness of this theory is explained by this engineering consideration: the body is invaded by discrete, specific, and external causal agents, and therapy accordingly consists in localized, physical interventions. Yet environmentists imply, to the contrary, that disease, even of the infectious type, is a function of maladaptation. They argue that most postnatal diseases result from discordance between an evolutionarily conditioned organism and environmental stresses that are in evolutionary terms novel. Speaking of infectious diseases, McKeown states that "for an understanding of the infections it is unsatisfactory to consider separately an organism and its host. They are living things which interact and adapt to each other by natural selection. The virulence of an organism is not, therefore, a distinct character like its size or shape: it is an expression of an interaction between a particular organism and a particular host" (1980, 45).

Here is the seed of a revolutionary (that is, neo-Hippocratean) concept of disease. Even in the case of infectious diseases, it is not the host-microorganism interaction that accounts for the disease, but a particular microorganism interacting with a host *under special conditions*. The particular mutagen (microbe) taken singly is not a pathogenic agent, as implied in the physical theory of disease causation. Rather pathogenesis is the product of the interplay of mutagen(s) and host-in-a-particular-state, a state induced by way-of-life factors. According to the environmentalist argument, to be medically useful this state needs to be specified with respect to some baseline. Specification of a biological baseline marks the environmental medicine difference, enabling it to define criteria of biological normality and so distinguish between normal and abnormal way-of-life factors.

That this interplay applies even to infectious diseases is an enviromedical motif. It informs an environmental report to the World Health Organization cited by McKeown which speaks of a "deadly combination" between certain microbes and children living in societies whose way of life is marked by malnutrition. It states:

> A debilitated organism is far less resistant to attacks by micro-organisms. Ordinary measles or diarrhea—harmless and short-lived diseases among

well-fed children—are usually serious and often fatal to the chronically malnourished. Before vaccines existed, practically every child in all countries caught measles, but 300 times more deaths occurred in the poorer countries than in the richer ones. The reason was not that the virus was more virulent, nor that there were fewer medical services; but that in poorly nourished communities the microbes attack a host which, because of chronic malnutrition, is less able to resist. The same happens with diarrhea, respiratory infections, tuberculosis and many other common infections to which malnourished populations pay a heavy and unnecessary toll. (Behar 1974, quoted in McKeown)

McKeown's comment on this report deserves quoting at length, for it embodies the revolutionary potential of the environmental medicine critique:

These and other investigations show the enormous importance of nutrition in determining the outcome of infection, and the tragic synergistic relation which exists between malnutrition and infectious disease. The World Health Organization report suggested that "we have given too much attention to the enemy and have to some extent overlooked our own defences." That is to say we have concentrated on specific measures such as vaccination . . . without sufficient regard for the predominant part played by nutritional state. "For the time being," it concluded, "an adequate diet is the most effective 'vaccine' against most of the diarrheal, respiratory and other common infections." (1980, 62–63)

A microbe is not *the* pathogenic agent in the production of fatal measles. It does not produce action by contact. Rather, it triggers action in something that is not one simple object (e.g., a body), but a pattern of relations, an integrated circuit, so to speak. The pathogenic action is intrinsic to the circuit, linked only in an indirect way to the stimulus (microbe) that set it off. Rather than a substantive mode whereby a pathogen invades a body, pathogenesis is described in a relational or communication systems mode. Instead of the enemy, the microbe is a trigger, a critical "fluctuation" made critical owing not to its intrinsic "virulence" (force) but to the state of the host. Only in combination with way-of-life factors affecting the host—in this case a way of life characterized by inadequate nutrition—can the microbe be said to produce the disease in question, fatal measles. Here is the "deadly combination" that forms the basis of the maladaptation or communications model of disease. Figure 5.1 is revised to show the structure of this "deadly combination" (Fig. 5.3).

This formulation is consistent with McKeown's contention that the virulence of a microbe is not a distinct character like its size or shape, but an expression of an interaction between a particular microbe and a particular host; that is, between a particular microbe and a host characterized by particular state variables. Gone are the engineering concepts

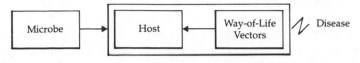

FIGURE 5.3

of *pathogen* as a discrete, specific, and external causal agent (force) and *patient* as an asocial, biological organism (particle or body) under the influence of that force. In their place (so environmental medicine implies) are the concepts of pathogen as an external stimulus or "fluctuation," and patient, or locus of disease, as a biopsychosocial system in an open energy exchange with the environment. The pathogenic "charge" or virulence of a substance (e.g., germ) is expressed as a ratio of mutagen to host-characterized-by-certain-state-variables. These variables ("stressors" or messages) are, in evolutionary terms, either normal or abnormal. They might represent either confrontation with a bear in Yellowstone Park or a bearish traffic jam in Asbury Park. In one instance normal stress reactions are available (e.g., "fight or flee"), in the other not. In one instance a bodily change is induced that is healthy. In the other a bodily change is induced that is not—that in combination, say, with a high-cholesterol diet (another way-of-life factor) predisposes to overt disease. Given these variables, the bear is a stressor (normal) and the traffic jam a distressor (abnormal). Writ large, this is the basis for a revolution.

The expressive inadequacy of the engineering model is here exposed. It cannot articulate the "tragic synergistic relation" of which McKeown speaks. For want of a vocabulary (Fig. 5.3) the roots of the disease are misdiagnosed, its treatment correspondingly incomplete. Only through a shift in framework-dependent concepts can a treatment protocol prescribe "vaccines" inoculating against the offending mutagen (microbe) and the abnormal way-of-life factor (diet) alike. And such a shift will require recognition of a circuit of interacting way-of-life factors in combination with external mutagens which together creates a critical fluctuation. This combination can produce change of state, disease. In clinically practical terms, this could involve looking, for example, to the increased incidence of a disease within a sociocultural framework and seeking an explanation for that increase by reference to departures from normality in any of the various way-of-life factors specified by the circuit.

What we see is that the traditional dichotomy between preventive and curative medicine leads to an insufficiently textured consideration of the notion of disease origins. This dichotomy, endorsed by biomedical and (ironically) enviromedical advocate alike, so generalizes the notion of disease origins as to include in its domain both etiological and risk factors but without properly distinguishing between the two. For example, while insect breeding grounds might defensibly be labeled risk factors with respect to contracting malaria, it is moot whether the same can be said for way-of-life vectors in the production of coronary heart disease. This blurring of the lines leads both to misdiagnosis of the cause of disease and to an unwarranted delimiting of the range of therapeutic options. Upon unpacking the notion of "disease origins," we see that way-of-life vectors, when they violate baseline boundaries, can in combination with traditionally recognized mutagens (microbes) be pathogenic. This was the import of the World Health Organization report as regards fatal measles. It is this "deadly" interactive combination that is the determinant of disease and hence a theoretically understood etiological factor.

Now we have a vantage point from which to identify a critical flaw in the additive thesis (détente) that joins prevention and cure. It is seen to rest on an interpretation that requires *causes* to be physical and other factors to be lumped together, somewhat arbitrarily, and termed situational or *risk factors*. At the same time, a major contribution of environmental medicine is that some so-called risk factors do *co-cause* disease. Such a distinction is possible, argues the enviromedicalist, with the provision that we can gauge whether bodily change induced by way of life is biologically normal or abnormal. As long as the concepts of disease and patient are treated in a social vacuum, there is no way to distinguish theoretically between the pathogenic role of environmental vectors like insect breeding grounds and social or way-of-life factors like a combination of malnourishment and crowded housing conditions. (Derivatively, there is no way to distinguish theoretically, as distinct from statistically, between a [social] stressor and distressor.) Failure to address this expressive limitation by formal realignment of concepts gives rise to the above-mentioned equivocation in the use of such terms as "influence on health" and "determinant of disease." We don't know what we are looking for because in the absence of an enriched vocabulary (Fig. 5.3) we don't know what to look for.

This can be further clarified by noting that while insect breeding grounds might be described as potentially harmful influences on health, they could scarcely be called determinants of disease—any more than could the proliferation of fast-food chains. On the other hand, if we assume an understanding of the way of life to which humans are biologically adapted, way-of-life factors like a high-serum-cholesterol diet coupled with sedentary lifestyle may (pending further experimentation) properly be described as determinants of disease—sufficient though not necessary determinants of coronary heart disease. As circumstantial evidence, common signs of these way-of-life factors, for example obesity and high blood pressure—but now coupled with systematically *different* way-of-life factors—may routinely fail to produce the referent disease. This was the burden of the WHO report documenting the absence of fatal disease in the case of well-nourished children exposed to microbes.

Powles advances just such a hypothesis. A physical theory of disease, he says, while giving support to the idea of specific therapies, failed to emphasize the importance of general resistance to infection:

> By contrast one could now describe the pre-industrial situation with respect to infection, as one of chronic predisposition to infection due to poor nutrition and environmental conditions. Thus the appropriate model for infectious disease need not, as is often suggested, be fundamentally different from that for the degenerative diseases. A fatal infection, like the occlusion of a coronary artery, is often a terminal event to which the individual involved is strongly predisposed by his social experience. (1973, 15)

The implied theoretical void in modern medicine—its inability to factor into the disease equation the role of social experience—Powles attributes to the limitations of what he calls individual biology. He finds remarkable the extent to which human population biology, for example evolutionary theory and medical ecology, has failed to influence medicine. Without a theoretical basis for dealing with biological phenomena at levels of organization above a single organism, modern medicine, he says, is without criteria for biological normality.

Given biomedical premises, we cannot measure the pathogenic potential of social factors inducing bodily change. "High," as in "high blood pressure," can have no theoretical meaning. As a result, says Powles, modern medicine "hesitates to call progressive health-compromising processes such as arterial degeneration, rising blood pressure and tendency toward diabetes 'diseases,' because they are associated with a way of life it feels bound to accept as 'normal.' " He notes the ongoing debate over the limits of normality in blood pressure: "The serious issue of whether a bodily change that is induced by our way of life and predisposes to overt disease should be regarded as pathological has been reduced to the trivial one of whether the distribution of blood pressures in the population is unimodal or bimodal. . . . With little understanding of the way of life to which man is biologically adapted, modern medicine is unable to predict the possible harmful consequences of departures from it" (1973, 14).

Consequently, medicine can only be continually "surprised" by contemporary events, theoretically defenseless in their wake. Powles cites the high correlation of cigarette smoking and lung cancer. Another instance is the correlation of diet and bowel cancer. "Until quite recently"—Powles is writing in 1973—"it was not widely suspected that large bowel cancer, a major cause of cancer death, might be associated with dietary habits that have become far removed from those of our forebears."[4] Again, citing the well-known Framingham study of heart-related diseases, Powles speaks of "naive interpretations" placed on the relative contribution of nature to nurture: "Epidemiological studies, say on ischemic heart disease, are carried out on populations with an industrial way of life which is implicitly assumed to be 'normal'; on the basis of findings a certain weight is accorded to the influence of heredity on the disease. The fact that these inherited characteristics may only become relevant to the aetiology of the condition under stresses that are in evolutionary terms novel—and that it is therefore the interaction between the stresses and the inherited variation in body build that is important—is often not acknowledged" (1973, 14–15). To underline what he regards as the fallacy of treating pathogenesis in a social vacuum, Powles recalls the analogy Cleave and Campbell (1966) develop in their discussion of the role of genetic factors in disease: "In populations that wear shoes the inherited variability of the build of the foot may well make some individuals more likely than others to develop bunions—but bunions only occur in populations that wear shoes."

It is highly instructive that Powles and other medical environmentalists[5] can speak so forcefully about the impact of civilization on the health of humans and the theoretical limitations of modern medicine in assessing this impact, while at the same time stop short of systematically recasting such foundational concepts as *etiological factor, locus of disease*, and appropriate medical *treatment*. Only by doing so can they show that the premises of environmental medicine subsume rather than peacefully coexist with those of mainstream medicine. Specifying the contents of a theoretical identikit for an approach to medicine, one keyed to providing a knowledge of "the importance of way-of-life factors in disease," Powles proceeds to grant the practical benefits of a division of labor. In doing so, however, he withdraws with the left hand what he has seized with the right: "It would however be unrealistic to expect all doctors to be expert not just in comprehending biological phenomena at an individual level but also at a population level. The principal concern of the clinician will continue to be the treatment of the sick" (1973, 22).

Once more, the specter of a dichotomy between curative and merely preventive measures arises. Powles acknowledges the significant gains made by today's dominant approach to community medicine, a statisti-

4. Citing a widely used text, H. Bailey and M. Love's *A Short Practice of Surgery*, whose fourteenth edition was published in 1968, Powles notes that in fifteen pages of discussion on cancers of the colon and rectum, "there is no discussion of aetiology and . . . no acknowledgement of the possibility that these cancers might be caused by our way of life and therefore be preventable."

5. See Dubos 1968, Boyden 1970, Cochrane 1972, and Burnet 1971.

cal methodology approach to the biology of human populations. At the same time, he points out that the correlated findings, once determined, do not speak for themselves: "It is only when their significance is assessed against a background body of theory (as occurs for example within the practice of clinical medicine) that they become important as guides to action." Significantly, he concludes that "the concentration of intellectual effort onto the development of the theoretical basis of community medicine is an urgent precondition for the articulation of an alternative 'etiological' strategy for the improvement of health" (1973, 23).

The materials for a revolution are at hand. Just this role of theory as a guide to action, in this case clinical action, underscores the imperative to formulate a background body of theory that serves enviromedical premises as pathophysiological theory serves biomedical premises. This is the outstanding item on the enviromedical agenda. Treatment is an artifact of theory. If the principal concern of the clinician is the treatment of the sick, then the propriety of this treatment must be assessed against one's background body of theory. And as the above series of figures and tables illustrates, treatment will differ qualitatively from one background body of theory to another. An essential curative treatment component within a "disease as maladaptation" model is, within a germ or engineering model, inessential—a cautionary measure, perhaps. In terms of the foregoing analogy, to treat the patient's bunion independently of the "abnormal" way of life (shoe-wearing) is, in the final analysis, inadequate. It is after-the-fact treatment, a temporary palliative, rather like giving aspirin for a migraine headache. Nevertheless, the distinction itself becomes intelligible only against the backdrop of a successor body of theory, one that can explain the role of shoe-wearing in the production of bunions. Otherwise, norms of therapeutic success continue to be measured against the standard of temporary alleviation of the condition. Only through translation of the theoretical premises into a clinical protocol will treatment dictate the temporary palliative *in combination with* a therapy aimed at mitigating the ill effects of the root (e.g., way-of-life) factor(s). And as Powles remarked vis-à-vis the bunion analogy, "Exactly the same point could be made with respect to heart disease, diabetes and some cancers" (1973, 15). The crucial point is that such a theoretical recasting is necessary to avoid the conceptual dilemma presented by the environmental medical position, which both embraces biomedical premises (germ theory, cure plus care, etc.) and necessarily rejects them (the baseline argument).

We see, then, that the line dividing "treatment of the sick" (diseased body) and "care of the ill" (sick person) is theory-sensitive. And this brings us full circle. It was the absence of a systematically articulated body of theory with its own enabling concepts of disease, patient, and therapy that led medical environmentalists to their otherwise puzzling conciliatory stance toward the medical biologists. Just this absence sanctioned Inglefinger's assessment that the insights of environmental medicine should have little effect on the kind of treatment that the able and conscientious physician gives his patients. On the other hand, weaving these insights into a theoretical fabric invites physicians to reexamine the reach of their diagnostic rule base. Moreover, the full dimensions of other extrabiomedical strategies suggest that, besides the enviromedical sanctioned social factors, other factors as well—genetic, behavioral, biospheric *and their synergistic interplay*—might be assessed and woven into a still more comprehensive disease mosaic. This is the burden of the latter part of this study. To the extent that each modality can be shown to have a measurable influence on health, today's physician will wish to reexamine the grounds for the kind of treatment he or she gives.

## The Medical Landscape: A Foundations Perspective

The medical landscape has been simplified by reference to several medical special interests, ranging from strictly reductionist biomedical physicians to nonmedical holistic practitioners. This range appears to satisfy the notion of comprehensive health care—prevention and cure. However, by examining two versions of extrabiomedical focus, holistic and environmental medicine, a critical contradiction in the "cure plus care" strategy surfaces. Proponents of détente argue persuasively for the extrasomatic basis for disease causation; yet they tacitly accept a physicalist theory of disease and abstain from directly challenging biomedical premises. For example, Hastings states: "The paradigm or model of holistic medicine has evolved in tandem with the critique of modern biomedicine. Each informs, stimulates, enlarges, and tempers the other. This model is, at least potentially, a corrective to the excesses of biomedicine, a supplement to its deficiencies, and an affirmation of its deepest and most enduring strengths" (1980, 15). The phrase "an affirmation of its [biomedicine's] deepest and most enduring strengths" is telltale. The implications of what the holistic proponents espouse would suggest rejection, not affirmation, of biomedical premises.

One reason the insurgents do not follow through with a sustained attack on foundational principles is because of the profound influence of the biomedical legacy on their own thinking. The very vocabulary of contemporary medicine—which the critics accept and use—secretes the classical science worldview on which biomedicine rests. So pervasive is this influence that even reform-minded elements in the medical community are circumvented from successfully proposing radical (nonbiomedical) approaches by virtue of biomedical presuppositions reflected in such content terms as *disease, cure, system,* and *cause.* No wonder conceptual revolutions are so rare—they must overcome the objections of the "experts" who have gained status via the reigning paradigm; and they must overcome the embedded bias of the language, which also reflects the reigning paradigm. In Table 5.1 we can see how the language of contemporary medicine encourages subtle dualisms as well as a complementary as opposed to a conflictual attitude among "competing" medical approaches.

The "cure plus care" proponents, by accepting the vocabulary of biomedicine, are restricted in their ability to offer a truly alternative medical model. We have noted the irony involved, because the implications of their findings suggest repudiating biomedical premises. Yet, by accepting and not redefining such terms as *cure, disease,* and *etiology,* they in fact invoke biomedical premises in the very process of proposing their alternative model. For example, look closely at the distinction between illness and disease. This assumes the need for care (to administer to illness) in addition to cure (to administer to disease). However, a recognition of the distinction between curing and caring can only be accomplished with at least implicit acceptance of a physical theory of disease—the cornerstore of biomedicine.

And consider the case of disease causation. To refer to etiological factors to indicate physical pathogens and refer to risk factors to indicate extrasomatic influences on disease invokes the image of the germ theory

TABLE 5.1   The Medical Debate

| BIOMEDICINE | | INSURGENTS |
|---|---|---|
| cure | vs. | care or prevention |
| diseased body | vs. | sick person (Kleinman) |
| etiological (physical) factors | vs. | risk or situational factors (mental-emotional triggers) |
| medicine per se | vs. | behavioral medicine |
| pathogens (physical agents) | vs. | disease triggers (psychosocial agents) |
| technical | vs. | nontechnical (Powles) |
| nonpersonal | vs. | personal (McKeown) |
| biological | vs. | emotional, existential (Powles) |
| technical mastery | vs. | helping to cope (Powles) |
| acute infectious | vs. | chronic degenerative |
| disease | vs. | illness (Kleinman) |
| disease mechanisms | vs. | disease origins (McKeown) |

as a basis for distinguishing the influence of the two factors in the disease process. If, for example, one had evidence that a risk factor is a cause of disease, then the traditional usage of the term *etiological factor* must be redefined to recognize an expanded etiological grid. Further, such a redefinition of etiological factor would dictate redefining the concept of disease as well as the concept of patient. While the insurgents' argument points the way to such a redefinition of key medical terms, this step is not taken. Rather, insurgents take the less revolutionary course of invoking a series of complementary terms such as found in Table 5.1.

The extent to which medical thinking is thoroughly infused with terms that invoke biomedical premises can be further seen in the distinction between "acute infections" and "chronic" diseases. We have already seen that environmental medical premises (as well as the premises of other insurgents) can refute the physical theory of disease by identifying infectious diseases as a subset of a wider disease spectrum. However, by virtue of the "cure plus care" thesis, antagonists never rise above the limitations imposed by their acceptance of biomedical terminology. Hence, they arrive at seemingly adequate compromises. For example, the extrabiomedicalists propose that preventive medicine, which focuses on disease origins, should complement curative medicine, which focuses on causal mechanisms. The dualisms (e.g., disease origins–causal mechanisms) built into the conceptual scheme fail to do justice to the interactive nature of the disease equation. Once again, the restrictiveness of widely accepted medical concepts is evident. We see the counterstrategists advance a position based on the molecular theory of disease causation when the drift of their argument is to refute the molecular theory.

We can now see how the limitations of the insurgents' program can be attributed, in part, to their refusal to attack the "implicit" inadequacy of "scientific medicine." "Scientific medicine," the insurgents could argue, does not address what is now known to be the full range of essential elements of disease. Rather, the insurgents allow the framework-laden language to draw them into a complementary relationship with biomedicine.

The failure to make their case on scientifically acceptable grounds is critical. From the perspective of the biomedical model and its two-tier foundations (see Chapter 3), the insurgents can only seem like *ad hoc* groups with narrowly conceived empirical evidence supporting their particular fiefdoms. With no reference to either tier 2 basic biophysical sciences or a tier 1 explanatory strategy, they can only be theoretically uninteresting, lacking the potential for comprehensive understanding. The insurgents react to the narrowness of biomedicine but themselves remain within normal science. They accept the biomedical definition of cure and try to add to it a scientific (clinical) approach to care. They provide no grounds for a successor. This accounts, in part, for why they have not had a dramatic impact on mainstream medicine. Rather, they appear to offer interesting clinical successes while not leading the way to a thorough reexamination of medical principles. The insurgents seem to embrace a piece of the truth but make no headway in the quest for a more adequate encompassing theoretical framework.

How extrabiomedical strategies are viewed provides an important link to understanding what impact they might have on the medical community. According to Hastings, Fadiman, and Gordon, "there is no specific holistic medical orthodoxy. . . . Rather, the holistic approach in medicine is a context and set of principles to guide our attitudes toward health, our therapeutic practices, and our relationships with body and mind, patients, the environment, and health care" (1980, xii). In spite of the ambitious range of factors just mentioned, it is understandable that the approach might be received lightly by a community which heretofore has been guided by principles consistent with classical physics and chemistry and the conduct of inquiry consistent with the canons of scientific method.

To the extent that there is debate within the medical community between the insurgents and biomedical advocates, it is a contest between groups of two different logical types. The biomedical model is a theoretically and scientifically grounded paradigm. The insurgents are an alternative medical strategy, no more than an additive arm to the institution of medicine. The debate, to the extent there is one, is not between equals. Yet it could be. The degree to which the insurgents find texture in areas (psycho- and socio-factors) that lie outside of the domain of biomedicine point to the conceptual inadequacy of biomedical premises. On these grounds, the cure the biomedical physician is proposing is not just additively inadequate but synergistically inadequate as well. Diagnosis and treatment are incomplete and subject to reexamination. The challenge facing the insurgents is to situate their findings within an alternative scientific paradigm—one that transcends the complementary dualisms that trap them and allows for the interactionism so evident in their findings.

To understand how the insurgents fall short in direct confrontation with the biomedical model requires examining the different ways in which the term *science* is used. This allows us to compare medical strategies from the perspective of how they rationalize the efficacy of their treatments. We may speak broadly of two usages of *scientific*, one as it applies in a theoretical or foundational context, the other as it applies in a practical, clinical context. To speak of today's Western (bio)medicine as scientific is to use the term in the first sense, the sense, for example, in which Thomas Kuhn speaks of "normal" science, the prevailing scientific "paradigm," "matrix," or "research tradition" in which a truly scientific medicine like biomedicine is embedded. In the case of an applied science like medicine, as will be discussed in Part Three, this first usage of *scientific* involves the integration of several components or tiers: (1) an explanatory strategy embodied in a set of methodological directives, (2) a body of basic physicochemical or biophysical sciences whose findings are consistent with this strategy and these directives, and (3) a body of applied (medical) sciences, the postulated behavior of whose entities are rationalized by (explained in terms of) the principles of the underlying basic sciences. Such a relationship is illustrated in Figure 5.4. Here the broken arrow stands for "animates the research strategy in the formulation of" and the unbroken arrow for "theoretically grounds the principles of."

The second use of "scientific" is commonly used in a clinical context, as in "the application of the scientific method to patient care" (Engel 1977a, 223), and is invoked for a different purpose. Here, extrabiomedicalist strategies test their procedures through hypothesis testing. For example, primary care techniques may be derived and validated according to strict tenets of the scientific method in the sense of experimental design procedures; however, in terms of the more encompassing sense of science—the theoretically encompassing (three-tiered) foundations sense—such findings may not necessarily be rationalized.

The different meanings attached to the term *scientific* are critical. The controversy between the "biomedical reductionist" and the "medical humanist" will never be resolved as long as insurgents fail to offer the

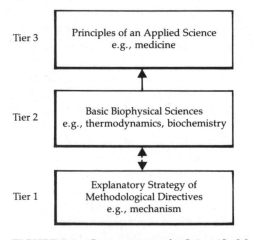

FIGURE 5.4   Components of a Scientific Model
for an Applied Science

medical enterprise a solution in the form of an alternative medical model—one that is comprehensive in the foundational sense of *scientific*. Such an alternative medical model would recognize that a concept of comprehensive health that is defined by the addition of clinically scientific care onto the edifice of biomedical care is unacceptable. It fails because it requires accepting physicalist premises regarding the patient as a complex biological system or organism, and this cannot be reconciled with what many findings in the medical literature suggest and the insurgents' critique asserts—that is, the patient is at minimum a biopsychosocial entity.

We now arrive at the major issue in the confrontation between the biomedical advocate and the sum of counterstrategies. It is the theoretical strength of the biomedical model that has gone unchallenged owing to the failure of the insurgents to offer a viable alternative that also can boast of such foundations.

## The Systems Option: A Conceptual Bridge

While the extrabiomedical strategies discussed thus far can be understood as a reaction on the part of patients and physicians to the limitations of biomedicine, the systems medicine movement stems from an active effort to change paradigms. Here, biomedicine is challenged at its reputed point of greatest strength—its scientific foundations.

> Protagonists of the biomedical model claim that its achievements more than justify the expectation that in time all major problems will succumb to further refinements in biomedical research. Critics argue that such dependence on "science," in effect, is at the expense of the humanity of the patient. The controversy cannot be resolved, however, as long as it is predicated, by advocate and critic alike, on the flawed premise that the biomedical model is an adequate scientific model for medical research and practice. (Engel 1981, 103)

Engel argues that the reductionist dogma of the biomedical model, a foundations issue, is responsible for the "distortions" introduced by limiting attention to the smallest isolatable components. Instead, says Engel, "the task is appreciably more complex than the biomedical model encourages one to believe" (1977*b*, 132).

Engel seeks redress by embracing a biopsychosocial model based on principles drawn from general systems theory (GST). His biopsychosocial approach to medicine is intended to offer an enlarged science of patient care. The major thrust of this approach is to reconcile the body that incurs disease with the person whose psychosocial dimensions can qualitatively influence the course of disease.

Engel takes the position that because the biomedical approach systematically ignores behavioral and psychological data, it is inadequate for the task. Denying that "the factor analytic approach of reductionism alone qualifies as scientific," Engel shoulders the burden of offering an alternative scientific paradigm. To this end he proposes "systems theory," which he describes as a new, nonreductionist paradigm "based on a . . . development in biology hardly more than 50 years old, the origin and elaboration of which may be credited chiefly to the biologists Paul Weiss and Ludwig von Bertalanffy" (1981, 102–103). Engel embraces the key premise of systems theory, which stipulates the mutual irreducibility of biological, psychological, and social systems. This permits him to propose a synoptic medical model whose aim is to "enable the physician to extend application of the scientific method to aspects of everyday practice and patient care previously not deemed accessible to a scientific approach. The success of this application can bring closer to reality the goal of the Flexner reform to educate a truly scientific physician" (1981, 102). Approaching clinical problems "from the more inclusive perspective of the systems-oriented biopsychosocial model, free of the constraints imposed by the dualistic and reductionistic approach of the biomedical model" (1981, 107) will attenuate the tension in medicine between curing the diseases and caring for the patient.

Engel describes systems theory as "best approached through the common sense observation that nature is a hierarchically arranged continuum, with its more complex larger units being superordinate to the less complex smaller units" (1981, 103–104). He projects this continuum schematically by nested squares such that each square in the hierarchy "represents an organized dynamic whole, a system of sufficient persistence and identity to justify being named. The name itself reflects the system's distinctive properties." To represent the hierarchy he projects the vertical stacking shown in Figure 5.5. The double arrows connecting the elements of the hierarchy emphasize its continuum character.

Engel intends this extended application of the systems concept to serve as the ground for converting the reductive factor-analytic approach into a nonsummative multifactorial approach that integrates psychological and biological factors (the top and bottom halves of the hierarchy) into a single scientific modeling of the disease process. The merit of this application is that it circumvents the arbitrary exclusion of those presumed pathogenic agencies inexpressible in a physicalist language. "Systems theory, by providing a conceptual framework within which both organized wholes and component parts can be studied, overcomes the centuries-old limitation and broadens the range of the scientific method to the study of life and living systems, including health and illness" (1981, 103).

Systems Hierarchy (Levels of Organization)

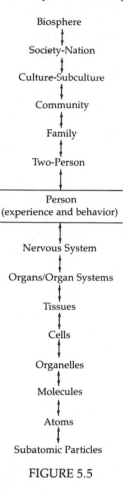

FIGURE 5.5

The transitional role that systems medicine plays is important. Unlike the alternatives discussed, it seeks to be scientific in the foundational sense. In Part Three, we argue that systems medicine falls short of this accomplishment owing to GST's shortcomings as a legitimate alternative paradigm.

## The Challenge to Theory

The debate between the biomedical advocates and possible alternatives is meaningful only to the extent that it addresses the question of whether the care given by the able and conscientious physician should change. With only a single model in the field, the clinician's choices are largely confined to operationalizing the dictates of that model; anything else would be irresponsible or *ad hoc*. But what of the responsibility of the medical theoretician and the researcher?

The point in articulating a theory is to fit known facts into a context, connecting them into a pattern of relations, "reducing entropy," in Jeremy Campbell's illuminating phrase. But except in relief of a contending theory, the detection of theory-wide entropy is for all practical purposes out of reach: how to distinguish anomalies from outstanding agenda items in the field? The insurgent's anomalies are the biomedical advocate's research program. It is not enough to allege, as do the insurgents, diagnostic inadequacies of a model for which the patient is "silent"—an amindful, asocial, biological organism. As the dialectic of their critique teaches, a further step must be taken. Proposed alternative foundations—a biopsychosocial patient—must be tailored to a background body of theory, one meeting general conditions for theory building. Short of this, entropy-pointing is literally pointless, and Inglefinger's conservative assessment is not only prudent but logically sound. In the face of alleged "surprises" (e.g., "diseases of civilization"), even the able and conscientious researcher should by and large stand pat, seeking to account for such phenomena within the theoretical umbrella of the inherited model. That is, he or she should issue promissory notes on the ability of the model eventually to resolve outstanding issues.

This bears on the second reason for articulating a theory. Not only does a theory seek to fit known facts into a context; it seeks also to generate new facts, facts not yet observed or findings not adverted to as significant. An ordering process, a theory "not only connects the known to the unknown; it also connects the unknown to the known" (Campbell 1984, 230). The advocates of the various insurgent strategies thus distinguish two types of surprising findings. There are the well-known findings in the medical literature which are surprising because they seem to breach the premises of the dominant model. Placebo effects are an illustration: suggesting a mindful patient, at face value they are at odds with the dualist premises of biomedicine. Here the biomedical researcher can plausibly take the hard science turn, invoking the logical possibility argument, and affirm that apparent mind-body events—the psychobiomedical explanation—will, before time is out, yield to a body-body (brain-body), or biomedical, explanation.

But besides the vintage findings yet to be explained, there are findings not yet made but whose discovery can be anticipated by virtue of being logically deducible from the premises of an alternative model. In this regard, on the basis of the enviromedical baseline argument, given a dramatic change in social organization (e.g., from agriculture to industry), we might anticipate the appearance of a novel disease or a significant fluctuation in the rate of an existing disease. Thus, medical environmentalists point to "afflictions of civilization" and to social "stressors," both previously undetected because formally unimaginable within the conceptual horizons of the conventional model. In a strictly biomedical textbook, no normative discussion of diseases of civilization would be warranted, any more, say, than would fast-food-induced indigestion. Medically, both are devoid of theoretical significance. Once introduced into the medical literature, however—for example, through statistical studies in epidemiology or through a maverick hypothesis ("stress-related" diseases)—promissory notes could be issued. The constructs could be deemed metaphorical or epiphenomenal concepts ("stress" becomes shorthand for certain hormonal discharges) or, in the case of afflictions of civilization and fast-food indigestion, regarded as of only statistical relevance.

With respect to each of these two functions of theory construction, the researcher can, then, by appeal to the ultimate reduction to physico-chemical explanation, "save the appearances": he or she can proceed without interruption in the face of apparently serious challenges. Consequently, in the case of an applied science like medicine, the only effective critique turns out to be one that challenges the background body of biophysical sciences on which biomedical science rests and from whose remarkable series of successes throughout the modern period the ultimate-reducibility argument derives its enduring strength. Just such a critique forms the subject area of Part Three.

Before turning to Part Three, in the next chapter we will examine in detail one other countermovement, behavioral medicine. It merits extended examination because of its proximity to the main corridors of biomedicine and, more important, because it represents perhaps the most sustained effort to date to integrate biological and behavioral knowledge in a single multidisciplinary approach.

# 6

## Hard Science Turn versus Self-organization: The Role of Psychosocial Factors in Disease Causation

In this chapter we will take a close look at the field of behavioral medicine by viewing its most recent branch, psychoneuroimmunology. This discipline, derivative of such earlier fields as psychosomatic medicine and psychoneuroendocrinology, is perhaps the most scientifically sophisticated attempt yet to include psychosocial factors in the disease equation. "In the spirit of holism," writes Stephen Locke, "but much more scientific and useful . . . is behavioral medicine, the clinical expression of psychoneuroimmunology" (1985, 172). As such, psychoneuroimmunology warrants separate examination from the previously discussed insurgents.

Our objectives in this chapter are twofold. First, by unpacking the psychoneuroimmunologist's research agenda, we will be able to see its foundational roots firmly in the natural science tradition while also attempting to give scientific standing to medical areas often excluded from biomedical research. As such, we see how psychoneuroimmunology successfully counters at least two major criticisms of the biomedical model. And second, by focusing on what the psychoneuroimmunologist pays attention to, we are able to identify medical phenomena that elude its research agenda. These excluded phenomena raise questions regarding the ultimate viability of that agenda and suggest a structural limitation. This structural limitation points to one of the major challenges any successor medical model must be able to overcome—and so meet the Kuhnian requirement for paradigm succession.

# Psychoneuroimmunology: Biomedicine's Farthest Reach

The exciting new discipline of psychoneuroimmunology has arisen within the last decade, devoted to providing "a link whereby psychosocial factors can be understood to play a role in influencing immune responses and processes of disease" (Ader 1981, xxii). The problematic giving rise to this new branch of behavioral medicine is offered by the immunologist Robert Good:

> Immunologists are often asked whether the state of mind can influence the body's defenses. Can positive attitude, a constructive frame of mind, grief, depression, or anxiety alter ability to resist infections, allergies, autoimmunities, or even cancer? Such questions leave me with a feeling of inadequacy because I know deep down that such influences exist, but I am unable to tell *how* they work, nor can I in any scientific way prescribe how to harness these influences, predict or control them. Thus they cannot usually be addressed in scientific perspective. In the face of this inadequacy, most immunologists are naturally uneasy and usually plead not to be bothered with such things. (1981, xvii)

Here we see crystallized the biomedical dilemma: the tacitly acknowledged recognition that psychosocial factors are indeed significant and the overtly acknowledged commitment to a scientific paradigm that does not comprehensively respond to this recognition. The task that psychoneuroimmunology sets for itself is to address these questions head on. That is, to track these acknowledged influences and to prescribe in a scientific way how to harness, predict, and control them. Hence, the task is to provide a map, in Good's words, of "the interaction of mind, endocrines, and immunity." As Good concludes: "It will be of greatest importance, at every step in the development of this science and the pharmacology that will no doubt follow from it, that precise quantitative measurements be made and that the experiments conducted—whether with humans or animals—be objectively designed, carefully controlled, and critically interpreted" (1981, xix).

Another expression of the aim of this field is voiced by S. M. Plaut and S. B. Friedman in an article revealingly titled "Psychosocial Factors in Infectious Disease." They say, "To the behavioral scientist, streptococcal disease is but one example of a host-parasite relationship where traditional cause-and-effect—streptococcus causes disease—appears only a partial explanation of disease, and the speculation arises as to whether psychosocial factors conceivably contribute to the development of disease" (1981, 3). Plaut and Friedman respond to this speculation in the affirmative: "Psychosocial factors do not influence disease in some mystic fashion. Rather, the physiological status of the host is altered in some way." They proceed to reference "numerous studies over the last two decades" demonstrating that psychological stimuli may have a profound influence on a wide range of physiological processes. They note that the assumption is made "that these physiological changes, acting simply or in combination, are the underlying mechanisms to which disease vulnerability or susceptibility is related" (5). It is grounding this assumption experimentally that constitutes for them the task of psychoneuroimmunology. Thus, they contend, "it is known that (a) psychological factors influence a wide range of physiological, hormonal, and biochemical responses; and (b) psychological factors influence the natural history of many disease states. However, the mechanism(s) by which psychological factors contribute to the etiology of any given disease is largely speculative" (6). Hence, the psychoneuroimmunological task—be both scientific and comprehensive. Psychoneuroimmunology "has grown out of the need to elucidate these mechanisms, and . . . demonstrate the extent to which the immune system may be subject to psychosocial influence."

Plaut and Friedman provide a lucid account of the shift in methodology animating behavioral medicine studies. This shift is highlighted against the background of the powerfully influential image of the germ theory of disease. The new theory was pioneered earlier in this century in the field of psychosomatic medicine and leads to what Plaut and Friedman call a multifactorial approach to etiology:

> "The model of disease causation provided by the germ theory," writes Cassel, "has accustomed us to think in monoetiological, specific terms." As Ader and Engel repeatedly emphasized, however, psychosomatic research "deals not with the role of psychosocial factors in *causing* disease, but in *altering individual susceptibility to disease.*" They and others have argued that the etiology of disease is best studied by a multifactorial or interactive approach. The relevant question is not *whether* a given disease is caused by a pathogenic agent *or* by psychological factors, but rather *to what extent* the disease can be related to each of a number of factors in the history, makeup, and environment of the organism. In statistical terms, we are asking what proportion of total variance is accounted for by each determining factor. Thus, if the "germ" is seen as a "necessary but not sufficient" determinant of disease, and as one of many interacting etiologic factors, "any distinction between psychosomatic and nonpsychosomatic disease is completely arbitrary." The term "psychosomatic disease" in fact loses its meaning, and justifiably so. (1981, 7)

Exemplified by Plaut and Friedman in Figure 6.1, this multifactorial approach identifies factors to be considered in a multivariate approach to the study of psychosocial influences in disease causation.

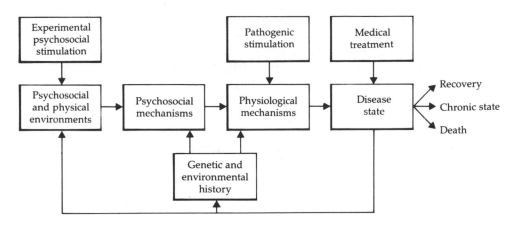

FIGURE 6.1

Source: Plaut and Friedman 1981, 4.

What Plaut and Friedman refer to as a germ theory account of disease causation Alastair Cunningham calls a function of human bilateral symmetry. This assessment refers to the preference for narrowly focused research characterized by "an 'all or nothing' approach to causality." Medicine, too, is affected by this bilateral symmetry limitation, according to Cunningham. Thus, he says:

> Cures have been found for most conditions where there is a single over-whelmingly obvious cause, notably the infectious diseases, but we are struggling with a formidable list of chronic ailments in which many factors can probably contribute to a disturbance of normal homeostasis, for example, cancer, cardiovascular disease, and autoimmune syndromes. We are simply not accustomed to the conceptual handling of complex entities where many factors, all vital, maintain a balance. The human body is one such entity, and disease (dis-ease) can be viewed as any persistent harmful disturbance of its equilibrium. (1981, 609)

For Cunningham, this equilibrium is formed by the three major body systems that form the subject matter of psychoneuroimmunology, the nervous, endocrine, and immune systems. This field, says Cunningham, promotes "the study of the interactions between these three [systems], . . . which is intrinsically fascinating and highly relevant to disease. It is also an area where we can test the explanatory power of our conventional reductionist techniques and try to devise new approaches where reductionism has failed." In order to characterize the difference between conventional reductionist techniques and new, nonreductionist approaches, Cunningham mentions a systems approach accord-

ing to which "with multi-level organized entities like the body, properties 'emerge' . . . at higher levels of organization that could not be
predicted solely by analysis of lower level parts (e.g., studying isolated
neurones would not allow us to predict consciousness). Mind can be
considered an emergent property of brain (at least if one takes an
interactionist philosophical position)" (1981, 610).

Recalling Figure 6.1 from Plaut and Friedman, Cunningham proposes to graphically answer the question he puts to himself: "What is
meant by 'understanding' the interaction between mind or brain and
immune system?" As we previously noted, this is the question to which
psychoneuroimmunology seeks to provide an experimentally grounded
answer. Cunningham states the psychoneuroimmunologist's task: "The
whole organism is an open system in dynamic interaction with the
environment. We need ultimately an overall theory connecting social,
psychological, and somatic events" (1981, 610). To represent these
interactions between immune system, body, mind, and environment,
Cunningham offers a "systems" figure (Fig. 6.2).

Reinforcing Plaut and Friedman's contention, Cunningham points
out that the concept of causality loses much of its meaning in such
complex, multivariate, interacting systems: "We can only try to uncover
a variety of factors which may exert some influence on the immune
response and hope that certain simple manipulations will be found to
have decisive effects" (1981, 614). To help identify some of the levels
through which an environmental stimulus, perceived by the mind, may
affect events in the body and eventually health and behavior, Cunningham offers the diagram in Figure 6.3. This figure represents an
attempt to show diagrammatically the kinds of interconnections experi-

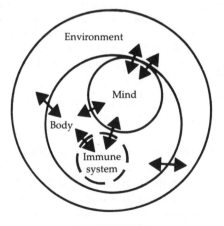

FIGURE 6.2

Source: Cunningham 1981, 610.

mentally established by workers in this fledgling field. Thus, it shows how " 'ideas in the mind' . . . [are] connected with effects in the immune system. . . . The animal conditioning experiments described by Ader are a good start" (1981, 616).

What are the mechanisms of these interconnections between these "ideas in the mind" and the immune system? According to Robert Ader and Nicholas Cohen, "We assume, initially at least, that the effects of conditioning are mediated via neuroendocrine changes that have the potential to influence afferent, central, and/or efferent immune processes." And,

> The application of conditioning techniques to the study of immunobiologic processes can be viewed as an extension of one of the more significant frontiers in the behavioral sciences, namely, the conditioning of visceral and autonomic responses and the conditioning of pharmacologic effects. Together with the wide ranging observations reported elsewhere in this volume, the results obtained thus far with regard to the conditioning of immune responses further substantiate the notion of an intimate relationship between the central nervous system and the immune system. (Ader and Cohen 1981; 315–316)

Speaking to the mechanism of conditioned immunosuppressants involved, they state, "In a field that already recognizes the potential of psychophysiological interactions in determining disease susceptibility, the conditioning of immune processes suggests a mechanism that may be involved in the complex pathogenesis of psychosomatic phenomena and bears eloquent witness to the principle of a very basic integration of biologic and psychological function" (1981, 316).

It is significant that Cunningham also should situate the significance of this young science in the context of the reductionist-nonreductionist debate. This is consistent with the somewhat eye-opening nature of the name given to this discipline and the routine use of such phrases as "psychophysiological" interactions in determining disease susceptibility (Ader and Cohen). As noted, Cunningham goes so far as to suggest that the field can test the explanatory power of our conventional reductionist techniques, holding out the promise that it might force the construction of "new approaches where reductionism has failed." Presumably, these approaches would center on what he calls "an interactionist philosophical position." Yet, equally significant in sketching such a position, which connects "social, psychological and somatic events," Cunningham locates the psychological component (mind) *inside* the somatic component (body) (See Fig. 6.2). This is consistent with Ader and Cohen's dual observation (quoted above) that in a field that recognizes the potential of psychophysiological interactions in determining disease susceptibility, (1) "The conditioning of immune processes suggests a mechanism that . . . bears eloquent witness to the principle of a very basic integration of

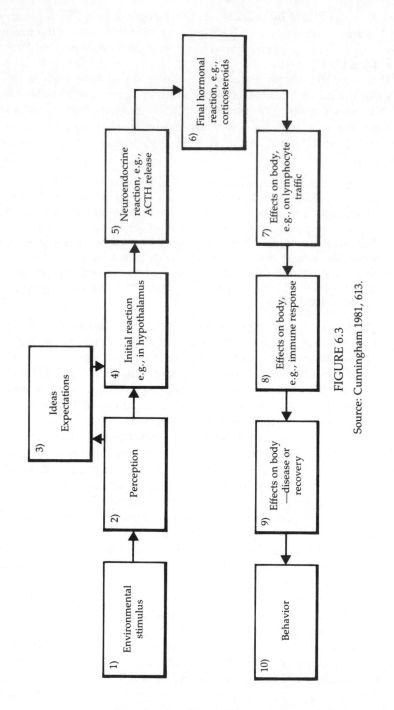

FIGURE 6.3

Source: Cunningham 1981, 613.

biologic and psychologic function," and (2) "The results obtained thus far with regard to the conditioning of immune responses further substantiate the notion of an intimate relationship between the central nervous system and the immune system."

The question arises whether the psychophysiological interactions mentioned ultimately refer only to interactions between the two somatic entities, the central nervous system and the immune system. Cunningham's diagram (Fig. 6.3) depicts some of the levels through which an environmental stimulus, perceived by the mind, may affect events in the body. Note that the "ideas" and "expectations" (box 3) perceived by the mind are of the sort characteristic of the behavioral conditioning experiments reported by Ader and Cohen:[1] that is, the sort of conditioning to which humans and animals alike are susceptible. For example, in conditioning an aversion to saccharin in rats, such actions were conditioning a suppression of immune response. Here, the animals had apparently learned to associate the offer of saccharin with immunosuppression. Speaking of the experiments conducted, Ader says, "All of these experiments were planned specifically to test the hypothesis that you can condition an alteration in immune reactivity. And that is a hypothesis that goes against traditional immunological thinking. As recently as ten, even five years ago, there were no readily accepted connections between behavior and the immune system" (in Anderson 1982, 54–55). We may surmise that "behavior" here refers to box 3 of Figure 6.3 ("ideas, expectations") and in Figure 6.2 to the circle enclosing "mind." This genre of experiment would seem to constitute a standard of what is meant in psychoneuroimmunology by such phrases as "psychophysiological interaction," "mind-immunity interaction," and "psychosocial-immunity interaction" in determining disease susceptibility. We are now able to identify two positions—a traditional reductionist position and a more contemporary (psychoneuroimmunological) nonreductionist, interactionist position and offer reasons for the superiority of the latter.

The first position is the one Ader mentions as characterizing traditional immunological thinking. According to this thinking, as recently as a decade ago "there were no readily accepted connections between behavior and the immune system." But such a position is challenged by the findings of psychoneuroimmunology. Here interactions between immune system, body, mind or brain, and environment have been mapped, linking behavior and the immune system. So, in contradistinction to "traditional immunological thinking," there is a second, nonreductionist position—the interaction of events pertaining to categories hitherto thought to be unrelated, the immune system and behavior.

1. See, for example, Ader 1976, 1977; Ader and Cohen 1975, 1982; Ader, Cohen, and Grota 1979.

It is important to see in what sense the psychoneuroimmunological position is both nonreductionist and interactionist. As will be shown, these terms are context-dependent, their meaning a function of the foundation principles embraced.

The new field may be described as follows:

> "Reductionism" implies the view that there are no experimentally verifiable connections between behavior and such body networks as the immune system. To the extent to which this new field has established such connections, it is (in this respect) nonreductionist and interactionist.

Therefore, the sense in which psychoneuroimmunology is nonreductionist and interactionist must be tempered lest it appear a more dramatic position than it in fact is. For the question arises whether behavior raised in the above context is to be understood as ultimately a brain event that is explicable without remainder in the language of neurophysiology.

That psychoneuroimmunology so understands behavior seems more consistent with statements in its literature, notwithstanding that, with reference to earlier immunological thinking, the new field is interactionist. That is, major body systems like the immune, endocrine, and nervous systems, demonstrably interact with one another; and, because of the centrality of the nervous system with brain functioning, this interaction has a manifestly behavioral component. To this extent, then, the new field of behavioral medicine is "an interdisciplinary field concerned with the integration of behavioral and biomedical science."[2] It might equally be described as an interdisciplinary biomedical field, but one concerned with the integration of behavioral and biochemical sciences within a broader framework. And this amounts to a qualified interactionist framework in which, while the role of the behavioral component in conditioning body systems is fully recognized, it is nevertheless subsumed under biomedical premises. In this sense, terms like "mind events" or "psychosocial factors" may be interpreted finally as shorthand for expressions that can, when necessary, be stated in a neurophysiological vocabulary. An implication of this interpretation for treatment strategies is suggested by statements like Good's when he speaks of "the development of this science and the pharmacology that will no doubt follow from it" (1981, xix). The mind-brain debate aside, the patient is an artifact of treatment.

The philosophical and scientific commitment of psychoneuroimmunology to ultimately physical explanations of psychophysiological

2. From the definition of behavioral medicine formulated at the National Institutes of Health–sponsored conference at Yale University in 1977, at which time the field was inaugurated.

interactions is subtle but clear. It is further illustrated in a popularized presentation of psychoneuroimmunology by one of its practitioners, Stephen Locke, co-authored with Douglas Colligan. Called *The Healer Within* (1986), it is subtitled *The New Medicine of Mind and Body*. The book provides a review of accumulated studies and numerous anecdotes that indicate or suggest a mind-immune connection. However, although the title and the material presented freely invoke the interconnectedness of mind and body, it is not always clear that the authors mean to distinguish *mind* from *brain*. There appears among the biopsychosocial themes a reductionist sentiment as well.

Along with the impressive accumulation of studies proposing a psychophysiological interaction, there is always some hedging:

> At this time we haven't been able to isolate specific immune control centers in the human brain. However . . . (p. 47)

> No precise mechanisms . . . only *factors* that affect susceptibility . . . (p. 136)

> . . . mechanisms of body and mind suggest . . . (p. 154)

These are a sampling of what we sense is the primary shortcoming of the psychoimmunologist's program—the subtle suggestion that the unanswered questions that psychoneuroimmunological research has generated can only be answered by reductionist findings—the *mechanism*. Speaking elsewhere, Locke outlines one of psychoneuroimmunology's current directions: " 'We are just beginning to flesh out some of the potential mediating pathways . . . ,' adding that a link between the nervous system and lymphocytes 'suggests at least a theoretical basis' for the mechanism of stress-mediated immune dysfunction" (in Risenberg 1986, 313).

Since the search is for mechanisms, the findings can only be stated in physical terms. The authors' chronicling of the psychoimmunology story indicates no redefining of mechanism in any meaningful way (for example, can the mechanism concept itself evolve with the findings so as to permit not just neurophysiological but psychoneurophysiological mechanisms?). Thus we can identify the paradigm-dependent, natural science methodological injunctions that the psychoneuroimmunologists have inherited. Their accumulated evidence does not lead to a questioning of foundations. In the sense that the term was distinguishable above, they are reporting on science (empirical findings), not Science (a foundations examination). So, Locke and Colligan begin with a revolutionary insight that "psychoneuroimmunological research suggests . . . that it may be time to retire the term *psychosomatic* altogether" (p. 61). They recognize that all disease has physical and psychosocial components. Such an insight alone demands a reassessment of the nature of causal mechanisms, one that entertains irreducible levels of organization that can interact. Yet they stay the course by always concluding that for want of the mechanism the evidence is "suggestive," "promising," and "encouraging."

Robert Good made the reluctant assessment above that, while he intuitively recognized the interactive relationship between mind and body, he found such a relationship unsupportable, given his commitment to the principles of science. He was suggesting that he (like many others) was forced into choosing between an "irrational" relationship and a rational one. One might ask: As the psychoneuroimmunology option unfolds, is one still forced into such a choice, or has an alternative model been projected that might transcend this dualism? As long as Good and Locke share the same definition of what constitutes science, they will both have to conclude that while the mind-body connection may eventually be proved beyond a doubt, the connections must be of an ultimately reductionist nature, because that is what makes it scientific: the paradigm trap. Further exemplifying psychoneuroimmunology's inability to bridge the gap between mind-body interaction and objective science (as well as the general acceptance of this gap) is the comment in a review of *The Healer Within* from the *New England Journal of Medicine*. The review editor states: "Maybe each generation must rediscover these timeless truths [mind and body go together] for itself while neurobiologists gradually uncover the details of this most complex aspect of human biology" (Moore 1986, 772).

We conclude that psychoneuroimmunology is not a true alternative medical model that challenges the biomedical edifice with its own deducible three-tiered approach. Foundations questions are not ultimately raised. According to Locke:

> Behavioral medicine is not based on any one system of healing; rather, it is an inspirational, eclectic attitude, a spirit that has come to perfuse twentieth-century medicine. Using the experimental, nondogmatic approach of behavioral medicine, psychoneuroimmunology researchers have learned to use the technique and therapies suggested by a broad mix of scientific experts. . . . (1986, 173)

We may now summarize the breakthrough implications of psychoneuroimmunology. Briefly, it counters two popular criticisms of the biomedical research agenda. It does so by proceeding in a manner that is interactionist (recognizing the interaction of major body systems and its relation to behavior) and nonreductionist (devising "new approaches where reductionism has failed"). All the while, it proceeds without violating biomedical foundation principles; that is, the behavioral component remains in principle explicable by neurophysiological events. At least, so far as our reading takes us, no systematic effort has been undertaken to advance the irreducibility of the "psycho" component to the "neuroimmunology" component in the discipline's name. As we will see in Part Four, by means of such systems concepts as "developmental antecedent" and "isomorphism" and in the context of a species evolution framework, Engel has recently paved the way for just such an effort. But his contribution, radical in its consequences for the continued viability of biomedical premises, has yet to be assimilated to the field of psychoneuroimmunology. Insofar, then, as biomedical foundation principles remain intact, we may say that, while the psychoneuroimmunological position supersedes the conventional reductionist position, its interactionism is in the final analysis still limited to bodily systems.

## Psychoneuroimmunology: Biomedicine's Limitations

Commenting on the implications of experimental findings in behavioral medicine studies, Ader writes:

> For years I've been studying psychosomatic factors in illness. Gastric lesions, infectious diseases, spontaneous tumor, diabetes, carcinogens. I can mix up a disease solution so potent that it will always elicit disease. But this kind of reductionist approach doesn't tell what real life is like. In real life, animals and people sometimes get sick and sometimes don't. It's not just disease agents that are involved; there are other factors, like age, genetics, sex, environment, early experiences, and so on. I'm interested in those other factors. (In Anderson 1982, 56)

Here we glimpse the psychoneuroimmunologist's notion of what Cunningham calls "new approaches where reductionism has failed." It is the "multivariate approach to the study of psychosocial influences on resistance to infectious disease," in Plaut and Friedman's words. Many of the agents other than the "disease agents" to which Ader refers are factors belonging to the first box of Figure 6.1, there labeled "experimental psychosocial stimulation." The "ideas or expectations in the mind" (Figure 6.3) interconnecting with the immune system are evidently of the sort that the experimental animal might have when it expects an unconditioned stimulus. Speaking broadly, they are of a Pavlovian sort, subject to behavioral conditioning and common to both humans and animals.

A closer examination of how the term *behavioral conditioning* functions in this discussion points to some very important distinctions. In particular, a research program that uses the term as it applies to animals and humans alike can conceal important differences. This can limit the explanatory potential of such a research effort. In this regard, it is interesting that among the references that Cunningham cites is one by

M. Cohn titled "Molecular Biology of Expectation" and another by O. C. Simonton and S. S. Simonton titled "Belief Systems and Management of the Emotional Aspects of Malignancy." Both the Pavlovian-type expectation referred to in Cohn's study and the belief systems in the Simontons' study ostensibly pertain to the psychological component of psychoneuroimmunology. But these two types of "psychological" events seem at face value to differ. To the extent that they do, we may be speaking of two qualitatively different positions, though both can be construed as nonreductionist.

The first of these nonreductionist approaches represents the psychoneuroimmunologist's position. We refer to it as "modified interactionism." This is the nonreductionism that experimentally documents the interactions linking psychosocial factors like "ideas and expectations" in Figure 6.3 and biochemical processes. These are the interactions to which Marvin Stein refers when he says, "The immune system itself is a highly complicated, fine-tuned system of cells all communicating with one another. The same is true of the central nervous system and the endocrine system. If you think in terms of the body and homeostasis, it shouldn't be any surprise if they are all interrelated" (in Anderson 1982, 53). Having delineated lines of communication between the central nervous system and the immune system, the psychoneuroimmunologist concludes that behavior, which has its locus in the cortex of the brain, can and does, via the limbic system and the hypothalamic-pituitary axis, affect immune response.

We will contrast modified interactionism with an unqualified version referred to simply as "interactionism." The dramatic distinction is that the latter version (breaking with biomedical tradition) assumes that all behavior is not ultimately reducible to and explainable in the language of neurobiology. That is, it postulates that human mental behavior is emergent behavior whose evolutionary substrate is primate "mental" behavior, different from but isomorphic with the former.

The contrast materializes when we compare a Pavlovian response to a conditioned stimulus (call it biofeedback I) with an altered mental-emotional state resulting, say, from a visualization technique common to the Simontons' therapeutic practice (call it biofeedback II). The psychoneuroimmunologist's concept of "idea or expectation in the mind" (Fig. 6.3) does not require a distinction between these two "mental events." But as we will argue, such a distinction is critical and serves to differentiate psychoneuroimmunology as presently conceived and a truly postbiomedical science, like that spelled out in Part Four.

The two previously mentioned articles, Cohn's "Molecular Biology of Expectation" and the Simontons' "Belief Systems and Management of the Emotional Aspects of Malignancy," may be used to help highlight the structural limitations of the psychoneuroimmunologist's approach.

The nature of the expectations built into the conditioned response experiments on rats and other animals conducted by Ader and his associates may well lend themselves to a molecular-biological analysis of the sort that Cohn's title suggests. Here the desired effects of the therapy administered turn on changing animal expectations through behavior conditioning techniques. The therapy consists in conditioning a specific immunological response such that administering a placebo (conditioned stimulus) brings about the unconditioned response to a pharmaceutical. In the case of the Simontons' regimen, the desired effects of the therapies administered turn on changing not just expectations but patient belief systems as well. The "conditioning" process seems to differ in certain essential ways from classical behavior conditioning techniques. Therapies include biofeedback, visualization, imagery, and cognitive affective learning. Fritjof Capra explains:

> For most cancer patients the impasse created by the accumulation of stressful events can be overcome only if they change part of their belief system. The Simonton therapy shows them that their situation seems hopeless only because they interpret it in ways that limit their responses. Patients are encouraged to explore alternative interpretations and responses in order to find healthful ways of resolving the stressful situation. Thus the therapy involves a continual examination of their belief system and world view. (1982, 357)

Whether or not these unconventional therapies work is not at issue. For present purposes, their importance is that to be operational they enlist not only the patient's belief system and worldview but the patient's *interpretation* of that system and view. In the psychoneuroimmunological literature cited, the conditioning experiments performed have involved conditioning of the sort to which animals and humans alike are susceptible. The patients' self-conscious interpretation of their condition is not implicated. Nowhere is it suggested that certain kinds of conditioning are, because of their uniquely human cognitive affective content, proper to humans alone. The issue here is whether techniques intrinsic to conditioning experiments like those conducted by the Simontons—techniques presupposing self-consciousness—apply uniquely to humans. Are some therapeutic measures, purportedly essential to treatment, such that humans alone are equipped to undergo them? If so, we need to distinguish between, first, behavioral conditioning applicable to both humans and animals and, second, a distinct species of conditioning applicable to humans alone, that is, beings capable of self-consciousness, or what Douglas Hofstadter calls "statistically emergent mentality" (1985, 654).

To appreciate this distinction, consider what is involved in the behavioral conditioning experiments common to psychoneuroimmunological studies involving placebo effect phenomena.

1. Subjects can be conditioned to initiate specific body processes previously thought to be autonomic (inaccessible).
2. Experiments establish a link between the brain and body system, and in particular, between the brain and the immune system—formerly believed to be autonomous.
3. There is no reason to regard the placebo effect as anything other than a brain/body phenomenon.
4. Not only do such experiments scientifically validate placebo effect phenomena (meeting the symbolic needs of the patient), but they can achieve a conditioned response sufficiently fine-tuned as to match a specific pharmacological effect. It is the latter discovery that constitutes the breakthrough findings in placebo research that experimentally connect the nervous system with the immune system.

From this experimental use of the placebo effect, we can draw the following inferences:

- The placebo involves the brain.
- The placebo effect may be a conditioned response and thus subject to external initiation.
- Behavioral conditioning of a desired conditioned response has led to the projected use of the placebo effect as a pharmacological substitute. It can thus become a viable therapeutic option in medicine per se.[3]

By way of contrast, let us examine the use of clinical biofeedback in regimens like those employed by the Simontons and others. The clinical use of biofeedback implies volitional control of interior body processes. Like behavioral conditioning techniques, it seeks to regulate heretofore inaccessible (autonomic) body functions. Unlike animal behavioral conditioning techniques, however, it implies a self-conscious, autocatalytic component. The therapist (or the patient) recruits the patient's intellect for medical purposes. This use of biofeedback responds to the following patient's needs/desires:

I will to have intimate access to and control of the dynamics of (some of) my physical functions by making knowledge of them part of the "exterior environment." I will this access and control *in order to:*

3. "These findings . . . suggest . . . that there is some heuristic value in analyzing a pharmacotherapeutic regimen in terms of conditioning operations. Based on the present paradigm in which conditioned stimulus presentations (placebo treatments) were substituted for some active immunosuppressive therapy, it may be hypothesized that the prescription of a noncontinuous schedule of pharmacologic treatment in contrast to an analysis of the effects of continuous regimens of drug (or placebo) would be applicable in the pharmacotherapeutic control and regulation of a variety of physiologic systems" (Ader and Cohen 1982, 1536).

- turn off useless pain
- tranquilize an alarmed heart
- instruct the body not to reject a transplanted organ
- recapture or banish an emotion

In general, clinical biofeedback is medically invoked in order to bring a harmonized body-mind under full and rational control and do so noninvasively. It is the setting of a goal and the self-conscious desire to achieve it that sets the stage for the *psycho-bio* interactive sequences that comprise what might accordingly be called "psychobiofeedback" (biofeedback II). We may contrast the psychoneuroimmunologist's behavioral conditioning objective of using the placebo effect as a pill substitute (a discrete series) and the psychobiofeedback objective of using the placebo effect, e.g., imagery and visualization, as a means of altering one's belief system (a continuous loop-structure or cybernetically circular process). Here the belief system is understood as one root of the dysfunctional body condition at which the behavioral conditioning technique aims. In addition to a strictly adaptive response to an external set of circumstances (as in behavioral conditioning),[4] biofeedback ("psychobiofeedback") can also be used as a self-differentiating activity involving a conscious mind-self inducing unconscious (autonomic) body-self processes.

This is the basis for contrasting a placebo effect that can be understood in the reductionist or modified interactionist language of neurophysiology and a different sort of placebo effect that cannot. While the first refers to external initiation (e.g., conditioned or unconditioned stimulus), the second refers to internal initiation or self-initiation (e.g., volitional control of internal body processes). This presupposes a *processor* and a *processed* in a self-reinforcing loop, where the italicized expressions designate different components of the *same* self-conscious entity. In this vein Barbara Brown says that "Only now are we learning that if we provide man with accurate and recognizable information about the dynamics of his functioning being as part of his external environment, he can then experience himself. That is, he can verify certain relationships between himself and the internal, non-external world, and then interact with himself" (1978, 4).

This ability to experience oneself and, moreover, to will to do so presupposes a novel primitive loop-structure whose component parts are a self-conscious mind-brain, a *he* (processor), and a nonselfconscious brain-body, a *himself* (processed). Thus, while conditioning is being tuned and retuned, biofeedback I, clinical biofeedback of the sort

---

4. Behavioral conditioning sets as its goal the (volitional) achievement of an *involuntary* (autonomic) response: "I want to stop smoking as an involuntary response."

referenced here is rather a consciously sought self-tuning, biofeedback II: "The process becomes completely internalized, and the control over the physiological function can be activated by intention, i.e., by voluntary control" (Brown 1978, 18).

In short, the experimental findings of psychoneuroimmunology lend themselves to the following interpretation with respect to mind-body issues: having disposed reductionistically of the role of placebos in behaviorally conditioned procedures, we have disposed reductionistically of the role of mind; mind need not be considered "an emergent property of brain." This accounts for the ready interchangeability of expressions like *mind* and *brain*, and *behavior* or *psychosocial factors* and *neurological processes*. But contrary to this interpretation, we have indicated one area of mind-body events not evidently captured in behaviorally conditioned experiments, clinical biofeedback. Here, recourse to a two-level language ("Through the use of biofeedback one is enabled to know oneself") is said to be necessary to adequately explain the process in a way not necessary to explain behavioral conditioning ("He/she/it was conditioned to respond automatically"). In certain forms of biofeedback, in other words, it is the *awareness* that our internal state is projected externally that distinguishes it from conditioning. Awareness that we can exercise and are exercising control over our biological processes, and a willingness to do so, is essential to advancing the process.

As a way of underlining this difference, the interactionist points to the fact that you cannot sensibly subject animals to the full use of clinical biofeedback. Or, to put it operationally, the design of clinical biofeedback for animals effectively translates into a behavioral conditioning experiment. There are essential elements in some uses of clinical biofeedback, then, that are not part of the behavioral conditioning experiment (e.g., *awareness* that the internal is projected to the external). The instigation of the process is itself a mental event. Brown gives voice to this added dimension: "And for the first time in therapeutics, complex mental processes are evoked to change the body's physiologic activities. This leads not only to learned control over 'involuntary' functions, but also to changing states of awareness and mental perspective" (1978, 26). This would appear to be a description of self-differentiation and self-organization. In Brown's estimate, the patient chooses to achieve a qualitative change that disposes him to react in a different fashion to future events; hence the significance of the title of her first book on clinical biofeedback: *New Mind, New Body*. Such a change, we suggest, can only be described in a two-level language. This is not a homeostatic adjustment capable of behavioral conditioning—it is a change in *program*, "a level shift as drastic as that between molecules and gases that takes place when thought emerges from billions of in-themselves-meaningless neural firings" (Hofstadter 1985, 649). Or, as we will argue in Part Three, as drastic as that between near-equilibrium and far-from-equilibrium (self-organizing) structures.

A final contrast:

1. A pill (like the stimulus in behavior conditioning) activates a process that sets off a chain reaction of physiological processes directed toward a preset goal.
2. Some uses of clinical biofeedback describe a continuous, on-line, two-way process likewise involving a series of physiological processes but whose subsequent direction is itself governed by a *reading* (reader) of these processes continually redirecting them in accord with a preset strategy or goal.

Hence, unlike the first case, the second case appears to involve *two* types of events, a series of *physiological* events and a series of *deliberative* events (which themselves have physiological correlates) that govern the direction of this series of physiological events.

One case describes a self-organizing or bootstrapping phenomenon, the other does not. The difference is between linear cause-effect (pill–sequence of biochemical events) and cybernetic circularity (decision-maker–decisions enacted biochemically). Whereas primitive elements of the first process are the *cause* (pill) and the *effect* (physiological chain reaction), the primitive element of the second process is the *feedback loop* whose components are the decision-maker and the physiological outcome of the decisions enacted. This outcome is the basis for a new decision; and so forth.

In informational terms, in the second but not in the first process, there is a continuous cumulative series: message sent concomitant with decision made to secure a goal; message received accompanied or manifested by physiological processes activated; message sent whose content is the result of activated processes; message received, the basis for new decision reached accompanied or manifested by message sent; and so on. We may say that the self-conscious governor and the governed physiological processes (sender-receiver) are chemically conjugate variables. This difference of process types reflects contrasting logics: the logic of probabilistic unidirectional causality versus the logic of negative and positive feedback mutual causality.

In summary, this chapter has distinguished three positions that respond to the explanatory challenge posed by the possible link between psychosocial factors and disease. The *reductionist* position we saw to be historically interesting but untenable given the experimental evidence over the last two decades—particularly the findings in the new field of psychoneuroimmunology. It is these findings that form the evidence supporting the *modified interactionist* position. Here the relationship between the nervous system or mind/brain and the immune system is well established. The strength of this position resides in the ease with which it is able to include in its explanatory framework the disease implications of "stressful" psychosocial factors by tracing the physiological mechanisms that such psychosocial factors initiate. Further, studies experimentally validating behaviorally conditioned responses that otherwise would have required active pharmacological treatment are among the kinds of brain/mind and immune system interactions that also can be accounted for via modified interactionist principles. However, the limitations of modified interactionism surface when the range of placebo effect phenomena is enlarged to include examples relating to a specifically human population (biofeedback II). These include placebo phenomena in which a two-level language is invoked due to the necessity of referring to such interacting primitives as process initiator or processor (mind-brain) and processed (body). *Interactionism* is the language that provides a nonreductionist account for the full range of events when one speaks of the specifically human psychological factors influencing disease. The burden of Part Three is to spell out the scientific grounds for such a language. Part Four deploys such a language and extends it to include also specifically human social and technological factors influencing disease.

# PART THREE

# The Second Revolution: Postmodern Science

With the existing [i.e., classical] laws of thermodynamics, science can do no better than to describe man as, in Monod's words, "the gypsy on the outskirts of the universe."
— Howard Brody
"The Systems View of Man"

Released from the arbitrary constraints imposed on science by the presuppositions of Cartesian and Newtonian "natural philosophy," all of the sciences—human and natural alike—have been free to rethink their assumptions and procedures, so as to allow for the scientist's own presence in, and involvement with, the world of natural phenomena and processes. In that sense, the whole range of theoretical sciences has, by now, begun to develop in the new, "post-modern" direction.
— Stephen Toulmin
"The Emergence of Post-Modern Science"

... the reception of a new paradigm often necessitates a redefinition of the corresponding science.
— Thomas Kuhn
*The Structure of Scientific Revolutions*

# INTRODUCTION TO PART THREE

Part Three is pivotal. It provides the theoretical and philosophical bridge that takes us from the foundations of biomedicine to the foundations of a fully articulated alternative infomedical model. As such, it presents a sustained attack on the foundations of biomedicine. While the medical countermovements critiqued medical practice, a tier 3 consideration, in Part Three the argument is aimed at tiers 1 and 2—the foundations upon which biomedicine is based.

To effectively challenge the biomedical model is to take issue with the logic of method or tier 1 foundations. To do this, one must counter the logical possibility or ultimate reducibility argument, the heart of the biomedical foundations defense. Such a challenge is the task of Chapter 7.

Briefly, the logical possibility argument claims that though a single-level, reductionist explanation may be difficult to achieve (particularly in the life sciences), there is the logical possibility that, when all the evidence is in, such explanations will be possible. Therefore, the task at hand is to stay with the natural science strategy rather than risk a wayward tack built upon less secure foundations. The logical possibility argument is neutralized by invoking the findings of quantum physics and irreversible thermodynamics. The single-level, reductionist agenda is impossible not so much in principle as in fact. Such an achievement, contemporary findings tell us, is a physical impossibility.

In Chapter 8, the revolutionary shift from a logic of method based on reductionism and dualism to a logic of method based on nonreductionism and interactionism is detailed. Such a shift provides the necessary two-level language that can be invoked to explain the range of specifically human population clinical events (biofeedback II). In the process, we offer the beginnings (tier 1' and 2') of a self-organizing systems alternative paradigm.

Briefly, the shift is from a cause-and-effect paradigm to a self-organizing systems paradigm in which a given response is not the direct result of some outside stimulus, but rather the result of rule-governed behavior that is a property of the system acting as a system. Hence, the alternative model is based on cybernetic feedback loops that interact to determine the future state of the system instead of the more traditional cause-and-effect view associated with an engineering model. We invoke support for the self-organizing systems infrastructure by reference to the findings of quantum mechanics, irreversible thermodynamics, and the emerging sciences of ecology and biogeochemistry.

In Chapter 9, certain philosophical questions are addressed. A self-organizing systems paradigm entails a two-level language and embraces an interactive pattern of relations. This raises questions concerning the relationship of mind-events and body-events. The self-organizing systems approach to dealing with the "mind-body" problem is clarified. This is presented in anticipation of criticisms that have been aimed at failed attempts in the past to expand the range of scientific understanding.

Finally, in Chapter 10, the infomedical model is presented. Just as the biomedical model rests on engineering concepts, so the infomedical model rests on cybernetic concepts. In detailing the infomedical model, key concepts from cybernetics (e.g., negative and positive feedback) and information theory (e.g., message, program, entropy, and noise) are defined.

Because of the pivotal character assigned in Part Three to the transition from one era of science to another—the classical or modern to the postclassical or "postmodern" era—we present this glossary:

*Modern science* refers to the scientific foundations of the first medical revolution. It developed during the 250 years from 1650 to 1900. Synonyms include *classical science, Newtonian science,* and the *natural science paradigm.* Its characteristics include reductionism, physicalism, determinism, and mechanism.

*Postmodern science* refers to the scientific foundations of the second medical revolution. It began early in the twentieth century and is still developing. Its disciplines include relativity theory, quantum mechanics, irreversible thermodynamics and ecology. Its characteristics include interactionism, emergence, loop-structure, and mutual causality.

# 7

## The Defeat of Biomedical Foundations

In Chapter 3 we got a glimpse of the formidable body of philosophical and scientific literature upon which the biomedical model is based. As such, we can view any successor to the biomedical model only to the extent that a compelling argument can be offered in support of alternative philosophical and scientific foundations. The balance of this chapter will examine the claim that there are such grounds for challenging the biomedical model.

## Criticisms of the Biomedical Model

Many people regard medicine to be in a state of crisis. It stems "from the logical inference that since 'disease' is defined in terms of somatic parameters, physicians need not be concerned with psychosocial issues that lie outside medicine's responsibilities and authority" (Engel 1977b, 129). René Dubos has argued that the alleged crisis is due to an insufficiently enriched theoretical vocabulary. Others charge that recently surfacing experimental findings fall outside the explanatory range of the prevailing medical framework and, more particularly, that possibly medicine has been uncritical in the way it has "bought" the natural sciences' conception of solution. One result of this explanatory shortfall is that research energies are increasingly directed toward aspects of disease most susceptible to the sophisticated biotechnologies at hand. "We have been looking through a lens of high power at a small segment of a large field," says Thomas McKeown (1979, 164). Insofar as the larger field is addressed, another result is that medical practice consists increasingly of therapies for which conditions but not reasons for success are known. Unaccounted-for experimental findings, many of them uncovered over the past several decades, point to limitations of the prevailing model. As such, the following premises might prove vulnerable:

1. Disease is a process accountable by deviations from the norm of biological parameters.[1]
2. Disease is best understood by means of sciences like pathophysiology, whose principles are themselves in principle rationalizable if not yet fully rationalized by sciences like molecular biology, biochemistry, and physics.
3. The human patient is conceptualizable as a biological organism ("whole body") such that, in Descartes's phrase, "were there no mind in it at all, it [the body] would not cease to have the same functions."
4. Disease cure is typically achieved physically (e.g., supplementing, reducing, or neutralizing).

The strength of these biomedical premises—a tier 3 consideration—is a function of the strength of the sciences upon which they are based—a tier 2 consideration. This, in turn, is measured by the adequacy of the methodological directives upon which these sciences are based—a tier 1 consideration. That reductionist/biomedical premises may not explain all medical events is not in itself sufficient grounds for abandoning the multitiered biomedical paradigm. Rather, as Richard Rudner points out, invalidation requires showing that "it is logically impossible for any such hypothesis to ever be formulated" (1966, 71). That some or even much clinical practice is not currently grounded by the sciences taught in today's medical curriculum does not imply that such practice will not or cannot be grounded. In essence this is the logical possibility argument and turns on the distinction between what is currently understood and what will be understood when all the evidence is in.

In the next section, we examine the logical possibility argument in more detail. This argument goes to the heart of the defense of the logic of method underpinning the scientific and philosophical foundations of the biomedical model. Thus, an examination of this defense provides a vantage point from which to view the claims of a potential successor model.

## The Logical Possibility Argument

In Chapter 3 we saw that philosophers of science such as Hempel, Nagel, and Toulmin view the methodological directives (Table 3.1) underlying modern theoretical science as virtually an analytic conse-

---

1. *Disease:* "A definite morbid process having a characteristic train of symptoms: it may affect the whole body or any of its parts, and its etiology, pathology and prognoses may be known or unknown."—*Dorland's Illustrated Medical Dictionary*, 26th ed. (1981).

*Disease:* "1. . . . an interruption, cessation or disorder of body functions, systems or organs. 2. A disease *entity* characterized usually by at least two of these criteria: A recognized etiological agent (or agents); an identifiable group of signs or symptoms; consistent anatomical alterations."—*Stedman's Medical Dictionary*, 24th ed. (1982).

quence of engaging in the conduct of empirical inquiry. For them the method they embody has achieved the status of a necessary condition for empirical inquiry to proceed. While the directives might be couched in terms that suggest they are provisional assumptions (e.g., Toulmin's methodological determinism) and so subject to revision, it is difficult to imagine that they truly view them as only provisional.

Biomedical premises derive in straightforward fashion from these directives. Some argue that these premises are too restrictive. However, apparent anomalies with respect to the biomedical model, for example placebo phenomena,[2] are interpreted quite differently: as signaling currently outstanding difficulties in the program to explain all phenomena, including psychological phenomena, by reference to deviations from the norm of pathophysiological and, by extension, biophysical parameters alone. So to call them anomalies is to commit what Nagel terms "an elementary blunder." It is to confuse what has yet to be explained with what cannot be explained. As Carl Sagan has said in a related context, the absence of evidence is not evidence of absence.

The reluctance to label a biomedically "unexplainable" event an anomaly is one product of the logical possibility argument. Nagel suggests the spirit of this argument:

> Organismic biologists are therefore on firm ground in maintaining that mechanistic explanations of all philosophical phenomena are currently impossible. . . . On the other hand, the facts cited . . . do not warrant the conclusion that biology is *in principle* irreducible to the physical sciences. The task facing such a proposed reduction is admittedly a most difficult one; . . . However, no *logical* contradiction has yet been exhibited to the supposition that both the formal and nonformal conditions for the reduction of biology may some day be fulfilled. (1961, 436)

While Nagel and others might dismiss the "anomalous evidence" of functionalists and neovitalists as examples of "elementary blunders," this is not to say that experimental findings might not be made to challenge the soundness of the logic of method that they endorse. This is a particularly important issue because the successor argument among competing paradigms ultimately takes place at the tier 1 level. Thus, the most fundamental directives of inquiry are at issue.

The choice of paradigms determines the kind of results that can be achieved. That a methodological strategy can have this effect is an argument advanced by Thomas Kuhn with reference to a scientific paradigm, a mixture of scientific principles, methodological attitudes, and resulting institutions and technologies. Such a paradigm, he says, can "insulate the

2. *Placebo:* "An inactive substance or preparation given to satisfy the patient's symbolic need for drug therapy and used in controlled studies to determine the efficacy of medicinal substances. Also, a procedure with no intrinsic therapeutic value, performed for such purposes."—*Dorland's Illustrated Medical Dictionary*, 26th ed. (1981).

community adopting it from problems that are not reducible to the puzzle form, because they cannot be stated in terms of the conceptual and instrumental tools the paradigm supplies" (1970, 37).

Defenders of the natural science paradigm counter that there are strong forces, based on convincing epistemological arguments and past successes, which determine the methodological strategy of medical researchers. This includes a mechanistic worldview, not only of physical nature, but of biological and psychosocial nature as well. As we have seen, such a view continues to have a powerful force in medicine today.

To the extent that our methodological strategies when writ large represent how we see the world, they can constitute a risk. Fully to appreciate this risk is to recall Hempel's formulation of the alternative to persisting in the search for basic physicochemical theories of biological and psychological phenomena. For the scientist to do otherwise, in Hempel's account, is "to resign himself to the view that the concepts and principles of physics and chemistry are powerless to give an adequate account of the phenomenon of life [and mind]." This recourse to the psychological language of resignation is revealing. Hempel seems to be saying that the life of rationality has been fostered by a persistent search for basic physicochemical theories of virtually all phenomena, even including in successive stages biological and psychological phenomena. In addition, because such a search has proved so fruitful, its dominant directives, reductionist and determinist, should not be lightly forsworn. This is the heart of the logical possibility argument. The capacity of this argument to stand or fall is crucial. Tier 1 assumptions and directives depend on the logical possibility argument, and the contemporary medical enterprise, biomedicine, depends on tier 1. The argument states:

1. There exists a formidable body of scientific knowledge that implies the possibility of an ultimate single-level physicalist language.
2. Further, the weight of modern science supports the injunction to proceed as if such a language will ultimately be formulated, even in the presence of those phenomena which appear to resist such formulation. In other words, persist, since ultimate success is logically possible, or, alternately phrased, has not been shown to be logically impossible to achieve.

Neither empirical generalizations nor scientific laws (like gravitational laws), these tier 1 directives function as strongly reinforced methodological or metascientific prescripts. The extent to which science progresses (understanding is achieved) in accordance with their application, the greater the warrant for strengthened faith in them. This faith, in turn, nourishes the worldview they imply. Called a scientific worldview because of the source of its credibility, a particular worldview thus preempts the notion of what it is to proceed scientifically and, in the descriptive (as distinct from the normative) domain, to proceed rationally. In this way a historically successful method appears to secrete the concept of a scientific worldview.

Not openly entertained by Hempel is the possibility of understanding becoming increasingly resistant to the application of this method. Were this to happen, what would be the prudent response? Suppose in the course of applying a reductionist and determinist method the world revealed appeared less and less consistent with the worldview implied. The option permitted to the scientist Hempel addresses is to persist nonetheless in the search for basic physicalist theories to explain all phenomena—or despair at the seeming futility of doing so. The question arises (though it is not raised by Hempel) whether sufficient empirical grounds could ever be marshaled to warrant reexamining one's initial methodological strategy. Might Hempel's scientist ever responsibly entertain the paradigm-independent option of applying extraphysicalist, nonreductionist "theories" for the guidance of research? Nagel refers to "certain broadly delimited features" that should characterize the directives instructing the search for explanations. These include mechanism, determinism, reductionism. The scientist is encouraged to persist in the assumption that explanations must ultimately yield to a framework defined by these features. He is enjoined, for example, to proceed as if the macroscopic level can ultimately be explained by means of the more "fundamental" microscopic level.

Such an assumption treads closely on the heels of matters that might be thought subject to scientific investigation. Thus the question whether there exists (or whether we can best organize our findings by assuming there exists) a single fundamental material level that is an absolute level has in our day come under growing scientific scrutiny. Assuredly the single-level assumption comports nicely with Occam's razor. Moreover, proceeding on its basis, as Nagel explains, has yielded impressive understanding in the past. Still, the question persists whether an accumulation of empirical evidence might ever license the scientist to call the assumption into question. (Granted that such evidence is garnered by application of a method based on the assumption.) There would seem to be no logical inconsistency in doing so as we are ever *in media res* when it comes to the pragmatic question of the soundness of methodological strategies.

In this century new postmodern sciences have appeared. These include quantum physics (the law of indeterminacy) and irreversible thermodynamics (the law of the irreducibility of levels). Development of these sciences appears to offer much the same kind of empirical and pragmatic impetus for advancing certain broadly delimiting features for characterizing directives instructing the search for explanations as development of Newtonian physics and classical thermodynamics offered in the seventeenth through nineteenth centuries. In this event Hempel's scientist's remarks might properly be characterized not in the psychological terms of resignation but in the heuristic terms of advancing a successor explanatory strategy. Much like an engineer charged with rebuilding the ship while at sea, such a scientist might be seen as invoking the experimental findings of science itself as a basis for offering alternative directives for its conduct. Ilya Prigogine suggests such a change in course:

> The idea of physics was always to look for a single fundamental basic level which would be an absolute level. For example, Newton's description was complete, there was no place for anything else, anything below or above, because essentially nature was simply a collection of particles moving according to the laws of dynamics. That was then the whole truth, a complete description of nature. The view which we reach now is that the microscopic level is reached from the macroscopic one but is in turn conditioning the macroscopic level. Therefore, there is no longer an absolute level of description. There are various levels, all interconnected in a much more complex fashion. Of course, this leads to a great change in epistemology because, before, the idea was to explain the macroscopic through the microscopic. That is partly true even now, but there is also the explanation of the microscopic through extrapolation of the macroscopic concept, and this again belongs to this interconnection of levels. (1979, 74–75)

This may be interpreted as a partial proposal for a revised strategy in the conduct of scientific inquiry. Substituting for the assumption of a "single fundamental level" expressible in the vocabulary of (classical) physics is the assumption of the interconnectedness of levels expressible in the vocabulary of irreversible thermodynamics. Rather than unidirectional causality, reductionism, and determinism, alternative directives for guiding research may be advanced. In the spirit of the foregoing remarks these countervailing directives might be termed cybernetic circularity, interactivation of levels, and stochastic transformation.

The scientist whom Hempel enjoins to persist, come what may, in the fundamental-level thesis is, in Kuhn's terms, being asked to keep faith with the prevailing "puzzle form." That is, persist in normal and, to extend this term, even "normative" science. Here, *normative* is understood as making one period's scientific successes the model for science as such. Prigogine was stepping out of that puzzle form. He was speculating on developments in postnormal or "revolutionary" science, gauging their potential implications for methodological directives like those advocated by Hempel and Nagel and plainly infusing classical science. If practicing science according to inherited directives is doing normal science, assessing the consequences of the findings of normal and conceivably postnormal science on the choice of an appropriate methodological strategy is doing something else. This takes us into the area of foundations of science or a variation of what Kuhn calls revolutionary science—metascience.

## The Task

A successor paradigm has to meet certain well-defined conditions as stipulated by the logic of theory succession. For example, its constituent sciences, like quantum physics and irreversible thermodynamics, must be shown to incorporate as special cases the basic sciences of the predecessor framework, like Newtonian physics and classical thermodynamics. That is, its persuasiveness turns on the same tests as that of its predecessor; its application has to yield all those scientific explanations yielded by application of the predecessor directives while at the same time at least some that are not. Also, a successor medical model must simultaneously provide:

1. A set of medical premises that define the model's tier 3 level. That is, disciplines incorporating the model's defining concepts of disease, patient, and appropriate therapy.
2. A body of basic empirical sciences whose principles underwrite the above premises. This constitutes the tier 2 level.
3. A logic of method consistent with the world properties that are implied by the above principles and premises. This constitutes the tier 1 level.

The task of meeting these conditions indicates the full complexity involved in effectively dislodging an existing paradigm. The objective of the remainder of this chapter and the rest of Part Three will be to address this task.

## The Argument for a Successor Paradigm

To critique the biomedical model is to take issue with the logic of method upon which it is based. Further, this logic of method implies acceptance of a certain worldview. Two world properties of this worldview were identified in Chapter 3: the fundamental-level world property and the external permanency world property. It is at the intersection of the tier 1 and tier 2 levels that the analysis will proceed. In this section we will argue that there is considerable evidence that calls into question the two world properties embraced by the logic of method of the natural science paradigm. A critique of these world properties proves to be the ground upon which a successor scientific paradigm can be offered. For, if the world properties prove to be inaccurate with respect to what our best knowledge tells us about the world, then the logical possibility of achieving the goals of a research program based on such an inaccurate worldview is unlikely.

The strength of the argument for identifying the enterprise of theoretical science with the general concepts expressed in Table 3.1 is that to proceed otherwise is to imperil the possibility of predictive-explanatory success, the hallmark of theoretical science. Yet some, perhaps many, would say that the appropriateness of directives like determinism and objectivity has been seriously challenged by findings in twentieth-century science. One of the leading exponents of the "new physics," Werner Heisenberg, remarks that "When we get down to the atomic level, the objective world in space and time no longer exists, and the mathematical symbols of theoretical physics refer merely to possibilities, not to facts" (1969, 64). That this raises questions about the propriety of adhering at least to one of the directives of Table 3.1 prompts the question: Are the findings on which Heisenberg's remark is based a challenge to the continued viability of theoretical science itself and its explanatory-predictive potential? Hempel's and Nagel's response is clear. Given their commitment, Heisenberg's remark appears at face value to challenge the possibility of theoretical science, or rather to "render the outcome of the enterprise incomparably different."

In what follows we argue that new findings do indeed render the enterprise radically, although not incomparably, different. The basis for the argument is found in the turnaround signaled by Heisenberg's remark. According to Morowitz, something altogether untoward has transpired in science in this century. Starting with the introduction of Einstein's relativity theory in 1905, the ordered mechanist world picture of classical physics was, he says, "unceremoniously upset." Because observers in different systems moving with respect to each other would perceive the world differently, they became involved in establishing physical reality. Devoid of the detached vantage point Newton's "single vision" had afforded, the scientist was losing the spectator's role and becoming an active participant in the system under study. With the next development the vision is further skewed. Morowitz explains:

> With the development of quantum mechanics, the role of the observer became an even more central part of physical theory, an essential component in defining an event. The mind of the observer emerged as a necessary element in the structure of the theory. The implications of the developing paradigm greatly surprised early quantum physicists and led them to study epistemology and the philosophy of science. . . . Heisenberg stressed that the laws of nature no longer dealt with elementary particles, but with our knowledge of these particles—that is *with the contents of our minds*.

Elaborating on the meaning of this italicized phrase, Morowitz says:

a complex system can only be described by using a probability distribution that relates the possible outcomes of an experiment. In order to decide among the various alternatives, a measurement is required. This measurement is what constitutes an event, as distinguished from the probability, which is a mathematical abstraction. However, the only simple and consistent description physicists were able to assign to a measurement involved an observer's becoming aware of the result. Thus the physical event and the content of the human mind were inseparable. (1980, 15–16)

One of the foundation stones on which the edifice of modern science was raised is, if not dislodged, at least nudged: the causal separation of observer and observed. Formulated above as the external permanency world property, it has had its tenability questioned from various quarters. One of the least understood implications of quantum theory, states John A. Wheeler, is the degree to which the observer has been written into the physical equation. " 'Participator' is the incontrovertible new concept given by quantum mechanics; it strikes down the term 'observer' of classical theory, the man who stands safely behind the thick glass wall and watches what goes on without taking part. It can't be done, quantum mechanics says. Even with the lowly electron one must participate before one can give any meaning whatsoever to its position and momentum" (1973, 1217). More recently, Bernard d'Espagnat has drawn the following conclusion from a body of elementary particle experiments concerned with correlations between distant events and the causes of those correlations—experiments growing out of the celebrated Einstein-Rosen-Podolsky "thought experiment": "The doctrine that the world is made up of objects whose existence is independent of human consciousness turns out to be in conflict with quantum mechanics and with facts established by experiment" (1979, 158). By present lights, it would seem, at least some theorists would categorically say that new information is generated by the experiment(er). Surprisingly (by classical expectations), the result of a quantum experiment gives information not already contained in the initial conditions, which specify only the probability of this or that event being observed. While the outcome of the experiment is undecidable, a decision is nevertheless made. In terms of the only available language for its description, the outcome is the product of the "objective state of affairs" and the experimenter's choice of how it is to be observed. In truth (the theory tells us), the only state of affairs is this subjective state of affairs.

We need not imply that an impersonal, acultural, objective experimental procedure cannot be prepared in quantum mechanics in order to conclude that the meaning of what counts as an objective-impersonal procedure has shifted as a result of the findings and principles of quantum mechanics. We need only assume that the physical meaning of *objectivity* evolves apace with the evolution of our understanding of the objects of inquiry. The kind of experimental objectivity that Galileo and Newton thought they could and should adopt toward macro-objects is not what Heisenberg and Niels Bohr believed to be possible vis-à-vis microreality. The concept of objectivity has experienced a profound, if subtle, transformation. We return to this general point in Chapter 9 in an examination of the development of the seventeenth-century concepts of matter and mechanism.

The point at issue is not a case of calling attention to a current difficulty in achieving the mechanistic ideals. Such an objection is neutralized by the logical possibility argument. Rather, the point here is that contemporary scientific findings indicate the impossibility of ever achieving such a goal. Thus, the mechanist is not being reminded of work still to be done. Rather, given the implications of the best under-standing of the phenomena available—quantum mechanics—it is not the logical but the physical impossibility of completing the work that is being asserted. According to Toulmin (this the "later" Toulmin), the reductionists' agenda "might be unrealizable, not, or not merely, be-cause it was out of human reach for practical reasons, but also because it was *misconceived in principle*" (1981, 85).

This point bears amplification. Under the entry "Quantum Mechanics," the *McGraw-Hill Encyclopedia of Science and Technology* states:

> *Uncertainty principle.* In classical physics the observables characterizing a given system are assumed to be simultaneously measurable (in principle) with arbitrarily small error. . . . According to the uncertainty principle (W. Heisenberg, 1927), accurate measurement of an observable quantity neces-sarily produces uncertainties in one's knowledge of the values of other observables.

> *Probability considerations.* The uncertainty and complementarity principles, which limit the experimenter's ability to describe a physical system, must limit equally the experimenter's ability to predict the results of measure-ment on that system (Gerjudy).

The greater the confidence in the "new physics"—the only available explanation of all the dynamic phenomena—the more suspect the mechanist's ideal.

The other natural-science world property referenced, the funda-mental-level property, is similarly embattled as a result of postmodern findings. Morowitz further chronicles the implications:

> By combining the positions of Sagan, Crick, and Wigner as spokesmen for various outlooks, we get a picture of the whole that is quite unexpected. First, the human mind, including consciousness and reflective thought, can be explained by activities of the central nervous system, which, in turn, can be reduced to the biological structure and function of that physiological

system [Sagan]. Second, biological phenomena at all levels can be totally understood in terms of atomic physics, that is, through the action and interaction of the component atoms of carbon, nitrogen, oxygen, and so forth [Crick]. Third and last, atomic physics, which is now understood most fully by means of quantum mechanics, must be formulated with the mind as a primitive component of the system [Wigner].

We have thus, in separate steps, gone around an epistemological circle—from the mind, back to the mind. . . . nevertheless, the closed loop follows from a straightforward combination of the explanatory processes of recognized experts in three separate sciences. Since individuals seldom work with more than one of these paradigms, the general problem has received little attention. (1980, 16)

The challenge to the fundamental-level thesis is indicated by a graphic of Morowitz's closed loop (Fig. 7.1).

From another quarter comes a further challenge to the fundamental-level ideal and hence further grounds for neutralizing the logical possibility argument. The emergence of life and the general appearance of increasing self-organization refer to another branch of the "new physics" complete with a mathematical symbolism for specifying the "underlying process" by which the interpenetration of levels suggested by Figure 7.1 occurs. Here G. Nicolis, P. Glansdorff, Prigogine, and others satisfy Hempel's predictive criterion for an acceptable scientific explanation (Glandsdorff and Prigogine 1971; Nicolis and Prigogine 1977). That is, their work specifies "underlying processes . . . definite enough to permit the derivation of specific implications concerning the phenomena that the theory [irreversible thermodynamics] is to explain." Yet at the same time the theory referenced opposes determinism. According to Nagel, "Given the state of a system for some initial time, the explanatory theory logically establishes a *unique* state for the system for any other time" (1961, 323; italics added). The new theory, predicated on asymmetrical or irreversible rather than reversible processes, systematically explains the existence of nonunique as well as unique states.

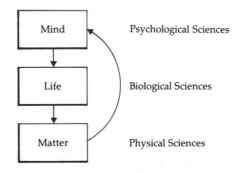

FIGURE 7.1

Thus our Hempel-antagonist scientist (speaking through Prigogine) can contrast a physical version of the world characterized by statistical thermodynamical situations alone, with a nonequilibrium thermodynamical version of the same situations. In other words, he can offer grounds for saying, "On the basis of the theoretical assumptions this is just what was to be expected—the theory explains it" (Hempel). This Hempel-antagonist scientist proceeds as follows: "In the frame of classical physics, and classical thermodynamics, there was essentially no place for life (and even less for mind!) except as a kind of chance product: at some moment, some molecules began to behave in a strange way, and then this fluctuation was propagated, etc.—and you find in authoritative books the idea that life is essentially a struggle against the laws of physics." In classical physics this duality between life and the laws of physics remains an outstanding promissory note. On the basis of new findings, an alternative to this duality is indicated: "A new satisfactory development is that this duality may be overcome. Self-organization comes in when the system is prepared to have it. This implies that the distance from equilibrium is sufficiently large that the description implies non-linearity and bifurcations. Then you can have self-organization which at equilibrium would appear as a miracle" (Prigogine 1979, 78).

This miracle may be interpreted as Nagel's "incomparably different something." That this overcoming of the duality of yesterday's physical laws does not represent merely a cashing in of one of the promissory notes of classical physics is indicated by the necessity for introducing concepts of nonlinearity and bifurcations and the mathematical formalism they entail. These concepts imply what the general ideals or principles for the guidance of research formerly expressed as causality and reductionism (Table 3.1) implicitly disallow. Namely, the existence of a world whose processes are irreversible, one with radical asymmetries. These asymmetries are the product of the "self-organization" referred to in the last passage. And this sense of self-organization appears incongruent with Nagel's sense of emergence as "entirely compatible with the belief in the universality of the causal principle, at any rate in the form that there are determinate conditions for the occurrence of all events."

To the question "Why should a system move away, or be away from equilibrium?" Prigogine replies:

> We live in a universe which permits strong non-equilibrium situations. We cannot imagine what a world in thermal equilibrium would be like. But we *live* in this world and therefore we have these non-equilibrium situations. In the evolution of polymers and biological molecules, we can find transitions which even increase the distance from equilibrium. Since each organization requires a threshold distance from equilibrium, we obtain in this an evolu-

tionary feedback, in which, with increasing distance from equilibrium, we go to higher and higher levels of organization. (1979, 79)

Here is the empirical basis for the concept of the emergence of order out of chaos, higher levels of organization out of lower orders. At face value it appears that this account of emergence according to the science of "dissipative structures" (irreversible thermodynamics) is in violation of Nagel's condition for emergent evolution. Emergence is explained not as a result of "strange" behavior via the law of large numbers; it is not "a struggle against the laws of physics." Rather it is explained in accordance with the laws of a new, reconstituted thermodynamical theory via the concepts of nonlinearity and bifurcations. Ostensibly, this is a theory that "permits a better integration of theoretical physics and chemistry with disciplines dealing with other aspects of nature" (Prigogine 1978, 785). Equilibrium (classical thermodynamics) is evidently half of the story. The full story includes nonequilibrium states as a *natural* state of affairs. The old duality is reputedly overcome at the cost of the condition that there be "determinate conditions for the occurrence of all events." In place of the determinate condition of Table 3.1 is the new condition of indeterminacy or stochastic transformation. It may be roughly described like this: "The laws of strict causality appear to us today as limiting situations, applicable to highly idealized cases, nearly as caricatures of the description of change. . . . The science of complexity . . . leads to a completely different view. . . . there is always the possibility of some instability leading to some new mechanism. We really have an 'open universe' " (Prigogine 1978, 785).

The logical possibility argument has now proven vulnerable on two fronts—the physical impossibility of achieving the mechanist agenda (the quantum argument) and the shortcomings of the single-level reductionist agenda (the interaction argument). In other words, the kind of world our present knowledge tells us that we live in, today's "science of complexity," is not consistent with the kind of world implied by the methodological directives of Table 3.1 and partly expressed by world properties 1 and 2. With respect to Figure 3.1 we can now specify what Nagel might have meant by the warning that to surrender the general ideal expressed by causality (and presumably other directives of Table 3.1) will transform the enterprise of modern theoretical science into something incomparably different. However, as the present account shows, "incomparable" is too strong a term. The findings of quantum mechanics and irreversible thermodynamics pertain to what we have called tier 2 language. These are basic sciences and comprise the substantive side of science. By reference to Figure 3.1, alterations at this tier impact tier 1, the procedural side of science. Thus, succeeding Figure 3.1

is Figure 7.2. For purposes of ready identification, changes noted at tier 2, namely the unanticipated experimental findings of the new "sciences of complexity," will be designated by the prime symbol, tier 2'; and likewise the corresponding, conjectured changes at tier 1, tier 1'. Now tier 2' and tier 1' formally subsume their respective predecessors, tier 2 and tier 1, in the qualified sense that quantum mechanics subsumes Newtonian mechanics and irreversible thermodynamics classical thermodynamics.[3] This relationship is expressed by the following proportionality:

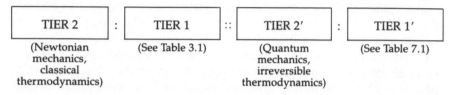

| TIER 2 | : | TIER 1 | :: | TIER 2' | : | TIER 1' |

(Newtonian mechanics, classical thermodynamics)        (See Table 3.1)        (Quantum mechanics, irreversible thermodynamics)        (See Table 7.1)

With reference to Figure 3.1, this subsumption may be alternatively illustrated as in Figure 7.2, this time also suggesting the historical relationship (the double-line arrow) between the elements of the forego-

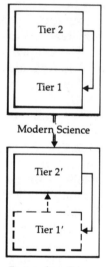

Modern Science

Postmodern Science

FIGURE 7.2

3. *Subsumption* and *special case* here and throughout are understood in Kuhn's sense: "Though an out-of-date theory can always be viewed as a special case of its up-to-date successor, it must be transformed for the purpose. And, the transformation is one that can be undertaken only with the advantages of hindsight, the explicit guidance of the more recent theory" (1970, 102–103). Thus, the transformation is an *approximation* of the predecessor theory.

ing proportionality. Here, the dashed, tier 1' rectangle indicates the still conjectural character of the logic of postmodern scientific method.

Thus, options seem not to be limited to either allowing inquiry to be guided by the concepts of Table 3.1 or succumbing to prescientific traps like subjectivism and neovitalism. We *can* point to tier 2 findings (now tier 2') as grounds for questioning the propriety of identifying the enterprise of theoretical science with the general ideals expressed by methodological policies exemplified by Table 3.1 (tier 1). But what successor policies should be put in their place? We return to this question in the next chapter. For now, the tier 1' box and arrow in Figure 7.2 may remain dashed lines. Looking at the two successor sciences referenced, quantum physics and irreversible thermodynamics, the counterpart concepts (Table 7.1) by which to approach the world tentatively suggest themselves as the basis for a logic of a postclassical science of complexity. Like their predecessors, these concepts imply a worldview, thus generating their own counterpart world properties, world properties 1' and 2':

1'  *Indeterminacy World Property*

The worldview implied by the successor logic of inquiry presupposes interactivating levels of reality. Levels of organization involve ontologically new entities beyond the level of elements from which the self-organization process proceeds. There is no absolute deterministic level of description.

2'  *Material Force World Property*

The worldview implied by the successor logic of inquiry presupposes a world in which ideas have a material impact on the structural lines of reality, are a "material force." There is no "external permanency" immune to the effects of ideation.

These alternative world properties cohere with an alternative logic of method and, derivatively, the foundations of an alternative medical model. Now that we have completed the first task of confronting and providing grounds for neutralizing the logical possibility argument, the stage is set for the second task—offering a three-tiered successor paradigm.

TABLE 7.1    Logic of the Postmodern Scientific Method

| CONCEPTS BY WHICH TO APPROACH THE WORLD | CONCEPTS BY WHICH TO APPROACH INQUIRY |
|---|---|
| Interactivation of levels<br>Open systems exchange<br>Cybernetic circularity (nonlinearity)<br>Stochastic transformation | Inquiry as an act that has an impact on that which is its subject |

# Biomedicine and the Logic of Scientific Method

We began this chapter by saying that arguments for the apparent restrictiveness of biomedical premises were not likely to be persuasive. By appeal to the logical possibility argument, one could counter that the arguments, if valid, entailed only one of two conclusions: Either (1) the methodological premises of the biomedical model are unduly restrictive and should be reexamined with an eye to their displacement by successor, nonreductionist premises, or (2) the arguments advanced point at best to current theoretical difficulties with respect to the biomedical strategy, targeting areas where further research is called for. Moreover, when the results are in, there is no overriding reason to doubt that many or all of these difficulties will be dispelled. The case of the earlier search for the source of infectious diseases and its subsequent successes exemplifies this need for perseverance. Therefore, the medical scientist should, to paraphrase Hempel, persist in the search for basic biomedical theories of pathological phenomena rather than resign himself to the view that the concepts and principles of physiology, cellular pathology, neurochemistry, and so on, are powerless to give an adequate account of the phenomena of disease. The attractiveness of this second option is enhanced by the commonly shared assumption that proposed nonreductionist strategies, like functionalist or neovitalist strategies, do not in the final analysis yield to scientific procedures.

This chapter has critiqued the attractiveness of this second option, not by committing the functionalist or neovitalist fallacy, but by subjecting the logical possibility argument to closer scrutiny. There are, we argued, empirical grounds for conducting scientific inquiry nonreductively. Insofar as this can be shown, there is an alternative to the dichotomy Hempel offers: either persist in the reductive strategy (on which biomedicine rests) or despair at the impotence of (medical) science. Rather, we can have it both ways: nonreductionism *and* science. This was the intended, combined import of Figure 7.2 and Table 7.1.

The relevance to contemporary medicine of this argument is pivotal. Biomedicine is linked to those "basic physico-chemical theories of biological and psychological phenomena" of which Hempel speaks. The principles of biomedicine, an "applied" science, are rationalized by and ultimately derive their validity from the "basic" physical and biophysical sciences underwriting them. For this reason it is useful to speak of a third tier, tier 3, consisting of applied sciences, like engineering and medicine. (Each of these applied sciences possesses in turn its own particular subdisciplines or sciences; for example, engineering has fluid mechanics and medicine pathophysiology, etc.) The legitimacy of their principles stems from the basic sciences of which they are the practical applications. The relationship between applied and basic sciences is two-way: practical successes in the applied, tier 3 sciences further strengthen confidence in the soundness of the laws of the basic, tier 2 sciences on which they rest. Thus we may speak of the engineering sciences that make possible today's successful space explorations as still another vindication of the Newtonian (and relativistic) laws of motion. Furthermore, the greater these successes, the more reason for confidence in the methods (tier 1) used to secure them. This mutuality is signified by redrawing Figure 3.1, this time (Fig. 7.3) alluding to applied, tier 3 sciences like medicine or engineering.

The mutually interlocking character depicted in Figure 7.3 illustrates the truth of the proposition stated at the outset of this chapter: To challenge the biomedical model (tier 3) is at once indirectly to challenge the network in which it is embedded, in particular the background body of scientific knowledge on which it rests. In symbols: tier 2 ↔ tier 1. Put another way, the biomedical strategy derives its support from more than the predictive-explanatory successes of biomedicine. It is part of an overall strategy extending into diverse domains of scientific inquiry and having deep historical, epistemological, and logical roots. An effective critique of the biomedical model therefore involves a stratified, multi-tiered challenge of the sort represented in Figure 7.4. Here the double arrow (⇒) signifies "is formally subsumed under" (and might also signify "historically grows out of").

## Conclusion

We saw that the biomedical model represented a formidable opponent to any rival model that sought to challenge its dominant standing. Biomedical premises and related disciplines such as pathophysiology, microbiology, and cellular pathology (which comprise the tier 3 level)

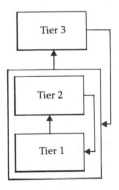

FIGURE 7.3

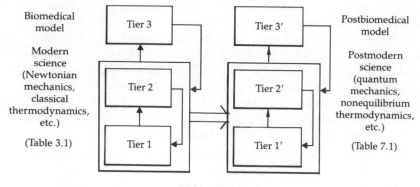

FIGURE 7.4

were shown to be erected on two solidly argued foundation levels. The tier 2 level consisted of Newtonian mechanics, classical thermodynamics, and so forth. At the tier 1 level the logic of scientific method that comprises directives for approaching both inquiry and the world was detailed and examined. The three tiers taken together reveal an internally consistent worldview. To rival the biomedical model, a potential successor (we argued) must not only offer its own internally consistent three-tiered worldview, but also show that it can at least equally successfully account for the successes of the biomedical model by subsuming its explanatory capabilities within its own apparatus. This subsumption was illustrated in Figure 7.4. It provides the rationale for bridging the gap between the premises of the biomedical and a postbiomedical model.

A conclusion based on the preceding presentation of material is that a successor medical model can be given serious consideration as a bona fide scientific model. It is by virtue of the articulation of tier 1' and tier 2' that such a model might be given scientific standing and, hence, credibility.

The argument in favor of the biomedical model rests on the strength of its underlying logic of scientific method. Here we saw that what started out as a directive instructing us to search for explanations possessing certain features came to function as a background generalization about the pervasive structure of the world. Adopting reductionism, mechanism, and determinism as principles for the guidance of research, neutral and value-free as the adoption appears, invited inferences tacitly importing the heuristic maxims as metaphysical principles. The world coheres to the worldview implied by these maxims, we said, only to the extent that sciences conducted according to them achieve their explanatory-predictive aims. Logical possibility arguments, in other words, are framework-dependent: principles guiding the conduct of scientific inquiry (heuristic goals) and the state of scientific knowledge (empirical findings) evolve together and are mutually adaptive and reinforcing.

It is at the juncture of heuristic maxims and scientific findings that the argument for the viability of a successor medical model began to gain credibility. It was pointed out that there is a body of knowledge by reference to which the implied biomedical ideal of an exclusively physicochemical or single-level description can be shown incapable of realization, not in principle but in fact. Further, this body of knowledge was shown to bear the same relation to the methodological strategy underlying a postbiomedical model (nonreductionist) as the classically formulated scientific body of knowledge bears to the strategy underlying the biomedical model. Hence there are empirical grounds favoring adoption of an alternative methodological strategy, one underwriting a postbiomedical model. In the balance of Part Three, a nonreductionist medical model will be articulated. Within this alternative, for example, nonreducible psychosocial issues are recognized to lie within, not without, medicine's responsibilities and authority.

# 8

# *The Revolutionary Successor: Self-organizing Systems Foundations*

In the last chapter the contours of a fully articulated alternative medical model were suggested but not elaborated. For example, the findings of postmodern sciences like quantum physics and irreversible thermodynamics (tier 2′) call into question the tier 1 logic of method (e.g., reductionism, dualism) and suggest in its place a tier 1′ logic of method (e.g., nonreductionism, interactionism). Such a shift in scientific paradigms can only be described as a revolution. Grounds for effecting this shift are the subject of this chapter.

In broad terms, a move from tier 1 to tier 1′ is a shift from a single-level to a two-level scientific language. Further, it is a shift from a linear causal, "atomic" paradigm, in which a given stimulus has a predictable response, to a mutual causal, "genetic" paradigm. Here a given response is not a direct result of the stimulus; rather it is the result of rule-governed processes that define the stimulated system. Because the final state of the system does not depend on initial or boundary conditions, reference to the stimulus is no longer sufficient to understand the response. Final state is a property of the system itself. Such a logic of method (tier 1′) and the paradigm it informs underpins and is reinforced by such otherwise diverse sciences as quantum mechanics, information theory, ecology, and thermodynamics. The term *self-organizing systems* is taken from the latter discipline. A self-organizing systems medical model incorporates such mutual causal processes, postulating the patient as a biopsychosocial entity in an open systems information exchange with the environment or, for short, as an information processing system. Hence, an information systems medical model or, for short, an infomedical model. Such a model provides expression for key tier 2 concepts like homeostasis, entropy, quantum of action, negative and positive feedback, and critical fluctuation. The centrality of these concepts (discussed below) is borne out by reference to the above sciences. Such a model also recognizes that a biomedical model/paradigm based on unidirectional causality cannot readily be reconciled with what many findings in the medical literature suggest and the holistic critique asserts—that is, the patient is a biopsychosocial system capable of renormalization and reorganization behavior. And the authenticated scientific grounds for saying so exclude the option of invoking the logical possibility argument.

What are these authenticated scientific grounds, the tier 1 and 2 underpinnings for a successor, infomedical model? Central to answering this question is explicating the notion of a self-organizing systems paradigm—the foundation of the successor model. To do this, its role is to be contrasted to that of the fundamental building-block paradigm—the foundation of the biomedical model.

Postmodern scientific findings point to self-organizing systems as a fundamental unit capable of scientific understanding. Self-organizing systems are entities that exhibit two principal dynamics: (1) self-renewal—the ability to continuously renew and recycle their components while maintaining the integrity of the overall structures, and (2) self-transcendence—the ability to reach out spontaneously beyond physical and mental boundaries in the process of learning, developing, and evolving. For those familiar with general systems theory (GST), much about the self-organizing system's paradigm will be familiar. Over the past several decades the GST dialogue has served as a general precursor for many of the important findings just alluded to. Questions and issues GST proponents have faced have bridged to a number of findings in today's postmodern sciences. Further, the GST position points to outstanding problems to which the classical, or modern, natural science paradigm can only issue promises. Examining GST premises, both their contribution to thought and their shortfall, helps to highlight the revolutionary promise of a self-organizing systems paradigm.

## General Systems Theory Strategy: A Bridge

Ervin Laszlo's description of systems properties is consistent with the self-organizing and information systems orientation. Briefly, Laszlo characterizes the study of "organized complexity" in terms of the invariant properties exhibited by systems (natural, biological, social, and cognitive) and hence as cutting across traditionally separated disciplines. The invariant properties of these systems include, first, the concept of wholeness. That is, wholes have combinatorial properties that cannot be produced by the parts acting alone. Second, these ordered wholes interact with their environment in ways that exhibit adaptive self-stabilization. That is, fluctuations both within and without the system set in motion forces that tend to bring it back to a stable or "steady state." Third, ordered wholes interact with their environment in ways that exhibit adaptive self-organization. That is, a system, when subjected to continued fixed perturbations or dramatic fluctuations driving it far from equilibrium, can reorganize itself and acquire new parameters—in other words, emerge to a new level of complexity or achieve a new equilibrium or steady state. Fourth, ordered wholes develop in the direction of increasing hierarchical complexity. Here wholes can be composed of subsystems and in turn be subsystems to larger wholes. In participating in intrasystemic and intersystemic hierarchies, fresh qualities can emerge in the form of increasingly complex and adaptive transformations.

An explanatory strategy embraces heuristic or pragmatically adopted metaphysical concepts by which to approach the world—ideals of natural order, Toulmin calls them. In the case of the natural science paradigm, we argued, they include reductionism, determinism, and linear causality and derive largely from the classical laws of motion. These directives define tier 1. And the predictive and explanatory successes refer to successes enjoyed in the physical and life sciences growing out of the seventeenth-century scientific revolution, ranging from physics, chemistry, and thermodynamics to today's molecular biology. These sciences characterize tier 2. Schematically described in Chapter 3, the relationship between tier 1 and tier 2 is reproduced in Figure 8.1.

In the course of the last three centuries, natural science directives have analytically eased themselves into the meaning of scientific method. Because these directives have so far passed the test of time, to stay the reductionist course has become the order of the day: "There is no limit to methodological reductionism and mechanism," says Gerald Edelman (1977, 8). Francis Crick, the codiscoverer of the genetic code, shares this conviction: "So far everything we have found can be explained without effort in terms of the standard bonds of chemistry—the homopolar bond, the van der Waals attraction between non-bonded atoms, the all-important hydrogen bonds, and so on" (1967).

We can now see how GST can be interpreted as a bridge to an authentic scientific alternative paradigm. Its proponents challenge the

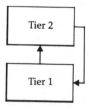

FIGURE 8.1

assumption that extrapolation of the model that led to successful prediction and explanation of mechanistic systems (e.g., integrable systems subject to the laws of motion) should be expected to provide comparable successes in the life, mind, and social sciences. Granting that much has been achieved by persisting in this assumption, the GST contention is that there is a limit on the kinds of achievement possible. M. Marney and P. E. Schmidt describe this limit:

> It is not to be denied that strict extension of the method of the exact sciences has led to impressive accomplishments in both microbehavioral studies of molecular biology and physiological psychology and in macrobehavioral modeling for economics and ecology. The point is simply that these attainments have been limited either to the consideration of elementary subsystems or to abstract reductions of the whole organisms (organizations) that are of ultimate interest in biology, sociology, psychology, anthropology, ecology, and economics. (1976, 190–191)

GST proposes that this method of the exact sciences be supplemented by an alternative method, nonreductionist and interactionist in orientation. Thus, the biologist Paul Weiss and the embryologist Conrad Waddington call attention to a wide variety of biological, ecological, and human population phenomena that display "emergent" or self-organizing properties. These are properties that, in Weiss's words, logically resist "exclusively reductionist tactics." By "reductionist tactics," Weiss means an atomistic or building-block approach to the analysis of living as well as nonliving systems. This approach presupposes that "the relevant macroinformation about nature must, and eventually will, be derived completely from adding up or piecing together the micro-informations about the smallest sample units" (1967, 801). For these advocates, an appeal to the succession of improbable mutations preserved in DNA as the genetic message governing the living structure is only a partial answer to the question of evolutionary growth. That is, to invest micro-objects (individual molecules or molecular chains) with the power to produce the macro-order that biology seeks to understand is, for them, to mistake the formulation of the problem for its solution: knowing the notation system (molecular biology) is not sufficient for understanding the rules governing that system (a theory of biology).

Only through a knowledge of the rules governing the system, its "grammar," can we come to an understanding of the kind of self-organizing behavior characteristic of embryogenesis and phylogenetic evolution. For GST advocates the need to posit such rules is in direct proportion to the insufficiency of the classical, neo-Darwinian explanation. Statistical laws of random process coupled with the principle of natural selection and applied to random mutations cannot, they say, account for the long-term modifiability of characteristic response common to developing embryos and evolving biological organisms.[1] Jeremy Campbell voices this reservation by distinguishing between a language's alphabet and its grammar: "Despite the immense abundance of recorded facts at the disposal of today's biologists, they have not succeeded in describing the living system, because they do not understand the many different kinds of internal rules in DNA, the algorithms by which genes are expressed. Biologists know the alphabet, but not the grammar of the genes; they can describe the surface, but not the principles which lie beneath the surface" (1982, 258).[2] Until these principles are known, argue systems theorists, there will be neither a theory of biology nor a theory of evolution in the full sense of the word.

The mainspring of this dissent from orthodox neo-Darwinian principles and the natural science paradigm they subserve is summarized in the observation that for some structures in nature—living structures are exemplars—micro- and macro-events form an interactive whole the full description of whose behavior exceeds the expressive capacity of the categories of a "mechanistic" vocabulary, even one as rich as molecular biology. According to Michael Polanyi, the operational principles governing the design and function of a machine cannot be deduced from a description of its hardware no matter how accurate and detailed. These operational principles and the boundary conditions that govern them, says Lila Gatlin describing Polanyi's position, "constitute a more fundamental definition of the machine than its mere hardware and circuitry. There is a hierarchy of control whereby these higher operational principles take precedence over the lower 'laws of physics and chemistry' which oversee the operation of the hardware in much the same manner as does a technician whose responsibility is restricted to keeping the machinery operating" (1972, 17).

For similar reasons, Weiss asserts that novel explanatory categories need to be introduced—novel with respect to classical science. These are categories that "objectively reflect the ascending scale of supplemental statements required for adequate description of corresponding objects in our experience" (1967, 805). For Weiss they are to be sought in a "field" or systems language embracing such concepts as wholeness, steady state, and goal-directedness. The two languages together, says Weiss, "complementary and co-equal," eventually will match the descriptive

1. As regards the neo-Darwinian explanation for the evolution of the eye, Gertrude Himmelfarb questions how mindless natural selection could have functioned in those initial stages of the eye's evolution when the variations had no possible survival value: "No single variation, indeed no single part, being of any use without every other, and natural selection presuming no knowledge of the ultimate end or purpose of the organ, the criterion of utility, or survival, would seem to be irrelevant" (1959, 337–338).

2. Invoking the same distinction, Bertalanffy makes a similar point: "Presently the genetic code represents the *vocabulary* of hereditary substance, i.e., the nucleotide triplets which 'spell' the amino acids of the proteins of an organism. Obviously, there must also exist a *grammar* of the code. . . . Without such 'grammar' the code could at best produce a pile of proteins, but not an organized organism" (1968, 153). See also Waddington 1975.

needs of the two types of structures science studies, the closed or essentially isolated systems of the physical sciences and the open systems of the life, mind, and social sciences.

GST focus is on the latter, open systems. An egg in the ocean, a cell in a tissue, a human individual in a society—each exhibits behavior inexplicable by reference to reductionist categories alone. An example common to open systems is the well-known "twinning" phenomenon. As the number of units comprising an open system keep on multiplying, whether by subdivision or accretion, after a point something happens that is indecipherable from the standpoint of statistical laws of random process. A critical mass forms and formerly free elements no longer behave independently. Geometrical space, invariant with respect to translations, undergoes a change. Weiss describes the process:

> All of a sudden a critical stage arises at which some of the units find themselves abruptly crowded inward, cut off completely from direct contact with their former vital environment by an outer layer of their fellows. The latter thereby acquire positions not only geometrically intermediary, but functionally mediatory, between the ambient medium and the now inner units. From then on, "inner" and "outer" units are no longer alike. A monotonic group of equals has become dichotomized into unequal sets. (1967, 819–820)

"With the emergence of the distinction between innerness and outerness, the $1 + 1 = 2$ rule becomes inapplicable," concludes Weiss.

The inapplicability of this rule imposes the need for a new concept of space and with it a new language, a field language, Weiss calls it. In this language, phenomena occurring in a region are determined by the structure of that region. Function and structure are reciprocal. Fresh units arising would thus be subject to new conditions, calling forth novel reactions. In stepwise sequence, the region takes on fresh qualities. Such self-ordering phenomena, so common in biological nature, press the classical concept of determinism to its limits. Statistical laws of random process (the law of large numbers) cannot be invoked. Weiss proposes a reason: "None of the component members of the group, all erstwhile alike, can know their future courses and eventual fate in advance; can know whether they would become 'inner' or 'outer' or intermediate. Nor does it matter for the resulting pattern as a whole." Consequently, "strict determinacy (or invariance) of a collective end state is fully reconcilable with indeterminacy (or variance) in detail of the component courses of events leading up to it." System and environment together conspire to produce order or determinacy out of freedom or indeterminacy. System does not adapt to environment; system and environment (subsystem and suprasystem) interactively co-adapt.

For this reason GST declares that for a full explanation of the behavior of natural structures additional macro or "systems" properties have to be recognized. Because a full explanation of the behavior of collectives possessing these systems properties cannot be achieved by means of the "method of the exact sciences," GST proposes a supplementary method or strategy, one applicable to closed systems, the other to open systems. It is not just that analysis of the behavior of open systems is more difficult and complex than that of isolated systems. Rather, the behavior of such systems is thought to be governed by a different logic. Magorah Maruyama sees this difference manifested in the contrast between the simple laws of cause and effect upon which classical science rests and the different model of causality upon which postclassical sciences rest. The two models reflect contrasting logics. One he calls the traditional mainstream "scientific" logic of unidirectional causality, and the other the logic of deviation-amplifying mutual causal processes. In the first, similar conditions produce similar effects; while in the second, similar conditions can result in dissimilar products, and greater order, not disorder, can ensue. This second logic and the model it subserves require a radically expanded vocabulary, one sanctioning concepts like quantum of action, position effect, and goal directedness. In Table 8.1 the two logics are differentiated, with certain characteristics of each noted. As we will see, this table exemplifies how GST mediates between the old and the new. While not resolving the questions it raises, it nevertheless poses important issues that must be satisfied by any serious challengers to the natural science logic of method.

For Maruyama, not only the laws of dynamics but those of thermodynamics call for reexamination. Only by adjusting each can the increased differentiation and complexity found in the evolution, growth, and life so common to biological and social phenomena be plausibly accounted for. This is the burden of the GST critique. Maruyama states the difficulty this way: "Under the assumption of the second law of thermodynamics, an isolated system in an inhomogeneous state will most probably be found in the future in a more homogeneous state. . . .

TABLE 8.1    GST Explanatory Strategy

| METHODOLOGICAL DIRECTIVES OR HEURISTIC CONCEPTS BY WHICH TO APPROACH THE WORLD | |
| --- | --- |
| *Closed (Isolated) Systems* | *Open ("Natural") Systems* |
| Reductionism | Interactionism |
| Mechanism | Holism |
| Determinism | Stochastic indeterminacy |
| Linear causality | Nonlinear causality |

any process such as biological growth which increases inhomogeneity was against the second law of thermodynamics and was an embarrassing problem for scientists." Rather than being resolved within the conventional framework, the problem was deferred: "This embarrassing question was temporarily ignored by the argument that an organism is not an isolated system. But what process and principle makes it possible for an organism to increase its structure and to accumulate heat was never squarely answered" (1963, 168–169).

The GST advocate declares that this process exceeds the explanatory range of the prevailing vocabulary. Although seeking to develop the germinal discipline of organismic or "open systems" biology as an empirical science growing out of GST principles, GST does not itself claim to be an empirical science. As Laszlo emphasizes, GST provides a second-order conceptual framework for the integration of first-order models of the world, that is, those constructed by the empirical sciences. Its data "come from the empirical sciences" (1972a, 32); they are not nor do they pretend to be deductive consequences of the principles of those sciences. Rather than formulating formal laws defining such sciences, GST suggestively describes conditions necessary for their formulation.[3]

In sum, GST proves to be an inadequate scientific basis upon which to base an alternative, nonreductionist paradigm. Unlike the tier 2 sciences of the natural science paradigm, GST does *not* rest on a model from which springs a "particular coherent tradition of scientific research" (Kuhn). Consequently, we may conclude that GST is better viewed as a metaphysical proposal or "world hypothesis." Though GST does not meet the second condition for paradigm succession—specifying a body of sciences guided by and consistent with an alternative tier 1 logic of method—the GST dialogue does highlight the importance of such an articulation. We can now turn to the task of satisfying this condition, which is a crucial step toward offering the self-organizing systems paradigm.

# Postmodern Explanatory Strategy: Successor Science Foundations

To achieve a bona fide alternative to the natural science paradigm requires referencing sciences that bear the same relationship to the successor strategy that the modern sciences bear to the natural science strategy. Stated as a proportionality:

3. "The open system model thus represents a fertile working hypothesis permitting new insights, quantitative statements and experimental verification." Still: "At present, we do not have a thermodynamic criterion that would define the steady state in open systems in a similar way as maximum entropy defines equilibrium in closed systems" (Bertalanffy 1968, 150–151).

tier 1 : tier 2 :: tier 1' : tier 2'

To exemplify this proportionality, representative directives contrasting modern and postmodern scientific strategies are listed in Table 8.2. These are methodological directives or heuristic concepts by which to approach the world.

Chapter 2 detailed the characteristics of modern science's logic of method. The remainder of this chapter similarly details the postmodern science's logic of method. In other words, tier 2' scientific practice will be referenced to give shape to tier 1' methodological directives.

## QUANTUM MECHANICS

The principles of quantum mechanics formally ascribe to the entities it studies the ordered wholeness property of GST. The denial of this property cannot be expressed in quantum mechanical terms. Additionally, its conduct of inquiry conforms to certain directives of Table 8.2, specifically the first two listed in the right-hand column. These two contentions are given expression in Toulmin's characterization of the strategy pursued in the physical sciences before and after the advent of quantum mechanics. Noting how one strategy presupposes what the other formally disallows—the separation of structure and function—Toulmin says, "Right up to 1925, scientists regularly distinguished

TABLE 8.2   Two Explanatory Strategies

| MODERN SCIENCE | POSTMODERN SCIENCE |
|---|---|
| *Fundamental Building-Block Paradigm* *(classical physics, statistical thermodynamics, molecular biology)* | *Self-organizing Systems Paradigm* *(quantum physics, nonequilibrium thermodynamics, biogeochemistry)* |
| Macro-level explained by micro-elements (group ←— elements) | Macro-/micro-level interaction (group ←—→ semigroup) |
| Function explained by structure (system adapts to environment) | Dual functional-structural adaptation (system-environment co-adaptation) |
| Determinism (chance and necessity: probabilistic laws of basically independent events) | Deterministic-and-stochastic description |
| Unidirectional causality (Similar conditions produce similar effects.) | Mutualistic causality (similar conditions may produce dissimilar products.) |

between the basic units or 'bricks' out of which material things were supposedly made, and the patterns subsequently to be found in the behavior of these units. The strategy of exposition in physical science was always to *begin* by defining the structure of material systems and then *afterwards* to investigate and discuss the laws governing the interaction of atoms, molecules, cells, or other constituent units" (1967, 828). Here we recognize a basic tenet of the fundamental building-block strategy, a strategy that, with the formulation of quantum mechanics, is radically altered. Toulmin explains:

> In strict quantum-mechanical terms, however, this distinction can now no longer be drawn. A physical system, or mechanism, is now specified by a wave-equation that characterizes in one step both the material constitution of the system and its mode of operation—both its structure and its activity. There is no procedure for specifying the one independently of the other, and to speak of either in isolation is a mere abstraction. (1967, 828)

Function cannot be unilaterally explained by structure, nor macro-level behavior by the dynamic interactions of micro-elements. This is not because of the apparent complexity of certain physical systems. Rather it is because in the only formalism available for describing the behavior of these systems, it cannot be expressed:

> The explanatory ideal that dominated physical science from the mid-seventeenth century until a few decades back—the model of solid, impenetrable, essentially inactive, unit bricks, exchanging energy and momentum by collision—has been displaced, even within physics, by a quite different explanatory ideal . . . and this requires us to consider the acitivities of a *whole system* in terms of the overall pattern of interactions by which it is defined and maintains itself—treating the system as the "product" of its component factors, rather than as the sum. (1967, 828)

Here is the appropriate response to the GST advocate's stated aim of providing an "ascending scale of supplemental statements . . . for adequate description of corresponding objects of our experience" (Weiss). Such supplemental statements are not an extension of or addition to existing statements (molecular plus organismic biological statements). Rather, a formal language is fashioned, a "whole systems" language, so to speak, in which the existing statements are recognized as partial explanations, abstract reductions. The complementarity between position and momentum in quantum mechanics is not due to a measurement apparatus limitation; it is a consequence of the quantum of action, the fact that the atoms are not able to interchange action except in multiples of a unit. They have, we might say, whole systems or "organismic" properties.

The burden of argument has shifted. The contention is not that it is logically impossible that a reductionist language describing these systems can be formulated (the thrust of the logical possibility argument). Rather, given the best language available for making sense of the experimental findings, what is being said is that it is pointless to try to do so—as we might say it is pointless in the language of Newtonian mechanics to try to describe the interior of the atom. Crudely, one event has not transpired, while another has: a comprehensive reductionist language has not been formulated, while a countervailing "whole systems" scientific language has. The logical possibility argument is not so much refuted as flanked. The phenomenological approach of GST is here gainsaid by a normative approach, whereby an accepted example of actual scientific practice (quantum mechanics) yields achievements that, in Kuhn's words, "some particular scientific community acknowledges for a time as supplying the foundation for its further scientific practice." The proposed successor strategy, tier 1', exemplified in Table 8.2, in the right-hand column, is coupled to a scientific language (tier 2'). This parallels the way that the predecessor explanatory strategy, tier 1, exemplified in the left-hand column, is coupled to an earlier scientific language (tier 2). Thus,

$$\text{tier } 1 : \text{tier } 2 :: \text{tier } 1' : \text{tier } 2'$$

where the prime notation again represents "formal successor to." And so, with reference to Figure 8.1, Figure 8.2 illustrates this proposed developmental successor.

IRREVERSIBLE THERMODYNAMICS
A comparable situation applies to other directives of Table 8.2. Thus, the self-organizing systems advocate cites additional sciences whose principles formally ascribe to their referent units other systems properties and, correlatively, presuppose right-hand-column directives. One such science addresses an issue regarded as a critical shortcoming of the building-block paradigm: what process enables a structure to increase its inhomogeneity, creating order out of disorder? In the natural science paradigm the structures studied were governed by laws that treated

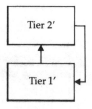

FIGURE 8.2

them as relatively isolated and near-equilibrium. Equations of motion for more than two objects moving under mutual influence, for example, were handled by piecemeal analysis such that the forces or bodies calculated were stipulated to interact in sequences of interacting pairs. Subject to the law of large numbers, such structures could only tend toward disorder or disorganization (equilibrium). Laws of thermodynamics decreed that the most probable state of the universe was that of a random distribution of events, each of which tends to behave with its own probability independently. In such a universe the important things were the atomic fundamentals, and the rest were derived concepts. Space was undifferentiated so that the average number of particles in any-sized small volume within a large volume could be expressed by Boltzmann's ordering principle. Random fluctuations could play only a minor or subordinate role and in many situations could be neglected. Pursuing inquiry according to directives like those of the left-hand column was therefore heuristically sound.

An alternative explanation became available only with the integration of the concept of complex, or far-from-equilibrium, structures with that of simple, or near-equilibrium, structures, and the fashioning of a unified mathematical language for describing the characteristic behavior of each (Nicolis and Prigogine 1977). When, instead of an equilibrium or near-equilibrium structure, we consider a far-from-equilibrium structure, "then an entirely different ordering principle applies, which may be called *order through fluctuation*" (Prigogine 1976, 95). Addressing the question "How can such chaotic behavior (reactive collisions in chemical systems) ever give rise to coherent structures?," Prigogine, Glansdorff, Nicolis, and others forged a language that explained the experimental findings of chemical kinetics and showed how, notwithstanding the second law of thermodynamics, organized or inhomogeneous states can develop out of homogeneous states. For nonlinear systems far from equilibrium they established mathematically that there was an unexpected aspect that had to be considered, unexpected by classical thermodynamical standards. The fluctuations are local events. Hence the need to introduce a supplementary parameter scaling the extension of the fluctuations: "This will be a new characteristic length determined by the intrinsic dynamics of the system and independent of the dimensions of the reacting volume. Thus, there is an essential difference in the behavior of the fluctuations depending on their spatial extension. Only fluctuations of sufficiently small dimensions obey [classical] Poisson statistics" (Prigogine 1976, 95). This is a key result, for it implies "that, conversely, only fluctuations of a sufficient extension can attain enough importance to compromise the stability of the macroscopic state considered. This leads, in turn, to the concept of a *critical fluctuation* as a prerequisite for the appearance of an instability."

A postmodern vocabulary recognizes that an event within the range of high probability, a small initial deviation (a critical fluctuation), can develop into a large deviation of low probability; that is, can compromise the stability of the macroscopic state. Or rather, it can develop into what, in the newly fashioned formalism, is a large deviation of high probability. Introduced here is a novel form of coherent behavior different from that conceptualizable in classical physics (e.g., ferromagnetism). A supermolecular property, it belongs uniquely to far-from-equilibrium structures. Because the triggers for the formation of these structures—small autocatalytic or cross-catalytic initial deviations—are probable events, the appearance of these structures is not now improbable. And the resulting instability creates conditions for the development for further coherent supermolecular totalities. Because of their free exchange of energy and materials with the environment, Prigogine calls them "dissipative structures." They are self-organizing energy-processing systems arising spontaneously as a natural response to fluctuations in an existing thermodynamic structure.

We now have an answer to the question of the precise "process and principle" enabling an open system—a chemical system in this instance—to increase its structure. Prigogine describes this principle as one by which "the instability structures the space-time in which the chemical processes responsible for the instability proceed. Inversely, the processes then become dependent on the behavior of the system as a whole. We come to concepts such as 'totality' of the system and its evolution through successive instabilities" (1979, 82). Fluctuations inherent in the statistical description, instead of spreading homogeneously throughout the whole reacting volume, are local and probable events. As such, they can function as a "critical mass" or quantum of action, serving as a principle of new organization, or morphogenesis. This is the breakdown of the conditions of validity of the law of large numbers: "The distribution of reactive particles near instabilities is no longer a random distribution. . . . [T]he system acts as a whole in spite of the short-range character of the chemical interactions. Chaos gives rise to order" (Prigogine 1978, 781–782). The coherent structure of the dynamics of the system as a whole coordinates the activities of the constituents. Invariance arises out of variance, order out of disorder.

While the new theory still has outstanding problems of its own, we can nevertheless now speak of the beginnings of an explanation for the evidently goal-directed behavior displayed in the evolution of complexity. Self-organization is a nonrandom (stochastic) but nonteleological process governed by the interaction of chance and necessity. As Prigogine and Stengers say, "Self-organization processes in far-from-equilibrium conditions correspond to a delicate interplay between chance and necessity, between fluctuations and deterministic laws. We expect that near a bifurcation, fluctuations or random elements would play an important role, while between bifurcations the deterministic aspects would become dominant" (1984, 176).

It is as if the new science were responding to Bertalanffy's call for "a general theory of non-linear differential equations, of steady states and rhythmic phenomena, a generalized principle of least action, the thermodynamic definition of steady states." Consider the claim of Prigogine and Stengers:

> At the root of nonlinear thermodynamics lies something quite surprising, something that first appeared to be a failure: in spite of much effort, the generalization of the theorem of minimum entropy production for systems in which the fluxes are no longer linear functions of the forces appeared impossible. Far from equilibrium, the system may still evolve to some steady state, but in general this state can no longer be characterized in terms of some suitably chosen potential (such as entropy production) for near-linear states. . . . Stability is no longer the consequence of the general laws of physics. (1984, 140)

To the extent that such a language (nonlinear thermodynamics) has, in the Nobel Committee's words, "fundamentally transformed and revised" its predecessor language (statistical thermodynamics), the more reason for confidence that a successor strategy like that suggested in Table 8.2 can underwrite the conduct of postmodern scientific inquiry.

Once again it is useful to recall that what is here at stake is satisfying Kuhn's condition for paradigm change—an ability to point to an "accepted example of actual scientific practice that some particular scientific community acknowledges for a time as supplying the foundation for its further scientific practice." At immediate issue is not whether such a practice is universally acknowledged or even whether the theory underlying it is complete and insulated from serious criticism from other sectors of the scientific community. Rather, for present purposes all that needs establishing is that the contemporary evidence for and credibility of Figure 8.2 is roughly equal to or greater than that of Figure 8.1; that an infrastructure is in place for a tier 3' (postbiomedical) model paralleling the infrastructure which has sustained and rationalized biomedicine (tier 3). For in the case of an applied science like medicine, as we said at the close of Part Two, the only effective critique of a prevailing model turns out to be one that challenges the background body of biophysical sciences on which that model rests. We may now turn to a final illustration of how this background body of biophysical sciences is currently being challenged and displaced by a successor body.

BIOGEOCHEMISTRY

As a final example, we may reference the emerging disciplines of ecology and evolutionary biology or biogeochemistry. For the self-organizing systems advocate, findings in these disciplines are likewise thought to be consistent with directives like those listed in the right-hand column of Table 8.2. In particular, the principles of these disciplines formally address the intrasystemic and intersystemic property of systems.[4]

Classical theory posits the phenotypic organism adapting to environmental fluctuations as the unit of evolutionary attention. Biological species answer to the question: What is the minimum unit of survival whose evolution calls for explanation? For Darwin the environment is therefore a given, the stage on which the drama of evolution ("the evolution of species") is played out. The organism adapts, the environment is adapted to. What nature "selects" is therefore the adaptive organism, the creatively responding mutant which meets (or not) the test of survival and which, through its reproductive potential, is or is not evolutionarily "fit." Deeply influenced by this choice of evolutionary module, the course of subsequent inquiry in the life sciences tended in an analytic-reductionist direction toward disclosure of the fundamental building blocks of the biological world. The essence of aliveness was thought reducible to its organismic fundamentals. With the late-nineteenth- and early-twentieth-century development of cellular biology and biochemistry, Darwinian theory became molecular biological theory, yielding in our time the remarkably precise elucidation of DNA, RNA, and proteins in cell growth and replication.

Adopting a different orientation, biogeochemistry experimentally traces the inseparability of life from the geochemical processes of Earth. Hence, it resituates the locus of life in a wider context. Its principles seek to give scientific warrant to the fourth systems property. Incorporating ecological findings that show the inseparability of organismic behavior and trophic cycles, biogeochemists adduce evidence for the inseparability of biochemical and geochemical cycles. Integrating these findings, they redefine the phenomenon of life as a "whole systems" property. Its fundamental building blocks are posited to comprise interdependent feedback loops connecting hierarchic, multilevel organismic *and* environmental structures and functions. Instead of the species (genotype) alone, the creatively responding mutant is now posited to be the cybernetically coupled species and its environment interactively inhabiting a single phase space. Interdependent negative and positive feedback loops describe intra-organismic pathways like those running from gene to chromosome and chromosome to cell. At the same time, they are

4. Laszlo describes this hierarchical property as follows: "Whenever a set of self-stabilizing and self-organizing systems share a common environment, their patterns of evolution crystallize some strands of mutual adaptations. . . . Systems on every level may exhibit the general properties of order, irreducibility, homeostatic self-stabilization, and evolutionary self-organization. The apex of any such hierarchy is itself a system, of which all other systems are subsystems" (1974, 223).

recognized as linking the more inclusive geochemical pathways of which the organismic pathways are now viewed as coordinative parts— "cut off from their matrix by our selective attention" (Bateson 1973, 459).

This scenario is spun in fine scientific detail by a multidisciplinary team of biochemists, ecologists, microbiologists, geologists, meteorologists, and oceanographers. Focus shifts from the evolution of the organism to the coevolution of organism plus environment. Through the prism of the emerging discipline of biogeochemistry the classical biological definition of life as a property of special molecular arrangements called cells is refocused. This definition is now regarded as demarcating not life per se but the limits of a definition of life accessible to molecular biology. Life does not exist and evolve simply because material conditions happened to favor it. Nor do biota evolve simply through the random and unpredictable process of mutation (imperfect genetic replications) and natural selection (the test of survival). Rather, findings in all these fields, from biochemistry to geology, indicate that terrestrial life alters the conditions to ensure its survival and works actively to maintain them (the "Gaia hypothesis").

In other words, the locus of life shifts from species to the total systemic creature. The concept of the evolution of species is differently staged. Instead of a reactive phenomenon (chemical modification of DNA elicited, for example, by ultraviolet light) or a random phenomenon (chance errors in genetic transcription), species evolution is recognized as an element of a larger pattern resulting from an active phenomenon, a self-organizing phenomenon. Now "self" casts a biospheric rather than organismic shadow. No longer are environmental fluctuations simply part of the arena in which the evolutionary drama is played out, a background condition.[5] They are reperceived as integral parts of the living biospheric web. They relate to the biospheric (as distinct from the genetic) unit of evolution as, in neo-Darwinian theory, organic "fluctuations"—like the formation of the circulatory system—relate to the organismic unit of evolution. Such macrofluctuations are endogenous, interacting elements of the circumambient unit, part of its *intérieur milieu*, Bernard might say.

In a series of papers written in the 1970s, biogeochemists James Lovelock and Lynn Margulis developed such an analogy with respect to one component of these environmental fluctuations, atmospheric fluctuations. The atmosphere, they argued, is the circulatory system of the biosphere. Summarizing their argument, Roger Bingham writes, "Gaia's

5. "Darwin saw the evolutionary process as a series of adaptations: plants and animals differ from one another in their hereditary endowments, and those variants which equip an organism specially well to cope with the *exigencies of the environment* will be preserved in the 'struggle for existence' and will thus become the prevailing type" (Medawar 1977, 154; italics added).

[the biosphere's] lifeblood is made up of gases and minerals that move in a continuous cycle, maintaining Earth's temperature, physical makeup, oxidation-reduction state, and acidity in the optimum condition for the support of life" (1980, 81).[6] This functioning of Earth's circulatory system is an expression of what Walter Cannon would call the wisdom of the body, now the biospheric body. From otherwise conceptually disparate and anomalous processes like the vast production of methane by bacteria and the cycling of essential minerals like iodine from marine algae to the land, Lovelock and Margulis conclude to the animating hypothesis of biogeochemistry: the atmosphere is manipulated and modulated on a day-to-day basis from the surface of the Earth.

Depending on the strength of the data leading up to this conclusion, the above-mentioned chemical modification of the DNA molecule by ultraviolet light to produce genetic "mutants" may not be just a chance phenomenon. It may be no more random than, say, the increase in the degree to which a developing embryo expresses specificities (e.g., diversification of cellular functions). Instead, the nature and intensity of the light (ultraviolet) admitted through the atmosphere may be consistently viewed as regulated from the surface of the Earth, now viewed as a finely tuned homeostatic system of feedback loops with the capacity to keep the planet a fit place for life. These loops are many and varied. Among them are photochemical pathways in the atmosphere linking solar radiation to atmospheric chemicals; photosynthetic pathways linking the atmosphere and the soil; and geochemical or "subduction" pathways linking, through the weathering of land nutrients in the Earth's crust, oceanic sedimentation to organisms.

Within this circuitous biogeochemical webwork, feedback loops can be isolated linking the ultraviolet light filtered by the atmosphere to the chemically modified DNA molecule of the referent organism. And rather than a given with which the organism has to cope, atmospheric events are now shown to be coordinative parts of the evolutionary process. Instead of an "exigency of the environment," the atmosphere is, in Lovelock's words, a biological construction, "not living, but like a cat's fur, or a bird's feathers, or the paper of a wasp's nest, an extension of a living system designed to maintain a chosen environment" (in Bingham 1980, 78). Species don't just adapt to environmental exigencies, say biogeochemists; they function coordinatively with them: the two are mutually explicative.

This is the thrust of biogeochemistry. The whole of nature is a vast self-regulating and recycling system of patterned energy and information flows, drawing energy from the sun and running itself without

6. For a fuller statement, see also Margulis and Lovelock 1974 and Lovelock 1979.

surpluses and waste. Life is recast as a circular process in which genes, cells, organisms, (individual) minds, ecosystems, and the wider environment continually feed information back and forth, enabling the system, at whatever heirarchic level, to regulate itself in response to changing external cues. In this precise sense, biogeochemistry experimentally underwrites the fourth systems property noted. The biogeochemist stipulates the environment and living organisms to be bound, inseparable parts of one set of linked planetary processes such that, in microbiologist Harold Morowitz's words, "the sustained activity of the global 'biogeochemical' system is more characteristic of life than are the individual species that arise, flourish for a time, and disappear in the course of evolution." As he explains:

> The life of any single organism is part of a larger-scale process involving the "metabolism" of the whole Earth. Continued biological activity is then a planetary property, an interrelationship of organisms, atmospheres, oceans and continents, all of which are in some sense alive. Without the part played by each of these components, life as we know it would, on a geological scale, grind to a halt. (1983, 21)

What is seen here is that the atmosphere may be consistently described as an integrated element in the overall process of adaptive self-organization. However, rather than a cosmic neovitalist claim, laws of biogeochemistry are invoked to scientifically underwrite the claim. So doing, they convert what in neo-Darwinian theory are merely external fluctuations—random atmospheric events—into internal constraints on the adaptively organizing self. The evolution of species is reconceptualized in biogeochemical terms. This reconceptualization may be expressed as follows:

> Species evolution is not a random or merely reactive phenomenon any more than is the evolution of the fertilized egg. Each process is part of an adaptive self-organizing event responsive to a survival need. The signal difference is that while in one case—the evolution of the egg—the referent self is a phenotypic organism, in the other case—the evolution of the species—it is the biospheric "organism," the biological species writ large. As the science of molecular biology (and embryology) seeks to explain the developmental stages of the fertilized egg, so too does the science of biogeochemistry ("geochemical biology") seek to explain the dynamic steady state of the atmosphere's composition.

The difference in the two choices of unit of evolution—the molecular biological choice and the geochemical biological choice—is between an account of the behavior of a single symbiont (genetics) and a host/organism symbiosis (epigenetics). In a strictly genetic account, that which is the root cause of evolution, e.g., the behavior of the molecular mechanisms of DNA and protein, is, in an epigenetic account, part cause and part symptomatic manifestation. For the biogeochemist, the behavior of such mechanisms is both catalyst and product of the photochemical, photosynthetic, and geochemical cycles alluded to above—an exemplar interaction of levels, system-environment co-adaptation phenomenon. Species and their molecular mechanisms not only react adaptively to environmental exigencies; they also function co-ordinatively with them. Briefly, this is the biogeochemistry contention. In a variation of Samuel Butler's aphorism: the DNA molecule (or the photosynthetic cycle) is the biosphere's way of perpetuating itself. And the science of geochemical biology accordingly subsumes the science of molecular biology as epigenetics, the study of the evolution of the host-organism symbiosis, subsumes genetics, the study of the evolution of the organism.

## Summary

The contrast between the modern natural science and the "postmodern" self-organizing systems infrastructure has been examined. With respect to the incompleteness of the Second Law ("what process or principle makes it possible for an organism to increase its structure and to accumulate heat"), the natural science infrastructure issues a promissory note: eventually the mechanism will be discovered accounting for open as well as closed system behavior, and this mechanism will be couched in a *single-level, reductionist language* (Fig. 8.3). The self-organizing systems infrastructure, on the other hand, references a body of postmodern sciences (tier 2') whose principles are consistent with a different strategy (tier 1') simultaneously explaining closed system (near-equilibrium) and open system (far-from-equilibrium) behavior. It does so with a *two-level, interactionist language* (Fig. 8.4).

Natural Science Infrastructure

Closed and (promissorily)
Open Systems

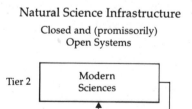

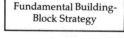

FIGURE 8.3

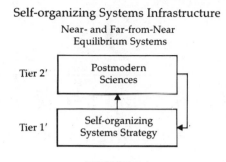

Self-organizing Systems Infrastructure
Near- and Far-from-Near
Equilibrium Systems

Tier 2′ — Postmodern Sciences

Tier 1′ — Self-organizing Systems Strategy

FIGURE 8.4

# 9

## From Engineering to Cybernetics: Philosophical Foundations of Infomedicine

The infomedical model, to be presented in the next chapter, adopts a multilevel vocabulary. As such it involves the interaction of a variety of levels, notable among them mind and body levels. In order to avoid confusion with discredited historical positions of the mind-body problem (e.g., Cartesian interactionism), we will first clarify the empirical basis for the many interactive arrows present in the infomedical strategy. We will show how infomedicine avoids pursuing an updated version of dualistic interactionism. Instead of the two options available in the seventeenth century—monistic materialism and dualistic interactionism, the sources of the classical mind-body debate—subsequent developments in science and technology have paved the way for a third option. This chapter argues that this option—cybernetic circularity—offers a way out of the mind-body impasse. Once clear of this impasse, the psycho-physical dualism immanent in biomedical practice can be succeeded by a psychobiological "holism."

## From Monistic Materialism to Cybernetic Circularity

Everyday words that come to play a prominent role in scientific discourse have a difficult double life. Often their connotations do not keep pace with the operational meaning given them in the science in which they figure or in the technology in which their meaning first took root. The words *matter* and *mechanical* are examples of this identity problem. Their connotations in everyday language and their developing meaning in the physical sciences are in ongoing tension, the former both influencing and dragging at the coattails of the latter. In Enlightenment times, terms like *matter, mechanism,* and *mechanistic explanation* were used in such a way that they came to imply reductionism. This was as much a matter of the emerging notion of scientific explanation and the contemporary state of technology as of metaphysical persuasion. To say of a phenomenon that it was mechanistic was to liken it to a clockwork and, later, to an engine. However complex, it could always be understood by reducing it to its basic building blocks and by looking at the mechanisms through which these interacted. Hence the explanation of its macrobehavior was ultimately reducible to (its content was explained by) a micro-level language. In the physics of the day a mechanical explanation of an event was a mathematical not a verbal one, typically a differential equation whose solutions were trajectories determined by the initial or boundary conditions. In this way *mechanism* and *matter* came to be associated with a cluster of concepts espoused on state-of-the-art technological or methodological, rather than metaphysical, grounds. These concepts were procedural directives by which to approach the world, and formed a working hypothesis (see Table 9.1).

Together with collateral directives by which to approach inquiry—objectivity, universality, self-correctiveness, and so forth—these directives came to define scientific method. Conducting research as if they characterized the natural world became the explanatory strategy that safeguarded science against the animism, subjectivity, and authoritarianism of prescientific (i.e., neo-Aristotelian) investigation.

Toulmin speaks to the centrality of this strategy at the dawn of the scientific revolution: "The men who initially stated the intellectual aims of modern science, and who conceived a strategy designed to fulfill them, began with very clear ideas about what *matter* is, what a *machine* or *mechanism* is, and so what a *mechanical* or *mechanistic* explanation must be" (1967, 823). Though propounding very different, often incompatible theories, these men—Galileo and Descartes, Newton and Boyle—"shared certain common assumptions—notably, a belief that all genuinely physical processes, arising out of the properties of matter alone, should ultimately prove explicable in 'mechanistic' terms" (Toulmin 1967, 823). As to the character of these terms, seventeenth- and eighteenth-century mechanistic explanation, says Toulmin, "recognized as authentic physical processes *only* transfers of momentum or energy by the contact or collision of solid, impenetrable particles." No conception then existed of "independent fields-of-force, no action-at-a-distance, no

TABLE 9.1  Mechanistic Worldview

|  |
| --- |
| Reductionism |
| Atomism |
| Determinism |
| Efficient causality |

patterns-of-organization more permanent than the pressure of 'aether-corpuscles' could maintain." A standard eighteenth-century exposition of Newtoniam physics, Ferguson's *Lectures*, states the classical limits of mechanistic explanation: "By the word *matter* is meant every thing that has length, breadth, thickness, and resists the touch. The inherent properties of matter are solidity, inactivity and divisibility. . . . That matter can never put itself in motion is allowed by all men" (in Toulmin 1967, 823). Here is the originative sense of *res extensa*.

Commenting on the consequences for the life sciences of these restrictive conceptions of mechanism and matter, Toulmin points to the inescapable difficulties that an exhaustive physical explanation of the processes going on in living things faced: "After all, the very idea of 'living' or 'self-propelled matter' ran counter to Ferguson's axiom, 'allowed by all men'—viz. 'that matter can never put itself into motion'. . . . A machine was simply an instrument for transmitting an outside action; it was not a prime mover" (1967, 824). By the later nineteenth century, with the newer technologies wrought by industrialization, the full force of the limits of these Enlightenment conceptions of matter and mechanism was felt. How could a material body or machine, in seventeenth-century terms, be spoken of as self-regulating, still less as calculating? These possibilities, says Toulmin, "involved flat contradictions. They were for the time being ruled out, not because seventeenth-century scientists had made any empirical discoveries that compelled them to take this position, but rather because of their own self-imposed definitions of the terms matter and machine."

To illustrate the difficulties encountered by these definitions, Toulmin cites a passage from Giovanni Borelli's strictly mechanical treatise, *On Animal Motion* (1680). Discussing the action of the muscles on the limbs, Borelli says: "Muscles are the organs and machines by which the motive faculty of the soul sets the joints and limbs of animals in motion. In itself a muscle is an inert and dead machine, which is . . . put into action solely by the access of the motive faculty" (in Toulmin 1967, 824). Since the muscles were only passive material instruments, says Toulmin, "the true source of animal motion had to be sought for elsewhere, outside the realm of material things." The result was animism in physiology and dualism in psychology:

> The "motive faculty of the soul" could not itself be the property of a machine, since a machine was never self-moving: still less could the reasoning powers of man. The Bodily Machine might serve as a passive physical instrument through which the Active Mind might interact with the world of Matter, but the Mind itself had to be something of quite another, non-Material kind. In short, the philosophical problems about Life and Mind (with capital initial letters) which have bedeviled biology and psychology from the seventeenth century on are not perennial features of our scientific tradition. (1967, 824)

Rather they stem from Enlightenment definitions of *matter* and *mechanism*. Still, these definitions have eased themselves into contemporary notions of what constitutes a scientific (i.e., physicalist) explanation. So, in the applied sciences, to credit an explanation as scientific, even today, carries with it the connotation that the behavior of the referent objects or processes can be ultimately expressed in a physicalist (physicochemical) language, where *physicalist* is understood as "single-level" and "reductionist" in the sense defined: all aspects of complex macro phenomena can be understood by reference to the properties and interactions of their micro constituents. Research policy continues in large part to be pursued accordingly.

What accounts for this durability of reductionism? Toulmin implies that, having played such a major role in launching the scientific revolution, the cluster of concepts implied by reductionism could not be lightly dismissed. At the level of working science, he says, "the standard definitions of matter and mechanism seemed indispensable to the new physics." He goes on:

> They had been adopted in the first place for convincing methodological reasons, as part of the revised alliance between physics and mathematics; and the payoff from this alliance, in terms of Newton's *Principia* alone, had been vastly impressive. So there were strong reasons for standing firmly by them—even though the price might be to exclude from science the study of Mind for certain, and possibly also that of Life. (1967, 825)

The dual concepts of matter as inert (mechanism) and action by contact or action by particles under the influence of a force (efficient causality) were bulwarks of modern science. Their retention, however, exacted a price, manifested most dramatically in the life and mind sciences. For out of this drama arose the modern psychophysical dilemma: either monistic materialism or Cartesian interactionism. Either contact is described as occurring between objects of the same logical type or between objects of different logical types—either between muscles and limbs (same type) or between "the motive faculty of the soul" and muscles-limbs (different types). (The soul, that is mind, is "something of quite another, non-Material kind," in Toulmin's phrase.) In the first instance, the description of the contact is single-level (monist) and physical (materialist). In the second instance, it is non-single-level (dualist) and psychophysical (interactionist). Methodological and epistemological options therefore tended to divide along either reductive materialist or nonreductive interactionist lines. These were the only seriously entertained, nonidealist options.[1] And because success in the physical sci-

---

1. Alternatives like behaviorism, mind-body identity theory, epiphenomenalism, and double aspect theory will here be understood as careful elaborations of monistic materialism. Thus the identity theorist seeks the neurophysiological correlate of the mental event with the aim of identifying the two, and so neutralizing the need for the nonphysicalist or "psycho" part of the psychophysical description.

ences had been achieved through adherence to the basic explanatory strategy of reductionist materialism (Table 9.1), it was natural to suppose that extrapolation of this strategy offered the greatest promise of comparable success in the life sciences. As noted, such a strategy had come to be identified with proceeding scientifically.

Meanwhile, however, knowledge of physical structures, and with it the state of technology, evolved. Machines and physical systems were recognized as capable of more and more unexpectedly complex behavior. Explanations became correspondingly stratified and decreasingly reconcilable with the reductionism characterizing the strategy of the early modern sciences. Speaking to one of these explanations, Toulmin states: "We live now with fundamental physical theories in which action by contact and collision have entirely lost their earlier significance. All the basic interactions of quantum physics represent species of field processes and . . . mechanical collision itself is now re-interpreted as the effect of force fields between the colliding bodies." He reports on a quiet conceptual revolution:

> Throughout the last 200 years the terms machine and mechanism have been shifting their meanings slowly, but in the long run drastically, and the aims and strategies appropriate to a mechanistic science . . . have shifted with them. . . . We can now recognize as machines and mechanical processes systems which the physicists of 1700 would unanimously have dismissed as "either miraculous or imaginary." . . . Faced with a mid-twentieth century computer, Descartes, Newton, and even Leibniz would have had no option but to say, "That's not what we mean by a *machine* at all!"

So,

> The Cartesian view of Mind as something quite distinct from Matter was a by-product of ideas about Matter and Mechanism that twentieth-century physics has abandoned; the axioms and definitions of seventeenth-century science made psycho-physical dualism . . . almost inescapable. (1967, 825)

Correspondingly, materialistic monism and its derivative, reductionism, became a most reasonable methodological strategy.

The kinds of behavior displayed by the physical structures studied today—whether in quantum theory, chemical kinetics, embryology, ecology, or computer science—are perhaps best described collectively as self-organizing or bootstrapping behavior. Yet the diverse formal languages by which this behavior is explained—e.g., quantum physics, nonlinear thermodynamics, information theory—can be characterized as neither dualistic interactionism nor monistic materialism. Psychophysical dualism is not at issue since human mental events (*res cogitans*) are not involved. And the rules or "grammar" governing the orderly series of processes by means of which, for example, cells specialize, ecosystems grow, or machines reason—in short, by means of which complex systems self-organize—while immanent in these processes are not reducible to the series of processes themselves. The concept of linear, efficient causality cannot account for the nonlinear interconnectedness characteristic of self-organizing behavior. Thus it cannot account for deviations that may be reinforced internally through positive feedback either in response to environmental changes *or spontaneously without any external influence.* The primitive unit of this self-generating mutual causal process is the complex loop structure of which the component parts— the governing influence and the governed series of orderly processes alike—are logically derivative.

The qualitative difference between the explanatory strategies characterizing the languages of these "postmodern" sciences and the languages of such early modern sciences as Newtonian (and relativistic) physics, statistical thermodynamics, and neo-Darwinian biology was symbolized in Table 8.2. For present purposes the two headings in that table—Fundamental Building-Block Paradigm and Self-organizing Systems Paradigm—may be relabeled here as Monistic Materialism and Cybernetic Circularity respectively. In Chapter 8, in which that table appeared, it was argued that the language most suitable for making sense of today's experimental findings is informed by a genetic or self-organizing rather than an atomistic or building-block explanatory strategy. There it was contended not that a reductionist language capable of explaining these findings cannot be formulated, but only that a fully scientific, albeit nonreductionist, language already has been formulated. With its formulation the perennial mind-body problem is not so much resolved as circumvented. For its tension has turned on the tenability of the logical possibility argument: as long as we can reasonably aspire to a fully mechanistic, or single-level, reductionist, scientific language, then mind-body events remain either problematic (dualistic interactionism) or promissorily eliminable in favor of body-body events (monistic materialism).

But now, in that language which offers reasonable grounds for circumventing the logical possibility argument, a new circumstance obtains: qualities once associated with vitalistic or mental (i.e., nonmechanistic) activity like self-motion, self-regulation and self-programming can be lawfully ascribed to physical, nonhuman, even nonliving systems. That is, they can be ascribed to the referent units of sciences like those just cited—quantum physics, nonlinear thermodynamics, and perhaps even computer science. Some "life" activities, even some activities traditionally associated with mindfulness (e.g., calculating and reasoning), can be explained by means of the laws and first principles of these disciplines. Hence the warrant for what is here termed cybernetic circularity: the bodily machine (physical system) is not "a passive physical instrument through which the Active Mind might interact with the world of Matter." Instead, the bodily machine may be something once unheard of: a self-organizing (cybernetic) unity which, as a complex system, can internally interact. Mutual causal loops within a system, rather than the initial trigger, can increase structuredness *within* a system. And even apart from the question of whether a system is open or closed, it is the internal interactions that are the responsible "causal" agents.

Contrary to Enlightenment language conventions, then, matter can be self-moving, a prime mover. A new class of physical systems has been identified and laws formulated describing their behavior. Besides the "simple" systems studied by the early modern sciences, there are "complex" systems. "Complexity," we quoted Campbell as saying, "is not just a matter of a system having a lot of parts which are related to one another in nonsimple ways. Instead, it turns out to be a special property in its own right, and it makes complex systems different in kind from simple ones" (1984, 102). John von Neuman had predicted in the early 1950s that a theory of complex systems would be quite unlike a theory of simple systems. And within two decades Ilya Prigogine and others had shown that laws describing the behavior of simple systems (the near-equilibrium systems of classical thermodynamics) are, locally, special cases of laws describing the behavior of complex systems (the far-from equilibrium systems of nonlinear thermodynamics). Campbell describes this subsumption by distinguishing between a *causal* (efficient causality) and a *genetic* (mutual causality) explanatory model:

> As soon as we have a system out of equilibrium, an organized system consisting of many parts, of which a living organism is a typical example, the simple laws of cause and effect let us down. They are too simple to be of much use. . . . When a cause produces an effect in an organized system, . . . the cause does not produce action by contact. . . . It triggers action in something which is not one simple object, but a pattern of relations. The action is intrinsic, linked only in an indirect way to the stimulus which set it off. (1984, 255)

Matter can be structured (a "pattern of relations") and irreducibly so.

The physicist Ernest Hutten makes this point by saying that the behavior of an organized system, the action of an organism, or human activity cannot be explained in terms of causal energy transfer alone. He speaks of an information model: "Information rather than causality describes processes within, or between, organized systems. The most general model of a natural process on which scientific explanation may be based is no longer the movement of a particle under the action of a force, but the storage (or organization) and the transmission of information within a system. This is the genetic model" (in Campbell 1984, 255).

This use of "genetic" corresponds to the bootstrapping or cybernetic circularity explanatory strategy of Table 8.2—there called the Self-organizing Systems Paradigm.

In sum, while simple systems—those studied by early modern science—are describable as "instruments for transmitting an outside action," complex systems—those studied by certain late modern sciences—are rather self-motivating instruments, capable of *internal* self-organization. Thus, were we to hypothesize a "sixth-generation" computer unmistakably displaying at least certain aspects of intelligent (mind) behavior—"artificial intelligence"—its explanation would now not involve a commitment to dualistic interactionism (psychophysical dualism), for the basic principles and formalism for explaining it are already in place. These are the "cybernetic circularity" principles of sciences describing "complex" (far-from-equilibrium) systems. Similarly, were we to project a medical science—call it pathopsychobiology—based on the premise that extrasomatic states can lawfully have an interactive influence on physiological states and drive a system into a new regime, this would not necessarily imply a commitment to dualistic interactionism. Systems capable of displaying such behavior, for example humans passing from morbidity to health through, say, certain applications of clinical biofeedback treatment, are now seen as special cases of complex systems displaying self-organizing behavior; that is, systems whose final state does not depend on initial or boundary conditions. (The matrix for such a science will be sketched in Part Four.)

It might be countered that what is here called the cybernetic circularity strategy—the genetic or self-organizing systems paradigm—is, because of its exclusively physicalist language, ultimately just a variant of monistic materialism. Edelman suggests this when he says, "As for the dethronement of mechanism by modern physics it is only a metaphor for a larger, more inclusive view that certainly does not imply a teleology or a mind that works outside the laws of thermodynamics or a basic procedure that is any different from that of their scientific predecessors" (1977, 8). With reference to what has already been said in Chapter 8, Edelman is certainly right to emphasize the lawlike and nonteleological character of modern physics and thermodynamics. Here is another instance of the elastic nature of concepts like *mechanism:* is today's bootstrapping approach to natural systems a repudiation of a mechanistic strategy for approaching the world, or does it further illuminate the full complexity of what it means to be mechanistic? Actually Edelman's statement may be interpreted as implying either one of two quite different propositions. Today's laws of thermodynamics certainly do not imply a teleology or a mind working outside of these laws. And the basic experimental procedures by which these laws are discovered do not differ from those of their scientific predecessors. Thus, the conduct of inquiry prevailing in thermodynamics both today and yesterday is governed by the directives of objectivity, universality, self-correctiveness, and so on. However, if by "basic procedure" Edelman means commitment to reductionist, building-block directives like those identified in Table 8.2 and characterizing the methodological approach to nature adopted by early modern science, then today's basic procedure would seem in important respects to be "different from that of its scientific predecessors." In Chapters 7 and 8 this difference was addressed. The new approach is reflected by Prigogine and Stengers when they state that "the units involved in the static descriptions of dynamics [classical *or* quantum physics] are not the same as those that have to be introduced to achieve the evolutionary paradigm as expressed by the growth of entropy. This transition leads to a new concept of matter, matter that is 'active,' as matter leads to irreversible processes and as irreversible processes organize matter" (1984, xxix). What are we to make of such a negentropic "mechanism"? Though not outside the laws of (postmodern) thermodynamics, contrary to what Edelman says, such a mechanism is in important respects different from that of its scientific predecessors.

Throughout the modern history of the philosophical mind-body debate, two conditions prevailed: either (1) it was believed that there was no *scientific* language that explained the evolutionary, negentropic behavior of matter, or (2), if such a language existed, it was believed ultimately to be framed in a building-block or reductionist (e.g., statistical thermodynamical) language. Only with the advent of the postmodern languages like those already referenced has a body of scientific theory been in place that seeks to explain (supplies a formalism for) the directive, self-organizing behavior of matter and does so in a nonreductionist interaction of micro- and macro-level vocabulary.

As a result, we are reminded that the position of monistic materialism has two quite separate elements. Distinguishing them permits us to differentiate that position not only from dualistic or Cartesian interactionism but also from a third position, called here cybernetic circularity. First, a monistic materialist account must be couched in a *physicalist* language (materialism); and second, it must be couched in a reductionist or *single-level* language (monism). Similarly, the position of dualistic interactionism has two separate elements. Besides being an *interaction-of-levels* language (interactionism), such a position must be couched in a *nonphysicalist*, i.e., psychophysicalist, language (dualism). And yet the contemporary scientific languages that best account for self-organizing behavior are both physicalist and interaction-of-levels languages. Prior to their formulation the two most attractive paradigm options were the fundamental building-block paradigm (monistic materialism) and the psychophysical systems paradigm (dualistic interactionism). And both encountered serious difficulties. Thus, while the language of dualistic interactionism dealt with complex systems like humans, it did not adequately explain how a psychic substance (mind) interacted with a physical substance (matter). And the language of monistic materialism, while it dealt adequately with simple systems—whose behavior could, for example, be accounted for by means of a probabilistic logic of basically independent events (the law of large numbers)—was inadequate to the explanation of certain behaviors of complex systems (e.g., twinning phenomena). Here promissory notes could only be issued. However, we are not now restricted to these two options. A third, independent option is available. Such an option would have appeared to the traditional mind-body philosopher as incomprehensible as the idea of a thinking machine to Descartes, Newton, and Leibniz. Faced with a postmodern non-single-level, yet physicalist, lawlike language, such a philosopher would have no option (e.g., cybernetic circularity) but to say, "That's not what I mean by *science* at all!"

To sum up: Notwithstanding that twentieth-century physics has abandoned the Cartesian view of mind as something quite distinct from matter, its legacy persists in the expressed need (so foreign to Aristotle and his followers) to have to *explain* how mind and matter can interact. That is the thorny issue of psychophysical interactionism. Prior to Descartes's time, there was no *scientific* rationale for dualism. Rather, the two broad premodern scientific, or metaphysical, options were holistic interactionism (e.g., the hylomorphism of Aristotle and his followers) and monistic materialism (e.g., Greek atomism). Each was taken as a bedrock metaphysical orientation, although with empirical warrant. Ideals of natural order, they were to be argued *from*, not *to*. Only with the formulation of seventeenth-century ideas of matter and mechanism does psychophysical interactionism call for explanation. For the first time, such a doctrine appears to commit a category mistake. For it conflicts with seventeenth-century notions of what it is to be physical: "the inherent properties of matter are solidity, inactivity, and divisibility." How can that which is neither solid, inactive, nor divisible (mind) enter into linear chains of cause and effect, involving at every stage the transmission of forces by contact, impact, direct pressures, and collisions alone?

The by-product of this impasse was that materialistic monism, initially introduced as an economical methodological directive, only derivatively and by reason of the explanatory successes of sciences employing such a directive metastasized into a metaphysical disposition. Its continued attractiveness has to be measured against its compatibility with Enlightenment science definitions of matter, machine, and mechanism. That twentieth-century physics has abandoned these definitions (in favor of independent fields of force, action at a distance, patterns of organization, etc.) therefore has far-reaching implications for the philosophical mind-body debate. There is no longer a need on scientific grounds to explain a methodological strategy based on nonreductionist, cybernetic circularity, any more than there was a seventeenth-century need to explain a methodological strategy based on a reductionist, materialistic monism. In a word, *dualism* is an artifact of seventeenth- and eighteenth-century scientific conceptions of matter and machine. And minus these conceptions, dualism may just as well be termed *cybernetic circularity* ("holism") inasmuch as, once more, it rests on the same logical footing as its methodological and metaphysical archrival, *monism*. Namely, it (holism) is an artifact of late-twentieth-century scientific conceptions of matter and machine.

## Dualism in Medical Practice: A Historical Perspective

It is difficult to overestimate the imprint of the classical natural science paradigm on medical thinking. Perhaps it is most evident in our dualistic patient concept. So completely did dualism separate mind from nature that the idea, even today, that there is a natural link joining physiological and psychological processes remains largely external to clinical practice.[2] The body, not the mind-body, is still the focus of medical attention. While we speak easily of the joining of the physical and life worlds, still, due in part to the continued sway of dualism, we speak much less familiarly of the joining of the living and mental worlds. Biochemistry is a well-established discipline, while "psychobiology" still calls for raised-eyebrow quotation marks around it. The idea of a seamless embodied mind, or mindful body, such that disease is a function of mind-body disequilibrium, remains alien to our cultural images. The Hippocratean idea that resting blood pressure, say—allowing for the various corporeal elements that contribute to it—is critically influenced by a person's harmonic dialogue with the social and physical environment has to be argued to, not from, in today's medical environment. We feel compelled to explain the premises of psychosomatic, or holistic, but not of somatic, or dualistic, medicine. That such an explanation would seem as unnatural in other cultures (e.g., China) as it seems natural in ours suggests that dualism, like its counterpart, holism, is a

2. "Hospital chaplains are today trained so as to feel no need to understand even the most rudimentary aspects of physical disease; instead they see their job as caring for the soul. Likewise psychologists can go through college and graduate school without any training in anatomy and physiology. And even the most elementary introductory courses in psychology and philosophy are not required to gain entrance to medical schools, though such schools do require advanced training in calculus, physics, and chemistry" (Lynch 1985, 7).

learned, not innate, response. That is, it reflects an ideology or cultural image. To trace the source of this ideology is to go back to the origins of classical science and even further, to Greek antiquity.

Thus, in the seventeenth century, when Descartes was formulating the philosophical foundations of the modern scientific movement, it was, we saw, the science of mechanics that shaped the edges of those foundations. His revolutionary ideal, following that of William Harvey, whose work on the hydraulic motion of the heart so influenced him, was that living bodies, whether animal or human, obey certain well-defined mechanical principles and ought to be studied according to the laws of physics. His epistemological problem was how to satisfy the dictates of a mechanical account of nature as formulated by Galileo, Kepler, and Descartes himself in the early years of the seventeenth century, an account brought to fruition in Newton's *Principia*. A scientific conception of nature could claim to be philosophically sound only if it was constructed around this mechanistic ideal of explanation. But such a description of nature imposed substantive and methodological constraints on any epistemology. According to this description nature consisted of causal, mechanical processes, conforming to deterministic, mathematical principles. Nature was a self-contained clockwork. "Force," "mass," and "motion" were the central concepts around which explanation had to turn. At the same time, a truly "scientific" attitude required that the scientist not only table his prejudices and come bias-free to his experiments, but also place himself and his rational theorizing outside the world of nature he was studying. He was thus to be doubly detached, detached from his prejudices and detached from the world of his subject matter. Scientific objectivity meant a one-way interaction with nature—the scientist as spectator.

But this placed the philosopher of nature at risk. If every action had a corresponding reaction, and if nonetheless the scientist's duty was to place himself outside the world of nature he was observing, how could these two imperatives be simultaneously served? How could his observations be without reaction? Either the rational behavior of the scientist was excluded from the world of matter, or the science of mechanics was partial and unsatisfactory. In this way, the statement of the problem and its solution were preordained. The dualistic die was cast: at the cost of the eminently fruitful mechanistic description of nature, rational processes seeking understanding of physical processes had to be categorically different and exempt from the laws governing the physical processes they tracked. So there was an "inner" and an "outer" world, a world of matter subject to scientific description and a world of mind doing the describing. The domain of causality was matter, while the domain of rationality was mind. And the possibility of a detached scientific observer required their separation.

In fact, this one-way interaction imperative was doubly sanctioned. It was sanctioned not only as a precondition for seventeenth-century science, but also by the theory-praxis dichotomy of ancient Greek thought. For Aristotle, it was self-evident that humans could look on nature without thereby intervening in its processes or otherwise influencing it. This was the basis of the highest mode of life, *theoria*, the detached life of contemplation. Therefore the idea that scientific objectivity entailed a one-way interaction with nature was supported not just by the dictates of the New Science but by the added weight of antiquity. The new and the old sciences came together in affirming the external permanency of the world, and the pervasiveness of dualism is best understood with reference to the sanctions of these two powerful Western intellectual influences.

Yet, while this one-way interaction was axiomatic for Aristotle—the precondition for the life of contemplation—for Descartes, who harbored a different (mechanical) description of nature, it was problematic. In other words, while Aristotle and Descartes shared a commitment to the external-permanency world property (one-way interaction), Descartes alone was committed to the first world property discussed above, the fundamental-level property. Consequently, he had to face the question "How can the human activity of observing escape the mechanical network of deterministic events?" If this activity escaped it, then the science of mechanics did not provide what it sought, a comprehensive description of the physical world. But if it did not, the universe described was not mechanical. And in either event the epistemological account did not square with the physical account. The solution? Cartesian mind-body dualism: the scientist studied the historical development of the universe from outside, explaining phenomena mathematically, without himself being a part of it. The book of nature was written in the language of mathematics, but it was not a book (text) whose meaning unfolded *in the course of* its interpretation, continually rewritten as a function of its circulation. Rather it was a book in the sense of a set of tablets given *from outside*.[3] Such a solution not only met the conditions of Greek natural philosophy but was likewise well adapted to the kind of celestial mechanics on which the reputation of the *Principia* rested. As Toulmin notes, "When Newton 'broke the code' of the Solar System . . . neither the astronomical observations to which he appealed in explaining the facts of planetary motion, nor the theoretical calculations which he himself performed, could have any effect on this motion" (1981, 80).

Here Descartes's dualism displays its scientific significance. For the external-permanency world property on which the methodological di-

---

3. Henceforth *this* sense of objectivity defines (descriptive) Western rationality. The "two cultures" debate has its origins in Descartes's solution.

rective of scientific objectivity rests conflicts with the universality of the mechanical processes described by deterministic principles. But it does so only if mind and matter are holistically related. That is, only if there are not *two* separate worlds ("substances"), an outer and an "inner" world—a world of matter *(res extensa)* and a world of mind or thought *(res cogitans)*. So the underlying imperatives compelling a dualistic solution are, first, the procedural imperative following from the method deemed appropriate to a scientific attitude and, second, a substantive imperative following from the science of mechanics of the time. The scientist had to be both detached from and external to the objects of his study. Toulmin succinctly characterizes these imperatives:

1. For purposes of scientific investigation and theorizing, it was the scientist's duty to place himself and his rational speculations outside the world of nature that was his subject matter.
2. Correspondingly, the scientific world picture that was gradually built up, by adopting this attitude and procedure, depicted nature as a self-contained, deterministic mechanism, from the influence of whose processes and forces humanity was somehow excluded or exempted. (1981, 71)

Here, in two imperatives—what we earlier termed the external-permanency and the fundamental-level world properties—are the roots of the dualism on which the natural science paradigm rests. They express the arbitrary constraints imposed on science by the presuppositions of Cartesian and Newtonian "natural philosophy" and, we proposed, they have infiltrated the foundations of all of the sciences—human and natural alike, not excluding medicine. Yet today neither imperative survives. This was the contention of Chapter 8. Nature is not best described mechanically, nor, according to our best lights, can the describer remain detached from the world he or she describes. Still, in medicine as elsewhere, dualism lives on. The patient of biomedicine, like the Newtonian natural world, is for most clinical purposes "silent." For example, animal models are still used to study stress-induced diseases in human beings. "Clinical" detachment remains a byword of practice. We need look only to the *Dorland's Medical Dictionary* definitions of disease and placebo effect to see the legacy of this dualism. Far from mind being a natural extension of the human body, as we might say the biosphere is a natural extension of the geosphere, the one a developmental antecedent of the other, mind continues to be regarded either as a different substance—the realm of psychiatry—or as ultimately explicable in body terms (the realm of molecular and genetic medicine). Except at the outer reaches of today's medicine (behavioral medicine), the patient is a "whole body" *(Dorland's)*, a biological organism effectively immune to the activity of mind. Correspondingly, *disease* remains a function of an eradicable physical condition, a deviation from the norm of somatic parameters.

The question facing today's medicine is "How should the repudiation of the scientific imperatives on which many of our leading biomedical concepts rest be translated into an altered medical agenda?" With the transformation of Newtonian into quantum mechanics, no longer need nature be conceived deterministically nor the observer as causally detached from the observed. New imperatives have succeeded the old. Briefly, they are as follows:

1. [T]he earlier conception of the scientist, as a rational onlooker detached from his objects of study, has been progressively displaced by a newer conception of the scientist, as a participant involved in the very processes about which he theorizes.
2. The scientific world picture . . . will be correspondingly less mechanical and deterministic. This picture will reintegrate humanity with nature—the human observer, as agent, with the natural processes that he both studies and influences. (Toulmin 1981, 92, 71)

Here is a successor world picture that allows us to recognize the rational activities, both of scientists and other human beings, "as active elements within the operations of nature" (Toulmin 1981, 71). Nature is mindful! Remarkably, mind is reintegrated into nature, not in some neovitalist sense but as a reciprocal element in a two-way coupling. Nature is seamlessly matter-mind, as we might say planet Earth is seamlessly biospheric. Through "biogeopsychocultural" pathways, the health of one (geosphere) is inextricably linked to the health of the other (biosphere). Further, this psychobiological, or interactionist, conclusion is as much a logical consequence of the quantum mechanical description of nature as was the biophysical, or reductionist, conclusion a logical consequence of its classical mechanical description. And an infrastructure is in place for explaining this unexpected finding (unexpected by classical standards).

Briefly, this infrastructure rests on the probabilistic interpretation of the second law of thermodynamics, according to which equilibrium is associated with maximum probability. When applied to particles, this means that equilibrium is uncorrelated particle motion. Since at thermodynamic equilibrium particles are uncorrelated units and behave in a chaotic way, the effect of nonequilibrium is to correlate these units, so converting chaos into order. An enabling idea, as argued in the previous chapter, this inference transforms a mechanistic into a self-organizing description of nature. Dramatically reperceived, *matter* is now "open" to a developmental or self-transcendent interpretation. Commenting on this description of nature, "in which order is generated out of chaos through nonequilibrium conditions provided by our cosmological environment," Prigogine says: "It leads to a conception of matter as active, as in a continuous state of becoming. This picture deviates significantly from the classical description of physics, of change in terms of forces and fields" (1984, 55). This turn, he adds, detours us from "the royal road opened by Newton, Maxwell, and Einstein." Although this road, further paved by Bernard, Virchow, Pasteur, and others, has shaped our concepts of patient and disease, it is the other, deviant road down which the findings of postmodern science take us. Along this road not taken lies today's medical opportunity: Given that we may now think of mind as continuous with body, how will this alter our patient concept? Relieved of the requirement to maintain a categorical separation between mind and matter, and enjoined to account for the developmental continuity of nature, how may this alter the way that we approach the patient and his or her disease? The answer to this question may bridge us to a hermeneutic or "genetic" (versus rationalistic or "atomic") medicine, whereby a given response is not a direct result of a stimulus, but rather the result of rule-governed processes that define the stimulated system—the psychobiological or, better, biopsychosocial system. The final state (e.g., health, disease) of the system does not depend on initial or boundary conditions (e.g., genetic predisposition). Reference to the stimulus (e.g., virus) is no longer sufficient to understand the response. Rather, final state is a property of the system itself: similar conditions (tubercle bacillus) can result in dissimilar products (tuberculosis or not tuberculosis) and greater order, not disorder, can ensue. In a word, what are the contours of a medicine in which final state is a stochastically emergent, self-organizing phenomenon, at once deterministic and probabilistic? The next chapter seeks to delineate these contours.

# 10

## From Engineering to Cybernetics: An Infomedical Model

In Part One we examined the biomedical model and its modern science foundations. We found that an engineering strategy was immanent. In this chapter, the infomedical model and its postmodern science foundations will be presented. Here, a cybernetics strategy is immanent. We invoke the language of information theory to capture the strategic advantages of a cybernetics approach based on a self-organizing systems scientific infrastructure. The rich, two-level vocabulary afforded by information theory offers explanations for events that are otherwise inexplicable in an engineering model.

## Infomedicine: Basic Concepts

Cybernetics deals with control and communication in systems formed by living organisms and their artifacts. It is the science of maintaining order in such systems. These systems have the property that selection of the state of any element of a system is influenced by the state of each of its other elements. Elements so linked by reciprocal influences form a feedback loop. Such a loop may be negative, or stabilizing, says Ramon Margalef, "like the one formed by a heating unit and a thermostat or the mechanisms regulating sugar level in the blood. Or the loop may be positive, or disruptive, like the spread of an annihilating epidemic" (1968, 2). Negative feedback loops are homeostatic and deviation-inhibiting. Positive feedback loops are deviation-amplifying and feed runaway processes. In addition to being destabilizing and disruptive, however, they can also be metastabilizing and homeodynamic, feeding self-organizing processes, like the growth of a village on a plain.

Organized structures carry with them information; that is, we can say something about them by virtue of their nonrandom nature of organization. Unorganized elements do not carry information. Their random nature defies description. Thus, a system's structure can be described, because of its orderly features, as well as determine within limits its future states. Information, in the context of cybernetics, refers to any after-the-fact restrictions on before-the-fact probabilities. "Any cybernetic system," says Margalef, "through the interactions of its parts, restricts the immensely large numbers of a priori possible states and, in consequence, carries information" (1968, 2). These after-the-fact restrictions that govern the interactions of its parts are the stored information or "grammar" of the system as distinct from its potential information or "alphabet." Together the system alphabet (freedom) and grammar (constraints) decree its range of activities, what it can do or communicate.

*Entropy* is a term used to measure the disorderliness of a physical system. When referring to energy, it characterizes the amount of "useful" energy. To be useful requires nonrandom structure. *High entropy* means high randomness, hence low amounts of useful energy. Since orderliness (low entropy) carries information—that is, we can describe it by virtue of its structuredness—we can see that entropy (inversely) measures information as well as energy. In information-theoretic terms, entropy is characterized by the rules by which potential information can be converted into actual activities ("messages"). Lila Gatlin illustrates this through a comparison of the potential and stored information in a library (1972, 49). She asks us to imagine each page of each book cut into single letter pieces and mixed in one jumbled heap. Here entropy unquestionably increases while stored information decreases. Stored information is constituted by letters ordered in word sequences according to formation rules, the words linearly ordered in sentence sequences according to rules of syntax, and these sequences themselves organized into carefully catalogued books and periodicals. High-potential information (alphabet soup) is actualized (message) only by the imposition of constraints. These constraints are instructions for use, rules delimiting possibilities: entropy reduction. Thus, high entropy means few rules and few restraints, which results in a high degree of randomness and low information content. On the other hand, low entropy means the presence of structure, rules, and nonrandom events and thus high information content.

Information is here understood in its etymological sense as an active agent, something that in-forms the material world, "much as the messages of the genes instruct the machinery of the cell to build an organism, or the signals from a radio transmitter guide the intricate path of a vehicle on its journey through space" (J. Campbell, 1984, 16). To inform, in this context, means to shape or reshape: messages from one level of organization are empowered to reshape and be reshaped by messages from another level of organization. So a *program* shapes computer behavior; and to psychoanalyze a computer is to scrutinize its programs. Analogously, to "psychoanalyze" (i.e., diagnose) a patient, in infomedical terms, is to scrutinize his or her programs and their interrelationships. These programs describe such diverse interactions as those between the immune, endocrine, and neurological systems (the province of psychoneuroimmunology) as well as bio-psycho-socio interactions (the more encompassing province of infomedicine). Here we see the applicability of the neo-Hippocratean premise, noted in the previous chapter, that bodily signs like resting blood pressure are a function of a person's overall harmonic dialogue with the environment. Infomedicine seeks to provide a vocabulary in which such a premise can be medically expressed. Therapy therefore consists in orchestrating these programs, with health reperceived as their adaptive interplay. In this way a behavioral state or a set of cultural values or belief systems, for example, just like a tumor, can actively maintain or reshape a physiological state, and vice versa, in a negative or positive mutual causal feedback process. This framework permits an explanation of otherwise puzzling findings in the medical literature such as the correlation reported by G. H. Edelstyne and K. D. McRae between psychosocial attitudes toward breast loss and the course and severity of neoplasia (1975, 30–33). It also helps resolve the difficulty voiced by Cunningham: "We are not good at multi-causal (chronic) but like single cause explanations" (1981, 609), where "single cause" may refer to multiple complex body systems but not to different *types* of systems, for instance psychological or sociocultural systems.

As Margalef states, "A cybernetic system influences the future, or bridges time, in the sense that the present state sets limits for or imposes patterns on future states. In this way, the present state is a bearer of information" (1968, 2). The rules governing the interaction of its state variables determine what forms the system might achieve. In this way it stalks the future, stochastically plotting it. For this reason, examination of the elements of the feedback-looped system conveys information about its probable future state and any of its elements. By coming to understand how messages from all significant levels of organization are processed (via programs) by the system, we can anticipate future states of health or disease. The informed physician can anticipate the onset and course of disease through "psychoanalyzing" patient programs in the above sense. This discloses the link between cybernetics and infomedicine. This link can be further clarified by reference to Figure 10.1, which graphically illustrates a feedback-loop perspective of the range of levels of organization that can influence the patient's state of well-being.

Describing various interactive parts of the health-relevant feedback-loop, the figure depicts an integrated communications circuit. Now the state of the biological organism (organ level) and the individual's mental-emotional environment (person level) are mutually functional. More generally, the state of any element over time influences and is influ-

The Infomedical Model

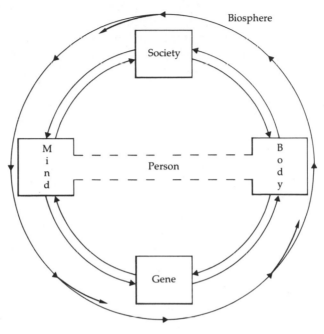

FIGURE 10.1

enced by the states of other elements of the system—genetic, interpersonal, biospheric, and so forth. To understand the grammar of the system—that is, the stored information that defines its interactions—is to recognize, stochastically, what is an "adaptive program" for the system as a whole. Examination of the elements of the mutual causal feedback-looped system therefore conveys information about the probable future state of the system and of any of its elements. For example, to know the genesis of the mutual adaptivity of society and body, and the relevant time scale of this adaptivity relation, is to be able to anticipate the repercussions on the body of a (relatively) sudden change in the parameter defining society. Thus, if it takes time scale $t$ for body to develop adaptivity to society 1, what is the likely repercussion on body in the event that society 1 self-organizes into society 2 in a time scale $t - n$? (Here, society 1 may be assumed to be a paleolithic, hunting-gathering society and society 2 a postneolithic, industrial-technological society; $t = 1,000,000$ years, and $n = 20,000$ years.) Answer: disequilibrium (dis-ease). And the therapeutic response? Again, the infomedical framework provides an answer: treatment designed to offset this disequilibrium through readjusting maladaptive programs.

What does such treatment look like? Since infomedical principles dictate the equilibration of body and society, therapies are designed to achieve this equilibration. For example, the infomedical physician prescribes a treatment for fashioning a mini-environment that simulates society 1 within society 2, a restructuring-of-some-environmental-situations therapy. (Such therapy has been successfully administered experimentally. See Powell et al. 1984.) Or again, in order to achieve the same end through a different means, the infomedical physician prescribes a treatment for refashioning the body into one now adaptive to the new society, society 2. Conceivably this might be achieved through a "Type C" behavioral learning therapy, whereby the inherited "fight-or-flight" body which is adaptive to society 1 is refashioned by means of a biopsychosocial technology (e.g., biofeedback, hypnotherapy, visualization) into a "flow" body adaptive to society 2. (See, e.g., Temoshok 1984.) The relevant point here is that in the first case, the infomedical model offers an *explanation* of the success of the behavioral adjustment therapy cited; whereas in the second case, this model, because of the excess empirical content characteristic of theories, indicates research directions otherwise pursued only serendipitously.

Here we see how the replacement of an engineering by a cybernetic framework dramatically alters the foundation concepts of diagnostics and therapeutics. No longer is disease conceived on the engineering concept of the movement by a particle (organism) under the action of a force (pathogen). (See Fig. 10.2.) According to this concept, the offending pathogen produces a dysfunctional biochemical reaction, the treatment for which may be the administration of a physical agent (e.g., chemical) designed to intercept the pathogen or counteract its biochemical effects.

Rather, in the successor framework, because the final state of the system does not depend on the boundary conditions, reference to the stimulus is no longer sufficient to understand the response. Now the final state is a property of the system itself. Its behavior is explained by reference not to the sum of its symbiotic parts (reductionism) but to something like the sums of all possible combinations of its symbiotic parts (interactionism)—the difference between the characteristic behavior of an ensemble in statistical thermodynamics (in principle reversible, deterministic) and of a dissipative structure in nonequilibrium thermodynamics (in principle irreversible, stochastically indeterminate). This is a revolutionary turn. For now the reputed cause of disease (e.g., a microorganism) triggers action in something that is not one simple object (or even one organismically complex object), but rather a pattern of relations, an "interaction of parts." These relations may include mutually irreducible organismic and extraorganismic elements. The action is intrinsic, linked only in an indirect way to the stimulus (microorganism) that set it off. Infomedically speaking, we might say that the patient is an information-processing system. The patient processes messages from a variety of levels of organization. These messages are mediated by the programs that are characteristic of the system. That is, the programs trigger action that is not a cause-effect reaction; rather, it is a feedback, loop-structured, interactive reaction. As such, the resulting state of the patient can only be understood in nonreducible, organizationally complex terms, as opposed to reducible, organizationally simple, single-level terms.

PATHOGEN ⟶ ORGANISM ⟋ DISEASE

FIGURE 10.2

To reflect this radical shift from an engineering to a communications model, Figure 10.1 may be mapped into a flow chart displaying the exchange of different, interactive messages—genetic, behavioral, social, biospheric. A rule base can be generated by assigning weights to elements from each message modality (level of organization) such that a probability value attaches to the pathogenic (or therapeutic) potential of their mutual interplay. Here the tentative findings reported by Edelstyne and MacRae, referenced above, will be instanced. As shown graphically in Figure 10.3, psychosocial attitudes toward breast loss in combination with the incidence of a (physical) carcinogen represent a socio-active program and a bio-active message respectively, impacting the patient. The patient, or locus of disease, is represented by the box as a whole.

In terms of the vocabulary provided by this matrix, Figure 10.3 may now be recast in successor terms (Fig. 10.4). Now curative medicine considerations fall within the brackets and preventive medicine considerations outside (to the left of) the brackets.

We now arrive at a new sense in which to understand disease and illness. Messages from many levels of organization inform the system. The system itself, as defined by the state of its interactive parts, may be far from equilibrium. In such a system, a small change in one of its parameters can result in a qualitatively redefined system. From the contributions to our understanding of complex structures made in the field of nonlinear thermodynamics, we recognize this as a state common to systems that exchange energy with the external environment. Hence, a cluster of interacting messages (bio-, psycho-, socio-, etc.) can act as a critical fluctuation that drives the system into a new regime. Such a new regime might be one of imbalance, maladaptation, or any other state customarily associated with disease or illness. Disease so understood leads to the following infomedical therapeutic insight:

The system, through self-understanding, has the potential to shape the messages that it receives through its impact on its own environment. Additionally, it has the potential to influence how it is in-formed by the surrounding messages through reprogramming itself (e.g., activating a change in beliefs, values, behaviors, etc.). Hence, the patient-as-decoder-of-information can gain (in some areas) cybernetic control to achieve a state of health through reestablishing either systemic stability or systemic reorganization.

This insight is further elucidated by means of some simple terms from the language of the communications engineer as in the loop structure diagram in Figure 10.5. The locus of health and disease (*L*), the human patient, is conceptualized as an integrated communications network. Rather than a biological organism, it is viewed as a geobiopsychosocial system:

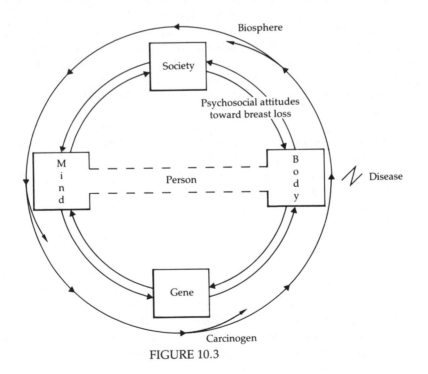

FIGURE 10.3

$L: \{G, B, M, S, E\}^1$

where the bracketed letters stand for the elements identified in Figure 10.1. The arrows in that figure represent Input, the descriptive terms represent Sources or Transmitters (when arrows are outward bound) or Receivers (when they are inward bound). As in the case of the integrated organism of the biomedical model, the system is a hierarchical structure with higher-level programs generating and controlling lower-level programs, its subunits thus in-forming and re-forming one another adaptively (health) or not (disease). This conceptualization may be usefully compared with that of the psychoneuroimmunologist for whom the locus of disease *(L)* is:

$L: \{P, N, I\}$

the letters now standing for Psychological, Neurological, and Immunological. Here, for example, depression (biobehavioral attitude) may activate neurological response (neurotransmitters), triggering some particular endocrinological process (hormonal discharge: catecholamines); these, in turn, suppress immune defenses (immunosuppressants). The resulting immunological incapacity further contributes, in its turn, to the depression, thus coming full circle. This cybernetic circularity disposes to and over time can produce disease:

$L: \{P, N, I\}$     disease

The diagnostic task of psychoneuroimmunology is seen as providing a "grammar" or mechanism that models the interconnections and control functions governing what is bracketed in the last equation. Accordingly, its therapeutic strategy is to trace the pathogenic path-

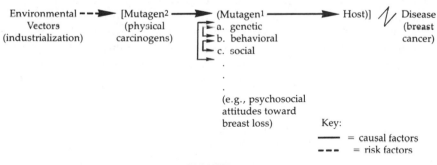

FIGURE 10.4

1. *E* = Environment (Biosphere).

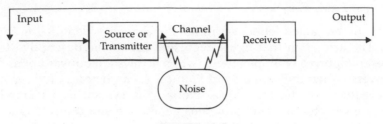

FIGURE 10.5

way(s) backward and intercept the offending message/problem (e.g., loss of job/depression). This might be done by "fooling" the patient (placebo) or by physically neutralizing the impact of the message by intercepting its concomitantly released neurotransmitter.

Analogously, the diagnostic task of infomedicine is to provide a grammar or mechanism that models the interconnections and control functions governing the subunits recognized within its hierarchical structure (the bracketed elements). For example, such a mechanism might first specify a physiological baseline or "program" by reference to which the virulence of a psychic or social "message" can be anticipated and measured. As psychoneuroimmunology seeks to elucidate the mechanism (rules govering the interconnections) describing the biochemistry of the psychoneuroimmunological system, infomedicine seeks to elucidate the mechanism describing the "biochemistry" of the geobiopsychosocial system. Here "biochemistry" is understood in expanded geopsychosocial as well as "bio" terms, inasmuch as the infomedical locus of disease (L), the human patient, designates a new or emergent way of being an animal in the world. (The number and type of elements included within brackets in either framework are in part a pragmatic matter depending on the promised fruitfulness of the evidence in behalf of the conjecturally introduced parameters.) Thus, the infomedical model seeks to achieve states of health by raising the principle of coevolution to the conscious and self-conscious level—we can influence the environment, both messages and programs, in which we must adapt to maintain our health.

The research agenda of the infomedical model is that of any medical model. It must separate (in all domains of significance) information from noise. Information is messages that have an impact on the state of health and well-being of the system; noise does not. Of course, what is information and what is noise are an artifact of the espoused model. In the case of the infomedical model, the "psychosocial underbrush" can be the source of important information. As the phrase suggests, from the biomedical perspective, such messages are noise. The infomedical research agenda is to come to understand the messages by which the system is influenced, as well as the programs that process the information, thus determining its impact.

The biomedical model recognizes bio-messages as the domain of information necessary to understand the health of the system. These bio-messages are processed by complex organismic programs. Looking at the biomedical model as a subset of the infomedical model, what is elucidated are bio-messages and bio-programs—extrasomatic messages are noise. A fully fleshed infomedical model recognizes messages emanating from diverse levels of complexity. The patient is an information-processing system with multilevel programs processing multilevel messages, whose interaction determines the systemic state (health and well-being of the system). To the extent that the nature of what is considered significant information is an artifact of the model, research agendas and what count as significant medical phenomena can shift dramatically from model to model. As we shall see in Part Four, identical experimental findings can yield radically different knowledge bases.

## Cybernetics: Basic Concepts

It is interesting that historically the field of cybernetics has struggled with some of the same issues confronting medical science—an adequate understanding of the interactions of complex systems. Cybernetics began by asking about the "fundamental concept of machine" and answered by stating, in W. Ross Ashby's words, "that its internal state, and the state of its surroundings, defines uniquely the next state it will go to" (1962). This means that the early cybernetic model of system was that of a "machine with input." Any fundamental change in the system's organization could not be ascribed to any cause within the system itself but, in Ashby's words, "must come from some outside agent, acting on the system S as input." As Bertalanffy notes, "to be 'self-organizing' the machine S must be coupled to another machine . . . that is, [S is] a system open to information but closed with respect to entropy transfer" (1968, 97). This contention of Ashby's that no machine can be self-organizing in that the "change cannot be ascribed to any cause in the set S characterizing the system but must come from some outside agent, an input" (in Bertalanffy 1968, 97), amounts to exclusion of self-organizing or self-differentiating systems. Systems can be adaptive (homeostatic) but not self-organizing (heterodynamic). The reason that such systems as "Ashby machines" are not self-organizing is traced by

Bertalanffy to restrictions imposed by the second law of thermodynamics:

> Self-differentiating systems that evolve toward higher complexity (decreasing entropy) are, for thermodynamic reasons, possible only as open systems—e.g., systems importing matter containing free energy to an amount overcompensating the increase in entropy due to irreversible processes within the system. . . . However, we cannot say that "this change comes from some outside agent, an input"; the differentiation within a developing embryo and organism is due to its internal laws [read: program] of organization, and the input [read: message] (e.g., oxygen supply which may vary quantitatively, or nutrition which can vary qualitatively within a broad spectrum) makes it only possible energetically. (1968, 97–98)

This early cybernetic definition of the "machine with inputs" proved to be a significant expansion of the machine concept with widespread applications to a number of fields. It is a concept both mathematically grounded and technologically implemented, and it characterized the spread of cybernetic principles in the early years. However, only the later, broadened definition of a machine, a machine with both inputs and its own "internal laws of organization," permitted the crucial distinction to be made between a system that adapts to the environment and one that self-differentiates within the environment. The basis of this distinction between other-directed and inner-directed systems led to the second phase of cybernetics called by Maruyama "Cybernetics II." Whereas the first phase ("Cybernetics I") dealt with negative feedback or deviation-inhibiting, adaptive behavior, the second phase dealt with the interplay of negative and positive feedback, deviation-inhibiting and deviation-amplifying behavior. And it is this interplay that accounts for the possibility of a system open both with respect to information and entropy transfer, namely a self-organizing system.

In this new, expanded framework, because the final state of the system does not depend on the initial or boundary conditions, reference to the stimulus (pathogen) is no longer sufficient to understand the response (disease). Applied to a medical model, this is the revolutionary turn referred to above—the basis for the second revolution. Information exchange, not unidirectional causality, describes processes in, or among, the various interacting systems now comprising the locus of disease. And the mechanism, or explanation, is sought not in the framework of classical physics or engineering but in the information-theoretic concepts of the storage and transfer of information within a system. These are the "rules" or programs informing the interaction of system elements. Compare Conway's Game of Life (in Gardner 1983).

The richness of a cybernetic/infomedical vocabulary contrasted with an engineering/biomedical vocabulary becomes apparent in explaining the "bootstrapping" events characteristic of clinical biofeedback. In the discussion of Chapter 6, we saw that the field of psychoneuroimmunology could explain, in a single-level reductionist language, the placebo effect that results from a behavior-conditioned response common to animals and humans (mind 1). This involved tracing the neurophysiological pathways among the body systems. Further, the explanation for this chain of events is consistent with Cybernetics I, or negative feedback, deviation-inhibiting behavior. Were this type of event representative of the full range of placebo behaviors, then the engineering/biomedical vocabulary would be adequate, and Occam's razor would dictate against a more complicated explanatory approach. But, as we noted, such conditioned behavior did not represent the full range of behavior in need of explanation. Clinical biofeedback, or rather, clinical psychobiofeedback, we argued, was not explicable in a single-level, engineering biomedical vocabulary. Here a change in mindset, a willful act, interacted with a physiological state and back again, in a feedback sequence that led to a new system state not predictable in a simple cause-and-effect sequence. This sequence was referred to as bootstrapping because of the qualitative change in system-state variables resulting from the qualitative change in mindset. The language describing these events, we said, required a vocabulary admitting multiple interacting levels of organization (mind 2)—a mindful person in loop-structured interaction with his or her biological components.

A cybernetically infomedical vocabulary can address this sequence by reference to nonreducible levels of organization—bio- and psychoactive messages mediated by bio- and psycho-active programs. Bertalanffy speaks to the theoretical basis of this framework by distinguishing two types of causality: "From the energetic viewpoint, in this case we do not find 'conservation causality' (*Erhaltungskausalität*) where the principle 'causa aequat effectum' holds, but 'instigation causality' (*Anschlusskausalität*), where an energetically insignificant change in $P_s$ (a 'leading part' coefficient in a Taylor series) causes a considerable change in the total system" (1968, 71). The pattern of relations forming such a system can be characterized by such general systems properties as allometry, progressive mechanization, centralization, and equifinality. Bertalanffy explains: "Any function of this pattern ultimately results from interaction of all parts, notwithstanding that in any given situation certain parts may influence it differentially and so be denoted as 'centers' for that function."

This provides a fresh context for disease. From the infomedical perspective, it is the value of these "centers" or "leading parts," not any fundamental difference in disease type, that accounts for the biomedical distinction between "acute" and "chronic" (or "degenerative") diseases. The infomedical model takes as its frame of reference all influences that can affect the locus of disease. The range of such influences can extend from the microscopic level of microbes and viruses to the macro level of the terrestrial-solar environment. The organic disease (disease recognized by the biomedicalist) is a manifestation of underlying messages that may be generated by various genetic, health-history, personality, sociocultural, and other programs. And disease is a function of maladaptation (pathogenic message-program mix). It is precipitated by prolonged distress and channeled through a particular configurational complex that gives rise to specific organic disorders—cardiovascular, neoplastic, and so forth.

Here we see how a successor diagnostic framework offers therapeutic redress not available to its diagnostically more restrictive predecessor. By expanding the spectrum of messages containing important information beyond bio-messages, it makes more informed diagnoses on the basis of which additional therapies present themselves. The effectiveness of these therapies can, moreover, be experimentally tested and integrated into clinical practice. Part Four offers a matrix for such an integration via an infomedical "expert system."

The defining insights of infomedicine can be summarized:

1. The locus of disease is a complex (i.e., coded), not a simple, system. Biomedicine (notably psychoneuroimmunology), recognizing the organismic system as complex is, in this sense, itself therefore susceptible of a partial infomedical analysis, a special case of infomedicine.
2. This locus comprises a variety of state variables or levels of organization—organismic as well as extraorganismic levels.
3. Message-program interactions within a feedback loop are reciprocal influences. They are capable of triggering either stabilizing (healthy) or destabilizing (dis-eased) processes. In the first case they are therapeutic agents, in the second pathogenic agents.
4. Each interacting level of organization constitutes stored information ("programs"); that is, each possesses its own instructions or "grammar." So messages can be decoded and mapped for potential mutual concordance or discordance as they pass between levels of organization. For example, the biological organism is evolutionarily coded to receive, with a minimum of maladaptation, messages (stimuli, fluctuations, stressors, mutagens) characteristic of a society marked by hunting-gathering (paleolithic) activities. Conversely, this organism is ill-coded to receive messages characteristic of a society marked by industrial (postneolithic) activities. Unless mediated, such messages can be maladaptive (trigger dis-ease).

From a fully articulated infomedical perspective, there remains a quantum gap separating the two models. The biomedical model recognizes the internalization of unconscious (autonomic) self-regulating processes, like the regulation of blood sugar levels in the body. But it does not formally recognize the internalization of self-regulating processes that initially require conscious decision-making, like the advertent regulation of "autonomic" nervous system functions sought, for example, in clinical biofeedback therapy. For this reason, programs involving self-conscious (intentional) decision-making cannot, within biomedicine, synergistically interact with unconscious, or autonomic, decision-making procedures. This was the weakness noted in the psychoneuroimmunologist's explanatory framework and hence a weakness in the biomedical explanatory strategy as illustrated in the bootstrapping sequence. And this is a defining difference between the two models.

An information-theoretic analysis of interacting messages characterizing the levels of organization forming the feedback loops that circumscribe the human patient and his or her morbidity levels dictates the therapeutic strategy of infomedicine. Briefly:

> Appropriate therapy is a systematic decoding-recoding process
> whereby the grammars governing the range of messages that can
> be sent from and received by a given level of organization or
> program can be modeled for mutual intelligibility.

The locus of disease is reconceptualized as an information processing system characterized by an integrated circuit in which diagnostic information is stored "just as a set of axioms and postulates stores the primary information from which a mathematical system is deduced. Therefore, if we wish to investigate the organization of living systems [read: patients (L)], we must investigate the ordering of the sequences of symbols which specify them" (Gatlin 1972, 23). A corresponding medical curriculum would identify and map the interactive relationships linking the various components of the disease equations—the "messages" and "programs" by which transmitters-and-receivers (i.e., the elements of Figure 10.1) intercommunicate. It will be recalled that any function of this circuit ultimately results from interaction of all the elements notwithstanding that certain elements may differentially influence the totality and so be variously characterized for that function. The adequacy of a model is gauged by the degree to which it can supply a map of the interconnected pathways along which breakdowns from within, as distinct from attack from without, travel. Here health is reconceptualized as the interplay of adaptive programs. It is a self-organizing "geopsychosociobiofeedback process," to coin an awkward but infomedically accurate neologism.

# An Infomedical Analogy

Information theory grew out of the efforts to solve certain practical, technological problems. Among them were wartime problems—specifically, how to hit a moving target like enemy aircraft. A historical look at this problem (see J. Campbell 1982, 25–30) can help to clarify the novel orientation of the infomedical model. This can be achieved by following the seemingly unlikely parallels between the infomedical practitioner and an anti-aircraft gunner.

During World War II, the British guns were nearly powerless to shoot down German bombers. Because they flew high and fast, it was difficult to determine where a plane would be after the guns were fired. The British response was to randomly spray anti-aircraft shells at the bombers, and they had little success in doing so. There was no rationalized procedure for reliable tracking and firing. This led to intense research to develop devices that could track a plane; compute its position, direction, and speed; and predict where it would be by the time the anti-aircraft shell had traveled from the gun to the target area.

The task facing the British gunners was how to reduce the uncertainty in a situation that was unpredictable—hitting a distant, waywardly moving plane. On a radar screen, the blips that trace the path of a plane are distorted by random electrical interference in the atmosphere, and the pilot of the plane also tries to confuse the gunners by purposely flying in an unpredictable manner. In other words, the task was to secure valuable information while being barraged by many messages—much of which contained noise. Noise is anything that corrupts the integrity of the messages. When a radio signal from the ground is bounced off an enemy plane in the sky, it scatters, and comes back to earth in a much weaker form. The weaker it becomes, the more it is contaminated by random noise in the atmosphere and in the circuits of the radar receiver itself.

The key to solving the unpredictability facing the British gunners was the postmodern insight that classical cause and effect must yield to the stochastic processes of chance and statistics. The noise in the radar was amenable to the same sort of mathematical treatment common to Brownian motion—that is, random behavior. "The link which relates the two concepts [radar noise and Brownian motion] is statistics, a branch of the theory of probability, the master principle behind some of the most profound discoveries of modern physics" (J. Campbell 1982, 27–28).

Thus, messages contain information that can be distorted by noise, and their full meaning is thereby not known completely in advance. This does not mean that we are totally at a loss as to what the possible outcomes are. The range of possible outcomes can be intelligently approached. Campbell notes that a sentence of English prose is a series of letters and words obeying certain statistical rules. It is internally consistent, so that if a person knows the rules, the sequence is not completely unpredictable. Given the first half of the sentence, it may be possible to guess the second half, or come near to guessing it, or at least to predict the next letter.

[T]he scientist must try to conquer uncertainty about the future by considering a range of different contingencies and assigning a suitable probability to each contingency. Then he or she can say what may happen, under this or that set of circumstances. (1982, 28–29)

The British gunners needed to know where the plane would be a few seconds after they fired to allow time for the bullets to travel. The probable path of the plane is treated as one of many possible paths. The task of separating messages from noise is accomplished statistically. Messages display a certain pattern, and the patterns change in a manner determined partly, but only partly, by their past history. The challenge became one of coming up with a device that could select the correct information and impose accurate probabilities on the content of the messages yielded.

The infomedical practitioner would recognize certain features of the British gunner's plight with his or her own. Patients occupy a range spanning from those severely diseased to those in good health. Decisions must be made regarding what has caused the patient's condition, what the patient's future state of health will be, as well as the impact of a variety of therapeutic options. The infomedicalist, like the British gunner, must make a clear break with determinism. The kind of exactness that a mechanist worldview assumes does not exist. In giving up determinism, the infomedicalist is able to move away from the strict requirement that physical messages—that is, messages from a single level of organization—are the only or the primary source of important information. This gives standing to messages that emanate from a variety of levels of organization, including now geopsychosocial messages. Biomedical practitioners, on the other hand, consider only messages that carry physically based information. Psychosocial factors only get in the way of the already complex undertaking of coming to understand the patient-as-biological-organism. Thus, in the biomedical view, psychosocial factors are noise. They confuse the issue.

The key determinants regarding the admission of a widened spectrum of messages is that they have an impact on the present and future state of the patient-as-system, the grammar or programs that process the messages are scientifically rationalized, and finally, a statistical relationship can be discovered between the message and its synergistic impact on the patient's future states. Here, as in the sentence of English prose, there is rule-governed behavior as well as an element of unpredictability. Thus, infomedicine recognizes a nondeterminist environment. Like the aircraft gunner, the practitioner is barraged by a great number of messages, some containing important information, some containing noise. Infomedicine recognizes that the uncertainty can be reduced by embracing an interactive disease equation that includes a fuller range of significant factors and the rule-governed behavior that determines their impact on the patient-as-information-processing-system. This range includes the statistical relationships of messages from multiple levels of organization. Campbell comments that "an actual message must be considered not in isolation but in its relation to all possible messages, just as the actual path of a plane is part of a pattern that includes other possible paths. This is a point of central importance in information theory, which is statistical to its very bones" (1982, 30).

An organic symptom, says the infomedicalist, represents the statistical confluence of messages from a variety of levels of organization, which together form an $n$-tuple matrix, the infomedical locus of disease. Disentangling these multiple strands and, based on a knowledge of the grammar of the geobiopsychosocial system, imposing accurate probabilities on the content of their messages defines the infomedical task. Its aim is to reduce the uncertainty of targeting the wayward pathogenic root(s) of a complex system, and so systematically convert noise into medically useful information. To paraphrase Campbell, the infomedical physician must try to conquer uncertainty about the course of pathogenesis by considering a range of different contingencies and, on the basis of a grammar of rules governing the behavior of the geobiopsychosocial system, assigning a suitable probability to each contingency. Then he or she can say what likely happened under this or that set of circumstances and treat accordingly. In Part Four construction of this grammar of infomedical rules begins.

# The Revolutionary Thesis: Infomedicine

With little understanding of the way of life to which man is biologically adapted, modern medicine is unable to predict the possible harmful consequences of departures from it. . . . The resulting inability to deal theoretically (as distinct from statistically) with biological phenomena at levels of organization above a single organism has left medical theory seriously deficient.

> —John Powles
> "On the Limitations of Modern Medicine"

The effect of change in one system, be it economic, social, political, cultural, or educational, upon all others, is now greater than ever before. There are strains and stresses which traverse the globe and tax the adaptive capacities of the individual.

> —Ervin Laszlo
> *The Systems View of the World*

And the candidate, looking on, begins to feel that great heaving, sun-blazing deathboard of a deck wallowing in his own vestibular system—and suddenly he finds himself backed up against his own limits. He ends up going to the flight surgeon with so-called conversion symptoms. Overnight he develops blurred vision or numbness in his hands and feet or sinusitis so severe that he cannot tolerate changes in altitude. On one level the symptom is real. He really cannot see too well or use his fingers or stand the pain. But somewhere in his subconscious he knows it is a plea and a beg-off; he shows not the slightest concern (the flight surgeon notes) that the condition might be permanent and affect him in whatever life awaits him outside the arena of the right stuff.

> —Tom Wolfe
> *The Right Stuff*

# INTRODUCTION TO PART FOUR

The revolutionary impact of a fully articulated alternative medical model is spelled out in Part Four. This is achieved by illustrating the consequences of choosing one strategy in favor of another. The comparison is carried out in Chapter 11 by visually examining two medical models, each embracing a different strategy. The first employs an engineering strategy founded upon a natural science infrastructure. The second employs a cybernetic strategy founded upon a self-organizing systems infrastructure. In the process, the dramatic differences in the concepts of disease, patient, and appropriate therapy are revealed, thus highlighting the sensitive nature of foundations choice.

Chapter 12 deals squarely with the most controversial aspect of the infomedical model and its self-organizing systems foundations. As the many interactive arrows of Chapters 10 and 11 indicate, the infomedical model embraces the idea that "mental events can cause disease." This source of immediate conflict between biomedicine and infomedicine is discussed through the voices of spokespersons for both camps as well as by bringing to bear empirical findings. In the process, the notion of "disease causality," and the foundational premises upon which the term rests, is unpacked.

The comparison of biomedical and infomedical concepts of disease causality clarifies the commitments embraced by each as well as how the vocabulary of each licenses the able and conscientious physician to proceed. Such a comparison highlights the risk of the biomedical commitment to translating complex cognitive states—beliefs, values, goals— into the language of the conventional cause-effect nosology. It may be not only impossible, but scientifically unsound.

Chapter 13 provides a view of the medical enterprise from an infomedical perspective. This view transcends the clinical practice of medicine to situate the enterprise in a larger, more universal role—its potential impact on the planet.

The four interactive components of a postmodern infomedical disease equation are identified. Bio-, psycho-, socio- and techno-active levels are examined as essential components for a comprehensive understanding of a patient's health and well-being. The argument for their inclusion is essentially an evolutionary one. Briefly, as the human species has evolved, the nature of critical imbalances that can be disruptive to health has evolved. How each component or level of organization can have such an impact is discussed. This spelling out of the four components of the infomedical model offers an explanatory model of broad scope. Events as seemingly unrelated (in a medical context) as negative attitudes and eco-imbalances are made sense of from a scientifically founded medical perspective.

Chapter 14 concludes by asking questions and raising issues that fall in the category of the "foundations initiative." Foremost among these is the prudence of keeping faith with a model that cannot and does not actively integrate extrasomatic factors as a central feature of the medical landscape. At issue is whether today's concept of scientific medicine represents an optimal range for today's health needs. The established patterns of medical thought are challenged: are old patterns being applied to new problems?

# 11

## Two Medical Strategies: Engineering versus Cybernetics

In Part Three an argument for paradigm succession was offered. In this chapter, we will contrast the familiar engineering strategy based on tier 1 and tier 2 natural science foundations with the unfamiliar cybernetic strategy based on tier 1' and tier 2' self-organizing systems foundations. When they are set side by side, their dramatic differences can be highlighted.

## Background

Nineteenth-century physicians were confronted with a body of formidable diseases mainly associated with poverty and difficult living conditions. Typical of these were diseases of malnutrition and the acute infectious diseases that plagued Western society. In coping with these diseases a particular medical strategy evolved whose orientation conformed to that of the natural sciences animating the scientific revolution. This strategy embodied certain working premises concerning the nature of disease, the patient, and the appropriate range of therapies. Among these premises, three may be singled out:

1. Disease is a function of a systemic physiologic disorder.
2. The patient is a biological organism or physiological system.
3. The primary determinants of disease are physical in nature, e.g., bacteria, lesions, viruses. Hence, appropriate therapies are also physical. Designed as counteractants, they include pharmaceuticals, surgery, and the like.

During the latter stages of this period, however, physicians were increasingly confronted with a new body of diseases. (See Figure 11.1.)

These diseases were mainly associated with affluence and technological complexity. Typical were the chronic degenerative diseases—cardiovascular disorders, certain cancers, rheumatoid arthritis, respiratory diseases—that came to be called "afflictions of civilization." The available explanatory strategy has proved less adaptive in alleviating these new diseases. Evidence has accumulated that some determinants of these diseases were nonphysical, extra-organic in origin. Since the available model acknowledged only physical disease determinants, physicians were left with three broad options in diagnosing and treating these so-called civilization- or "stress"-related diseases. The first two are consistent with an engineering approach to disease, and the third with a cybernetic approach. In accord with these three options, physicians could do one of the following:

1. Define these nonphysical factors as risk factors or triggering agents of disease belonging to "preventive" and "rehabilitative" medicine and continue to concentrate on eradicating the well-defined physical disease determinants.
2. Acknowledge the influential role of the nonphysical factors in the production of disease and develop an expanded but still single-level, reductionist vocabulary for dealing with them.
3. Acknowledge the influential role of the nonphysical factors in the production of disease and adopt an alternative explanatory strategy that would formally recognize the scientifically rationalized place that such factors had. This would entail a conceptual revolution in medical foundations.

The second option, although representing an expansion of the biomedical model, still adheres to biomedical premises. Its thrust is to translate the experimentally documented, nonphysical disease determinants (stressors, behavioral stimuli) into a vocabulary making reference only to the neurophysiological processes concomitant with or precipitated by these stimuli. Thus, while it pushes back the boundaries of disease determinants to include nonphysical, behavioral pathogens in addition to physical pathogens, it explains them in physicalist and reductionist terms: it seeks to identify them with biochemical processes.

The third option adopts a different explanatory strategy with its own, alternative set of working premises. Rather than reductionist and single-level, these premises are nonreductionist, specifying the interaction of micro and macro levels. Such premises include the following:

1. Disease is a function of a systemic biopsychosociologic disorder.
2. The patient is a psychophysiologic unity in an open systems relationship with the social (and physical) environment.

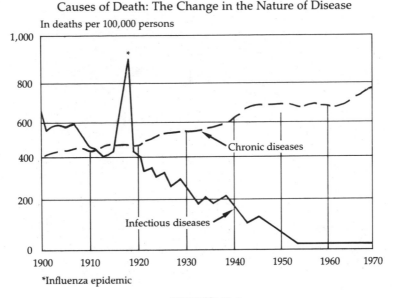

Causes of Death: The Change in the Nature of Disease

*Influenza epidemic

FIGURE 11.1

3. The primary determinants of disease are mutually activating physical, behavioral, and social agencies. As such, appropriate therapies
   include physical, behavioral, and social "counteractants" used synergistically.

These premises augur the formulation of a scientific medicine in a
nonreductionist or interactionist language. Briefly, the strategic difference is that in one strategy mind (and culture) is a by-product of
biological organization ($Q1a$ $Q1b$, . . .). In the other strategy mind (and
culture), having developmentally arisen out of biological organization, is
an irreducible component of a primitive, mutually activating, biopsychosocial loop structure ($Q_1$, $Q_2$, . . .). In order to contrast the model based
on this strategy with the dominant biological organism medical model
(the biomedical model), it is here called the self-organizing systems
model.

   In what follows these different strategies and the models they beget
will be further examined and mutually assessed. The first two strategies
mentioned are engineering strategies based on biological foundations
and reflect current practice. The second represents an enlargement of
the first to take account of today's prevalent stress-related diseases.
Hence, these will be termed strategies E and E' (E = engineering). The
third strategy mentioned is a cybernetic strategy based on self-organizing systems foundations; hence strategy C (C = cybernetics).

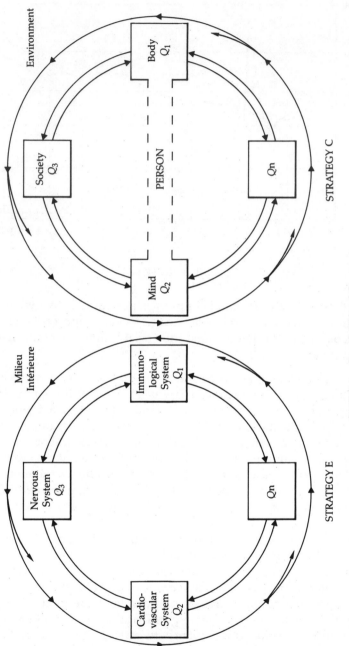

SLIDE 1   Two Medical Strategies

# Competing Medical Strategies: An Illustrated Argument

## SLIDE 1 NARRATIVE

Here the two strategies—engineering and cybernetic—are viewed in their most general form. Both are systemic in orientation. The system of Strategy E embodies the biological organism. The system of Strategy C embodies the biopsychosocial unity in open exchange with the environment. In presenting each strategy, an undefined element in the system $(Q_n)$ is included to indicate the unlimited number of potentially significant interacting variables.

SLIDE 2   Disease Concept Illustrated by Two Explanatory Strategies

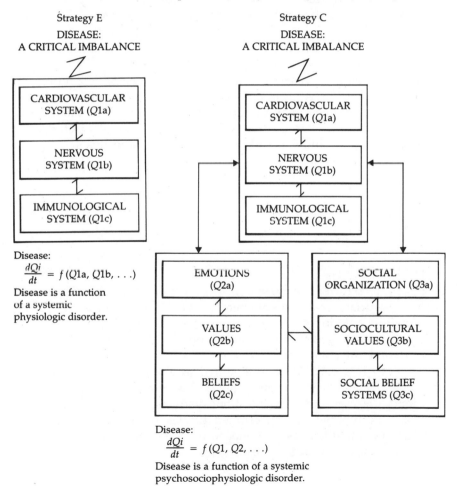

Strategy E
DISEASE:
A CRITICAL IMBALANCE

CARDIOVASCULAR SYSTEM ($Q$1a)

NERVOUS SYSTEM ($Q$1b)

IMMUNOLOGICAL SYSTEM ($Q$1c)

Disease:
$$\frac{dQi}{dt} = f\,(Q1a,\ Q1b,\ \ldots)$$
Disease is a function of a systemic physiologic disorder.

Strategy C
DISEASE:
A CRITICAL IMBALANCE

CARDIOVASCULAR SYSTEM ($Q$1a)

NERVOUS SYSTEM ($Q$1b)

IMMUNOLOGICAL SYSTEM ($Q$1c)

EMOTIONS ($Q$2a)

VALUES ($Q$2b)

BELIEFS ($Q$2c)

SOCIAL ORGANIZATION ($Q$3a)

SOCIOCULTURAL VALUES ($Q$3b)

SOCIAL BELIEF SYSTEMS ($Q$3c)

Disease:
$$\frac{dQi}{dt} = f\,(Q1,\ Q2,\ \ldots)$$
Disease is a function of a systemic psychosociophysiologic disorder.

## SLIDE 2 NARRATIVE

For brevity of exposition, Slide 2 represents a blow-up of the three rectangles of Slide 1 marked $Q_1$, $Q_2$, $Q_3$. The slides that follow will likewise constitute a limited extrapolation of the strategies presented in Slide 1.

In Strategy E, disease is defined as a function of a systemic physiologic disorder. Disease can be mathematically expressed:

$$\text{Disease:} \quad \frac{dQi}{dt} = f(Q1_a, Q1_b, \ldots)$$

where $Q1_i$ represents any body system, organ or function, for example the nervous or cardiovascular system. Thus, disease is a function of mutually interacting physiologic systems.

In Strategy C, disease is defined as a function of a systemic biopsychosociologic disorder. It is mathematically expressed:

$$\text{Disease:} \quad \frac{dQi}{dt} = f(Q1, Q2, Q3, \ldots)$$

In this definition, $Q1$ represents the physiologic system, $Q2$ represents the psychologic system, and $Q3$ represents the sociocultural system. Each of these systems may be further broken down into subsystems, thus $Qja$, $Qjb$. . . . Here disease is a function of mutually potentiating psychophysiologic and sociocultural systems. Without this synergy the disease may not occur.

## SLIDE 3 NARRATIVE

Strategy E recognizes the cause of disease to be a physical pathogen. As such, appropriate treatments are perceived to be correspondingly physical in nature: antibiotics, serums, vaccines, etc. Thus, disease is successfully viewed as a physiologic phenomenon, and therapeutic interventions assume the patient as a physical entity.

Strategy E is particularly well suited to diseases that characterized the subject of nineteenth-century medical attention, notably nutrition-deficiency diseases and acute infectious diseases like pneumonia, tuberculosis, and typhoid. The presumed causes of these diseases were isolated and identified as pneumococcus, tubercle bacillus, etc., predominantly physical pathogenic agencies.

SLIDE 3     Exemplar Strategy E: Disease-Cure Process

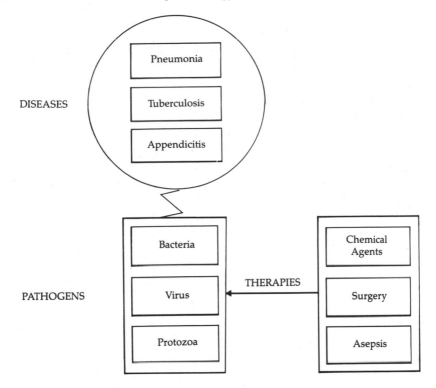

## SLIDE 4 NARRATIVE

Strategy C recognizes the causes of disease to be multifactorial and interdependent, ranging from physical to mental, emotional, and sociocultural agents. Appropriate treatments are perceived to be correspondingly multimodal and interdependent—for example, chemical therapy, support, and behavioral learning therapy administered in combination. Thus, with reference to Strategy E, disease is reconceived as an interactive biopsychosociologic phenomenon, and therapeutic interventions assume the patient as a psychophysiologic unity in an open systems relationship with the social environment.

Strategy C is particularly well suited to diseases that command twentieth-century medical attention, notably chronic degenerative diseases like heart disease, cancer, hypertension. The presumed causes of these diseases comprise a complex network of interdependent genetic, biochemical, environmental and psychosocial factors. In other words, the Strategy C disease-cure process shows how psychosocial and physical states work together in the onset, course, and cure of disease.

SLIDE 4    Exemplar Strategy C: Disease-Cure Process

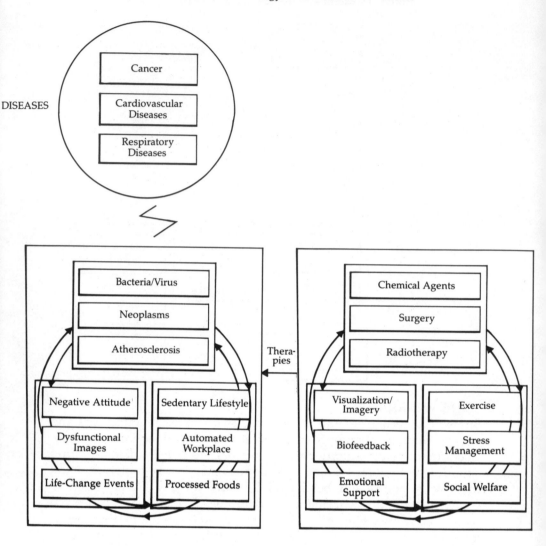

## SLIDE 5 NARRATIVE

Using Strategy E, the etiology of a contemporary disease (atherosclerosis) can be delineated as illustrated. The precipitating causal event of atherosclerosis is seen as intimal vessel injury, which leads to fibrin and lipid deposits, which further lead to placque formation, clot formation, and eventually to an occlusion of a coronary artery.

SLIDE 5    Exemplar Strategy E: Etiology

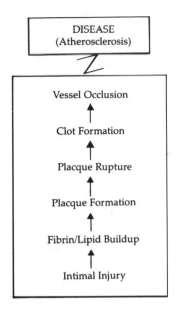

## SLIDE 6 NARRATIVE

In order to account for the novel source of the characteristic twentieth-century diseases, the concept of stress was introduced. Its physiology was traced and incorporated into the etiology of these diseases. The resulting etiology yielded an enlargement of Strategy E analysis, called here Strategy E'. This illustrates the physician's second option, mentioned earlier, in which the physician assigns a role to extraphysiologic factors and develops an enlarged physicalistic vocabulary for dealing with them. In this strategy the initial event is no longer an intimal vessel injury but extraphysiologic stimuli ("stressors"), which, consistent with biomedical premises, can be reduced to a chemically mediated nervous system reaction. This reduction process is represented by the dashed box on the right. This reaction is treated as a putative causal factor (represented by the dashed arrow) in the production of the disease, in the present instance atherosclerosis.

Unlike Strategy E, Strategy E' seeks to account for a stress component in the etiology of a contemporary disease. It does so by reducing it to its physiological correlate states.

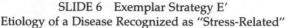

SLIDE 6   Exemplar Strategy E'
Etiology of a Disease Recognized as "Stress-Related"

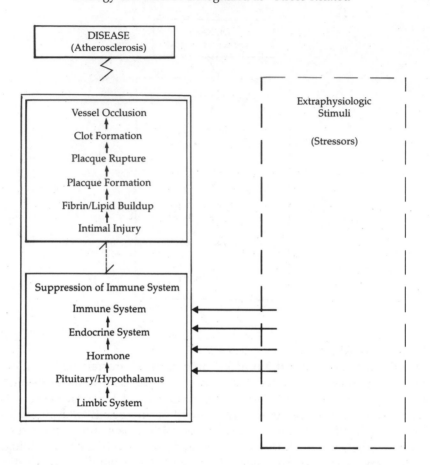

## SLIDE 7 NARRATIVE
Strategy E etiology of a contemporary disease dictates the kinds of therapies here identified. The end result of the pathogenic process in Strategy E is the occlusion of a coronary vessel, myocardial infarction. Recognized and accepted therapies are here illustrated, streptokinase, angioplasty, etc. Appropriate therapies are seen as an artifact of the disease concept (definition of disease).

## SLIDE 8 NARRATIVE
Strategy E' etiology of a contemporary disease calls for therapies that take into account both components of the disease process, the cardiovascular system component of Strategy E and the stress-related nervous

SLIDE 7    Exemplar Strategy E: Etiology and Therapy

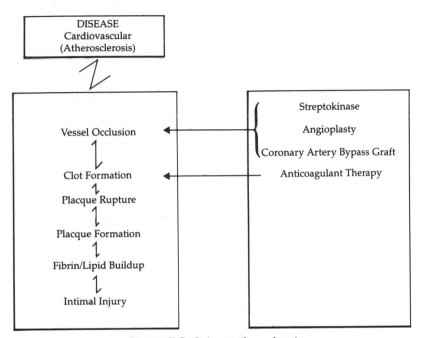

Strategy E Goal: Arrest atherosclerosis
by means of revascularizing the vessel,
the primary source of atherosclerosis.

system component proper to Strategy E'. Therefore, Strategy E' incorporates as a proper subset the etiology of Strategy E.

In Strategy E', "stress" is recognized as a contributing cause of disease, the stressor having a physiologic correlate. Thus, in order to stem this pathogenic agent, the tactic is to block the production of the endogenous chemical recognized as the source of the body's stress reactions. A current illustration of this tactic is described in a *Time* cover story on medicine, "Stress: Can We Cope?" (June 6, 1983): "In late 1981 scientists at the Salk Institute synthesized the remarkable chemical that triggers the body's stress reactions. . . . the substance, called corticotropin releasing factor (CRF), is produced in the hypothalamus, a tiny but powerful structure sometimes called 'the brain's brain.' Having duplicated CRF, the Salk scientists now hope to produce a modified version of the chemical that would actually block the body's reaction to stress." Whether or not their particular efforts prove successful, because the tactic followed by these "Salk scientists" is representative of Strategy E', here we will let "anti-CRF" symbolize the therapy type sought.

SLIDE 8    Exemplar Strategy E'
Etiology and Therapy of a Disease Recognized as "Stress-Related"

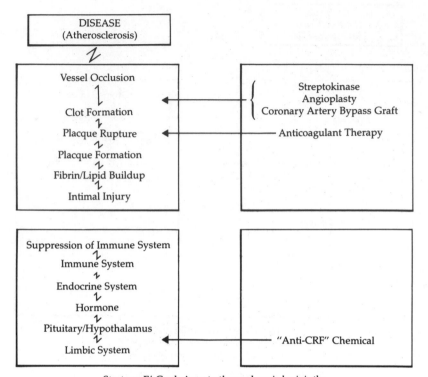

Strategy E' Goal: Arrest atherosclerosis by jointly
(a) revascularizing the vessel and (b) blocking "CRF"
production, the primary source of atherosclerosis.

## SLIDE 9 NARRATIVE

The etiology of a contemporary disease as seen in Strategy C is a function of the interaction of physiologic, psychologic, and sociologic systems. Here the precipitating causal event is multimodal, involving the mutual potentiation of systems. This illustrates the physician's third option, previously mentioned, in which the physician acknowledges the presumed role of the extraphysiologic factors and develops an alternative explanatory strategy with its own unified vocabulary for dealing with them. Now disease is seen as the synergistic product of interacting systems ($Q1, Q2, \ldots$). Therefore, the etiology of Strategy C incorporates as proper subsets the etiologies of Strategies E and E'.

Strategy C etiology of a contemporary disease calls for a combination of therapies that acknowledges each of the modalities identified in the production of disease: physical, behavioral, and sociocultural. Appropriate therapies for Strategy C may then range over streptokinase, visualization, and social behavior learning administered in combination. Dosages of each are scaled to the particular diagnosis of the disease under consideration. Because of their ability to activate one another, the joint effect of these therapies is more than the sum of their effects when administered independently.

SLIDE 9   Exemplar Strategy C
Etiology and Therapy of a Disease Recognized as an "Affliction of Civilization"

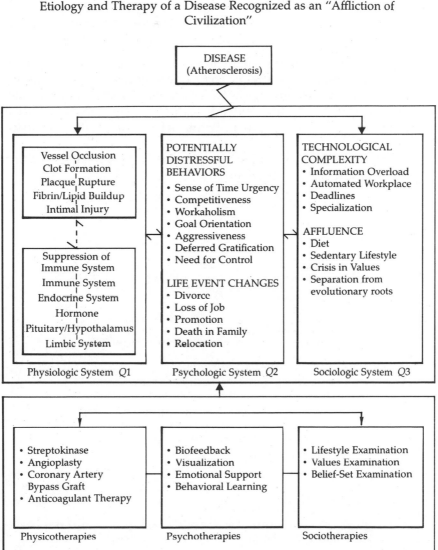

## SLIDE 10 NARRATIVE

The implication of Strategy E' can be expressed in a reductionist (fundamental micro-level) vocabulary in two propositions:

1. The role of stress (behavioral stimuli) in the production of disease can be interpreted as a brain-body interaction: a neurochemical hormonal release can produce a dysfunctional physiologic stress reaction.
2. Effective treatment is drug therapy aimed at blocking the neurochemical stress reaction.

The implication of Strategy C can be expressed in an interactionist (interaction of micro and macro levels) vocabulary in two propositions:

1. The role of stress (behavioral stimuli) in the production of disease can be interpreted as a mind-body interaction:[1] psychosocially induced anxiety can produce a dysfunctional physiologic stress reaction, which can in turn exacerbate the anxiety, which can then produce . . . , and so on in a mutual causal positive feedback process.
2. Effective treatment includes behavioral therapy aimed at blocking the psychosocially induced anxiety.

### SLIDE 10

#### TWO PREMISES OF PATHOGENESIS: STRATEGIES E' AND C

E'   Neurochemical hormonal release (e.g., "CRF") can produce
dysfunctional physiologic stress reaction:
BRAIN-BODY INTERACTION.

C    Psychosocially induced anxiety (e.g., high demand–low
control workplace) can produce dysfunctional
physiologic stress reaction: MIND-BODY INTERACTION.

#### CONSEQUENT STRATEGY THERAPIES

E'   Chemical therapy (e.g., "anti-CRF" drug) administered
to block neurophysiological stress reaction.

C    Stress management theory (e.g., relaxation)
administered (with or without chemical therapy)
to block psychosocially induced anxiety.

---

1.  See Chapter 9 for a discussion of the difference between the philosophic position of Cartesian interactionism and the cybernetic circularity of Strategy C.

SLIDE 11 NARRATIVE

In Slide 10, two premises of pathogenesis and consequent therapies were identified for Strategy E' and Strategy C. In Slide 11 we see the disease spectrum that is implied by these strategies.

The illustration indicates that the two strategies conflict in a significant way. Because they define "acute disease" differently, they therefore differ in terms of what the root cause of the disease is and, importantly, what it is that is the responsibility of the physician to treat. The significance of these two orientations to disease can be highlighted by contrasting (in simplified terms) the treatment rationale and procedures in dealing with atherosclerosis. This contrast will indicate why the heavy (etiological factor) line is more extensive in the Strategy C than the Strategy E' disease spectrum.

The Strategy E' physician recognizes two important elements within the acute disease area. The first element is the physical manifestation of atheroclerosis, which begins with the intimal injury and concludes with vessel occlusion. The second element is the stress-related discharge of the "CRF" chemical, which impacts the limbic system and may lead to suppression of the immune system. (Both of these elements are depicted in Slide 8). Counteracting these two elements of acute disease defines the task of the Strategy E' physician. (Given a medical emergency, priorities would dictate immediate administration of strategy E therapies.) Since both elements are physiological in nature, the proposed therapy would consist of administering streptokinase, etc. (see slide 8), for the first element and, an (hypothesized) "anti-CRF" chemical to counter the second element, the stress-related discharge. Upon successfully dealing with these two elements, the limits of the responsibility of Strategy E' physician have been reached. The patient, having regained the strength to move out of intensive care can anticipate moving into the rehabilitative medical phase. Here, the health care professional is likely to review the "risk factors"—diet, sedentary lifestyle, work pressures, etc.—that may have contributed to the condition.

The Strategy C physician also recognizes two elements in the acute disease area. As in the Strategy E' analysis, the physical manifestation of atherosclerosis (vessel occlusion) is recognized as requiring immediate medical attention. The second element, however, is defined in behavioral terms, in recognition of the expanded spectrum of what constitutes acute disease. This difference turns on the issue of what qualifies as an etiological factor. The strategy C physician would recognize as an instance of the second element the interaction of a stressful situation and a specific personality profile. Thus, regarding the first element of acute disease, the Strategy C physician would follow suit with the Strategy E' physician and administer streptokinase, etc., for the physical manifestations of the disease. But he or she might also administer a behavior therapy, e.g., clinical biofeedback, for the second element. Depending on the particular diagnosis, the Strategy C physician would define the "destructive personality" factor as an etiological factor and within the physician's responsibility. Such responsibility is mandated by the model.

The difference between the Strategy E' designation of stress as a risk factor and the Strategy C designation of it as an etiological factor is significant. In Strategy E' it is designated as a risk or complicating factor on the basis of statistical findings in epidemiological studies correlating certain personality types with the incidence of atherosclerosis. Significantly, such findings are *ad hoc* with respect to the Strategy E' theoretically recognized causes of disease. In Strategy C it is designated as an etiological factor on the grounds that behavioral variables are theoretically recognized as potentially significant pathogenic agents. The prospective benefit of the latter option is that which accrues to any scientific theory: the theory seeks to fit known findings (e.g., epidemiological findings) into a context, connecting them into a pattern of relations. In addition, it indicates where new findings may be sought; and these too will be part of the pattern and, in the present context, may enlarge medicine's inventory of effective therapies. That the two therapeutic strategies will have a different impact on the patient is illustrated in Slide 12.

SLIDE 11

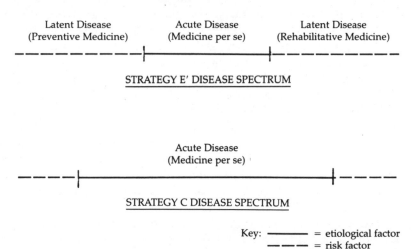

| Latent Disease | Acute Disease | Latent Disease |
|---|---|---|
| (Preventive Medicine) | (Medicine per se) | (Rehabilitative Medicine) |

STRATEGY E' DISEASE SPECTRUM

Acute Disease
(Medicine per se)

STRATEGY C DISEASE SPECTRUM

Key: ——— = etiological factor
— — — = risk factor

SLIDE 12 NARRATIVE

In Strategy E', therapeutically desired effects [△] can be achieved through the clinical use of chemical interventions [↘] upon autonomic body functions [B].

In Strategy C, roughly comparable therapeutically desired effects [△] can be achieved through the clinical use of biofeedback intervention [↘] upon autonomic body functions [B].

The mechanism accounting for the chemical–autonomic body function interaction is well documented in neurophysiological literature and need not be further referenced here. On the other hand, clinical biofeedback is a relatively new phenomenon whose precise mechanism is still controverted. However, any descriptive account of the process will necessarily include a description of cybernetic circularities involving both neurophysiological and intentional components (which themselves will of course have a neurophysiological correlate). One representative description of this "black box" cybernetic process is given by Barbara Brown:

> . . . there is an internal, presumably a cerebral, information-processing system capable of discriminating productively useful information and activating physiological mechanisms to achieve specific, directed changes in physiologic activity. . . . The element that is common to biofeedback seems to be the development of a keen awareness of internal events; the difficulty in the concept is that such an awareness can be specific to pinpoint accuracy yet inexpressible by conventional means of information. The communication of the awareness may be solely by the physiologic change, i.e., a biological communication. . . . The process becomes completely internalized, and the control over the physiological function can be activated by intention, i.e., by voluntary control. (1978, 22–23, 18)

Whereas the top visual is consistent with reductionist premises, from the Strategy C viewpoint the bottom visual clearly is not. One may designate the box and circle variously; mind and body, mind-brain and brain, intention and physiologic function, etc. The Strategy C contention is that, however designated, they are mutually irreducible. That is, they belong to different logical types: the "internal, presumably a cerebral, information-processing system capable of discriminating productively useful information and activating physiological mechanisms to achieve specific, directed changes in physiologic activity," i.e. Ⓜ, is irreducible to the "physiologic activity" it activates, i.e. Ⓑ. Hence, interactionist premises would be mandated in order to account for the demonstrated efficacy of clinical biofeedback treatment.

SLIDE 12

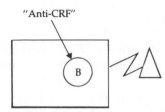

"Anti-CRF"

STRATEGY E' THERAPY

Biofeedback Signal

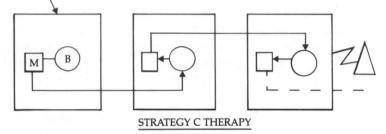

STRATEGY C THERAPY

## SLIDE 13 NARRATIVE

Slide 13 contrasts the outcomes of Strategy E' and C therapeutic care to the stress-related disease under consideration—in this case, hypertension as often instrumental in the production of atherosclerosis. Because of the chronic nature of the disease, the dashed lines signify likely successive reappearances of the disease (or, alternatively, recurrences of the disease symptoms) over time as one after another life event triggers a dysfunctional stress reaction.

According to Strategy E', an illustration of the proper therapy to combat the (physical) stress reaction syndrome would be, ideally, the administration of, for example, an "anti-CRF" drug. The purpose of this drug is to achieve a certain desired physiological state (Δ). Such procedures are theoretically rationalized by the premises of Strategy E'. Should the disease and its attendant stress reaction reoccur, the procedure would be reinitiated. While it might be necessary in subsequent incidences of the disease to strengthen the "anti-CRF" dosage, the procedure remains essentially the same. Nothing in the procedure lessens the likelihood that the disease and its attendant symptoms (stress reaction) might reoccur in the future.

The Strategy C approach shares with E' the same commitment to combat the physical stress reaction. To do this, the strategy C physician uses a combination of behavioral (e.g., biofeedback) and/or physical (e.g., pharmaceutical ["anti-CRF"]) therapy options. These two therapeutic options are used alone or interactively to combat the stress reaction and achieve the desired physiological state. In addition, the Strategy C physician has a second agenda, and that is to achieve a change in the patient's *behavioral* response to future stressful situations. This agenda is administered through behavioral learning therapy, termed here psychobiofeedback to indicate the theoretically rationalized goal in behalf of which the biofeedback process is being used. Here the goal is to internalize over time a different behavioral pattern on the part of the patient to ongoing or stockpiling stressful life events (loss of a job, bereavement, deadlines, etc.). This sought-for change in behavioral response is illustrated by the increasing size of the rectangle ($\square$) until the desired behavioral state is reached, noted by $T_n$. Within each time frame, the long- and short-term therapy of Strategy C is illustrated. Short-term therapy may combine biofeedback with traditional E' treatment to achieve the desired physiological state. (For brevity, the drug therapy is not illustrated in the C strategy.) The distinctive feature of Strategy C is the long-term goal of psychobiofeedback to gradually internalize the patient's modified behavioral response pattern to the ever-present stressful life event, thereby avoiding the stress reaction and the repeated need for more short-term therapy. The goal of psychobiofeedback is achieved at the point that the behavioral learning process is internalized, i.e., has become part of the patient's habitual behavioral pattern.

This twofold agenda of Strategy C constitutes the quantum difference. In Strategy E' there is no formally rationalized defense against the likely reoccurrence of the stress reaction. While, to the contrary, Strategy C, recognizing the stress reaction in certain diagnoses to be a product of a behavioral disposition to a life event, addresses the behavioral roots of this reaction: it theoretically rationalizes a twofold therapy that gets both at the dysfunctional physiological stress reaction as well as the behavioral source of that reaction. So doing, it thwarts what, in the Strategy E' perspective, are the likely chronic reoccurrences of the disease. In this respect, Strategy C recognizes a different time frame for the disease. Namely, the disease is said to span the period between the dysfunctional behavioral disposition ($T_1$) and the formation of the functional behavioral disposition ($T_n$). Stress-related diseases are not chronic diseases per se, any more than infectious diseases. Rather, they are "acute" diseases whose therapy necessitates an enlarged time span (enlarged by E' standards) to treat the disease's behavioral roots. Thus the different segments shown are viewed, within the C perspective, not as discrete reoccurrences of the disease but as a continuum measured by the duration of a single protracted disease state subject to curative measures directed at both physiological (short-term $\triangle$) and behavioral (long-term $\square$) symptoms. Unlike the E' perspective, then, the disease cure can only be represented by the realization of the triangle in combination with the comparably sized rectangle. Anything less is to address the symptoms, not the cause, a distinction possible only within the C perspective.

Hence, the treatment protocol of each strategy is such that the difference in their outcomes (a) is experimentally measurable and (b) is short-term in E' ($\triangle$) and short-term and long-term alike in C ($\triangle$, $\square$). Furthermore, were the E' strategist apprised of this "long-term" disease remedy, he or she would embrace the strategy that entailed it. That the E' strategist is not formally aware of it is explained by the fact that, without a behavioral component in his or her model, there is no reason to strategize ways of getting at this long-term behavior-oriented solution.

With respect to the disease in question—hypertension—the C strategist predicts and theoretically rationalizes that its treatment protocol will both alleviate the disease symptoms (stress reaction $\triangle$) and thwart its reoccurrence. The E' strategist can predict and theoretically rationalize only the alleviation of symptoms. The quantum difference may be expressed by saying that both C strategy contentions and only the single E' contention are experimentally borne out. So, to use the idiom of Strategy E', while one strategy systematically addresses the "acute" dimension of the disease, the other systematically addresses both its "acute" and "chronic" dimensions.


SLIDE 14 NARRATIVE
In Strategy E, disease is defined as the product of the interactive effects of pathogenic perturbations ( $\uparrow$ ) of the various physiologic subsystems ($Q1a$, $Q1b$ . . .). Treatment procedures are accordingly defined as the products of the interactive effects of therapeutic perturbations ( $\uparrow$ ) of the same physiologic subsystems.

In Strategy C disease is defined as the product of the interactive effects of pathogenic perturbations ( $\uparrow$ ) of three different major systems ($Q1$, $Q2$, $Q3$). Treatment procedures are accordingly defined as the product of the interactive effects of therapeutic perturbations ( $\uparrow$ ) of the same three major systems.

Invoking the analogy of an iceberg, the waterline separating tip from base divides the domain of the etiologic factors (causal determinants of disease, $\uparrow$ ) and risk factors (occasions of disease, $\uparrow$ ). Consequently, it divides the domains of scientific medicine or medicine per se and preventive/rehabilitative medicine.

In the top illustration (Strategy E), the waterline divides the physio-

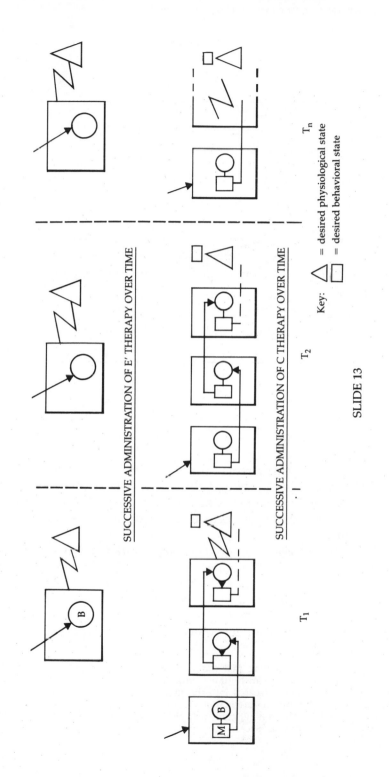

SUCCESSIVE ADMINISTRATION OF E' THERAPY OVER TIME

SUCCESSIVE ADMINISTRATION OF C THERAPY OVER TIME

$T_1$     $T_2$     $T_n$

Key: △ = desired physiological state
□ = desired behavioral state

SLIDE 13

SLIDE 14

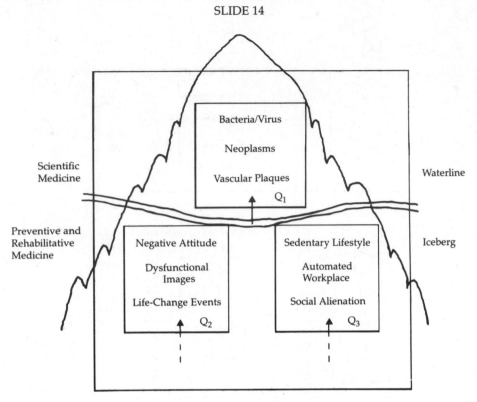

Strategy E

logic and the other two systems—the psychologic and sociologic. Consequently, from the perspective of the bottom illustration (Strategy C), essential arcs connecting the systems are severed such that the resulting diagnostics and therapeutics focus exclusively on just one dimension of a unified whole.[2]

The clinical consequences of choosing a Strategy E or a Strategy C perspective are depicted in Slides 15 and 16. The first slide depicts a sample expert system printout of a Strategy E protocol for atherosclerosis, with its expectations of a single type of pathogenic agency ($Q1$). The second slide depicts a sample expert system printout of a Strategy C protocol, with its expectations of a combination of types of pathogenic agencies ($Q1$, $Q2$, $Q3$).

2. It should be understood that the waterline as drawn is intended only to be contrasted with the more shallowly drawn Strategy E waterline. Its position is relative, depending on the state of research into the multifactorial causes of disease. As more factors are identified, future representations would be adjusted accordingly. The present representation seeks only to highlight a few of the most widely researched and hence easily identified extrasomatic factors.

SLIDE 14 (cont.)

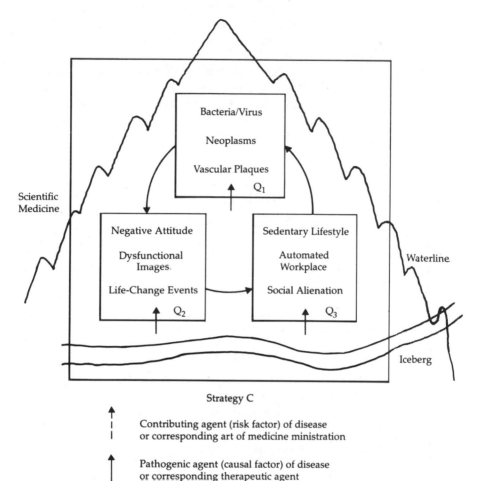

Strategy C

↑  Contributing agent (risk factor) of disease
or corresponding art of medicine ministration

↑  Pathogenic agent (causal factor) of disease
or corresponding therapeutic agent

## SLIDE 15 NARRATIVE

***A Hypothetical Strategy E Expert System: Atherocin I.***[3] Atherocin I specializes in the diagnosis and therapy selection for patients with atherosclerosis. Its goal is to provide sound therapeutic advice using available Strategy E information to identify all known significant contributing disease factors. Its model of logic is the use of "production rules" which represent facts and their interrelationships. The Atherocin I knowledge base consists of some finite number of such rules. Essentially, each rule is an IF . . . THEN statement, which encompasses a set

3. Adapted from description of MYCIN, Freiherr 1983, 37, 38.

of preconditions to justify a conclusion. For example, IF the patient has crushing substernal chest pain; is pale, cold, clammy, diaphoretic, nauseated with 12-Lead EKG, S-T elevation in Leads II, III and AVF; THEN there is suggestive evidence (.7) that the patient is evolving an inferior myocardial infarction.

Atherocin I is able to identify symptomatic and electrocardiographic evidence of myocardial infarction; prescribe appropriate analgesic, seda-tive, antiarhythmic, and pacemaking therapies; and explain, in detail, its advice. When recommending a diagnosis or therapy, Atherocin I lists the rules and cites literature references used in the decision-making process.

SLIDE 15    Strategy E Expert System
ATHEROCIN I

**HOW DO YOU USE THE TYPE OF THE HEART DISEASE?

THE FOLLOWING RULES USE:
    THE TYPE OF THE HEART DISEASE

132, 114, 176

WOULD YOU LIKE A SUMMARY OF ALL THE PARAMETERS CONCLUDED BY THESE RULES?

**NO

WHICH OF THE RULES DO YOU WISH TO SEE?

**132

RULE 132
--------

IF:    1) THE DISEASE WHICH REQUIRES THERAPY IS HEART DISEASE, AND
       2) THE TYPE OF HEART DISEASE IS ATHEROSCLEROTIC, AND
       3) THE HEART CATHETERIZATION DOCUMENTED SEVERE TWO-VESSEL DISEASE, AND
       4) THE PATIENT HAS EXERCISE INTOLERANCE, AND
       5) THE PATIENT HAS ANGINA WITH EXERTION, AND
       6) THE PATIENT HAS EKG EVIDENCE OF AN OLD INFERIOR MYOCARDIAL INFARCTION, AND
       7) THE PATIENT HAS A 70 PACK/YEAR HISTORY OF CIGARETTE SMOKING, AND
       8) THE PATIENT'S FATHER DIED AT AGE 47 OF HEART DISEASE, AND
       9) THE PATIENT HAS DIABETES CONTROLLED BY ORAL AGENTS

THEN:  THERE IS SUFFICIENT EVIDENCE (.7) THAT INDEROL 40 mg. q6h AND DILTIAZEM 10 mg. q8h WOULD INCREASE EXERCISE TOLERANCE AND RELIEVE ANGINA.

AUTHOR: FM
JUSTIFICATION:  BETA-BLOCKING AGENTS AND THE CALCIUM-CHANNEL BLOCKING AGENTS INCREASE EXERCISE TOLERANCE AND RELIEVE ANGINA.

LITERATURE:

(Adapted from a MYCIN printout, a computerized consultant on certain infectious diseases that diagnoses, recommends therapy, and justifies decisions.)

SLIDE 16    Strategy C Expert System
ATHEROCIN II

**HOW DO YOU USE THE TYPE OF THE HEART DISEASE?

THE FOLLOWING RULES USE:
THE TYPE OF THE HEART DISEASE

132, 114, 176

WOULD YOU LIKE A SUMMARY OF ALL THE PARAMETERS CONCLUDED BY THESE
RULES?

**NO

WHICH OF THE RULES DO YOU WISH TO SEE?

**132

RULE 132
--------

IF:    1) THE DISEASE WHICH REQUIRES THERAPY IS HEART DISEASE, AND
      2) THE TYPE OF HEART DISEASE IS ATHEROSCLEROTIC, AND
      3) THE HEART CATHETERIZATION DOCUMENTED SEVERE TWO-VESSEL DISEASE, AND
      4) THE PATIENT HAS EXERCISE INTOLERANCE, AND
      5) THE PATIENT HAS ANGINA WITH EXERTION, AND
      6) THE PATIENT HAS EKG EVIDENCE OF AN OLD INFERIOR MYOCARDIAL INFARCTION, AND
      7) THE PATIENT HAS A 70 PACK/YEAR HISTORY OF CIGARETTE SMOKING, AND
      8) THE PATIENT'S FATHER DIED AT AGE 47 OF HEART DISEASE, AND
      9) THE PATIENT HAS DIABETES CONTROLLED BY ORAL AGENTS
     10) THE PATIENT IS MALE, 59, UNIVERSITY PROFESSOR, AND
     11) THE PATIENT IS MARRIED, WIFE AND TWO DAUGHTERS ALL ATTENDING THE
PATIENT, AND
     12) THE PATIENT HAS TYPE-A PERSONALITY, AND
     13) WIFE REPORTS THAT PATIENT HAS FELT EXTREME TENSION AND ANXIETY FOR
THE PAST THREE MONTHS, AND
     14) PATIENT'S HAND GESTURES SHOW SENSE OF LOSS OF CONTROL, AND
     15) PATIENT SERVES ON SEVEN COMMITTEES, THREE INTRA-UNIVERSITY, TWO
UNIVERSITY-INDUSTRY, AND TWO MULTINATIONAL CORPORATION BOARDS, AND
     16) COLLEAGUE EXPRESSED CONCERN ABOUT PATIENT'S ANXIETY REGARDING HOW
HOSPITALIZATION WILL IMPEDE COMPLETION OF CURRENT RESEARCH PROJECT.

THEN:  1) THERE IS SUFFICIENT EVIDENCE (.8) THAT INDEROL 40 mg. q6h, DILTIAZEM
10 mg. q8h AND RELAXATION THERAPY 20 min. q8h WOULD INCREASE
EXERCISE TOLERANCE AND RELIEVE ANGINA, AND
      2) THERE IS SUGGESTIVE EVIDENCE (.6) THAT FAMILY MEMBERS' AND COL-
LEAGUES' VISITS SHOULD BE LIMITED TO 15 MIN. TWICE PER DAY AND
THAT THEY SHOULD BE INFORMED OF REASONS FOR LIMITATION AND INSTRUCTED
IN DESIRED BEHAVIORS IN PRESENCE OF PATIENT.

AUTHOR: FM
JUSTIFICATION: TYPE-A PERSONALITIES ARE DISPOSED TO NEED TO DISPLAY CONTROL OF
SELF AND ENVIRONMENT IN THE PRESENCE OF FAMILY AND CO-WORKERS. THIS
DISPLAY ACTIVATES PHYSIOLOGIC PROCESSES THAT THE BETA-BLOCKER IS
DESIGNED TO DEACTIVATE, HENCE COUNTERACTING DESIRED EFFECTS OF THE DRUG
THERAPY. INCREASED BETA-BLOCKAGE MAY LEAD TO UNDESIRABLE SIDE EFFECTS.

REFERENCES: R. ROSENMAN AND M. FRIEDMAN

SLIDE 16 NARRATIVE

*A Hypothetical Strategy C Expert System: Atherocin II.* A correlate of Atherocin I, Atherocin II, based upon the premises of Strategy C, would take the form illustrated in Slide 16. Atherocin II, like Atherocin I, specializes in diagnosis and therapy selection for patients with atherosclerosis. Its goal is to provide sound therapeutic advice using available Strategy C information to identify all known significant contributing disease factors. Its model of logic conforms to that of Atherocin I. Its knowledge base consists of some finite number of production rules. Each rule is an IF . . . THEN statement that encompasses a set of preconditions to justify a conclusion. Here one of these rules of the embryonic rule base can be exemplified. For example, IF the patient has a Type A profile and IF the patient is under heightened work pressure and the patient has crushing substernal chest pain and is pale, cold, clammy, diaphoretic, nauseated, with 12-Lead EKG S-T elevation in leads II, III, AVF; THEN there is suggestive evidence (.8) that the patient is evolving an inferior myocardial infarction.

Atherocin II is able to identify symptomatic evidence of interacting physical, psychological, and social pathogenic agencies of the atherosclerotic process leading to myocardial infarction; prescribe joint physiologic and behavioral therapies; and explain, in detail, its advice. When recommending a diagnosis or therapy, Atherocin II lists the rules and cites literature references used in the decision-making process.

SLIDE 17 NARRATIVE

A strength of the medical model that is based on Strategy E—the biomedical model—is the degree to which it constitutes a fully scientific medicine. That is, the principles of the sciences which comprise biomedicine, such as physiology, pathology, bacteriology, are themselves grounded in empirically validated basic physical and biophysical sciences—statistical thermodynamics, molecular biology, etc. (tier 2). The explanatory strategy animating these basic sciences includes such methodological directives as reductionism and determinism (tier 1). Moreover, the principles of these basic sciences are consistent with those directives in that the greater the degree of the empirical confirmation of these principles, the greater the reason for continued confidence in the soundness of those directives. Hence, the double arrows linking tier 1 and tier 2. In addition, the greater the degree of the therapeutic successes yielded by the applied medical sciences (tier 3), the greater the reason for continued confidence in both the basic sciences and their explanatory strategy on which the applied sciences rest. Hence, the double arrows linking the coupled tiers 1 and 2 with tier 3.

It is this complex, mutually reinforcing, three-tiered structure that makes the biomedical model a scientific model. These are the necessary conditions that must be satisfied by any medical model in order to qualify as scientific.

SLIDE 17   Components of a Scientific Model for an Applied Medical Science

STRATEGY E

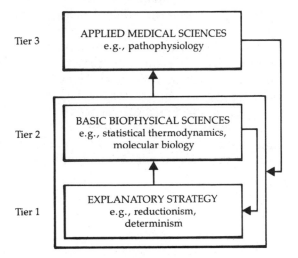

SLIDE 18   Components of a Scientific Model for an Applied Medical Science

STRATEGY C

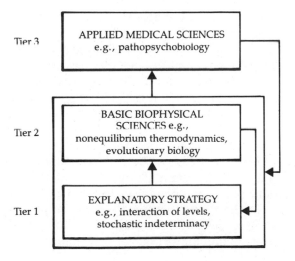

SLIDE 18 NARRATIVE

Slide 18 indicates how the medical model based on Strategy C might satisfy the necessary conditions stipulated in the narrative for Slide 16 for a model to qualify as scientific. That is, the principles of the sciences that comprise a Strategy C approach, such as "pathopsychobiology," are themselves grounded in empirically validated basic physical and biophysical sciences. These latter sciences range from evolutionary, i.e., post-neo-Darwinian, biology to nonequilibrium thermodynamics (tier 2). The explanatory strategy animating these basic sciences includes such methodological directives as interactionism and stochastic indeterminacy (tier 1). The principles of these basic sciences are consistent with those directives such that the greater the degree of the empirical confirmation of these principles, the greater the reason for continued confidence in the soundness of those directives. Hence, the double arrow linking tier 1 and tier 2. Finally, the greater the degree of the therapeutic successes yielded by the applied medical sciences (tier 3), the greater the reason for continued confidence in both the basic sciences and their explanatory strategy on which the applied sciences rest. Hence, the double arrows linking the coupled tiers 1 and 2 with tier 3.

# Conclusion

Strategy E' recognizes risk factors in the production of stress-related diseases like atherosclerosis. These may include life-change events "ranging from overwork and quarreling to loss of a job to a death in the family." The E' response to this recognition is to address the derivative physiological reaction to the stressful situation. This approach treats the life event as a risk factor—the cause of stress, not the cause of disease. It is the chemical stress reaction that is considered the cause of disease and thus the focus of therapy. This is consistent with the premises of an engineering medical model that defines disease, etiology, and therapy in physical terms—action by impact. This is the E' strategist's story of stress, and it is limited to a physiological stress reaction story.

According to the C strategist's story of stress theory, therapy also entails behavioral learning. Therapy includes internalizing "flow" behavior in the presence of situations inhibiting fight-or-flight and so preventing the chemical stress reaction. Such a strategy capitalizes on the cybernetic insight that certain life events in interactive combination with dysfunctional behavioral responses to them are the cause of stress and that this, in further interaction with significant psychosociobiological variables, is the cause of disease. Hence, according to the Strategy C stress story, counteracting the stress reaction chemically and *not* behav-

iorally fails to medically address a significant etiological factor—specifically, those life factors which do not permit of fighting or fleeing because
of the nature of social or psychosocial organization. According to this
story, chemical therapy alone is after-the-fact therapy, that is, treatment
of symptoms, not causes.

According to Strategy C, the research agenda would be to subsume
chemical options as one element in an increasingly refined array of
therapeutic options. Such a research agenda would require development of a psychosociobiological morphology whereby such variables as
life-change events, social organization, and psychological makeup interact in ways that measurably influence health and disease.

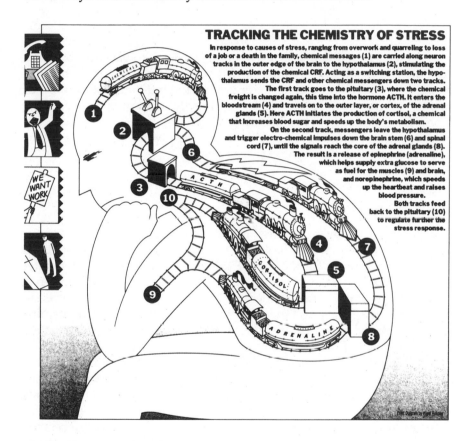

**TRACKING THE CHEMISTRY OF STRESS**

In response to causes of stress, ranging from overwork and quarreling to loss
of a job or a death in the family, chemical messages (1) are carried along neuron
tracks in the outer edge of the brain to the hypothalamus (2), stimulating the
production of the chemical CRF. Acting as a switching station, the hypothalamus sends the CRF and other chemical messengers down two tracks.
The first track goes to the pituitary (3), where the chemical
freight is changed again, this time into the hormone ACTH. It enters the
bloodstream (4) and travels on to the outer layer, or cortex, of the adrenal
glands (5). Here ACTH initiates the production of cortisol, a chemical
that increases blood sugar and speeds up the body's metabolism.
On the second track, messengers leave the hypothalamus
and trigger electro-chemical impulses down the brain stem (6) and spinal
cord (7), until the signals reach the core of the adrenal glands (8).
The result is a release of epinephrine (adrenaline),
which helps supply extra glucose to serve
as fuel for the muscles (9) and brain,
and norepinephrine, which speeds
up the heartbeat and raises
blood pressure.
Both tracks feed
back to the pituitary (10)
to regulate further the
stress response.

From *Time*, June 6, 1983.

# 12

## Disease Causation: Two Explanations

The interaction of different levels of organization (bio, psycho, socio) is a central feature of the infomedical framework for explaining medical events. The claim that there are, for example, mind-body interactions or mental events that "cause" disease directly confronts conventional biomedical thinking. The following discussion focuses on both the biomedical and infomedical positions on this pivotal issue—the claims and counterclaims regarding disease causality.

## Background

A debate sparked by an editorial in the *New England Journal of Medicine* concerning the role, if any, of the psyche in promoting disease serves as a useful springboard for examining the question posed in this chapter and pursued in the next: Is disease causation an essentially unidirectional or multidirectional phenomenon? Correspondingly, what is an appropriate diagnostic and therapeutic strategy? In our next chapter this question takes the form: Is disease causation an essentially determinate or indeterminate phenomenon?

In this editorial Marcia Angell raised the question whether disease is a reflection of mental state (1985*a*). The editorial was prompted by two studies that appeared in the journal within several months of each other, one on cancer and the other on heart disease (Cassileth et al. 1985; Case et al. 1985). The findings of each raised questions concerning mental state as a significant factor in treating disease in its later stages. From this, Angell generalized: "The fact that these well-designed studies were negative raises the possibility that we have been too ready to accept the venerable belief that mental state is an important factor in the cause and cure of disease." Angell's strongly phrased biomedical reductionist position provides an opportunity to examine the status of this controversy over disease causation. A close examination of her position is revealing. For example, it serves to identify the paradigm-dependent criteria for evidence.

Interestingly, even studies that argue against "other level" (e.g., mental) causal factors are reluctant to close the door completely on such interaction. For example, the Cassileth study says that its findings are consistent with the speculation "that psychosocial factors have a role in causing or influencing the course of malignant disease under some circumstances and in some persons" (1985, 1555). And the Case study allows that its results "do not invalidate the effects of all emotional factors on coronary disease," citing approvingly a study that asserts such an effect (1985, 741). Still, in Angell's estimate, "The literature contains very few scientifically sound studies of the relation, if there is one, between mental state and disease." She sets the tone for this debate by concluding that "it is time to acknowledge that our belief in disease as a direct reflection of mental state is largely folklore" (1985*a*, 1572). Although this is perhaps stronger language than most biomedical proponents would use, it nevertheless sets the biomedical reductionist position in sharp relief. To appreciate this orientation, it is helpful to consider the conventional estimate of the solution to an earlier disease once believed to be associated with psychosocial factors, tuberculosis. Doing so will help clarify the way terms like *causal factor, disease determinant,* and *pathogenic agent* are used in disease research.

Once described as a disease of excessive feeling, tuberculosis is in biomedical terms a model of what Susan Sontag in *Illness as Metaphor* calls the "myths" that come to surround particularly dreaded diseases of unknown origin. Many believe that such myths, like those surrounding cancer today (a "disease of depletion"), need to be dispelled, and "Interestingly, when the cause of such a disease is discovered, it is usually relatively simple and does not involve psychological factors. For example, the elaborate construct of a tuberculosis-prone personality evaporated when tuberculosis was found to be caused by the tubercle bacillus" (Angell 1985*a*, 1571). This use of the verb *caused* is telling when it is contrasted with its use by proponents of a more holistic approach. Hence, we can identify two uses of the term:

1. The tubercle bacillus *causes* tuberculosis.
2. Mental state (e.g., a disease-prone personality) is a major factor in *causing* specific diseases.

The meaning of this use of *cause*, whereby the tubercle bacillus is said to cause tuberculosis, is brought home when we recall the problem that the discovery of the bacillus resolved. Historically, seventeenth- and eighteenth-century clinical investigators left nineteenth-century tuberculosis researchers with two sets of problems. The first involved the questions "What *is* the disease tuberculosis?" and "How do we identify patients who suffer from it?" According to the historian Lester King, only after having an answer to these questions did the second set of problems present itself: "What factors will necessarily bring it about?" and "What is its proximal cause?" (1982, 218). Answers to these questions awaited the development of the successive eras of pathology, microscopy and bacteriology. Not until the last third of the nineteenth century was clinical observation sufficiently refined for solving the first set of problems. Jean-Antoine Villemin showed the contagious nature of tuberculosis, and Robert Koch demonstrated the specific organism, the tubercle bacillus, adding, says King, "a crucial limiting condition to the causal network" (1982, 218). None of the remote causes identified to that time—catarrh, scrofula, hemoptysis, the anatomical tubercle—would lead to tuberculosis unless the specific tubercle bacillus was present. "This discovery allowed physicians to speak with complete confidence about the disease entity." But, adds King, this was not a solution to the second set of problems: "This criterion, however had negative value only and did not involve any causal necessity. If the patient did not harbor the bacillus, he did not have tuberculosis; but if the bacillus was present in the body, he did not necessarily have the disease" (1982, 218).

This appeal to the history of tuberculosis helps fix the precise role assigned to the tubercle bacillus. The bacillus was not found to be *the* cause of the disease (its proximal cause) but *a* cause, albeit a singular one in that it was an indispensable factor in its pathogenesis. In logical terms this may be expressed by saying: If $T$ (tuberculosis), then $A$ (tubercle bacillus): $(T \rightarrow A)$. But the converse does not of course follow: If $A$, then $T$: $(A \rightarrow T)$. And only when both conditions hold can we speak of *the* cause, the proximal cause of the disease. In the case of tuberculosis, as in virtually every disease, this comprises a network of factors.

For convenience of reference we may distinguish symbolically the three relevant causes mentioned:

Proximal cause:              $(T \rightarrow A)$ and $(A \rightarrow T)$
Indispensable-factor cause: $(T \rightarrow A)$ but not $(A \rightarrow T)$
Remote cause:               Neither $(T \rightarrow A)$ nor $(A \rightarrow T)$ but
                            $(T \rightarrow B)$,

where B denotes host susceptibility.

The clinical importance of these disease equations will be immediately apparent. For without them we cannot address such practical questions as "Among those harboring the bacillus *(A)*, why do some contract tuberculosis while others do not?" The answer is expressed in the following disease equation by $(A + B)$:

EQUATION 1
    $(A + B) \nrightarrow T$ (Tuberculosis)

With reference to our symbolism, $(A + B)$ can be expressed as a proximal cause:

$$[ (A + B) \rightarrow T ] \text{ and } [ T \rightarrow (A + B) ].$$

But observe that $B$ (host susceptibility) is an elastic concept. We might speak of fibrous tissue as a cause or, again, of cellular processes that account for the fibrosis. Always there are next-level questions to be asked. Data increase in amount, the conceptual framework slowly changes, and the pattern that we call disease gradually takes on new boundaries. Again, this expansion is illustrated from the history of tuberculosis. We may take as a baseline the finding of the prominent eighteenth-century physician William Cullen that any disease that seemed to result in phthisis (tuberculosis) acted by producing an acrimony that in turn produced tubercles. Trying to bring order into a confusing mass of phenomena, Cullen had to fall back on general explanatory concepts like acrimony which, as King observes, to our modern ears sounds like a catch-all. And in fact, "With the further growth of knowledge during two hundred years the single vague concept became subdivided into several more precise terms each of which served a portion of the total explanatory function. . . . Ferments and acrids, quite satisfactory at one time, gave way to more precise concepts of bacterial infection" (1982; 29, 198–199). Such historical developments support the biomedical advocate's reluctance to deviate from the biology of the disease. Staying the course has proved productive in the past.

Today's concepts always appear, in the succeeding era, as catch-alls. Acrimony is in this respect the rule, not the exception. With the arrival of the bacteriological era, medical researchers had advanced from concepts like acrimony to that of the tubercle bacillus. As a result of the work of Virchow, Villemin, Koch, and others, a wide diversity of syndromes in both animals and humans could be shown definitively to be different strains of a single disease. And this served, in turn, to generate still further questions, questions of pathogenesis:

> How do the different forms of the disease arise? What factors are responsible for the remarkably varied appearance that can occur in different cases? The answers involve not merely bacteriology and pathology, but also a new but closely related science, immunology. And with the study of immunology we enter the fifth phase of the history of tuberculosis. (King 1982, 64)

Now the study of tuberculosis came to focus on such interacting concepts as virulence, native and acquired resistance, and hypersensitivity. While the clinical disease depends on the presence of the bacillus, emphasis shifts to what Claude Bernard called the *milieu intérieure:* what renders the patient vulnerable in the presence of this agent? The tubercular infection is explained through immunological mechanisms. Acrimony breaks down into such modern topics as the physical chemistry of blood proteins, hypersensitivity reactions, and their correlations with lymphocytes and protein moieties.

As each successive era produces next-level questions, investigation burrows ever more deeply, at each stage extending the levels of organization of the configuration we call disease (tuberculosis): person (emaciation), organ (exulceration), tissue (necrosis), cell (bacillus), and so on. What causes the symptom at the person level may be posited as itself caused by something at the tissue level, and so on. Determinants or etiological factors at one stage (humor, acrimony, caseation, tumor, bacillus) at a later stage are symptoms or accompaniments: What causes the tumor? What makes the bacillus virulent? And conversely, as the hierarchy of organizational levels expands, what were recognized as complicating or risk factors, e.g., emphysema, may be built into the disease equation. This sequence of historical eras inversely matches a hierarchy of explanatory levels in the study of the disease and gives support to today's molecular theory of disease causation (see Table 12.1).

From this serpentine growth of the conceptual framework in which tuberculosis is viewed, we see that the tubercle bacillus is the cause of the disease only in the qualified sense of Equation 1: the combination of the tubercle bacillus *(A)* and host susceptibility factors *(B)*, defined immmunologically, produces tuberculosis *(T)*. Hence, B might be said to define a tuberculosis-prone organism.

With reference to the two numbered propositions above, we may now subdivide the first one to read:

TABLE 12.1   Hierarchy of Explanatory Levels

| HISTORICAL ERAS | TUBERCULOSIS (a case study) | | EXPLANATORY CONCEPTS |
|---|---|---|---|
| | Clinical observation | (hectic fever) | |
| | Clinicopathology | (tubercle) | |
| | Microscopy | (blastema) | |
| | Bacteriology | (bacillus) | |
| | Immunology | (*milieu intérieure*) | |

1a. The tubercle bacillus causes tuberculosis.
1b. Bodily state, "the immunological status of the patient," is a major factor in causing tuberculosis.

Combining these, we have our disease equation: $(A + B) \not\!\!/ T.$

Where does this series of next-level questions stop? King offers this perspective:

> The clinical disease depends on the presence of the bacillus, to be sure, but in the present immunological era greater importance rests on what the older physicians called the internal factors. These we now interpret as the multiple features that we lump together as the immunological status of the patient. These relate to the topics of susceptibility, resistance, and reactivity. And these, in turn, are affected by other factors. (1982, 68)

What other factors? At first this succession of factors would seem to be limited only by our knowledge and the boundaries of the patterns that our ideology or strategy permits us to call disease. Given a biomedical strategy, we might further enlarge our hierarchy by tracking molecular or genetic factors that explicate the mechanisms forming the tuberculosis-prone organism. In fact, "There are already portents of the next stage, which may prove to be the era of heredity, wherein perhaps hereditary factors will determine the immunological factors that will in turn determine the pathological picture and clinical course" (King 1982, 68). Our organizational hierarchy is accordingly deepened; the *milieu intérieure* is further plumbed:

| Immunology | *Milieu intérieure* |
|:---:|:---:|
| ↓ | ↑ |
| Genetics | ("TB gene") |

Probing still further, we might imagine an elementary particle level of analysis, though at present molecular and genetic biology represent innermost frontiers of biological research. Have we, then, with genetics reached the bottom line? From the perspective of a biomedical strategy, the answer would seem to be yes—thus, today's molecular theory of disease causation.

So far, our analysis shows that reservations regarding other-level factors in disease causality are both in accord with biomedical injunctions as well as with general trends in disease research. However, questions continue to arise regarding other-level disease factors. Decades of research findings continue to mount. The *New England Journal of Medicine* editorial that discounts such findings can be interpreted as a statement of the biomedical counterposition. The persistent question is whether there are leveraging "external" or psychosocial factors in *addition* to internal or biological factors, a relevant *milieu extérieure* as well as *milieu intérieure*. Interpreting the concept of immunology in its most general, etymological sense of susceptibility, might we meaningfully speak of the bio-immunological and the "psycho-immunological" status of the human patient? In this event, disease would result from the *interplay* of the patient's bio-immunological and psycho-immunological states, mutually interacting internal and external factors. Calling these conjectural external factors C, the disease equation would now be enlarged to read:

EQUATION 2:

$$A + (B \times C) \mathcal{N} T$$

Essentially, this is the counterclaim of today's growing body of medical studies that propose a pathogenic role for psychosocial factors. In defense of biomedical reductionism, Angell cites Bernard Fox's extensive critical review of this literature as it pertains to the genesis of cancer (1978). Fox offers reasons for saying that these studies "are less convincing than many seem to think," noting that "Most studies have not . . . described a rationale for relationships sought" (1978, 45). Still, he is reluctant to dismiss the potential significance of external factors in the genesis of cancer. He sees difficulties in research design as an overriding issue, not the very legitimacy of psychosocial factors. Interestingly, he offers little support for the position that when the cause of a disease like cancer is discovered, "it is usually relatively simple and does not involve psychological factors" (Angell 1985*a*, 1571). In fact, Fox's own provisional model on the role of premorbid psychological factors and/or stress in the initiation of cancer seems closer to Equation 2 above. Thus, "At a first approximation, with a given susceptibility and a given exposure to a carcinogen, the excess probability of tumors provoked by stress over that expected will be a linear function of the dose of stress" (1978, 109).[1] Here, the carcinogen corresponds to an indispensable factor cause *(A)*, the given susceptibility to an internal factor *(B)*, and the stress (or psychological factor) to an external factor *(C)*. Thus, $A + (B \times C) \mathcal{N} N$ (neoplasm).

The confrontation between biomedical reductionists and the proponents raising other-level questions ("psycho-immunologists") crystallizes over the issue of causation. What are the grounds, both experimental and scientific, which allow one to say that such-and-such is a cause of disease?

The classical point of reference for normative criteria are Koch's

1. "Psychological factors and/or stress that produce particular changes in the body are likely to make it easier for similarly particular cancer sites to succumb to internal or environmental carcinogens" (Fox 1978, 111). In a later study, Fox further moderates his claim for the role of psychological factors in influencing medical outcome: "They do so in small degree, only in certain people, and under circumstances specific to their coping capabilities, hormone response, tumor status, genetics, and psychological states" (1984).

celebrated postulates. Briefly, these are that the agent must be present in every case of the disease; it should occur in no other disease as nonpathogenic; and, once isolated in a pure culture, it should be able to induce the disease anew. In the hundred or so years since their formulation, however, the path leading to pathogenic agents in viral and other infectious and noninfectious diseases has broadened considerably. Except for a number of animal diseases, very few diseases besides tuberculosis and tetanus have been found to meet such stringent postulates. Alfred Evans speaks of the "particular irony" of Werner Henle's discovery in 1968 of the causative relationship of the Epstein-Barr virus to infectious mononucleosis. Henle, the grandson of Koch's teacher, Jacob Henle, who had himself explicitly anticipated Koch's postulates, formulated his criteria of immunologic proof "without fulfilling a single one of the postulates set up by his grandfather and by Robert Koch" (1978, 252). Chronicling the successive limitations that researchers have found necessary to impose in their efforts to track the circuitous route from causative agent to disease, Evans concludes that, while fulfillment of these postulates is reasonable grounds for accepting a causal role of a suspected agent, lack of fulfillment should not exclude such a relationship. His explanation elucidates the etiological complexity of many of today's slow viral and chronic neurological diseases, including cancer. It is worth quoting at length:

> Causation in both infectious and non-infectious disease involves a complex interplay of agents, environmental, and host factors. The latter include the host's immunologic status, genetic background, socioeconomic level, hygienic practices, behavioral patterns, age at the time of exposure and the presence of coexisting disease. Different qualitative and quantitative mixes of the agent, environment, and host may result in the same clinical and pathological diseases under different circumstances. (1978, 254)

This depicts pathogenesis as the complex interplay of physical agents and environmental and host factors. This prompts the question "If not Koch's postulates, then what are the criteria that internal, or physical, factors must fulfill in order to qualify as causative?" Evans cites amendments to Koch's original criteria that researchers over the past century have found necessary to make. These include the addition of epidemiological and immunological elements of causation, multiple causation, and different causes at different settings for the same syndrome.

Evans's historical perspective documents a changing definition of the term *cause*. Practical considerations have dramatically relaxed criteria that researchers ask a putative agent to satisfy to count as causative. As a result, the concept of disease and its causation is complexified.

# An Expert System View of Causation

To arbitrate the claims between biomedical reductionists and the psychoimmunologists requires a closer look at the pivotal term *cause*. A helpful way to clarify how this term is used in etiological research is to see how it has surfaced in the field of artificial intelligence as applied to medicine. Here, all assumptions, premises, and framework-dependent biases surface as they are built into decision-making programs for clinical use.

## PROJECT RX: AN OVERVIEW

One important result of efforts to assist medical decision-making via computational models of intelligent behavior, often called "expert systems," has been to make both researcher and clinician alike methodologically more self-conscious concerning the links between the data and the rules that rationalize diagnosis and treatment. Now we possess a technique for automating the process of generating and testing hypotheses about causal relations in medical data banks. Hypothesized links between disease states and their conjectural pathogenic agents are therefore subject to more formal scrutiny, as are hypothesized links between disease remission and its therapeutic agents. Robert Blum's "Project RX" is a prototype of this procedure for grounding and expanding clinical rules by automating the process of generating, testing, and validating hypotheses about causal links. Blum describes his project as aimed at emulating "the usual method of discovery and confirmation of medical knowledge that characterizes epidemiological and clinical research. . . . [it] is a prototype system for automating the discovery and confirmation of hypotheses from large clinical data bases" (Blum 1982, 165). Ordering the sequential steps involved, the project aims at showing that a formal logic underlies clinical diagnostics and therapeutics and exposing that logic. To illustrate, Blum asks us to consider the following hypothetical scenario:

> Suppose a medical researcher has noticed an interesting effect in a small group of patients, say unusual longevity. He carefully examines those patients' records looking for possible explanatory factors. He discovers that heavy physical exertion associated with occupation and sports is a possible factor in promoting longevity.
>
> Interested in pursuing the hypothesis that heavy physical exertion predisposes to long life, the medical researcher consults with a statistician, and together they design a comprehensive study of this hypothesis. First they analyze the results of the study on their local data base, controlling for factors known to be associated with longevity. Having confirmed the hypothesis on one data base, they proceed to test the hypothesis on many other data bases, modifying the study design to allow for differences in the type and quantity of data.
>
> Having confirmed the hypothesis, they publish the result, and other

researchers proceed with further confirmatory studies, attempting to elucidate the mechanism of the "exercise effect." When future researchers study other factors that influence longevity, they control for physical activity.

To demonstrate this cycle in which knowledge gradually evolves from data through a succession of increasingly comprehensive studies, Blum draws a feedback loop (Fig. 12.1), noting that "At each stage of discovery and confirmation existing medical knowledge is used to design and interpret the studies" (1982, 165–166).

Besides a medical data base, the RX program consists of four major parts: the discovery module, the study module, a statistical analysis package, and a knowledge base. To indicate the character of their interrelations Blum offers a second loop (Fig. 12.2), this time a discovery and confirmation loop:

> The discovery module produces hypotheses "*A* [causes] *B*." The hypotheses denote that in a number of individual patient records, "*A* precedes and is correlated with *B*." Information from the knowledge base is used to guide the formation of initial hypotheses.
> The study module then designs a comprehensive study of the most promising hypotheses.
> The statistical analysis package is invoked by the study module to test the statistical model.
> The knowledge base is used in all phases of hypothesis generation and testing. . . . Newly incorporated knowledge is appropriately labeled as to source, validity, evidential basis, and so on. As the knowledge base grows, old information is updated. (Blum 1982, 165–167)

The Evolution of Medical Knowledge

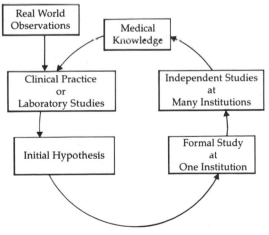

Source: Blum 1982, 166.

FIGURE 12.1

Discovery and Confirmation in RX

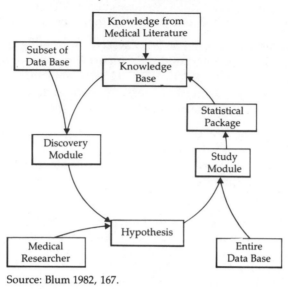

Source: Blum 1982, 167.

FIGURE 12.2

Underlying the discovery and study modules is an operational definition of causality possessing three properties. Blum elaborates these three properties as (1) time precedence: $A$ generally precedes $B$; (2) covariation or association: the intensity of $A$ is correlated with the intensity of $B$; (3) nonspuriousness: there is no known third variable $C$ responsible for the correlation. The importance of this definition will emerge below when we examine the model-sensitive character of the application of computer-assisted decision-making (CADM) procedures like RX.

"These three properties," says Blum, "are the foundation of the RX algorithm." He explains:

> Causality can never be proven using observational data. The persuasiveness of a given demonstration simply depends on the extent to which the three properties have been shown.
>     The function of the *discovery module* is to find candidate causal relationships. The discovery module exploits only the first two properties of causal relationships to do this: time precedence and covariation. (1982, 173)

Applying this exploitation of the causal relationship properties, Blum enters the following hypothesis. It forms the basis of the RX Project:

> Prednisone *(A)* elevates cholesterol *(B)*.

The study module parses this hypothesis by matching the tokens in the input string to determine their classification in the knowledge base. The pattern that matches is: *variable relationship variable*. "Prednisone" and "cholesterol" are the variables and "elevates" is the relationship. The program encodes them as follows:

> Prednisone is a known concept.
> It is classified as a Steroid which is a Drug which is an Action.
>
> Elevates is a known concept.
> It is classified as a Relationship.
>
> Cholesterol is a known concept.
> It is classified as a Chemistry which is a Lab-Value which is a State. (1982, 176)

The study module is "the core of the RX algorithm." Its function is to take as input a causal hypothesis which can be gotten

> either from the discovery module or interactively from a researcher. It then generates a medically and statistically plausible model of the hypothesis, which it analyzes on appropriate data from the data base.
>
> The study module is patterned after a sequence of steps usually undertaken by designers of large clinical studies. Its design may be considered an exercise in artificial intelligence insofar as it emulates human expertise in this area. (1982, 175)

As its activities indicate, the study module is model-independent. It parses the hypotheses fed it from the medical knowledge base and applies statistical techniques for assessing the validity of the causal relationship posited by the hypothesis. The medical knowledge base, a subset of the knowledge base, is distinct from the statistical package. For Blum's RX Project the medical knowledge base is itself a subset of the American Rheumatism Association Medical Information System (ARAMIS), a vast collection of detailed longitudinal rheumatism patient information. "Its first-order subtrees are *states* and *actions*, which in turn are broken down into *signs, symptoms, lab findings, diseases* and into *drugs, surgery,* and *physical therapy*." Significantly, Blum adds that "the categories of diseases and other entities follow the conventional nosology based upon organ systems and/or pathology found in any standard textbook of medicine" (1982, 169–170). Here he cites the widely used Harrison's *Principles of Internal Medicine* as providing the medical knowledge base for the RX Project.

We see that although the system's internal workings are model-independent, its sources of data are not. This means that not only the data but the permissible kinds of data (state variables) fed into the knowledge base are model-dependent. As we will show, this dependence imposes constraints on what are well-formed sentences within the system's inferential apparatus. Its admissible actions and states (in the present instance, Drug and Chemistry) are physical, as likewise are any prescribed therapies. That is, actions, states, and therapies are consistent with a particular nosology, specifically that embodied in Harrison's *Principles*. We shall return to this point in a moment.

Blum stipulates that the purpose of constructing RX was in the first instance the development of methodology. He proceeds to furnish an overview of this methodology. As the project's title indicates, its aim is to provide a means for establishing causal ties between pathological states and their pathogenic roots; and, conversely, between treatment protocols and subsequent change from diseased to healthy state. These methods read like a basic text in statistics: a causal hypothesis with controls for confounding influences. Through deployment of this methodology, Blum is able to derive certain concrete results and so, as he says, modestly add to the medical knowledge base: "The effect of prednisone on cholesterol, strongly supported by this study, has been reported only a few times previously. No previous study has recorded the reproducibility of the effect over time or the interpatient variability as was done here" (1982, 185).

For present purposes it is useful to highlight the conditions that had to be satisfied to validate RX's hypothesized causal relationship and so enter it into its medical knowledge base. Doing so helps clarify the extent to which RX is and is not model-neutral. Each causal relationship (*A* causes *B*) entered into the study module is represented by a set of features that include intensity, frequency, direction, setting, validity, and evidence. Here validity is of special importance. It is measured, says Blum, on "a 1 to 10 scale distinguishing tentative associations from widely confirmed causal relationships" (1982, 172). This distinction between tentative associations and widely confirmed causal relationships is crucial. Noting that the validity score is a component of every causal relationship stored in the knowledge base, Blum characterizes it as "summarizing the state of proof of a relationship." He proceeds to describe the scoring procedure:

> The highest score that a study based on a single nonrandomized data base can achieve is 6. Higher scores can be obtained only from replicated studies, the highest scores requiring experimental manipulation and known mechanisms of action. A score of 6 means that "strong correlation and time relationship have been demonstrated after known covariates have been controlled in a single data-base study." (1982, 183)

The distinction between an *empirically confirmed covariation* and a *causal relationship* is built into the program and evokes Blum's earlier reminder that causality can never be proven using observational data. Programmatically, this means that possession of the above noted properties—time precedence, covariation, and nonspuriousness—carries with it a validity ceiling of 6. For a validity score converging on 10—the imputation of a bona fide causal relationship—two further properties need to be present, two additional conditions satisfied. All told, for full-fledged causality to be imputed to an *A/B* relationship, five conditions can be distinguished:

1. Time precedence
2. Covariation
3. Nonspuriousness
4. Replicability—experimental manipulation
5. Known mechanism

Satisfaction of conditions 1–3 yields a validity score between 1 and 6, a score in the neighborhood of 6 answering to "strong correlation and time relationship . . . after known covariates have been controlled in a single data-base study." For a validity score between 7 and 10, conditions 4 and 5 have additionally to be satisfied.

It is noteworthy that only the first four conditions pertain to direct experimentation procedures. The fifth condition signals the presence of a background framework. In order to furnish "a known mechanism of action," an appeal to "conventional nosology" (e.g., Harrison's *Principles*) is relevant. Since this nosology—in its broadest terms the biomedical model—underpins all the CADM programs or "expert systems" assembled to date, as a rule this mechanism may be taken for granted. It forms the background condition for the application of such systems, the more so once replicated studies and experimental findings have further substantiated earlier findings and raised the validity score to the 7–9 range. By this stage of the study its theoretical orientation has fully asserted itself; observations incorporated into the data base, for example, have been selected according to a relevance criterion.

The conclusion RX reaches on the basis of its experimental findings illustrates this general background condition. These findings, based on a sample data base containing the records of fifty patients with systematic lupus erethematosus (SLE), generated the following threefold conclusion: "Prednisone is thought to cause an increase (in cholesterol) . . . the time of delay is 'acute' (less than one average internist interval), and . . . the effect is highly statistically significant (p = .0001)" (1982, 184). These new links and details, and in particular the putative causal relationship between prednisone and cholesterol elevation, are duly incorporated as rules into the expanded knowledge base.

## An Alternative View of Causation

"Prednisone causes cholesterol" can be added to the medical knowledge base as a result of meeting the data base conditions 1–6 and the nosology conditions 7–10. Let us now examine the evidence for "Mental state causes coronary heart disease," a variation of the second proposition noted earlier. We may inspect this proposition by focusing on the results of an independent panel appointed by NIH to assess claims that such a connection exists.

In 1977, "recognizing the need for a comprehensive, impartial, and objective review" of the data regarding the impact of behavioral and environmental factors upon the cardiovascular system, the National Heart, Lung, and Blood Institute undertook a two-stage process to determine the efficacy of this research and its relevance to the prevention and control of coronary heart disease. After a careful review of the evidence, the panel declared that although "a primary causative role of type A behavior in the pathogenesis of coronary atherosclerosis has not been established," nevertheless it constitutes "an independent risk factor for coronary disease, on a par with hypertension, high serum cholesterol level and smoking" (1981). The question remains whether the evidence cited warrants this distinction between causative role and risk factor. To answer this question, we need to look closely at what the panel perceived to be the status of the evidence.

Raising the central question, "Does the behavior pattern characterized as type A play an etiologic role in atherosclerosis?" the study declares, "There is no evidence, even suggestive, that type A behavior contributes either directly or indirectly to the primary event: the formation of atheromata" (1981, 1207). All the same, the panel proceeds to reference "the classic work implicating the sympathetic nervous system and the adrenals in emotion and stress," and "more recent work on the regulation of the circulation and lipid mobilization, platelet aggregation and other processes potentially related to atherogenesis" (1981, 1207). Here it cites several experimental studies that show cardiovascular injury induced by sympathetic catecholamines. This raises the question whether, by means of a simplified diagram (Fig. 12.3), we might point to "suggestive" evidence for an "indirect" contribution by a type A behavioral syndrome to the formation of atheromata.

While the panel clearly believes the evidence cited falls short of establishing the links represented in this figure, it nevertheless acknowledges that the evidence implicates certain patterns of behavioral traits in collaboration with other environmental and host factors, mediated by the sympathetic nervous system, as significantly correlated with the disease. Thus the panel declares:

> The initial intuition of patterns of behavioral traits aggregating in some persons with CHD . . . has been repeatedly confirmed as a scientifically valid association of the broad behavioral type and CHD. (1981, 1211)

> More than 2 decades of research have solidly established that type A behavior pattern is associated with and is predictive of CHD. . . . (1981, 1209)

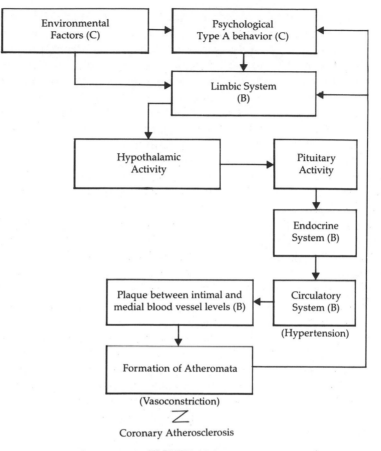

FIGURE 12.3

Several [studies] have reported . . . arteriographic findings . . . [that] support the hypothesis that type A patients have a more diffuse process that develops simultaneously in several vessels and that evolves more rapidly than do type B patients. This conclusion, if categorically established, would be important in relating behavior-associated physiologic mechanisms to the atherosclerotic process. (1981, 1209)

The panel notes some weaknesses to this latter argument, most notably one study that fails to find the postulated correlation.

Now, when we associate these findings and others with what Evans chronicles as the broadening of the causal concept during the period between late-nineteenth-century investigations into infectious diseases and mid-twentieth-century investigations into slow viral infectious and chronic neurologic diseases, we are tempted to conclude that they offer a matrix for fulfilling the newer criteria. In particular, criteria that recognize (in the case of viral diseases) "that the same clinical picture could be produced by a variety of different agents, that different agents predominate under different epidemiologic circumstances, and that the host response to a given virus [read: behavioral syndrome] would vary from one setting to another" (Evans 1978, 251). Admittedly, a mechanism is not securely in place, but this may reflect in part the fact that, as the panel asserts, "the basic pathophysiology of the development of atherosclerosis is not understood" (1981, 1209) and "the exact causal relationship between CHD and myocardial infarction is not known" (1981, 1208). With such a void in the pathophysiologic infrastructure, it is difficult to ascertain just what sort of psychophysiologic data are being sought that would provide suggestive evidence that Type A behavior contributes, directly or indirectly, to the formation of atheromata. It is not clear that the behavioral syndrome as a noncausal (i.e., risk) factor is being contrasted with anything—a causal, but not indispensable, factor. That is, the *only* known factors are either indispensable factor causes (e.g., vasoconstriction) or risk factors (e.g., organic factors, psychological factors).

Assuredly, there can still be and are a number of outstanding research questions. Is Type A behavior a factor "only in collaboration with other behavioral or physiologic factors, such as frustration, depression, job pressure, or an enhanced response of catecholamine activity" (Case et al. 1985, 741)? Does the Type A concept need to be "deglobalized"?: do hostility and unexpressed anger predominate over a heightened sense of time pressure (Dembroski et al., in press)? What precisely are "the chemical, neural and other physiologic mechanisms that could produce or exacerbate CHD as a consequence of a behavior pattern or life style" (Review Panel 1981, 1207)? Insofar as these questions and others remain unanswered, the panel is quite correct to call for further research into the missing links in the chain (or loop structure) connecting patterns of behavioral traits and CHD. But in this case "independent risk factor" might be understood merely as signifying that (1) the basic pathophysiology of the development of atherosclerosis is not understood, and (2) because there is suggestive evidence that a behavioral variable is implicated, the research agenda is to be converted into a search for the basic pathopsychophysiology of the development of atherosclerosis.

Certainly, from the perspective of Equation 2, this is how the evidence appears. That equation implies that the patient is a psychophysiologic unity and disease is a function of biopsychosocial maladaptation. It therefore assumes that certain behavioral as well as other factors are causally implicated in the pathogenesis of atherosclerosis. And the research task becomes to determine what proportion of total variance is accounted for by each of the interacting factor types. From this perspective, what the evidence suggests is, first, "a scientifically valid association of the broad behavioral type and CHD." And second, by means of the role of the sympathetic nervous system in emotion and of circulating catecholamines in precipitating cardiovascular complications, it suggests also "behavior-associated physiologic mechanisms to the atherosclerotic process." In short, it suggests the broad outlines of a mechanism by means of which way-of-life vectors, specifically Type A behavior, play a causal role in CHD.

Hence, rather than "no evidence, even suggestive, that type A behavior contributes either directly or indirectly to the . . . formation of atheromata," the evidence cited might be interpreted as indicating a mechanism incorporating variables like those of Figure 12.3. And it bears repeating that this conclusion—that the behavior pattern contributes to CHD only indirectly and the evidence for it is only suggestive— does not add up to the conclusion that the behavior pattern in question is a risk (as distinct from a causal) factor. We may symbolize a risk factor (R) as:

$$R \xrightarrow{\quad p \quad} [A + (B \times C) \not\vee D],$$

where this means: If $R$, then the probability that the disease process will be initiated is increased by $p$. But as the foregoing distinctions indicate, a difference in kind, not degree, separates the two factor-types. A causal factor, however remote (nonproximal), cannot be converted into a risk factor.

In summary, by bringing together and critically evaluating "all available research and theory linking behavior to coronary heart disease . . . and provid[ing] recommendations to the National Heart, Lung, and Blood Institute concerning future research" (1981, 1199), the panel has performed an invaluable service. Among other things, it has brought us to the brink of an important foundational question. While stopping short of proclaiming that the Type A behavior pattern "is of prime etiologic significance" in CHD, the panel clearly entertains such a possibility. It advocates that further experimentation be undertaken that might incontrovertibly ground this possibility.[2] And the implications of this for key biomedical premises are profound. For such a possibility implies a disease model like that depicted in Figure 12.3 (essentially a refinement of the panel's Model 1—p. 1203) according to which CHD is a function of biopsychosocial maladaptation and the CHD patient is, therefore, a psychophysiologic unity. Moreover, this psychic component of the patient cannot be assimilated to animal models of mental

2. As a result of the panel's recommendations, a five-year study of nearly one thousand volunteers was commissioned by the NHLBI to test whether altering Type A behavior reduces cardiac morbidity and mortality in postinfarction patients. Six months before the official end of the study, a review by government experts decided that the results were so clear that the study was ended and all participants in the control group began receiving psychological counseling (Friedman et al. 1986).

behavior for, as the panel declares, the syndrome in question qualifies "what are probably *uniquely human behavioral phenomena*" (1981, 1212; italics added).

As regards the career of biomedicine, this declaration, coupled with the above possibility, has revolutionary potential. For if we think of the science of medicine as the systematic diagnosis and treatment of disease, then this revised disease equation enlarges the scope of medical responsibility by an order of magnitude. Evans's criteria for disease causation reflect the results of a gradually shifting disease concept over the past hundred years or so. And the panel's orientation reflects the culmination of this shift. The early concept was that of disease as caused by a physical agent, like a bacterium or virus, invading or permeating the organism. From this relatively straightforward "germ theory" image, research led to a concept of disease as caused by a physical agent in combination with a network of interacting factors internal to the organism. And as the etiological roots of the diseases studied were found to branch still more extensively, research expanded to include the interaction of factors both internal and external to the organism. These included epidemiological and behavioral as well as systematically interrelated biological factors. But this enlarged equation—Equation 2—does not simply introduce an additional parameter $(C)$ into the disease equation. It recasts the loop structure by which disease is described, changing the boundaries of the patterns we call disease. Recall the contrasting "iceberg" images depicted in Slide 14 in the previous chapter. If disease is the product of environmental, behavioral, and somatic states, adequate diagnosis requires assessing the synergy of these states.

Accordingly, our working concept of the patient, a function of the disease concept, is altered. From being a biological organism subject to the depredations of a physical organic agent, the patient is reperceived, first as a complex organism consisting of different, interacting organizational levels, a biological *system*. And next, as these biological factors, notably immunological factors, are experimentally linked to other bodily and extrabodily factors—endocrinological, neurological, behavioral—internal and external factors come to be seen to mesh in a psychophysiological system. The rise of stress theory is a recent effort to harness this recognition. This progressive complexity in the patient concept is reflected in the sequence of disease equations marking the successive eras of bacteriology $(A \not\sim D)$, immunology $([A + B] \not\sim D)$, and psychoneuroimmunology $[A + (B \times C)] \not\sim D$, where the left-hand side of the equations symbolizes a developmental understanding of the patient.

The Cartesian dualism on which much of the biomedical edifice has been erected has been bridged. Or, at least, near the heart of the biomedical enterprise the twin pillars of biomedicine are undermined: interactionism threatens reductionism; and holism (psychobiology) threatens dualism (biology plus psychology). Primary determinants of disease are acknowledged as at least potentially coactivating physical and (uniquely human) behavioral agencies. Correspondingly, appropriate therapies might include physical and behavioral counteractants used synergistically. To assume that treating one agency is part of curative medicine (etiological factor) while treating the other is part of preventive medicine (risk factor) may be to cut off an essential arc in the pathogenic grid. There is a single causal nexus stretching as far "back" as our data and concepts take us. And, to judge from the panel's orientation, currently these may take us back to "a complex interplay of agents, environmental and host factors," where "environmental" now includes uniquely human psychological factors. Calibrating the differential strengths of the actors in this interplay defines one of today's leading research and clinical tasks. At its frontiers, then, biomedicine is biopsychosocial medicine. Or, because the implications of this finding have yet to be fully internalized, it is incipiently biopsychosocial medicine.

# The Nosology Issue

The reductionist, the proponent of biomedicine, and the interactionist, the proponent of infomedicine, differ over the notion of disease causality. For each, their position is a function of the medical model they embrace. To highlight the model-dependent nature of the debate, we may contrast RX's conclusion that "Prednisone causes cholesterol" with a hypothetical program testing the causal relationship between a different set of variables. In this program variables will consist of a cognitive-affective syndrome $(A')$ and an organic disease state $(B')$. Call this the RX II Project.

PROJECT RX II
Project RX II is designed to test the hypothesis: $A'$ causes $B'$. For the sake of argument, we will assume that a statistically rigorous experimental procedure conforming to the RX methodology has established a 1–4 validity score for the $A'/B'$ relationship virtually identical to that for the prednisone/cholesterol relationship $(A/B)$ in RX. How could RX II, but not RX, deal with this finding? What conclusion would it deduce? To answer this question is to see the role that the "conventional nosology" plays in the application of CADM programs like RX.

We have seen that, no matter how statistically significant the covariation, until condition 5 is satisfied, we cannot associate the agent (e.g., prednisone) with the etiology of the dysfunctional state (e.g., high serum cholesterol). That is, we cannot conclude that prednisone is a *causal* factor in the production of the dysfunctional or "diseased" state.

The reason for this is clear. Satisfaction of conditions 1–4 is consistent with *A* being a *carrier* for *B*, not a causal agent in its production. The species of insect that uniquely and always carries the microorganism responsible for a particular infectious disease can serve as an illustration of such a carrier—with the provision that the discipline of microbiology has not yet been developed nor the concept "microbe" forged. That is, because satisfaction of conditions 1–4 cannot yield an *explanation* for the *A*/*B* covariation, a "known mechanism of action," we cannot validly conclude that *A* is a causal (etiological) factor. At most, we can conclude that it is a situational or risk factor as regards *B*, although a very powerful one.

This indicates that when RX concludes that prednisone is thought to cause—not predispose to—an increase in cholesterol, the program has implicitly or explicitly appealed to a nosology like that embodied in Harrison's *Principles* for provision of a known mechanism elucidating the causal link. It indicates that a rationale is available for explaining the empirically observed covariation: knowledge of the chemistry of the drug coupled with knowledge of the biochemistry of the blood of SLE victims furnishes a *reason*, or mechanism, for the inferred pathways linking the ingestion of prednisone to cholesterol elevation.

But what if such a rationale is not available; then to what is RX to appeal? Harrison's *Principles*, for example, will not license a causal *A'/B'* relationship. Of course, the two chief hardware components of RX (and RX II)—the discovery and study modules—are model- or nosology-neutral. The operations of the discovery module deal mainly with temporal precedence and correlation, and those of the study module with spuriousness and nonspuriousness of correlation. The causality with which these modules deal, therefore, is of the strictly operational sort identified with conditions 1–4. However, the data base and subsequently the knowledge base (and medical researcher) components are model-dependent in that both selection and interpretation of data are guided by the conventional nosology and fed into the program from outside. This means that the nosology implicit to the data and knowledge bases on which the discovery and study modules draw for their operations licenses as well-formed only certain *variable relationship variable* instances and precludes others as ill-formed. So, "Drug-Action (prednisone) causes Chemistry-State (cholesterol)" is licensed as well-formed. Here the variables conform to types (physical) that the nosology recognizes as properly interactive. But a psychological or cognitive-affective state, for example a behavioral syndrome like *A'*, could not interact with one of the organic states of a biological organism—short of the former being translated into exclusively neurophysiological terms. The very expression crosses categories and so would be rejected by the program.

In short, the conventional nosology underwrites a mechanism that explains why the drug prednisone can elevate serum cholesterol blood levels, an explanation framed in languages like pathophysiology, microbiology, and pharmacology. These languages describe in biochemical detail the net effect of the interaction of the chemical components of prednisone with the blood chemistry of SLE patients. Thus, "Prednisone (variable) elevates (relationship) cholesterol (variable)" is a well-formed sentence in the language that underwrites the application of the RX algorithm, internal medicine. (And, when the other four conditions are satisfied, this sentence can be validly converted into its lawful counterpart: "Prednisone causes an increase in cholesterol.") This is the model's conventional nosology that Blum describes as "based upon organ systems and/or pathology found in any standard textbook of medicine." It is the state variables of that nosology—in a word, biomedicine—to which the otherwise neutral RX algorithm is applied.

The same background condition cannot of course be assumed for the cognitive-affective syndrome/organic disease *(A'/B')* correlation. Even hypothesizing that the other four properties, 1–4, obtain in equivalent strength, there is no known mechanism of action in the conventional nosology by which a mental state (variable) can be said to cause (relationship) organic disease (variable). A proposition so conjoining them is ill-formed inasmuch as it crosses categories in the way that "Mind event causes body event" crosses categories. The above-mentioned languages (pathophysiology, etc.) do not afford an explanatory mechanism (except in the reductionist sense already examined in Part Three). This distinction grounds one important methodological difference between being a causal and a risk, situational, or complicating factor.

Consequently, the second expression (Mental state causes organic disease) could be accorded well-formed status in RX only by adjusting its admissible state variables in the data and knowledge base boxes. That is, by replacing such languages as pathophysiology and its cognates, which underwrite the conventional nosology with successor languages, which underwrite as well-formed expressions of this second sort. In other words, by undertaking the formidable task of supplanting an institutionalized, multitiered working model by a successor model—fomenting revolution.

We can now further understand the basis for the mixed reactions in the medical community to experimental studies like those conducted over the past quarter of a century seeking to show a vital link between the cognitive-affective syndrome named Type A and the incidence of coronary heart disease. A plausible case can be made that these studies have experimentally demonstrated that "Type A behavior *strongly predisposes to* coronary heart disease," where the italicized expression signifies satisfaction of conditions 1–4. Our impulse, therefore, is to say, with the principal investigator of these studies, Meyer Friedman, that it has been experimentally shown that "Type A behavior can *cause* coronary heart disease."[3] On the other hand, there is a general reluctance on the part of the medical community as a whole to amend coronary heart disease treatment on the basis of what would otherwise appear to be a rather impressive array of epidemiologic, clinical, and pathologic studies.[4] Why is this so? Conceivably, were such evidence marshaled in behalf of a chemical rather than a cognitive-affective therapy, treatment would be appropriately amended. That is, there is a tendency within the medical community to apply the Inglefinger criterion (see Chapter 5) and conclude that (curative) medical practice will be influenced very little as a result of research findings on Type A behavior. Such findings (implies the criterion) show only that a certain type of behavior is a complicating or risk (as distinct from a causal) factor and, therefore, pertains more to preventive/rehabilitative medicine than to scientific/curative medicine. Just this language is used by the authors of one of these studies: "These data suggest that type A behavior can be altered in a sizable fraction of postinfarction patients and that such alteration is *associated with* a significantly reduced state of nonfatal myocardial infarctions" (Friedman et al. 1984, 237; italics added).

According to our analysis, this is a quite proper conclusion on the part of the investigators and, correspondingly, the medical community's response to these findings is likewise appropriate. Accordingly, Friedman is ill-advised to infer, as he does on occasion, that the evidence indicates that Type A behavior counseling *causes* a reduction of coronary heart disease recurrence. This inference betrays a misapprehension of the roles of preventive and curative medicine, and of their conceptual offspring, risk (situational) and causal (etiological) factors. This convention is attested to by noting that in the face of identical experimental evidence, RX and RX II would reach different conclusions. RX concluded that the drug in question was thought to *cause* a certain correlative event; whereas, with respect to the cognitive-affective behavior in question, RX could conclude only that such behavior was thought to *dispose to* or otherwise be associated with the referent correlative event. Only by reprogramming RX with an alternative nosology (that is converting RX into RX II) could it conclude that the interplay of the drugs and behavior is thought to *cause* the reduction in the disease state. The difference follows not from a difference in the strength of the experimen-

3. "Type A behavior can now be regarded, alone among risk factors, as a primary causal agent in the pathogenesis of coronary heart disease" (Friedman and Ulmer 1984, 30). The chapter in which this statement occurs was written by Friedman alone.

4. E.g., Haynes, Feinleib, and Kannel 1980, 37; Williams et al. 1982, 483; Blumenthal et al. 1978, 634.

tal evidence but from the semantic requirements of the strategy imposed by the nosology in whose behalf the program is enlisted.

Here the question arises: what are the practical consequences of not being able to entertain both options? Can we judge the merit of a strategy on the basis of the effectiveness of the therapies it dictates? Because the range of explanatory mechanisms sought is a function of the strategy selected, the infomedical model provides a norm for evaluating strategy selection: one strategy is preferable to another by the measure that (a) it derives from a scientifically grounded explanatory mechanism, and (b) this mechanism rationalizes more effective therapies in the treatment of a given disease.

Let us suppose that certain findings in the medical literature have, at face value, implicated a variety of levels of organization in the disease process. So, in the case of RX II, implicated are psychological ($Q2$) and social ($Q3$) as well as physiological ($Q1$) levels.[5] Within a strategy like that governing RX, resolution can proceed only toward translating these surplus, extrasomatic levels into their concomitant somatic counterparts. Only then can the referent pathology-inducing process be manipulated physically (e.g., pharmaceutically) to redress its pathogenic effects. RX investigation is in this respect unidirectional, proceeding from a reported pathogenic behavioral or social syndrome to its resolution into a single-level physicalist language. This strategy imperative derives from what Dubos calls one of the bulwarks of scientific medicine, namely the conceptualization of the patient as an organism that can be described in the language "of elementary structures and mechanisms." It leads to a disease concept earlier described by the formula $dQi/dt = f(Q1a, Q1b, \ldots)$, where $Qi$ designates physical variables. This concept fosters a language which, although susceptible to intrasystemic (as distinct from intersystemic) mutual causal analysis ($Q1a$, $Q1b$, . . .), is nevertheless single-level. Since this unidirectional orientation governs the application of CADM systems like RX, we will call it the RX strategy. Schematically:

$$\ldots Q3, Q2 \quad \xrightarrow[\text{orientation}]{\text{research}} \quad (Q1a, Q1b, \ldots)$$

RX Strategy

---

A different disease concept, $dQi/dt = f(Q1, Q2, \ldots)$, exacts a different research orientation. At the expense of conceptual economy,

5. E.g., Jenkins 1976, 987, 1033; Fox and Newbury 1984.

research orientation now may be broadened to permit alternative logical configurations, such as the multidirectional orientation of the nosology to which RX II is applied. Call this the RX II strategy.

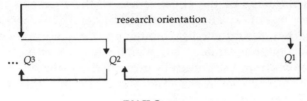

RX II Strategy

Here the model-neutral infrastructure of RX is enlisted (as RX II) in the service of a less economical, level-diffuse nosology. Or rather, it might be so enlisted on the provision that a successor nosology, based upon organic *and* extra-organic systems, can be articulated. For only in this event is condition (a) above satisfied. The beginnings of such an articulation take place in Chapter 13.

# 13

## Disease Causation:
## Determinacy versus Indeterminacy

### Illness as Metaphor or Metaphor as Illness

Our text in this chapter is from Susan Sontag:

> One's mind betrays one's body. "My head and lungs have come to an agreement without my knowledge," Kafka said about his TB in a letter to Max Brod in September 1917. Or one's body betrays one's feelings, as in Mann's late novel, *The Black Swan*, whose aging heroine, youthfully in love with a young man, takes as the return of her menses what is actually a hemorrhage and the symptom of incurable cancer. The body's treachery is thought to have its own inner logic. (1979, 39)

Can mind so betray body, or body betray feelings? The premises of biomedicine say no. Those of infomedicine say yes. Here, we shall examine the nosological grounds for these two contrasting answers.

### Biocultural Medicine:
### Accounting for the Human Factor

In the preceding chapter we suggested that a biomedical nosology (condition 5) like Harrison's *Principles of Internal Medicine* is going to be hard pressed to link mental events to organic disease even in the face of empirical evidence (conditions 1–4) suggesting such a connection. Thus, there is no "rationale for relationships sought." This was Fox's criticism of similar behavioral studies in cancer research. Either the two categories interact or the co-presence of mental and bodily events indicates only that we do not yet know enough about the biochemical substrate of the apparent mental events to explain them in the language of neurophysiology. Certainly, this is the thrust of Herbert Spector's estimate. A neurophysiologist at NIH, Spector says, "The new research makes it clear. Attitudes can matter. The focus now should be on discovering the mechanisms involved—the question is: What is the biochemistry of all this?" (in Goleman 1985, 13).

In this vein, in announcing plans for the construction of a Center for

Molecular and Genetic Medicine at Stanford University, Nobel laureate Paul Berg observed that "almost all human disease is genetic in origin" (in L. Hofstadter 1985, 2). The implication is that sufficient knowledge of the role of molecular mechanisms (protein molecules encoded by master genes, for example) in producing human disorders will explain them and so lead to a cure. Disease is physiology gone astray. And "abnormal development"—the patient's immune-deficient state—ultimately results from deranged molecular processes. But it needs to be repeated that this is an ideological, not an empirical, issue.

Since there is no experimental way of resolving this issue, closer inspection of the premises on which such studies are undertaken is called for to resolve the nosological issue both Project RX II and the NHLBI panel raise. Thus we may distinquish two ideologies: reductionism and nonreductionism, or interactionism, and consider the status of the evidence for each:

   *a.* *Reductionism*

Psychosocial mechanisms can *de jure* be explained by (reduced to) biophysical mechanisms, such that disorders due to abnormal development can be prevented or treated by understanding biophysical mechanisms.

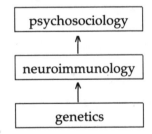

   *b.* *Interactionism*

Biophysical and psychosocial mechanisms can *de jure* be explained by their mutual interaction, such that disorders due to abnormal development can be prevented or treated by understanding the nature of their interaction.

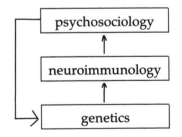

The status of the evidence for reductionism and interactionism alike is necessarily circumstantial and indirect. With respect to reductionism, the nature of this evidence is well known and need not be restated here: biophysical mechanisms cannot *de facto* explain all psychological and psychosocial phenomena. Nevertheless, by assuming that *de jure* they can and proceeding on this basis, an impressive medical landscape has taken shape, today's scientific medicine.

While acknowledging the truly impressive accomplishments of today's medicine, the interactionist maintains that, all the same, certain abnormal developments in people can be explained only by reference to their irreducibly human characteristics. Hence, the need to subsume biomedical premises under a more comprehensive set. To distinguish it from biopsychosocial medicine, the interactionist refers to this wider set of premises as *biopsychocultural* medicine. This neologism is introduced only to acknowledge the earlier point that biomedicine is not only a biological but, at its frontiers, a biopsychosocial medicine. That is, biomedicine has the resources to recognize mental and social phenomena of one kind and formally integrate them into its research and practice. This point is exemplified by today's field of behavioral medicine and in particular psychoneuroimmunology, whose premises are biopsychosocial while consistent with biomedicine. That is, the phenomena it studies can ultimately be rendered in exclusively physicalist languages like neurophysiology, immunogenetics, and pharmacology. Hence, the choice of the term *biopsychocultural*—for short, *biocultural*—underlines the interactionist contention that, while many mental events and psychosocial phenomena are common to both humans and animals and so subject to biomedical premises, others are proper to humans and so transcend the explanatory scope of these premises; they call forth biocultural premises. Among such singularly human events the interactionist points to the use of behavioral counseling and clinical biofeedback techniques to modify patient *values* and *worldview* ("psychobiofeedback"); and, again, to certain peculiarly *cultural* phenomena as distinct from the social phenomena of other biotic communities.

To explain the synergy between biological and psychological factors ($B \times C$), represented in Equation 2, the interactionist posits a hierarchy of organizational levels stretching from elementary particles at one end to the person and human culture and beyond at the other. Because this position, interactionism, is less well known and provides a beginning nosology within whose premises biocultural medicine can be practiced, we will outline it here. Doing so indicates the kind of task that meeting Blum's 7–10 validity score condition implies. At the same time, it offers a way out of the reductionist impasse evoked by the panel's reference to uniquely human behavioral phenomena.

The systems concepts of isomorphism and developmental antecedent are applied throughout the successive levels of this hierarchy, reflecting the evolutionary heritage of each element of the system. In this way the interactionist seeks to account for successive re-editions of such basic adaptability and self-regulating modes as are readily observable at each system level, cell no less than person. For the interactionist, these re-editions are transmitted through the genetic code and preserved precisely because they have successfully accomplished the ends of adaptation in the past. In systems terms they are called isomorphisms, a concept suggested by our tendency to use terms such as *know* and *recognize* when referring to living systems as rudimentary as cells and unicellular organisms. George Engel remarks that "cells *do* retain information; they *do* have 'memory', cells *do* 'recognize' particular inputs and in response they *do* 'know' to 'behave' in certain, often complex, ways, ways 'remembered' because they had worked in the past" (1985, 12–13). From this he infers that "elements of communication and information already manifest at the cell level may be recognized as developmental antecedents of similar more complex processes at the mental level."

This concept of developmental antecedent provides the evolutionary basis of the interactionist claims for the continuity of biological and psychological processes. Exemplifying this continuity is the notion of symbolic process. Here the interactionist uses *symbol* in its information-theoretic sense of compacting into a pattern multiple pieces of information to convey a particular message. Originating at the intracellular level, symbolic processes manifest throughout the hierarchy. Thus within a cell there are effector molecules that accumulate when the cell is exposed to a particular environmental condition. Because they come to represent that environmental state and so "inform" the cell how the environment has changed, Gordon Tomkins calls effector molecules within these cells "metabolic symbols," instancing cyclic AMP (cAMP) whose concentrations within the cell rapidly fluctuate with glucose changes in its environment. In response to these environmental changes, cAMP phases in metabolic processes that are adaptive for glucose depletion, thereby protecting the cell from impending deficiency in its supply of glucose.

As we move up the hierarchy, the interactionist cites as a further isomorphism behavioral as well as metabolic symbols. Engel states: "In E. coli, for example, cAMP also promotes flagellin synthesis, thereby enabling the bacterium to become motile and move away from the glucose-depleted environment" (1985, 14). In this way, notes Tomkins, the symbolization process allows "a relatively simple environmental change to bring about a complex, coordinated cellular response" (1975, 761). As this extension implies, these re-editions emerge in ever more sophisticated and internalized forms as we progress up the evolutionary ladder. "In effect, symbols of external events increasingly become part of the internal processes of the organism and through such internal representation provide a means whereby needs may be assayed before action is taken" (Engel 1985, 14–15). The greater the capacity to symbolize external events and manipulate them internally, the greater the ability to exercise freedom from these events, to gain autonomy. This self-differentiation process appears as a natural survival impulse in species evolution. Strata of stability developmentally build upon and internalize strata of stability—the bio-level builds upon the geo-level, the psycho-level upon the bio-level, the culture level upon the psycho-level—each successor level affording not only greater control over and freedom from environmental fluctuations but greater protection against total breakdown.

Engel cites Freud's operational designation of thinking as an experimental kind of action to try out the appropriateness of responses as isomorphic with the operation of metabolic symbols intracellularly. Here the link between biology and psychology is forged. From metabolic symbols we can successively trace behavioral (conscious) and then cognitive-affective (self-conscious) symbols; from molecular accumulation to organismic locomotion to human cognition, each a developmental antecedent with respect to its successor. But note that they do not replace one another; instead they presuppose and build upon one another: "Higher system level processes do not replace the lower system level processes for which they are isomorphic. Rather they continue as part of integrated organismal adjustment. Thinking is not reducible to chemical events in the brain any more than intracellular operation of metabolic symbols means that the cell is thinking" (1985, 15). While thinking requires as its substrate chemical events in the brain, it is not explained by them. For comparison, consider the origins of the overall orderliness that emerges in an ant colony. While depending on the armies of food-carrying, trail-building, and other ants that make it up, no individual ant or group of ants "knows" the colony's overriding plan. The colony as a whole has a kind of knowledge—how to grow, how to move—that is nowhere to be found in the individual ants. In systems terms, the individual ant's behavior is a developmental antecedent of the behavior of the trail-building group to which it belongs. The two sets of behaviors are isomorphic. And so the various behaviors of the different constituent groups themselves are developmental antecedents of the behavior of the colony as a whole, each an isomorphism of the other. There are successive gradations of "know," each isomorphic with yet not explicable by the other. For "ants" we could here substitute "cells," including neural cells. Here is the infomedical sense of holism.

Consider now in more detail the comparison of cAMP in a cell, as the symbol indicating depletion (loss) of a particular glucose supply in its environment, with the internal representations of the depletions (losses) a person experiences during bereavement. Illustrating the isomorphism of *loss* throughout the hierarchy, the comparison highlights the psychobiology inherent in interactionism. It places in perspective the interactionist concept of the patient as a psychobiologic unity whereby psychological processes organically arise out of but are not reducible to biological processes. Engel describes the complex sense of loss he experienced upon his father's death:

> For me, not only were the "supplies" that I lost upon my father's death multiplex and peculiar for me, but also their internal representatives derived not just from my father-relationship but from the whole history of my social relationships since birth. But note that my social relationships actually had their beginnings in a biological context, in the transition at birth from the biologic mutuality of transplacental nutrition to the social mutuality of oral feeding at my mother's breasts. In that process the recurring cycles of hunger-feeding-satiation that I experienced as a neonate not only were regulators of my earliest social relations, they also established a permanent linkage between processes implicated in maintaining cellular nutrition and processes implicated in sustaining human relationships, literally linking cAMP and feelings that reflect human ties. (1985, 16–17)

The birth canal bridges biology into psychosociobiology.

A wide difference in complexity separates intracellular and cognitive-affective symbolic processes. Yet, because of their mutual isomorphism, "it is not by chance that when we feel threatened or endangered there is secretion of epinephrine, a substance that stimulates cAMP production and mobilizes metabolic stores. Such a connection reflects our evolutionary heritage, to be prepared for substrate depletion upon any disturbance of harmony within our ecological niche" (Engel 1985, 17). It reflects this heritage both ontogenetically and phylogenetically. We are psychobiological creatures not in any abstract philosophical sense but by reason of our evolutionary heritage integrating each successive organizational level into a single ecosystem. This interactionist theme links psychobiology and diagnostics. For example, psychobiology serves to explain the mutual interplay, noted in Fox's provisional model, of biological and psychological levels. Rather than being related summatively, they interact in a self-regulating (or self-deregulating) way because they evolved such that depletion (e.g., bereavement) activates hormonal discharges; and these, in turn, may enhance (or depress) cognitive-affective state. Moreover, the resulting state may help restore hormonal balance, affecting immune defenses; and so forth. The process describes a mutual causal negative and/or positive feedback circuit:

> The very fact that my apprehending of my father's death includes use of symbolic processes historically connected since my birth with regulation of

biological supplies in itself predetermines that connections could exist even at the level of molecular symbols. Obviously our inner world of symbols is not a separate world unto itself, as Cartesian dualism would have us believe, it is an integral part of a complex multi-layered network intimately involved in biological regulation even at the cellular level. (Engel 1985, 18–19)

Psychological stimuli are internalized biological stimuli, isomorphic of one another, within a single multilayered hierarchical organization. Here is the nosological ground for the fact that, as the panel concluded, "More than 2 decades of research have solidly established that type A behavior pattern is associated with and is predictive of CHD." We may begin to speak of a "rationale for relationships sought" and so surmount the level of mere data base studies.

To appreciate the clinical application of this nosology to diagnostics (and therapeutics), the interactionist asks us first to recall the layering and decreasing specificity of symbols as we move up the systems hierarchy. While specificity is greatest at the lowest system levels—for example, molecular symbols—it becomes progressively more idiosyncratic as higher psychological levels are attained. For example, while only a single interpretation is possible in the behavior of cAMP as a symbol indicating depletion (loss) of a particular supply in a cell's environment, the internal representations of the depletions (losses) experienced when Engel's father died were systematically ambiguous. This is because "Implicit in such a perspective is the meaning to the organism of the particular life event or circumstance, a meaning in part determined by what has gone on before in the life of that organism" (Engel 1974, 1092). In the case of the cell, cAMP controls symbolization processes natural to the cell, protecting the cell from an impending deficiency in its life-support system—glucose depletion. To frustrate these processes is to frustrate a natural function; doing so therefore produces a disorder, a "disturbance of harmony." The specific "disease" the cell suffers as a result of this disorder (glucose deficit) is in part determined by the "meaning" to the cell of that particular event or circumstance—"what has gone on before in the life of that [cell]." Since in the case of the cell this "prehistory" is minimal, the final common pathway is for the most part predetermined: protracted glucose depletion (A) is virtually a proximal cause of the "disease" (D):

$A \mathrel{\rlap{\hspace{0.1em}/}{\rightarrow}} D$

The specific disease the human suffers as a result of this disorder (emotional deficit) is likewise in part determined by the meaning to the person of that particular life event—what has gone on before in the person's life, both biologically *(B)* and psychologically *(C)*. However, since in the case of persons this prehistory is maximal, now the final common pathway is correspondingly indeterminate. Here the inherent indeterminacy of the interactionist position comes into focus. We may paraphrase Engel (1985, 23):

> Such a perspective is both deterministic and probabilistic. It is deterministic in the sense of recognizing that *particular* conditions (A) are *necessary* for a specific disease (D) to occur; just as without the tubercle bacillus, tuberculosis cannot develop. It is probabilistic in the sense that merely the presence of the *necessary* conditions does not suffice for the particular disease to occur. Rather, whether and when the particular disease occurs depends on the probability of occurrence of other factors (B, C), in the proper quantity and at the proper times.

Disease is the product of an interactive mix, a thesis with which we are now familiar. Had some predisposition not interactive with the emotional loss experienced been present, no disorder would have developed. Or, adds Engel, "Had the interactions been slow or multilayered and the clinical signs of the evolving disorder long in emerging, then a time relationship, and hence a connection with the [emotional loss], would have remained inapparent, e.g., slow course of tuberculosis or neoplasia. Or had some other vulnerability of the moment taken precedence, exposure to an infectious agent, for example, then a one-time illness episode may have been the result" (1985, 24). In short,

$$A + (B \times C) \nrightarrow D$$

where the final common pathway depends on the precise composition of the mix, whose differential assay in each instance is critical to effective diagnosis and treatment.[1]

This helps account for the amendments to Koch's criteria found necessary in the century-long research into disease causation since Koch; thus such amendments as: different causes at different settings may occur for the same syndrome. It explains the otherwise perplexing, almost "anything goes" character of today's etiologic norms as encapsulated in Evans's conclusion that "Different qualitative and quantitative mixes of the agent, environment, and host may result in the same clinical and pathological disease under different circumstances." Little wonder that Fox cautions us that research design in tracking etiological

1. This indeterminacy is the infomedical explanation for what Engel says "is common to the epidemiological studies that show that persons suffering bereavement or facing a job loss have a higher morbidity and mortality; to the retrospective and prospective studies that show increased incidence of illness among individuals reporting many life changes during the preceding months; and to the finding that persons already ill report a high incidence of psychological giving up in the period preceding disease onset. These all doubtless include instances of final common pathways, some not yet elucidated" (1974, 1092). This commonality accounts for the necessary diffuseness of the stress concept: stress is simply a measure of the meaning of an event or circumstance to the host, whether dysfunctional (distress) or functional (eustress).

roots is "a most difficult type of knowledge." Or that for almost any data base study reporting one finding we can likely cite another that fails to find the postulated correlation. From an infomedical standpoint, this is not necessarily a sign of an ill-designed study (though it may be), nor a reflection of a weakness in contemporary research techniques generally. (Nor even of the fact that there are some 20,000 medical journals published annually, each with its several scores of studies, totaling something in the neighborhood of a million studies appearing a year.) Rather, it merely reflects the interactionist point that systems properties like allometry, centralization, and equifinality come into play when assaying differential strengths of mutually influential factors for a given pathogenic function. From this we can infer that studies reporting arteriographic findings that support a hypothesis like that suggested by Figure 12.3 may be consistent with studies that fail to find the postulated covariations. This is because either the covariations do not exist or different interactive mixes here result in different (or no) pathologic manifestations. And to point to this inherently fuzzy state of disease causation is simply to repeat that the interactive programs and messages producing disease (or health) are indeterminate in the designated sense. That is, they define a probability distribution governed by stochastic processes.

The discussion thus far has suggested the scientific defensibility of proposition 2 stated early on in the previous chapter—that mental state is a major factor in causing disease. As a key to this, we have introduced the notion of the *meaning* to the host of a particular event or circumstance. It is instructive to observe that this concept has an *objective*, not merely subjective, application: how does the particular event or circumstance *(A)*—whether glucose- or emotion-depleted environment—relate quantitatively and temporally to the host's interacting biological *(B)* and psychological *(C)* history? To assess this and prescribe accordingly is to practice not just biomedicine but "biocultural" medicine and so participate in a medical revolution. A prototype for the practice of this medicine is offered in the section following the next ("A Clinical Application").

# Mental States/Physical States: The Infomedical Connection

The comparison of RX and RX II clarifies the commitments embraced by each, we said, as well as how the vocabulary of each licenses the able and conscientious physician to proceed. Such a comparison highlights the risk of the biomedical commitment to translating complex cognitive-affective states—beliefs, values, goals—into the language of the conventional nosology. We noted that it may be not only impossible, but scientifically unsound.

To see this is to recognize the difference between a determinacy and an indeterminacy model of disease causation. In biological medicine the unit of pathogenicity tends to be localized to a physical agent, organic condition, or biochemical process. In biocultural medicine the pathogenic action is intrinsic to the pattern of relations, linked only in an indirect way to the stimulus (microbe) that set it off. The latter is a critical "fluctuation" made critical owing not to its intrinsic "virulence" but to its relation to the host, a host-in-a-particular-state. This contrast entails differences not only in research aims but in the interpretation of experimental findings. In the biocultural model, experiments are designed not primarily to isolate a particular pathogen as capable of producing disease in the host with a view, say, to developing an appropriate counteragent (vaccine). This is but the tail end of the research story. Instead, attention is directed toward isolating the interplay of mutagen(s) and a host-characterized-by-certain-state-variables. In the vocabulary of self-organizing systems, only the latter, a host-in-a-particular-state, can form a critical mass. And the former, for instance a microbe, as catalyst, may trigger the complex pattern of relations into a new organizational state—thus from health (near-equilibrium) to disease (far-from-equilibrium).

The minimum unit of pathogenicity is accordingly enlarged, with a corresponding indeterminacy of focus. This is illustrated by contrasting a biological and biocultural interpretation of the evidence for the relation between mental state and atherosclerosis, as symbolized by Figure 12.3. Looking at the upper half of that figure, depicted are the conjectured relations between mental state and hypertension. In a biocultural diagnosis of hypertension, the prospective causative agent—that for which an appropriate antidote (vaccine) might be sought—is not a physical or organic agent (e.g., fibrin-lipid buildup in the arteries) or a behavioral agent (e.g., a cognitive-affective disorder). Nor are mutagens like stressful life events and fatty deposits viewed as conceivably linked in a direct causal manner, in the sense that one always leads to the other. Rather, they are viewed as capable of functioning causatively only as *channeled through* a host inhabiting a particular biopsychosocial "space." Only in combination with a pattern of relations forming the disease host can they trigger a cross- or autocatalytic process whose end result is protracted high blood pressure, essential hypertension. Further, this hypertensive state can itself exacerbate the psychosocial state in feedback fashion.

Standard accounts of this feedback loop system abound in the literature of stress theory and emotional disorders. We saw them described by the panel as "the classic work implicating the sympathetic nervous system and the adrenals in emotion and stress and more recent work on the regulation of the circulation and lipid mobilization, platelet aggregation and other processes potentially related to atherogenesis." In very general terms these studies document the ability of the central nervous system to activate a stress reaction as a result of sensory and cognitive stimuli (perceived information). Kenneth Pelletier summarizes these findings when he observes that "Psychological stress can initiate hypothalamic discharges and stimulate the pituitary during the second-ary, sustained stress response to secrete hormones which in turn stimulate the appropriate endocrine glands. Some of these endocrine secretions are distributed through the bloodstream to the brain, where they further excite the brain or stimulate specific parts of the hypothala-mus" (Pelletier 1977, 68). This loop structure is shown in Figure 13.1.

Here cortical arousal, hypothalamic activity, sympathetic discharge, endocrine functions, and the bloodstream are linked in a closed feed-back loop. Usually oriented toward maintaining homeostasis, "stressful stimuli" can disrupt this loop. Under certain psychosocial circumstances such disruption can, moreover, be anticipated. In this way the biocultural model offers a rationale for dysfunctional "stress reactivity" as an essential psychophysiological process. Speaking to this rationale, Pelletier notes that humans are equipped with much the same physiol-ogy as animals to cope with stress. That is, when subjected to major stress, both are roused to a fight-or-flight reaction. But herein lies the

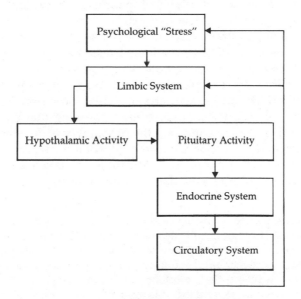

FIGURE 13.1

specifically human, or biocultural, problem. Humans can create culture and so supersede the "natural" rules. One by-product is psychophysiologic maladaptation. Roughly speaking, whereas an animal can deal with a threat through fight or flight, a human being in a civilized society very often cannot. "In our complex society with its highly refined codes of acceptable behavior, fighting and fleeing are often not considered appropriate reactions to stressful situations," says Pelletier. We are made to bide our time. Consequently the more combative and time-oriented we tend to be, the more likely we are to internalize our distress. "He who desires but acts not, breeds pestilence," wrote Blake prophetically. Failing to otherwise channel this combativeness, the distress builds up. Its physiological correlate is damaging. "Since the negative psychological state persists, the physiological stress response also continues. It is under these circumstances, when a stress response is prolonged and unabated, that the biochemical changes associated with stress become potentially detrimental to health" (1976, 69–70).

A certain personality configuration coupled to a social organization that is, in evolutionary terms, maladaptive has a pathogenic potential. A complex social organization when channeled through a particular personality syndrome can thus render autonomic responses dysfunctional. And the resulting prolonged stress reactivity can translate into hypertension. To illustrate this pattern of relations Figure 13.1 may be given its biocultural version, as in Figure 13.2.

Now we can anticipate how an indeterminacy model of disease causation characterizes the relationship between hypertension and atherosclerosis (Figure 12.3). The two diseases are related analogously to the way prolonged stress reactivity is related to hypertension—via a complex loop structure. They are linked not in a direct or linear causal chain, but by a mutual causal feedback circuit. We know that a narrowing of the arteries due to fibrin-lipid buildup and the consequent loss of vessel elasticity would tend to elevate blood pressure. Relevant to a biocultural etiology are data base studies showing that elevated blood pressure, in turn, tends to increase the probability of developing arteriosclerotic symptoms. Crucial here is the interplay between the hypertensive and atherosclerotic conditions, an interplay posited to account for the statistically significant covariation in the two diseases. Pelletier notes that:

> Although experimental evidence demonstrating a positive link between the two diseases has not been conclusive, most of these experiments seem to ignore the fact that a closed-loop feedback system exists between the two. One negative trigger affects another and creates a downward spiral which ultimately increases the probability of coronary failure. . . . Once this degenerative cycle is initiated, it is difficult if not impossible to reverse its progress. (1976, 168)

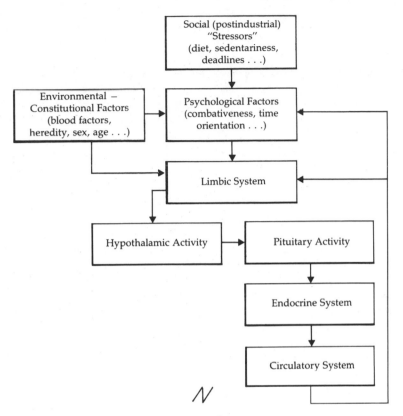

Hypertension

FIGURE 13.2

In the framework of infomedicine this closed-loop feedback system and the indeterminacy immanent in it *is* a positive link between the two diseases. In such a system no part can have unilateral control over the whole. The pathogenic (as well as therapeutic) characteristics of the system are immanent, not in some part but in the system as a whole. It is the hypertensive host-in-a-particular-biocultural-state that is susceptible to coronary failure. The model is inescapably probabilistic (stochastically indeterminate) in that whether and when the particular disease occurs depends not only on its necessary conditions ("microbe") but also "on the probability of occurrence of other factors, in the proper quantity and at the proper times." (For example, in Figure 13.2 some of these "other factors" are symbolized by the loop-structure role of the "environmental-constitutional" box.) A particular combination of biological, psychological, and cultural components, conditioned by certain environmental factors, forms the relevant unit of pathogenicity. A probability distribution of final common pathways therefore characterizes the relationship between a pathogenic loop and the disease state. Further, this relationship *defines the infomedical meaning of a positive causal link*.

Here is the import of the model's premise that final state does not depend on initial conditions. A given response is not the direct result of some outside stimulus but rather of rule-governed behavior which is a property of the system acting as a system. Given this "genetic model" sense of positive link, the same experimental evidence that, in one model, may demonstrate a positive causal link, in another, may not. Nor is this indeterminacy—with further experimentation, controlling for other variables—eliminable. Therefore, we might speak of the model's "indeterminacy principle" analogously to its use in quantum mechanics: the more complex (e.g., mindful) the disease host, the more essentially diffuse the etiological analysis. This is just to say that the referent pathogen in Figure 13.2 is the closed-loop feedback system itself. Here is the context in which the full research story unfolds.

In mathematical terms, this difference in the way a positive link is measured in a biological and a biocultural model may be characterized as the difference between a well-conditioned and an ill-conditioned problem. This refers to whether small changes in certain beginning conditions will make only small changes in the end result (a well-conditioned problem) or whether small changes can make disproportionately large, even catastrophic—or no—changes in the end result (an ill-conditioned problem). The difference in complexity of symbols (programs) in biological systems (for instance, lab animals) and biocultural systems (humans) makes diagnoses of a body system/disease relationship and a mind-body system/disease relationship differ as the solution to a well-conditioned problem differs from that of an ill-conditioned problem.

From the biocultural perspective, then, some confusion pervades the ongoing debate over the relationship of attitude and health. For example, on the question of the links between emotions and disease, Angell says, "I'm not saying that there is no point in pursuing this research, but I am saying the conclusions don't follow from the findings. I'm still waiting for proof that the way we think has a major clinical impact on the immune system. The studies so far are inadequate" (in Goleman 1985, 21). Interestingly, this is not pitting the relative adequacy of studies seeking to show the existence of links between thinking and the immune system against studies seeking to refute the existence of these links. Rather the prevailing biomedical model simply *assumes* the latter. Thus, only after the appearance of a vast body of circumstantial evidence connecting mental factors and disease has been reported[2] does

2. *Mind and Immunity* published in 1985 by the Institute for the Advancement of Health contains an annotated bibliography summarizing almost 1,400 scientific reports showing, in the words of the Institute's director, "connections between mental factors and disease" (in Goleman 1985, 25).

the need even arise for studies showing that the way we think does *not* have a major impact on disease.

But this raises the question of adequacy and proof. We can see why the debate volleys back and forth almost monthly from position to counterposition. Given the number of researchers and journals in the field, it is not surprising that each side can confidently claim support for its position. For example, within less than two months of the time that Angell wrote, the *Lancet* reviewed studies linking psychological factors and cancer, and concluded that counseling and psychological support may be as important as many medical measures ("Emotion and Immunity" 1985, 135). Cited were the findings of the 1979 study by M. S. Greer and others, represented in Table 13.1. As with our previous figure of a (projected) mental state–heart disease relationship, this table can be readily grafted onto the familiar emotions-cancer armature (Figure 13.3).

If we imagine the Greer findings enlarged by subsequent data base studies indicating that uncontrollable psychological events are associated with immune responses,[3] as the *Lancet* editorial implies, would biomedical reductionists now be disposed to alter their position? Is the proof they seek materializing in these studies? Clearly these are rhetorical questions. For the tactical strength of their position is that, starting from a biomedical orientation—today's prevailing orientation—the bur-

TABLE 13.1   Relation of Emotions to Cancer

| Psychological response three months after operation | AFTER 10 YEARS | | |
| --- | --- | --- | --- |
| | Alive, with no recurrence | Alive, with cancer | Dead |
| Denial: "Despite the operation I don't believe I really ever had cancer." | 5 | 0 | 5 |
| Fighting Spirit: "I'm going to conquer this thing." | 6 | 1 | 3 |
| Stoic Acceptance: "Keep a stiff upper lip—don't complain." | 7 | 1 | 24 |
| Helplessness, Hopelessness "There's nothing to be done; I'm as good as dead." | 1 | 0 | 4 |

Source: Greer et al. 1979

3. Keller et al. 1983; Laudenslager et al. 1983; Locke et al. 1984.

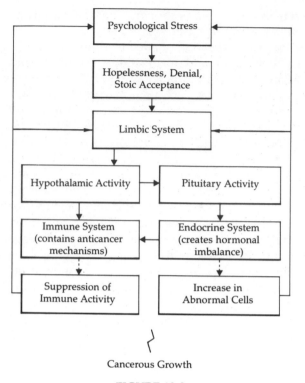

FIGURE 13.3

den of proof is on the opposing side. A mechanism (positive causal link), not just significant covariation, must be shown to connect mental events and organic dysfunction. Short of this, logically (it is assumed) a small body of well-designed counterexamples (e.g., the Case and Cassileth studies) would serve to undercut the counterposition and call into question the scientific adequacy of the studies reporting significant covariation. Such is the rationale of the biomedical position for which a nosology is already in place.

But we have questioned whether such a rationale is warranted in the present case. Does it rely for its force on an etiological model (deterministic) that the model being tested challenges? The question is relevant because whereas the molecular theory of disease causation—the biological model—invites relatively predictable covariations, this is not the case for the interactionist theory of disease causation—the biocultural model. Consider that when testing covariation among only body systems, say between the central nervous system and the immune system—as in many studies with laboratory animals—RX requires a high degree of replicability and experimental manipulation before investing the relationship with Blum's *empirically confirmed covariation*. But what if, as in

RX II, we are testing covariation between a body system and a mind system, between (say) human mental state and the immune or cardio-vascular system? For reasons just noted, this is a relatively new species of data base study. And we saw in the contrast between the way cAMP guides cellular behavior and the way mental-emotional attitudes guide human behavior that symbols (programs and messages) are more complex and predictability less as we move up the systems hierarchy. This follows from their layering and decreasing specificity. Yet today's studies testing covariation between upper levels of this hierarchy (human emotions) and lower levels (biochemical processes) are conducted (unwittingly) as if one can expect the same kind of determinate covariation that the biomedical model encourages. That is, experimental design procedures applied in these studies, studies to test emotions/nervous-system/disease covariation, are consistent with the molecular theory of disease causation. They are designed as if the problem were well-conditioned, not ill-conditioned. And this orients what will count as proof, so predisposing the outcome of the debate.

This last point needs to be underlined. "It is not enough," says Angell, "to point to the plausibility of a chain of events leading from emotional stress to increased adrenal activity to immune suppression to cancer. . . . Each link of this chain must be carefully demonstrated." And the apparent inability to do so leads to Angell's "negative assessment of the quality of much of the research that has been done on this issue and, especially, of the exuberant interpretations of it" (1985b, 1359). "My guess," she concludes, "is that any direct effect of mental state on disease is relatively small; otherwise, we would not be having so much difficulty demonstrating it" (1985b, 1358). But we need to ask whether this use of "direct effect" belies the assumption of a deterministic model. What, precisely, is the nature of the demonstration sought? What would such a "chain" or mechanism look like? Would it include psychic processes? And how would they "hook up" with bodily processes? Rolf Adler notes that while it is true that studies demonstrating direct connections between mental state and disease are lacking, expecting such connections "reflects the state of psychosomatic medicine 30 or more years ago. Modern researchers in this field don't expect to observe a direct and overriding connection between mental state and disease" (1985, 1358). Instead, the field is defined by what he calls a "multifactorial concept of disease" such that psychosocial factors represent "neither a necessary nor sufficient prerequisite for disease"; their influences are "subtle." This distinction between direct connections and implied linear causal chains, on the one hand, and a multifactorial disease concept and feedback circuits, on the other, is, in the present idiom, the difference between a relatively deterministic and an indeterministic model of disease causation.

If a probability distribution defines the notion of an empirically confirmed covariation, then findings of well-designed experimental studies measuring a change-in-mental-state/change-in-disease-state relationship can be expected to vary within a stochastically defined range. And as a result of applying determinate correlation standards (RX correlation criteria 1–4) to indeterminate processes (RX II variables), significant correlations will be lost. This is the biocultural contention. And from *this* standpoint we can anticipate the kind of "volleying back and forth" debate to which we have grown accustomed over the past decade or so, each camp citing equally reputable (given RX correlation criteria) scientific studies. In fact, we would expect mediators of the debate to strike a note of detente and conclude, as do Norman Cousins and Barrie Cassileth, that "few things are more important in the care of seriously ill patients than their mental state. Even so, patients should not be encouraged to believe that positive attitudes are a substitute for competent medical attention" (in Goleman 1985, 25).

It turns out, then, that from the perspective of a successor model, even the application of the first four of Blum's criteria is nosology-sensitive. That is, their application needs to be adjusted to nosological requirements in that change-in-mental-state/change-in-disease-state relationships are stochastically indeterminate and so intrinsically complex. This alters standards of what counts as a positive link. And entente among participants in the ongoing "conversation" turns on the appropriate concept of disease causation as it applies to that "large portion of the world's illness" that is behavior-related (Hamburg 1983, 969). Were Angell and Adler to reach agreement here, they might further agree not only that the connection between mental state and disease "is unlikely to be overriding" (Angell 1985b, 1358) but that in today's multifactorial (indeterminacy) model the connection between *any* states—whether bodily or mental—is unlikely to be overriding because of their complex mutual potentiation. Only then might each take the infomedical turn and agree that this progressive diffusion of etiological focus (complexity) is desirable. A by-product of self-organizing systems, it reflects our evolutionarily won humanness: a human medicine dictates an indeterminacy model of disease causation.

# A Clinical Application

We have pointed to the infomedical importance of the meaning of an event or circumstance to the host and suggested that it could be captured on an intersubjective scale and put to clinical use. We saw that symbols, or programs, activate processes (messages) throughout the hierarchy, triggering a pattern of relations. To be able to read this pattern is to have a means, or "technology," for seeing into the entrails of patient state: a psychobiologic "CAT scan." One component of such a means is offered by the system for analyzing cancer imagery developed by J. Achterberg and G. F. Lawlis. Called "Image CA," it is a projective test for accessing symbols and harnessing them as change agents, on the recognition that the immune system reacts to messages from the brain.

The patients' graphic and verbal imagery is used as a reflection of their attitudes about the disease and treatment, as well as their belief in their innate ability to overcome the disease via immunological and other systems. The act of extracting this imagery takes place in a conducive environment where the patient listens to tape-recorded relaxation instructions. In this relaxed state, "a very brief type of education is provided to inform the patient of the disease process, of how treatment might be working to the patient's advantage, and finally, the idea of host defense, or the immune system, is presented. The listener is then advised to imagine these three factors in action" (Achterberg 1985, 188).

Typically, the properties of natural recovery are represented by immunological defenses in the form of white blood cells capable of overcoming cancer cells. "Imagery that takes into consideration what is known about physiology," says Achterberg, "can be said to become a ritual that incorporates the values of a modern age" (1985, 107). While the imagery is guided, it is not programmed in the sense of suggesting to patients that the cells be represented by anything in particular. "Those ideas that spring from the depths of their psyche are drawn by the patient, and then described in an interview, structured with such questions as, 'Describe how your cancer cells look in your mind's eye' and 'How do you imagine your white blood cells fight disease?' " (188). The combined results of the interview and the drawings are tabulated on the basis of fourteen dimensions for quantifying the components of the imagery. Each dimension is scored on a 1–5 scale, and the net product determines a total imagery score.

> The dimensions include the vividness, activity, and strength of the cancer cell; vividness and activity of the white blood cells; relative comparison of size and number of cancer and white blood cells; strength of the white blood cells; vividness and effectiveness of medical treatment; choice of symbolism; the integration of the whole imagery process; the regularity with which they imaged a positive outcome; and a ventured clinical opinion on the prognosis, given the previously listed thirteen factors. (Achterberg 1985, 188–189)

As these dimensions indicate, imagination can serve a diagnostic role only if certain common factors can be identified. Image CA extracts common factors in terms of the *features* of the symbols (i.e., size, activity, numbers, etc.) since, Achterberg observes, the *kind* of symbol chosen was not uniformly predictive of outcome.

In two studies conducted under the auspices of the National Cancer

Institute, disease state at the time the scores were tabulated was checked against disease state two months later. In each case it was found to be significantly predictive, both of marked deterioration and remission (Achterberg and Lawlis 1978). Achterberg puts the significance of this outcome in perspective: "The scores are just a shape put on the imagination—it was the images themselves that so accurately predicted the future" (Achterberg 1985, 189). The imagery is but a visual/verbal representation of patient attitudes about the disease and treatment. And the attitudes the imagery reflects (e.g., resignation, nondirected struggle, purposeful action) translate as psychobiologic messages into body function. In constructing and intentionally reconstructing the imagery, the patient is at once directing body processes. The total imagery score is the numerical shape of these processes. Achterberg interprets the results:

> The symbols that so quickly emerged into consciousness when the questions were asked were as much a part of the patients' lives as the symptoms were part of the disease. The symptoms were symbols, the symbols symptoms. (The two words have essentially the same meaning—a concrete or tangible object that stands for an intangible idea.) And they both deserve equal respect for influencing the course of lives. (1985, 191)

From an infomedical perspective, this convertibility of symbol and symptom is not surprising, inasmuch as the images, reflecting patient attitudes (the meaning of the disease to the patient), are programs that convey messages; and message transmission is a coordinated psychobiologic event. At the human level, these symbols are isomorphic with what, at the cellular level, is the production of cAMP. An effector symbol mobilized in response to external fluctuations, cAMP can guide cell body behaviors. So too, mental-emotional attitudes, an effector symbol mobilized in response to external fluctuations, can guide human body behaviors. Attitudes (meanings) both reflect body functions (symptoms) and influence those functions (prognosticators, provocateurs). In an ecological idiom, attitudes (reflected in imagery) and body functions are mutually causative and reactive: the medusa and the snail.

We can best understand this symbol-symptom convertibility by viewing Achterberg and Lawlis's experiments as the projection onto a human screen of Ader and Cohen's animal experiments. Ader and his colleagues have shown that white blood cells (T-cells) can be trained in the same fashion as Pavlov's dogs. When an immunosuppressant agent that inhibits T-cells, like the cytotoxin cyclophosphamide, is paired with a harmless stimulus, like saccharin, the T-cells learn to respond to the saccharin as if it were the cytotoxin itself. Mortality rate is related to the amount of the harmless solution consumed (Ader and Cohen 1982).

Decisive is the *meaning* to the experimental rats of the solution; and this is influenced by "what has gone on before in the rats' lives" (i.e., the conditioning). To this and not the solution per se T-cells respond. In Image CA terms, the rats *image* or symbolize what they are consuming as a cytotoxin; this is the message from the brain to which the immune system (T-cells) is programmed to react. The meaning of the event to the patient, a "psychological" factor, in this case overrides the influence of the chemical properties of the substance administered, a physical or biological factor. Or the two interact to produce a surprising (biomedically speaking) result.

So Achterberg and Lawlis's findings (Achterberg and Lawlis 1978, 1979, 1980, 1981, 1984) are an isomorphic re-edition of Ader and Cohen's results. The two senses of *meaning*—the "meaning" of the solution to rats and the meaning of the disease and its treatment to humans—are developmentally successive and isomorphic of one another. The total imagery score encodes the latter meaning. Noteworthy here is the meaning to the patient of the disease and its treatment. Inasmuch as our inner world of symbols is "an integral part of a complex multi-layered network intimately involved in biological regulation," this meaning is itself a symptom. So, too, the "meaning" to Ader's experimental rats of the solution given them: meaning can direct biology. To redirect this meaning (symbol)—make saccharin mean the cytotoxin (via biofeedback, meditation, behavioral counseling, conditioning, etc.)—is tantamount to treating symptoms. For in this special respect it *is* treating symptoms. And we recognize exclusively human psychoneuroimmunology (biocultural medicine) as governed by the same principles as human-and-animal psychoneuroimmunology (biopsychosocial medicine): the immune system reacts to messages from the mind-brain.

A single-case instance of this convertibility of symbol and symptom appears in the study of R. G. Smith and his colleagues in which, according to the authors, "the data confirmed the hypothesis that [the subject of the experiment] could voluntarily modulate her immune responses by a psychic mechanism" (Smith et al. 1985, 2111). The authors describe the experiment as a single-case study design in which the subject, an experienced meditator, was skin-tested weekly with a skin test reagent. "After baseline immunologic studies, she was able, as hypothesized, to significantly reduce both the induration of her delayed hypersensitivity skin test reaction and in vitro lymphocyte stimulation to varicella zoster" (2110). Then she was able to allow her reaction to return to baseline and, in addition, to reproduce the entire sequence nine months later. "To our knowledge," conclude the authors, "these are the first published data of an intentional direct psychological modulation of the human immune system." The mechanism employed?

During the phase 2 periods of the original and repeat experiment, [the subject] would usually reserve about five minutes of her daily meditation for attention to the study. First she would dedicate her intention concerning the study for universal good instead of individual advancement. She would also tell her body not to violate its wisdom concerning her defense against infection. Finally she would visualize the area of erythema and induration getting smaller and smaller. Soon after each phase 2 injection, she would pass her hand over her arm, sending "healing energy" to the injection site. (Smith et al. 1985, 2111)

Here a psychic mechanism, tantric generation meditation and visualization of specific physiologic processes—literally a psychoneuroimmunologic mechanism—explains the apparent "intentional direct psychological modulation of the human immune system." Programs (visualization) convey messages, and message transmission, we said, is a coordinated psychobiologic event. The authors caution that the results cannot be generalized to all humans. Nevertheless, "Perhaps other people have the ability to [auto-] modulate their immune response or to develop the capacity to do so." And the more likely this is, "Perhaps, also, intentional modulation can be used therapeutically to increase or decrease immune response, depending on the particular disease state." In any event, "These data, along with the previously cited results, should allow for many new carefully designed studies to be undertaken" (1985, 2111).

We see here an illustration of Toulmin's conceptual phylogeny. The concept *mechanism* is permitted to range over novel landscapes apace with new, "surprising" findings. Tantric generation meditation is introduced as one of the allowable parameters interacting with erythematic and other bodily processes whose simultaneous values define system state. The mechanism formed by these interdependent parameters produces state-transition behavior, namely intentional automodulation of the immune system from "diseased" to healthy state. We wind up speaking of something that at face (i.e., first scientific revolution) value sounds oxymoronic: a self-conscious, or psychoneuroimmunologic, mechanism. (Already biomedicine had stretched the seventeenth-century concept to apply to *living* mechanisms, for instance conscious, or neuroimmunologic, mechanisms.) Wasn't the intent of the revolution to hammer out a language in which the qualitative, vitalistic, and "tacit" dimensions of experience could be made quantitative, physicalistic, and explicit—or, as the term came to be called, "scientific"? Nature, proclaimed Galileo, sounding the revolution's rallying cry, is written in the language of mathematics. And mathematics objectifies the subjective.

Would the biomedical advocate acknowledge a chain formed of a psychic or intentional element linked to physiologic or neuroimmunologic processes? Or does the term *linked* in such a sentence collapse under its own weight? From the infomedical standpoint, to answer yes is to mistake a limitation of one's inheritance for a limitation in nature: paradigm gridlock. To speak of a psychoneuroimmunologic chain or mechanism is not arbitrarily to invent a new term or stretch an old term beyond its breaking point; it is to try intellectually to reconcile a paradigm limitation and a newly discovered reality.

The foundations question persists: do the biomedical model's (RX) knowledge base requirements deprive the medical practitioner of actual and potential diagnostic and therapeutic applications—for instance via coupling known psychic and immunological mechanisms for treatment of autoimmune-related diseases? Only in the vocabulary of RX II is illness in part, quoting Sontag, "what speaks through the body, a language for dramatizing the mental: a form of self-expression" (1979, 43). "The illness is speaking for me because I have asked it to do so," Kafka observes (in Sontag 1979, 43). "Illness is in part what the world has done to a victim, but in larger part it is what the victim has done with his world, and with himself," writes Karl Menninger infomedically (also in Sontag). And because the function is symmetric, what applies to our illness applies equally to our well-being: symbol (program) as illness; symbol as health.

Put simply, meaning, a psycho-active message, is a change agent. Interacting with other, bio-active messages ($B \times C$), it can be massaged (treated) to therapeutic purpose. And despite its relative indeterminacy,[4] the Image CA experiments and this single-case study alike indicate that meaning can be serviceably objectified and quantified, rendered partially algorithmic. Clinically speaking, symbols in the form of psycho-active and socio-active programs process messages that have consequences, are a "material force." And disease, in significant and measurable ways, is a reflection of mental state.

## Blushing: An Analogy

At the start of the chapter we quoted a neurophysiologist who remarked that since research shows that attitudes can influence health, attention should be directed to the question of "what is the biochemistry of all this." However, we have seen that human disease cannot always be referenced through an understanding of its molecular mechanisms. Typically we will also want to know what caused the molecular mechanism to go awry, the more so as regards today's so-called diseases of choice, lifestyle-related diseases. Advocates of infomedicine contend

4. "Diseases have taken on idiosyncratic cultural meaning and they are each person's unique response to his or her lifestyle" (Achterberg 1985, 106).

that, with respect to their causal roots, there are effectively two categorically distinct types of diseases. First, there are diseases pertaining to cardiovascular disorders, many cancers, and respiratory ailments, to name a few, that afflict animals and are predominantly biological in origin. And there is another class of diseases with the same names, and these afflict humans alone and are predominantly biopsychocultural in origin. The two classes differ by the order of magnitude that separates cognitive-affective behavior in humans and in animals.

Illustrating this difference, advocates cite clinical studies of human hypertension. These studies, they note, reveal a direct influence on resting baseline blood pressure levels of such variables as one's psychological orientation (the effect of environment), social state (the effect of status), and interpersonal relationships (the effect of person) (Graham 1966, Lynch 1974, Long 1982). Analyzing these findings, James Lynch concludes that "overall reduction in resting blood pressure levels of hypertensive patients could be effected by altering their way of communicating with their social and natural world" (1985, 182). Psychosocial events mesh with physiological events to produce disease (hypertension). And, conversely, intervention in psychosocial (in combination with biological) variables is therapeutically sound (Thomas 1986).

For this reason, advocates urge that attention be directed not to the underlying biochemistry but to the underlying psychosociobiology of disease. However, confounding this task is the abiding Cartesian legacy of the mutually noncommunicative sciences of biology, psychology, and sociology or cultural anthropology. Our very language militates against the initiative to join together what the seventeenth-century scientific revolution has rent asunder. We cannot speak psychosociobiologically (i.e., bioculturally) without committing a neologism. We are, however, reductionistically fluent. Microbiologist John Leavitt, formerly of N.I.H., illustrates this fluency: "If we can define the molecular nature of cancer, then that information can tell us what the common denominator [in the cancer cell] is. And understanding that defect should allow us to define a universal cure for cancer."

Curiously, pronouncements like this go unremarked. The conditional expressed here is valid only if the characteristic cause of human cancer is biological and not biopsychocultural. Doubtlessly, the cause of some human cancers derives from a genetic defect present before or a mutation occurring during fertilization. But, by reason of natural selection pressures, these are rarities. What gives credibility to pronouncements like Leavitt's, and Berg's cited earlier, is the ease with which our language and disciplinary categories invite us to visualize mechanistically and reason reductionistically. We can picture links leading from an embattled DNA command tower to cellular processes run amok, like typewriter keys whose letters have been jumbled. To give voice to ideology (a), schematized at the start of the chapter, we need only mention the sciences listed and their relative hierarchical order. But to give voice to ideology (b), we need to visualize cybernetically and be prepared to say something like "psychoculturobiology," an unspeakable task. The idiom and categories that invite one visualization pattern disinvite its counterpart. Accordingly, animal models prevail, and *biopsychocultural* remains ineffable.

We get some sense of this linguistic monarchy when we try to script the psychologist instructing the neurophysiologist: "Since research shows that the release of neural transmitters can influence health, attention should be directed to the question of what is the psychology of all this." To help unseat this royalty, infomedicalists propose the analogy of blushing as a "disease." Experimental evidence for the genesis of "lifestyle-related" diseases like human hypertension, a link to cardiovascular disorders is, they say, better understood by means of a biocultural model (blushing condition) than a biological model (infectious disease). Diagnosing such diseases has more in common with how we might diagnose a person who blushes inadvertently than with how we might diagnose a typhoid-affected animal. Thus, they ask us to extrapolate the incongruity of the conditional: "If we can define the molecular nature of blushing, then that information could allow us to define a cure for blushing."

Let us pursue this analogy a bit further. The vocabulary of blushing invites an interactionist model (ideology b above). Its grammar permits recognition that the roseate facial coloration is only the bodily expression of a psychocultural syndrome, "a language for dramatizing the mental." (Recall Aristotle's definition of human feelings as "words [*logoi*] expressed in human flesh.") Therefore, to say that when a person blushes (develops hypertension) his or her body is saying something meaningful is not to make a statement that calls for experimental verification. It is not to make an empirical claim but to utter a truism. This is the way the rules governing the vocabulary of blushing operate: "I blush" just means I express a certain biopsychocultural syndrome. Nor is this to say that blushing is not always accompanied by select biochemical processes, only that it cannot be explained in terms of these processes. They do not define the meaning of the "pathology." Were the body denied its expression—through ingestion of an "anti-blush" drug—the "patient" would not thereby be cured of blushing. In short, blushing (the roseate cheek coloration)—unlike animal typhoid, say— *means* something. It has a semantic, or psychosocial, as well as a physiological dimension. Animals don't blush, nor do infants, nor people in social isolation. It takes a culture for blushing to occur.

So, in terms of our analogy, proponents of infomedicine may say that animal hypertension and human hypertension, for all their important commonalities, are *different* diseases in just the sense that animal "psychology" is different from human psychology. For them, our disposition to place quotation marks around words like *mind* and *culture* when applied to animals and animal communities underlies the difference between animal diseases and human diseases of choice. They liken the physical expression of blushing to a sentence (signal) in that to erase the sentence—through an anti-blushing drug, for instance—is not to eradicate its meaning: the immaterial proposition survives the physical sentence. (Were the body denied its natural expression, it would likely seek another, apparently unrelated pathway for that expression—an "allergy.") For this reason, rules governing the grammar of blushing (and, by analogical extension, today's diseases of civilization) cannot be decoded at a center for molecular and genetic medicine. Infomedically speaking, the "text" (body) and what it says (meaning) are as disparate as the languages of biology and sociobiology or, more accurately, culturobiology. And as the analogy is meant to illustrate, the full etiological story incorporates the question: How can we get at the psychocultural roots of the dysfunctional biochemical mechanism?

Short of raising this question, we are not likely to realize our goal—to cure the disease. To redress its ravages, the infomedicalist first generalizes Lynch's experimentally derived conclusion regarding hypertension: if we allow for the various structural or corporeal elements that contribute to blood pressure, hypertension "is also determined by a person's overall harmonic dialogue with the environment" (1985, 183).[5] More particularly, it is also determined by the dissonance between what is manifesting physically (sustained blood pressure elevations) and what the person perceives to be manifesting ("I am not agitated"). Essential to effective therapy is a means to reconcile the two: assist the patient to get "in touch" with who he or she is, an embodied mind. In infomedical terms, when normal transmitter channels are closed off, psychosocial signals can be redirected along physiological channels and so translated into biological language and sent as organic (e.g., dermatological) signals. The purpose of treatment, which may combine perceived self-efficacy, self-hypnosis, and imagery, is to heighten the patients' mental-emotional sensitivity, to make them aware of the events taking place within them—"to listen to their skin," in Theodore Grossbart's phrase.

This idea that a person is a new way of being an animal in the world is based on the infomedical premise that only a human being possesses a corporeal "language for dramatizing the mental." The brain minds the body, where this informational theoretic use of the verb "mind" applies uniquely to humans as a result of mutually potentiating levels of self-conscious mental organization and conscious (or unconscious, auto-

5. The analogy of blushing is taken from Lynch.

nomic) neural organization. The wisdom of the human body differs from the wisdom of the animal body by the margin separating self-conscious and merely conscious behavior. Infomedicine seeks to therapeutically leverage this difference. Whereas a biological being is normally in harmonic (i.e., symbiotic) dialogue with the environment, only a biocultural being can engage (self-consciously or not) in prolonged disharmonic dialogue with the environment.This is true to the extent that psychosociology (culture) can war with biology (nature). Diseases of choice have to be reperceived in part as enacting a drama whose text is the body. "The body's treachery is thought to have its own inner logic." Disease is drama; the physician is medical hermeneuticist.

## Conclusion

Historically, in the case of infectious diseases it seemed beneficial to be able to narrow the resolution of focus from agencies like tropical breeding grounds and insects to microbes and viruses. It was the difference between being able to prescribe relatively vague, precautionary measures like avoidance therapy and precise, curative measures like antibiotics. It was also the difference between possessing a statistical "black box" knowledge of infectious disease and a perspicuous "glass box" knowledge whereby investigators could seek precise mechanisms of action; and so achieve understanding. This led in turn to increasingly effective treatment—from Salvarsan to penicillin.

This century-and-a-half-long trajectory from a broader environmental to a laserlike biochemical context of disease became the prototype of medical scientific explanation. As Dubos states, "This shift occurred simultaneously in medicine and in the various fields of general biology. For example, the Darwinian approach to evolution was replaced by studies focused first on chromosomes, then on genes, finally on molecular genetics" (1965, 209). The harvest of this narrowing of medical focus from the broader environmental to the more channeled biochemical context of disease was adoption of one of the central tenets of biomedicine, the widespread assumption "that complete understanding of man's problems will eventually emerge from the detailed knowledge of the structures and functions which are common to all living things" (1965, 210). This assumption informs the RX strategy, displayed above.

We can only surmise what path scientific medicine might have taken had the leading disease burden during its formative years been not infectious and nutritional diseases but today's so-called afflictions of civilization. From the vantage point of hindsight what we see today is a well-entrenched infrastructure with a remarkable series of successes to its credit. For want of an alternative strategy, this infrastructure is now asked to cope with a species of disease whose sources appear to be quite different from the sources of those diseases whose cure was the touchstone for the development and eventual adoption of that infrastructure. Hence the contemporary dilemma: whether to pursue a strategy capable of making use of the powerful biotechnical resources and skills invested in that infrastructure, or a strategy that lacks a comparable infrastructure but, at least at face value, is well suited to the diseases at hand.

That other options might fruitfully be entertained suggests a need for a foundations component in medicine. This will be further examined in the last chapter. Application of the conventional nosology, the prevailing strategy, must proceed concurrently with periodic reexamination of that strategy in the light of subsequent findings, or earlier findings reperceived in a fresh light. In this way the foundational, or second-revolution, question presents itself: could a body of evidence *ever* arise that would invite the medical enterprise to reexamine the prudence of keeping faith with its current strategy? And how would the enterprise discover that a threshold had been crossed? As the hard science turn illustrates, short of raising the foundations question, the *only* available evaluation of the medical enterprise is the two-step ritual of (1) saluting recognized successes while (2) flagging yet-to-be successes through issuing promissory notes on biomedical capital.

Now the potential gains and losses of adopting the biomedical strategy are exposed. It rests on a concept of disease that generates a distinction between risk and causal factor that is based in part on whether the factor is physical or nonphysical. That is, while a risk factor may be physical (high cholesterol intake) or behavioral (a cognitive-affective disorder), a causal factor can only be physical (microorganism). Thus, any nonphysical factor shown to be a statistically significant covariant of a dysfunctional organic process can, by virtue of a strategic constraint, only be a risk or situational or complicating factor. This is because within the conventional nosology it cannot be part of any "known mechanism of action"—condition (a). By this fact alone it cannot be an etiological or causal factor. And this is a definitional, not empirical, constraint.

But as evidence for "diseases of civilization" or "stress-related" diseases mounts, there is a consequent stockpiling of situational or risk factors—and with it, of promissory notes. This means that the domain of preventive medicine expands and with it the domain of *ad hoc*, state-of-the-art treatment. So we have seen over the past generation a dramatic rise, even within established medical circles, in the use of therapies without formal status in the conventional nosology. These include not only nutritional and exercise regimens—which might be argued to have a basis, hitherto untapped, in biomedicine—but also a wide range of "holistic" therapies from relaxation to behavioral counseling to transactional psychophysiological therapies.

It might be thought that it matters little under what rubric treatment is prescribed, whether preventive or curative medicine, as long as the appropriate therapy is administered. But this overlooks a significant fact. When behavioral factors, like a cognitive-affective disorder, are designated risk factors, and their antidotes (for example, behavioral counseling) are therefore adopted as part of preventive medicine measures, these measures are of necessity administered in a theoretical vacuum. Their rationale can only be based on statistical correlations, not a scientific nosology. Without a mechanism for tracking risk factors to their etiological roots, the therapies of this branch of preventive medicine represent a holding action, awaiting developments on the research front to explain, via causal pathways, *why* its variables place us at risk. By definition, this branch of preventive medicine dealing with psychosocially oriented therapy is a repository for those statistically significant observations currently recalcitrant to explanations in the prevailing nosology. Once its state variables (risk factor) are subsumed under that nosology, ipso facto they become causal factors (e.g., "germs" after the development of microbiology). And that branch of state-of-the-art preventive medicine is assimilated into curative medicine. The shift, therefore, is more than terminological. Now a mechanism of action, a network of interconnected causal pathways (nosology) articulates the disease process, explaining why risk factors are not just risky but pathogenic. And what in biological medicine is ad hoc therapy, in biocultural medicine is scientifically rationalized medicine.

But beyond this, any mechanism possesses a surplus of empirical content and so functions as a heuristic device for suggesting novel intervention options. We will remember how this heuristic potential expanded biomedical horizons in the last century. When interest turned from the role of environmental agents (situational factors) to that of microbiological agents (etiological factors) in the production of infectious diseases, biomedical analysis replaced statistically based, demographic and epidemiological analyses. The results were increasingly sophisticated bacteriological and biochemical investigations—cellular, chromosomal, genetic—tracing neurophysiological pathways that linked the conjectural agents to the intimate structures and mechanisms of living organisms.

Earlier we quoted Kenneth Schaffner as saying that biomedical theories were bona fide scientific in that they "admit of all the important features of theories in physics and chemistry: . . . [they] are testable and have excess empirical content, they organize knowledge in inductive and sometimes even deductive ways, . . . and they are applicable for prediction and control in crucially important areas such as . . . health-care delivery" (1980, 88). By replacing only the infrastructure, the same claim might be made for infomedical theories. Infomedicine too is capable of organizing knowledge in inductive and even deductive ways, as well as applying to prediction and control in health care delivery. Biomedicine progressed by explaining macro-objects of interest in terms of their micro-structure. Infomedicine explains micro-objects (and macro-objects) of interest in terms of their ecostructure. Insofar as this heuristic potential can be shown to attach to infomedical explanation, Zucker's claim too that "where there is truly no physiological problem, there is no disease" (1981, 146) can be paraphrased. Thus, infomedically speaking, "Where there is truly no biocultural problem, there is no disease." Reviewing biomedical successes, Zucker noted that they were due to the strategy of looking to micro-structure as the best explanation for macro-behavior. He added: "[P]redictability will increase as one uses more and more of the micro-level to explain the macro-level" (1981, 149). As the biomedicalist's touchstone is genetics and molecular biology, the infomedicalist's touchstone is ecology and evolutionary biology. For the infomedical model, therefore, the proper study of the physician is not, as Murphy suggested, targeted primarily toward biochemistry. Instead, more ambitiously, it is distributed across the spectrum of each of the foregoing sciences, from geobiochemistry and ecology to information theory and their cognates. The revolutionary implications of such an ambitious articulation are offered in Chapter 14.

# 14

## *The Infomedical Revolution*

Part Two argued that détente—the joining together of biomedical cure and holistic care—did not work. Such an approach, in any guise, is conceptually confused. It asks that we simultaneously accept the patient as a biocultural being at one level and a physiologically complex organism at another level. Herein lies a major contribution offered by the infomedical alternative. An interactive thesis is not layered on top of a reductionist thesis. Rather, the interactive thesis wells up from the self-organizing foundations upon which it is built. Thus, the infomedical approach avoids the hazards of détente by subsuming biomedical findings within its explanatory framework.

This chapter will examine significant levels of organization that impact the state of health and disease of the patient. These levels of organization conform to the commonsense levels of the world we live in—biological, psychological, social, and bionoospheric. The explanatory range of the infomedical model is revealed by exploring the impact of these levels on the patient. With each level, the laws of infomedicine and their interactive foundations become more evident.

## Background

Claude Shannon, a major pioneer in the field of information theory, stated that "the human being acts as an ideal decoder." The infomedical model begins with the assumption that the human patient is such an ideal decoder—a cybernetic system whose state of health (or illness) is the product of both its internal organization and external messages that may derive from a variety of levels of organization, e.g., physical, psychological, or social.

The goal of the infomedical model can be generalized briefly as the accumulation of two levels of cybernetic understanding. The first level is to understand the "programs" or "grammar" that govern the interactions of the internal workings of the patient-as-cybernetic-system. Here, the rules governing the interactions of the parts are modeled. The second level is to understand which messages "inform" the system and the nature of this impact. To inform, in this context, means to shape or reshape—literally to in-form or re-form. Messages from one level of organization can reshape and be reshaped by messages from another level of organization. As such, messages cannot be understood in isolation. Therefore, one must take into account both the environment in which the message circulates and the state of the system. Interpreting these messages turns them into information that the doctor or patient can then use to counter the disease/illness state.

Infomedicine expands the spectrum of messages recognized as important to the health and well-being of the system beyond biomedicine's bio-messages. Bio-messages are physical. They include too much or too little of some critical substance and intrinsically damaging agents. The latter cause disease states through contact with the organism-as-patient. Infomedicine's message spectrum includes psycho-messages and socio-messages as well. In this way, the infomedical model formally recognizes that a behavioral state, set of cultural values, or belief system, for example, can actively maintain or reshape a physiological state, and vice versa, in a negative or positive causal feedback process. The infomedical contention is that by expanding the spectrum of medically relevant messages beyond bio-messages, we make more informed diagnoses and self-diagnoses. This becomes the therapeutic goal of infomedicine—to increase the range of information so that both the physician and the patient-as-decoder-of-information have what they need for cybernetic control and maintenance.

# Postmodern Disease Equation: Significant Levels of Organization

### BIO-ACTIVE MESSAGES AND PROGRAMS

We begin by subsuming biomedical laws into the infomedical framework. The biomedical model offers a comprehensive rationalization for the disease-producing effects of physical pathogens. It does so by recognizing the human system as a complex (as opposed to simple) organismic system as well as the fact that physical pathogens can interact in disease-producing fashion. From another perspective, such an analysis is a partial infomedical approach. Absent is consideration of the systemic impact of messages from extraphysical levels of organization. When such a consideration is built into the analysis, the biomedical constraint of focusing only on bio-messages becomes a special case of infomedicine. We may now rephrase the two biomedical laws offered in Chapter 2 as a subset of a series of infomedical laws:

*Infomedical Law 1*

Human diseases reflect the outcome of an interaction between the programs defining the physiological responses of state variables by which the system is composed as well as the bio-active information processed by these programs.

And:

*Infomedical Law 2*

Change in the state of one physiological variable mutually activates an appropriate change in another physiological variable.

## PSYCHO-ACTIVE AND SOCIO-ACTIVE MESSAGES AND PROGRAMS

The bio-active messages and programs comprise one component of the infomedical disease equation. Psycho- and socio-active messages and programs comprise the next two levels or components. These two components will be discussed together because the lines of demarcation between the two are often blurred. Divorce and retirement serve as two examples of life events that impact the individual at both a personal (psychological) and social level.

We can expand the relevant message/program spectrum to include the following four infomedical laws:

*Infomedical Law 3*

Human diseases reflect the outcome of an interaction between the programs defining the responses of the state variables (including biological and psychological) by which the system is composed as well as the information (messages) processed by these programs. Whatever the proximate (physical) cause of disease—viral, genetic, metabolic, or neoplastic—the psychological state is a codeterminant of prevalence, cause, and outcome.

*Infomedical Law 4*

Change in the physiological state (bio-messages and programs) mutually interacts with a change in the psychological state (psycho-messages and programs), conscious or unconscious, and, conversely, change in the psychological state, conscious or unconscious, mutually interacts with a change in the physiological state.

*Infomedical Law 5*

Human diseases reflect the outcome of an interaction between the bio- and psycho-active messages and programs with cultural messages and programs in a mediating role. Whatever the proximate cause(s) of disease—physical or psychological—the way in which society is organized is a determinant of prevalence, cause, and outcome.

*Infomedical Law 6*

Change in the nature of social conditions (socio-messages and programs) mutually interacts with changes in the psychophysiologic state, whether self-conscious or unselfconscious, and, conversely, change in the psychophysiologic state, whether self-conscious or unselfconscious, mutually interacts with changes in the nature of social conditions.

With the emergence of mind, a medically significant psycho-active factor joins the somatic component in the disease equation. In this way, members of the human community are subject to diseases that do not threaten members of other biotic communities. With the emergence of qualitatively more complex social structures, a socio-active series of factors (sedentary lifestyles, "unnatural" working environments, alienation, deadlines) enters the disease equation. This can be accounted for, in part, by natural psychophysiological responses (the results of species evolution) no longer dovetailing with the heightened pace of social change. Thus, we see that as the human system evolves to greater complexity, so too is the message spectrum that impacts its system state enlarged.

## TECHNO-ACTIVE MESSAGES AND PROGRAMS

Because of the nature of the coevolutionary process, and in particular the looming world-reshaping role now being played by humans, there is reason for designating another level of organization that critically interfaces in mutual feedback fashion with the bio-, psycho-, and socio-active levels. This level further extends the list of etiologically emergent elements in the disease equation to include techno-active factors. This formally recognizes that humans, in the course of cultural development, can and have dramatically impacted (i.e., qualitatively changed) the environment in which they must adapt to maintain their health. This suggests the following two infomedical laws:

*Infomedical Law 7*

Human diseases reflect the outcome of an interaction between natural selective pressures (terrestrial body, biosphere) and cultural selective pressures (terrestrial mind, noosphere). Whatever the predominant proximate cause(s) of disease—physical, psychological, or social—the nature of human decisions and actions (terrestrial mind) is a determinant of prevalence, cause, and outcome.

*Infomedical Law 8*

Change in the state of the physical environment or terrestrial body (biosphere) mutually interacts with a change in the state of the cultural environment or terrestrial mind (noosphere), whether self-conscious or unselfconscious; and, conversely, change in the state of the cultural environment or terrestrial mind (noosphere), whether self-conscious or unselfconscious, mutually interacts with a change in the state of the physical environment or terrestrial body (biosphere).

The importance of offering the techno-active component resides in the transcendent perspective it provides to the medical profession. It provides a bridge from the very important "narrower" concerns of the medical practitioner for the individual patient to the wider concerns of the planet. The techno-active component of infomedicine takes medicine out of the offices and hospitals and situates the profession in the universe. As a result, this transcendent perspective gives meaning to Dubos's vision: "In its highest form, medicine remains potentially the richest expression of science because it is concerned with all the various aspects of man's humanness" (1965, 220).

These components of a postmodern disease equation are made intelligible by the premises underwriting the self-organizing systems or infomedical model. Recognition of these interacting levels of organization enables the conscientious and able practitioner to identify important messages and programs that help provide a comprehensive understanding of the patient (read: patient-as-information-processing-system).

## The Infomedical Contention

An understanding of the revolutionary implications of the infomedical postmodern disease equation is possible by reviewing the logic for each of its component parts. In contrast to the exclusively physical (bio-active) orientation espoused by biomedicine, the importance of psycho-active agents is based on a major difference between members of the human community and members of other biotic communities: their mindfulness. This yields a concept of the patient and treatment in contrast to the dualistic orientation of biomedicine. In the systems language described by the differential equations invoked earlier to define the patient, recognition of psycho-active factors represents an "extension" in the concept of the human patient. This extension is defined by the emergent level of organization—mindfulness—and its inclusion as part of a mutual-causal feedback loop. It is designated by an additional, interacting state variable $(Qi)$ of the systemic whole. Whereas the animal (or tree) patient—the biological organism—is represented by

$$\frac{dQn}{dt} = f(Q1a, Q1b, \ldots),$$

the human patient—the person or psychobiological being—is represented by

$$\frac{dQn}{dt} = f(Q1a, Q1b, \ldots Q2 \ldots),$$

where $Q2$ stands for this additional level of complexity. By definition, the two systems differ qualitatively.

From the socio-active perspective, members of the human community differ in still another vital respect from members of other biotic communities. This difference relates to the nature of the social structures that humans erect. Because of the dominance of the natural environment over species evolution, members of other biotic communities are, in the course of socialization, further integrated into nature. Natural responses are made to dovetail with environmental conditions; growing in host-parasite fashion, the two are literally made for each other. The natural environment (host) dictates the course of species evolution (parasite). Or rather the two, related symbiotically, are unselfconsciously coevolutionary. According to the socio-active contention, this relative dominance of natural environment over species evolution was profoundly modified in the evolution of humankind. Human species evolution moves along two fronts at once, one biological, the other cultural. By means of the second front, cultural adaptation, humans have been able to insulate themselves from the natural environment and exploit it. Over time they have created artificial environments to whose altered conditions, however, they were, in the biological dimensions $(Q1a, Q1b, \ldots)$, ill-adapted. For a full accounting of the disease process, this added state variable in health adaptation has to be factored into the disease equation. The health implications of messages and programs derived from the emergence of social structure as a significant level of organization is the basis of the socio-active argument. Humans must cope with the conditions of a changing social environment $(Q3)$ that, with respect to their biological makeup, is anachronistic. There is, then, in addition to the original biological dimension, represented by $(Q1a, Q1b, \ldots)$, and the mindful dimension $(Q2)$, the social dimension $(Q3)$. With respect to our original formula, the socio-active definition of disease is rewritten:

$$\frac{dQi}{dt} = f(Q1, Q2, Q3)$$

It is understood that each state variable can itself be resolved into subsystems ($Qia$, $Qib$ . . .).

This disparity between humans' inherited biological apparatus—designated by the value assigned to $Q1$—and today's altered social conditions—designated by the value assigned to $Q3$—is invoked to account for altered conditions conducive to disease. Dubos refers to this contemporary medical burden as "diseases of civilization." The socio-active argument does not imply that human biology is not changing in response to the changing, artifactual environment; only that the principles of natural selection take hold at orders of magnitude slower than principles of cultural selection.

The techno-active argument takes the socio-active argument a step further. Acknowledging the disparity between yesterday's and today's environmental conditions, the techno-active perspective emphasizes the specifically human origin of and growing responsibility for this disparity. Disease, from the socio-active perspective, is a function of maladaptation, a matter of shifting social environmental conditions disrupting an individual's adaptive capabilities. The techno-active position maintains that due to the unique adaptation mode of humans, in the course of their cultural development they have embarked on a wholesale change of environmental conditions, both social and physical, that characterize the environment in which humankind must adapt to maintain health. If for most of history the growth of human population and artifacts was slow and its impact on earth ecology comparatively small, with the rise of industrialization this condition was measurably reversed. The successive domestication of stone, wood, and skins (the tool industry) and, later, of animals (husbandry) and plants (agriculture) and, later still, of thermal energy (industrialization) has had a leveraging terrestrial effect. The product of this civilizing process—one scientist-philosopher terms it the *hominisation* of the planet (Teilhard de Chardin 1959, 164)—forms the mainstay of the techno-active argument: in the course of civilizing the planet humans are altering its structural contours. Through their cultural choices they are empowered to refashion the earth in their image. The coevolutionary process is gradually becoming self-conscious.

We can now identify the revolutionary potential of the infomedical model. It not only extends the range of medically significant information but also extends the conceptual reach of the medical enterprise to include the concerns of the planet.

Infomedicine embraces the premise that humans are engaged in collectively co-creating the environmental conditions to which they must adapt in order to avoid disease and maintain health. Infomedicine recognizes that the nature of our social organization, the social environment, is a source of potential pathology and so, too, is the nature of the organization of today's physical environment itself. And this organization is in essential ways the product of human decisions and actions. Called cultural adaptation by anthropologists, increasingly the totality of these decisions and actions vies with the processes of natural or biological adaptation to coproduce today's terrestrial environment, the "new earth."

Infomedicine in its most cosmic form extends beyond the province of the medical profession. An example of techno-active infomedicine being practiced today provides a means for seeing both the medical implications of bionoospheric dis-ease and how therapeutic redress is beyond the traditional scope of medical practice. In the past few years a group of American doctors has begun speaking out in graphic terms about the dangers of nuclear war. This group, the Physicians for Social Responsibility (PSR), and a related group called the International Physicians for the Prevention of Nuclear War have dedicated their efforts to campaign for nuclear disarmament. They see this as the only way to avoid a medical tragedy beyond any possible cure; hence, social action is seen as a cure for a disease that has not yet struck. These groups have attempted to arouse the public conscience and raise its consciousness regarding the devastation that could become "the last epidemic," a new phrase that has come into being with the emergence of the bionoospheric entity. Similar consciousness raising is starting to take shape in response to human activities that cause depletions in the ozone layer. We may anticipate that infomedically oriented physicians will take the lead in developing appropriate therapeutic responses to this biospheric "lesion."

In summary, the infomedical perspective can be translated into the stimulus-response idiom as shown in Figure 14.1. Here, two formerly distinctive environments converge: the natural environment (biosphere) and the cultural or artifactual environment. The latter principle, called the noosphere by Teilhard de Chardin, is the product of collective mind—ideas, values, technologies, and institutions. Together, the two environments form the *bionoosphere.* This qualitative transformation can be represented schematically as in Figure 14.2.

Here we see the infomedical "patient" writ large. Derivatively we

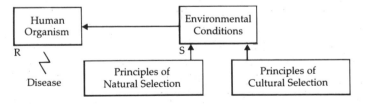

FIGURE 14.1

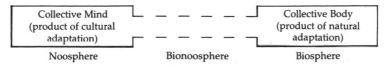

| Collective Mind (product of cultural adaptation) | | Collective Body (product of natural adaptation) |
|---|---|---|
| Noosphere | Bionoosphere | Biosphere |

FIGURE 14.2

can understand the infomedical human patient as a biocultural being. The infomedical contention recognizes that shifting conditions in the terrestrial or ecomental environment that result from human intervention in natural geochemical cycles or in the genetic composition of bacteria, for example, have to be acknowledged as potentially disequilibrating, both to the bionoospheric "patient" and residually to the individual human patient having to adapt to these anachronistic conditions. Such shifting conditions necessitate change of collective lifestyle therapies, thus readjusting the ratios of interacting ecosystems. Because we humans—not fate or nature or the gods—are collectively responsible for the conditions by which health is maintained or disease incurred, responsibility for these conditions ultimately rests with us. By virtue of the consequences, this is a medical responsibility and so a necessary part of a comprehensive medical synthesis.

# 15

## *The Invisible College and the Foundations of Medicine*

In the introduction to this book, we said that the concepts underwriting today's medical practice reflect the problem set from which they arose. This set was formed largely by nineteenth- and early-twentieth-century challenges posed by nutritional and infectious diseases. Although the problems have changed, the equipment we bring to the task (premises, methodological tools, technologies) is by and large the legacy of the earlier challenge. The foundations initiative enjoins periodic reexamination of the fit between the problem set and the strategy designed for its resolution.

The issue of strategy change is not, of course, as straightforwardly conceptual as these remarks imply. The issue does not turn on just the worthiness of a strategy based on its ability to convert a given amount of currently unusable data ("noise") or still-to-be-discovered data into medically useful information. There are external as well as internal constraints on embracing a successor model—even one that promises to excel in such a test.[1] Our concepts, our research orientation, and clinical practice all organize themselves around the puzzle forms set by the received framework. Beyond this, our social structures—hospital associations, medical suppliers, allied health services, insurance programs, legal sanctions, federal policies—are embedded in the institutional mesh of the model in place. To suggest replacing a model therefore is to suggest dismantling a broadly institutionalized infrastructure ("tier 0") providing multiple essential health support services to millions nationwide. Our earlier figure depicting the complex, three-tiered conceptual structure embodied by any working model may therefore be further complexified by linking it to the realpolitik, signified by tier 0 in Figure 15.1.

Mediating between tier 0 and the large square above it is institutionalized medicine as reflected in its professional organizations (schools,

1. Paul Starr (1983) contends that politics, not science, largely influences the type of medicine practiced in America today.

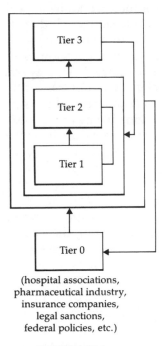

(hospital associations,
pharmaceutical industry,
insurance companies,
legal sanctions,
federal policies, etc.)

FIGURE 15.1

faculties, associations, journals). This is the "invisible college" which legitimizes the premises and explanatory presuppositions that remain implicit but uniquely characterize clinical practice, research strategy, admissions policies, and curriculum. The more this college is firmly established, the more the thought patterns of its sanctioned model become second nature and the more disposed its members to treat new challenges in terms of patterns developed in response to earlier (successfully resolved) challenges. Describing the pluses and minuses of such a disposition, Edward de Bono invokes the image of a river bed:

> An obvious advantage of this type of system is that things go on building up with a useful continuity. The disadvantage of the system is that it becomes very difficult to change the old patterns. The established patterns are like the streams and rivers that are formed on the surface of the land by the action of rain. Once the streams and rivers have become established they tend to become self-perpetuating as they drain off into themselves whatever rain falls on the land. (1983, 64)

At some stage the line blurs between what would count as counterevidence to the continued fluency of the model and simply new challenges to be resolved in its terms. For example, there is no way to determine by further empirical investigation whether, with regard to the brain system, more structural knowledge of its basic units—neural cells—and their interconnections will dispel the need for principles of hierarchical organization to account for its uniquely self-conscious behavior. Yet resolution of this question is preordained. For only in a vocabulary other than neurophysiology can the levels question be framed. Such a vocabulary is not conventionally sanctioned. We can thus anticipate the likely outcome of pursuing a strategy that seeks to incorporate self-organizing behavior into a single-level vocabulary. This is exemplified in the passage cited earlier from Douglas Hofstadter. To account for the self-consciousness displayed by the human brain, Hofstadter posits "a self-reinforcing 'resonance' between different levels." Still, he has no doubt that ultimately we will achieve "a totally reductionist but incomprehensible explanation" (1980, 709). The reason for this conclusion lies not in any empirical constraints but in the dictates of the language chosen for framing the explanation. In the reductionist vocabulary there is no way to express this "resonance." (Hence, the quotation marks around it.) It is a mystical (ineffable) concept, like emergence or self-organization. Because it cannot be said, it cannot be realized. ("Whereof one cannot speak, one must remain silent.")

This processing of new information by concepts already in place—new rain drained off into existing stream beds—can be seen in the way we assimilate today's diseases to concepts developed in response to yesterday's disease burden. We may recall that, historically, biomedical concepts arose in the course of late-nineteenth-century efforts to combat the major disease threat of that period. The nineteenth century was a period of intellectual ferment in medicine. Hippocratic medicine was out of touch with advances in the biological sciences. At the same time, a number of basic medical sciences were developing—physiology, cellular pathology, bacteriology—whose concepts were well suited to the task at hand. This development and the events leading up to it had eroded confidence in the predecessor "humors" and environmental medicine strategies. The time was ripe for fashioning new medical tools. Consequently, the notion of disease as caused by a physical agent (the "germ theory") grew apace with the discovery of covariations among cellular derangement, the presence of microbes, and infectious disease. The synthesis of chemicals designed to counteract the effect of these pathogens—"magic bullets" aimed at microbes—strengthened confidence in the new strategy. Its clinical application led to a dramatic decrease in the incidence of infectious diseases, in proportion to which its fundamental concepts came to be regarded as definitive of disease.

By the mid-twentieth century the dramatic reduction of the diseases that a century earlier had rallied the medical community behind the construction of a strategy adequate to the challenge erased any residual doubts about its working efficacy. By reason of the conceptual and technical tools that became a standard part of the professional training of physicians, the concepts of this strategy, biomedical concepts, "became ever more firmly established and controlled the way they looked at present situations." These concepts formed the pattern in whose image disease was perceived.

This development accounts for a reluctance to comply with recommendations that medicine extend the range of its care to include today's major illnesses. Such recommendations are thought to challenge the ramparts of scientific medicine, now defined by reference to concepts found so useful in the effort to stem infectious disease. Exemplifying this reluctance are the comments of one of the deans of the invisible college, the former editor of the *New England Journal of Medicine*, Franz J. Inglefinger. Speaking to a growing interest in a health movement that had mushroomed during the previous decade, holistic medicine, Inglefinger strikes a cautious note:

> The doctor should not be expected to play a major role in changing whatever lifestyle may be seriously detrimental. He has enough to do if he takes care of the crisis illnesses that do occur, and if he keeps up to date with the various scientific facts known about their nature and management. Hence, I would not consider the failure of the doctor to practice holistic medicine as substantive evidence of inferior medical practice. (1978)

The laissez-faire quality of these scaled-down expectations is dramatized when we substitute the word *infection* for *lifestyle* in the first sentence: "The doctor should not be expected to play a major role in changing whatever infection may be seriously detrimental." What makes one proposition acceptable and the other not is our commitment to a historically conditioned concept of scientific medicine. The notions of scientific medical practice and treatment of infectiouslike diseases, having evolved together, define one another. Hence, although doctors should be expected to play a major role in altering certain kinds of conditions like infections, it does not follow that they should play the same role with respect to conditions that contribute to the occurrence of diseases that do not conform to this pattern. Their science may not equip them to do so. Exemplar diseases, diseases like those encountered when scientific medicine was taking shape, are conceptualized as produced by an intrinsically damaging agent or too much or too little of some critical factor. The doctor's role is to select a supplement, a biochemical agent or surgical intervention that will counteract the damaging physical condition. (See Fig. 15.2.)

Inglefinger's comments suggest two sorts of disease, not one. There are acute diseases, like infections, tractable to the practice of scientific medicine, and there are diseases beyond the scope of scientific medicine. The latter might include any variety of diseases, ranging from

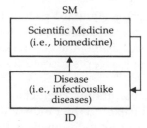

SM

ID

KEY: Upward arrow = "gives rise to"
Downward arrow = "proves increasingly effective in the treatment of"

FIGURE 15.2

psychosomatic illnesses to diseases of stress. Using Inglefinger's term, we might call the latter lifestyle-related diseases (LD) and the former infectiouslike diseases (ID). This division is further strengthened by Inglefinger when he converts what might be regarded as a shortfall of scientific medicine (SM), its incapacity to do much for this second variety of disease, into one of its triumphs: "Ironically, the present emphasis on eliminating 'bad' lifestyles and opting for the temperate life reflects the success of scientifically based medical practice in controlling acute illness and thus uncovering the importance of degenerative diseases and medicine's relative inability to do anything about them" (1978). Here is the basis for distinguishing two sorts of disease, "acute" and "degenerative." While one is subject to scientific medicine, the other is not—is subject, perhaps, to health care approaches like holistic medicine (HM). (See Fig. 15.3.)

It stands to reason that the doctor should not have to take responsibility for caring for patients with diseases that fall outside the range of his or her professional competence—the practice of scientific medicine. The foundational question is whether such a division represents an optimal solution to today's health needs. Or is the admission of the importance of a new type of disease for which today's prevailing model (SM) cannot do much presumptive evidence that we should reexamine that model?[2] If the framework developed in response to an earlier challenge is ill-suited for application to a new disease threat, what is today's responsibility to entertain a successor framework, much as was done in the last century?

So relativizing the current concept of scientific medicine to a chance encounter with a particular disease threat (Figure 15.2) permits us to

2. An epidemiological and statistical study has concluded that the "war against cancer" of the past thirty-five years must be judged a "qualified failure" (Bailar et al. 1986, 1231; see also Cairns 1985). The conclusion has prompted rebuttals by spokespersons for the National Cancer Institute and others. So we need to suspend final judgment on the validity of the conclusion. However, one thing the study has not prompted, so far as we can tell, is public discussion of the foundations question concerning the adequacy of the model in terms of which the war is being conducted.

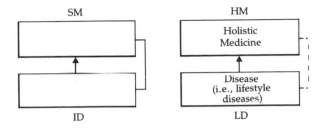

FIGURE 15.3

reconsider the inevitability of the premises of today's model. What might have happened, we may ask, had the nineteenth-century medical community chanced instead upon today's lifestyle-related diseases, diseases of the sort that Inglefinger refers to? Would our dilemma now be one of reconciling the central role of *psychosocial* pathogens in the prevailing "biocultural" model with the incongruous but empirically well-documented correlation of *physical* agents and today's chief disease assailant, infectious and nutritional diseases? This "what if" serves to remind us of the range of today's commitment to biomedical concepts. In the final analysis, their worthiness is measured by their clinical usefulness as regards the diseases at hand. There is no overriding conceptual (as distinct from infrastructural) reason to wage today's war with weapons fashioned for yesterday's battle.

Still, with an infrastructure already in place, it is difficult, psychologically, to entertain the foundational task of reviewing the premises of today's model. Not only are we still understandably flushed with its recent successes but, as Inglefinger's remarks also show, criteria of success are internally determined, and with but a single model in the field we have no way to assess failure. "It is not the ideas that we do not have that block our thinking but the ideas that we do have," says de Bono. "It is always easier to find a new way of looking at things if there is no fixed way already established" (1972, 66). Established patterns, he says, represent the natural development of a pattern: "They come about through the self-organization of information as it comes in. The chance nature of the encounter with certain types of situation, the chance sequence in which the pieces of information are collected, all affect the development of the established pattern" (1983, 160). For this reason, "the natural pattern may not be the best one," he concludes. "In a sequence system the final arrangement of available information is very unlikely to make the best use of that information. This is because the best possible use would be made if all the information had arrived at once and the sequence of arrival played no part" (1972, 60).

In a sequence system we arrive at Figure 15.3, the left and right sides of the figure reflecting the chance sequence in which the pieces of information were collected. Had all the information arrived at once, we might instead be looking at Figure 15.4, in which the best possible use of all the information is made.

Here is a foundations parable for our time. Insofar as our concepts are the spectacles by which events become information, to the extent that our concepts form sequentially—so are not optimally arranged—it is prudent periodically to take the foundations turn: examine the adequacy of the edifice we inhabit, the apparatus we use—not just for solving our problems but for seeing what information there is.

Let us conclude by applying the Inglefinger criterion to this book's thesis:

> The clinical question is, So what? What is the clinical importance of a link between the mind and the body?

For an answer we may turn the floor over to a senior professor at the "college": "The answer is that counselling in the acute phase of disease and psychological support in the chronic may be as important to outcome as many other therapeutic measures now undertaken" ("Emotion and Immunity" 1985, 134).

A corner has been turned. Within the college itself, faculty are beginning to speak the unspeakable. Has mind-body dualism been quietly interred? "[Experimental] results . . . indicate an effect of psychological factors on cancer and are compatible with an effect via immunological mechanisms" ("Emotion and Immunity" 1985, 133). Has the Hygeian circle, sundered in the seventeenth century, been rejoined? The psyche ("psychological factors") is being spoken of as having a direct impact on the soma ("cancer"). Psychological factors are imputed to modify the immunologic mechanisms of the host and alter the course of disease. That which has been shown experimentally to be true of animals (Ader 1981) now is said *mutatis mutandis* to be also true of humans.

What are the implications of this extraordinary contemporary event?

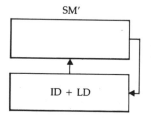

FIGURE 15.4

From a foundations perspective, the critical fluctuation has occurred. "The relation between emotion and immunity may prove to be another strong argument for a return towards whole-person medicine" ("Emotion and Immunity" 1985, 134). If mind can directly affect body and if psychotherapy (e.g., counseling, psychological support) may be as important to outcome as physical therapy (e.g., chemotherapy)—and, moreover, if these two contentions are experimentally validated and can be scientifically underwritten (Part Three)—then scientific medicine has bridged into the postmodern era: medicine's second revolution.

# Bibliography

BOOKS

Achterberg, Jeanne. 1985. *Imagery in Healing*. Boston: Shambhala.

Achterberg, J., and Lawlis, G. F. 1978. *Imagery of Cancer: A Diagnostic Tool for the Process of Disease*. Champaign Ill.: Institute for Personality and Ability Testing.

———. 1980. *Bridges of the Bodymind: Behavioral Approaches to Health Care*. Champaign, Ill.: Institute for Personality and Ability Testing.

———. 1984. *Imagery and Disease*. Champaign, Ill.: Institute for Personality and Ability Testing.

Ader, Robert, and Cohen, Nicolas, eds. *Psychoneuroimmunology*. New York: Academic Press.

Ashby, Eric. 1978. *Reconciling Man with the Environment*. Palo Alto, Calif.: Stanford University Press.

Bailey, H., and Love, M. 1968. *A Short Practice of Surgery*, 14th ed. London: Lewis.

Bateson, Gregory. 1973. *Steps toward an Ecology of Mind*. New York: Ballantine.

Benson, Herbert. 1979. *The Mind-Body Effect*. New York: Simon and Schuster.

Bernstein, Richard. 1983. *Beyond Objectivism and Relativism: Science, Hermaneutics and Praxis*. Philadelphia: University of Pennsylvania Press.

Bertalanffy, Ludvig von. 1968. *General System Theory*. New York: George Braziller.

Black, D.A.K. 1968. *The Logic of Medicine*. London: Oliver and Boyd.

Boulding, Kenneth. 1964. *The Image*. Ann Arbor. University of Michigan Press

Boyden, Stephen V., ed. 1970. *The Impact of Civilization on the Biology of Man*. Canberra: Australian National University Press.

Brinton, Crane. 1963. *Ideas and Man*. Englewood Cliffs, N.J.: Prentice Hall.

Brod, Craig. 1984. *Technostress: The Human Cost of the Computer Revolution*. Reading, Mass.: Addison-Wesley.

Brody, Howard. 1980. *Placebos and the Philosophy of Medicine*. Chicago: University of Chicago Press.

Bronowski, Jacob. 1973. *The Ascent of Man*. Boston: Little, Brown.

———. 1959. *The Common Sense of Science*. New York: Vintage Books.

———. 1965. *Science and Human Values*. New York: Harper and Row.

———. 1977. *A Sense of the Future*. Cambridge: MIT Press.

Bronowski, Jacob, et al. 1963. *Technology: Man Remakes His World*. New York: Doubleday.

Brown, Barbara. 1974. *New Mind, New Body*. New York: Bantam Books.

315

————. 1978. *Stress and the Art of Biofeedback.* New York: Bantam Books.

Burnet, Macfarlane. 1971. *Genes, Dreams, and Realities.* Aylesbury, England: Medical and Technical Publishing Co.

Bury, J. B. 1932. *The Idea of Progress.* New York: Dover Publications.

Campbell, Bernard. 1976. *Humankind Emerging.* Boston: Little, Brown.

Campbell, Jeremy. 1982. *Grammatical Man: Information, Entropy, Language, and Life.* New York: Simon and Schuster.

Capra, Fritjof. 1982. *The Turning Point.* New York: Bantam Books.

Carlson, Rick J. 1975. *The End of Medicine.* New York: John Wiley.

————, ed. 1976. *The Frontiers of Science and Medicine.* Chicago: Henry Regnery.

Carter, Richard. 1983. *Descartes' Medical Philosophy: The Organic Solution to the Mind-Body Problem.* Baltimore: Johns Hopkins University Press.

Cassirer, Ernst. 1951. *The Philosophy of the Enlightenment,* trans. Fritz C. A. Koelln and James P. Pettegrove. Princeton, N.J.: Princeton University Press.

Cleave, T. L., and Campbell, G. D. 1966. *Diabetes, Coronary Thrombosis and the Saccharine Disease.* Bristol: Wright.

Cochrane, A. L. 1972. *Effectiveness and Efficiency: Random Reflections on Health Services.* London: Oxford University Press.

Crick, Francis. 1967. *Of Molecules and Men.* Seattle: University of Washington Press.

De Bono, Edward. 1983. *The Mechanism of Mind.* New York: Penguin Books.

————. 1972. *Po: Beyond Yes and No.* Middlesex, England: Penguin Books.

Descartes, René. 1927. *Selections,* ed. R. M. Eaton. New York: Charles Scribner and Sons.

Dickey, Lawrence D., ed. 1976. *Clinical Ecology.* Springfield, Ill.: Thomas.

Dobzhansky, Theodosius. 1964. *Mankind Evolving: The Evolution of the Human Species.* New Haven: Yale University Press.

Dodge, A. W., and Martin, R. W. 1970. *Social Stress and Illness.* South Bend, Ind.: University of Notre Dame Press.

*Dorland's Illustrated Medical Dictionary,* 25th ed. 1978. New York: W. B. Saunders.

Dossey, Larry. 1982. *Space, Time and Medicine.* Boston: Shambhala.

Dubos, René. 1959. *The Mirage of Health.* New York: Harper.

————. 1968. *Man, Medicine and Environment.* London: Pall Mall Press.

Dubos, René; Pines, Maya; et al. 1965. *Health and Disease.* New York: Time-Life Books.

Elsasser, W. M. 1957. *The Physical Foundations of Biology.* New York: Pergamon Press.

————. 1966. *Atom and Organism.* Princeton, N.J.: Princeton University Press.

Farb, Peter, et al. 1969. *Ecology.* New York: Time-Life Books.

Foucault, M. 1972. *Naissance de la clinique: Une archéologie du regard médical.* Paris: Presse Université de France.

Fox, B. H., and Newbury, B. H., eds. 1984. *Impact of Psychoendocrine Systems in Cancer and Immunity.* Lewiston, N.Y.: C. J. Hogrefe.

Freiherr, Gregory. 1983. *The Seeds of Artificial Intelligence: SUMEX-AIM.* Bethesda, Md.: U.S. Department of Health, Education, and Welfare, National Institutes of Health.

Friedman, Meyer. 1974. *Type A Behavior and Your Heart.* New York: Alfred A. Knopf.

Friedman, Meyer, and Ulmer, Diane. 1984. *Treating Type A Behavior and Your Heart*. New York: Alfred A. Knopf.

Gardner, Martin. 1983. *Wheels, Life, and Other Amusements*. New York: W. H. Freeman.

Gatlin, Lila. 1972. *Information Theory and the Living System*. New York: Columbia University Press.

Glandsdorff, P., and Prigogine, I. 1971. *Thermodynamic Theory of Structure, Stability, and Fluctuations*. New York: John Wiley.

Grossinger, Richard. 1980. *Planet Medicine: From Stone Age Shamanism to Post-Industrial Healing*. Garden City, N.Y.: Anchor Press.

Harding, Sandra. 1986. *The Science Question in Feminism*. Ithaca, N.Y.: Cornell University Press.

Heisenberg, Werner. 1969. *Physics and Philosophy*. New York: Harper and Row.

Hempel, Carl G. 1966. *Philosophy of Natural Science*. Englewood Cliffs, N.J.: Prentice-Hall.

Himmelfarb, Gertrude. 1959. *Darwin and the Darwinian Revolution*. New York: Norton.

Hofstadter, Douglas. 1980. *Gödel, Escher, Bach*. New York: Vintage Books.

———. 1985. *Meta-Magical Themas*. New York: Basic Books.

Hull, David L. 1974. *Philosophy of Biological Science*. Englewood Cliffs, N.J.: Prentice-Hall.

Jencks, Christopher, and Reisman, David. 1968. *The Academic Revolution*. Garden City, N.Y.: Doubleday.

Jenkins, C. D.; Zyzanski, S. J.; and Rosenman, R. H. 1979. *Jenkins Activity Survey Manual*. New York: Psychological Corporation.

Josephson, Eric, and Mary Josephson, eds. 1962. *Man Alone: Alienation in Modern Society*. New York: Dell.

Kaplan, Abraham. 1964. *The Conduct of Inquiry*. Scranton: Chandler.

King, Lester B. 1982. *Medical Thinking: A Historical Preface*. Princeton, N.J.: Princeton University Press.

Kuhn, Thomas S. 1962. *The Structure of Scientific Revolution*. Chicago: University of Chicago Press.

———. 1970. *The Structure of Scientific Revolutions*, 2nd ed. Chicago: University of Chicago Press.

LaPatra, Jack. 1978. *Healing*. New York: McGraw-Hill.

Laszlo, Ervin. 1972a. *Introduction to Systems Philosophy*. New York: Harper and Row.

———. 1972b. *The Systems View of the World*. New York: George Braziller.

———. 1974. *A Strategy for the Future: The Systems Approach to World Order*. New York: George Braziller.

Lee, D.H.K., and Kotin, P., eds. 1972. *Multiple Factors in the Causation of Environmentally Induced Disease*. New York: Academic Press.

Lee, Russell. 1965. *The Physicians*. Chicago: Time-Life Books.

Locke, S., and Colligan, D. 1986. *The Healer Within: The New Medicine of Mind and Body*. New York: E. P. Dutton.

Lovelock, James E. 1979. *Gaia*. Oxford University Press.

Lynch, James J. 1985. *The Language of the Heart*. New York: Basic Books.

McKeown, Thomas. 1979. *The Role of Medicine: Dream, Mirage, or Nemesis*. Princeton, N.J.: Princeton University Press.

McLuhan, Marshall. 1969. *Counterblast*. New York: Harcourt.
Margalef, Ramón. 1968. *Perspectives in Ecological Theory*. Chicago: University of Chicago Press.
Markley, O. W., et al. 1974. *Changing Images of Man*. Menlo Park, Calif.: Stanford Research Institute.
Marti-Ibañez, Felix. 1961. *A Prelude to Medical History*. New York: M.D. Publications.
Monod, Jacques. 1972. *Chance and Necessity*. New York: Vintage Books.
Moore, Ruth. 1964. *Evolution*. New York: Time-Life Books.
Nagel, Ernest. 1961. *The Structure of Science*. New York: Harcourt, Brace, World.
Naisbett, John. 1984. *Megatrends*. New York: Warner Books.
Nicolis, G., and Prigogine, I. 1977. *Self-Organization in Non-Equilibrium Systems*. New York: John Wiley.
Pelletier, Kenneth. 1979. *Holistic Medicine*. San Francisco: Delacorte Press/ S. Lawrence.
———. 1977. *Mind as Healer, Mind as Slayer*. New York: Dell.
Pepper, Stephen. 1959. *World Hypothesis*. New York: Open Court Press.
Pirsig, Robert M. 1974. *Zen and Art of Motorcycle Maintenance*. New York: Bantam Books.
Prigogine, I., and Stengers, I. 1984. *Order Out of Chaos: Man's New Dialogue with Nature*. New York: Bantam Books.
Randall, John Herman Jr. 1940. *The Making of the Modern Mind*. Boston: Houghton Mifflin.
Reiser, Stanley J. 1978a. *Medicine and the Reign of Technology*. New York: Cambridge University Press.
Rosenberg, Jay. 1974. *Linguistic Representation*. Boston: Reidel.
Rudner, Richard. 1966. *Philosophy of the Social Sciences*. Englewood Cliffs, N.J.: Prentice-Hall.
Russell, Bertrand. 1948. *Human Knowledge: Its Scope and Limits*. New York: Simon and Schuster.
Russell, E. S. 1936. *The Interpretation of Development and Heredity*. Oxford: Oxford University Press.
Segerberg, Osborne. 1974. *The Immortality Factor*. New York: E. P. Dutton.
Selye, Hans. 1956. *The Stress of Life*. New York: McGraw-Hill.
———. 1974. *Stress without Distress*. New York: E. P. Dutton.
Simeons, A.J.W. 1960. *Man's Presumptuous Brain*. New York: E. P. Dutton.
Slater, Phillip. 1977. *The Wayward Gate*. Boston: Beacon Press.
Sontag, Susan. 1979. *Illness as Metaphor*. New York: Random House.
Starr, Paul. 1983. *The Social Transformation of American Medicine*. New York: Basic Books.
*Stedman's Medical Dictionary*, 22nd ed. 1972.
Teilhard de Chardin, Pierre. 1959. *The Phenomenon of Man*. New York: Harper & Bros.
Thomas, Lewis. 1979. *The Medusa and the Snail*. New York: Viking.
Toulmin, Stephen. 1953. *The Philosophy of Science*. New York: Harper & Row.
———. 1961. *Foresight and Understanding*. New York: Harper & Row.
U.S. Department of Health, Education, and Welfare. 1975. *Forward Plan for Health*. Washington, D.C.: Government Printing Office.

Waddington, Conrad. 1975. *The Evolution of an Evolutionist.* Edinburgh: Edinburgh University Press.
Wechsler, Henry, et al. 1982. *The Horizons of Health.* Cambridge: Harvard University Press.
Weil, Andrew. 1972. *The Natural Mind.* New York: Houghton-Mifflin.
Weiss, Paul, et al., eds. 1971. *Hierarchically Ordered Systems in Theory and Practice.* New York: Hafner.
Weiss, S. M., et al., eds. 1981. *Perspectives on Behavioral Medicine.* New York: Academic Press.
Wheeler, John A., et al. 1973. *Gravitation.* San Francisco: W. F. Freeman.
Wigner, Eugene. 1967. *Symmetries and Reflections.* Bloomington: Indiana University Press.
Wolfe, Tom. 1980. *The Right Stuff.* New York: Bantam.
Woolridge, P.S., et al. 1968. *Behavioral Science, Social Practice and the Nursing Profession.* Cleveland: Case Western Reserve University Press.


ARTICLES
Achterberg, J., and Lawlis, G. F. 1979. "A Canonical Analysis of Blood Chemistry Variables Related to Psychological Measures of Cancer Patients." *Multivariate Experimental Clinical Research* 4 (nos. 1 & 2): 1–10.
———. 1981. "Imagery and Terminal Care: The Therapist as Shaman." In *Behavior Therapy in Terminal Care,* ed. D. Sobel. Cambridge, Mass.: Ballinger.
Ader, R. 1976. "Conditioned Adrenocortical Steroid Elevations in the Rat." *Journal of Comparative Physiology and Psychology* 90: 1156–1163.
———. 1977. "A Note on the Role of Olfaction in Taste Aversion Learning." *Bulletin of the Psychonomic Society* 10: 402–404.
———. 1981. Preface to *Psychneuroimmunology,* ed. R. Ader and N. Cohen. New York: Academic Press.
Ader, R., and Cohen, N. 1975. "Behaviorally Conditioning Immunosuppression." *Psychosomatic Medicine* 37: 333–340.
———. 1981. "Conditioned Immunopharmacologic Responses." In *Psychoneuroimmunology,* ed. R. Ader and N. Cohen. New York: Academic Press.
———. 1982. "Behaviorally Conditioning Immunosuppression and Murine Systemic Lupus Erythematosus." *Science* 215: 1534–1536.
Ader, R.; Cohen, N.; and Grota, L. J. 1979. "Adrenal Involvement in Conditioning Immunosuppression." *International Journal of Immunopharmacology* 1: 145–145.
Adler, Rolf H. 1985. Letter to the Editor. *New England Journal of Medicine* 313 (November 21): 1358.
Anderson, Alan. 1982. "How the Mind Heals." *Psychology Today* (December).
Angell, Marcia. 1985a. "Disease as a Reflection of the Psyche." *New England Journal of Medicine* 312 (June 13): 1570–1572.
———. 1985b. "Reply." *New England Journal of Medicine* 313: 1359.
Ashby, W. Ross. 1962. "Principles of the Self-Organizing System." In *Principles of Self-Organization,* ed. Foerster and Zoph. New York: Barnes & Noble.
Bailar, John C., and Smith, Elaine M. 1986. "Progress against Cancer." *New England Journal of Medicine* 314(19):1225–1232.

Beard, Charles. 1932. Foreword to J. B. Bury, *The Idea of Progress*. New York: Dover.

Beckner, Morton O. 1972. "Biology." In *The Encyclopedia of Philosophy*, reprint ed. New York: Macmillan Publishing Co.

Beecher, Henry K. 1955. "The Powerful Placebo." *Journal of the American Medical Association* 159.

————. 1960. "Increased Stress and Effectiveness of Placebos with Increased Stress." *Science* 132.

————. 1961. "Surgery as Placebo: A Quantitative Study of Bias," *Journal of the American Medical Association* 176: 1102–1107.

Behar, M. 1974. "A Deadly Combination." *World Health*, February–March.

Benson, Herbert, and MacCallie, D. 1979. "Angina Pectoris and the Placebo Effect." *New England Journal of Medicine* 299.

Benson, H.; Alexander, S.; and Feldman, C. L. 1975. "Decreased Premature Ventricular Contractions through the Use of Relaxation Response in Patients with Stable Ischemic Heart Disease." *Lancet* 2: 380–382.

Berliner, Robert. 1977. "Medical Education and Scholarly Inquiry." In *Beyond Tomorrow: Trends and Prospects in Medical Science*, Seventy-fifth Anniversary Conference. New York: Rockefeller University Press.

Bingham, Roger. 1980. "The Maverick and the Earth Goddess." *Science Digest*, November–December.

Blum, Robert L. 1982. "Discovery, Confirmation, and Incorporation of Causal Relationships from a Large Time-Oriented Clinical Data Base: The RX Project." *Computers and Biomedical Research* 15.

Blumenthal, J. A.; Williams, R. B.; Kong, Y.; Schonberg, S. M.; and Thompson, L. W. 1978. "Type A Behavior Pattern and Coronary Atherosclerosis." *Circulation* 58.

Brody, Howard. 1973. "The Systems View of Man: Implications for Medicine, Science, and Ethics." *Perspectives in Biology and Medicine* 11, no. 1 (Autumn).

Brody, Howard, and Sobel, David S. 1980. "A Systems View of Health and Disease." *Holistic Health Review* 3, no. 3 (Spring).

Brody, J. 1974. "Philosophy of Science." *Encyclopaedia Brittanica*, 15th ed. Chicago: Encyclopaedia Britannica.

Brooks, Harvey. 1980. "Technology, Evolution, and Purpose." *Daedalus* 109 (Winter).

Cairns, J. 1985. "The Treatment of Diseases and the War against Cancer." *Scientific American* 253(5): 51–59.

Case, R. B.; Heller, S. S.; Case, N. B.; et al. 1985. "Type A Behavior and Survival After Acute Myocardial Infarction." *New England Journal of Medicine* 312: 737–741.

Cassileth, Barrie R. 1985. "Reply." *New England Journal of Medicine* 313: 1356.

Cassileth, Barrie R.; Lusk, E. J.; et al. 1985. "Psychosocial Correlates of Survival in Advanced Malignant Disease?" *New England Journal of Medicine* 312: 1551–1555.

"Coronary-Prone Behavior and Coronary Heart Disease: A Critical Review." 1981. *Circulation* 63: 1199–1215.

Cunningham, Alastair J. 1981. "Mind, Body, and Immune Response." In *Psychoneuroimmunology*, ed. R. Ader and N. Cohen. New York: Academic Press.

Dembroski, T. M., and MacDougall, J. M. In press. "Beyond Global Type A. Relation of Paralinguistic Attributes, Hostility, and Anger in Coronary Heart Disease." In *Stress and Coping*, ed. T. Field, P. McCabe, and N. Schneiderman. Hillsdale, N.J.: Erlebaum.

Department of Health and Social Security. 1971. *On the State of Public Health, The Annual Report of the Chief Medical Officer . . . for the Year 1970.* London: H.M.S.O.

d'Espagnat, Bernard. 1979. "The Quantum Theory and Reality." *Scientific American* 241 (November).

Dinnerstein, A. J., and Halm, J. 1970. "Modification of Placebo Effects by Means of Drugs: Effects of Aspirin and Placebos on Self-Rated Moods." *Journal of Abnormal Psychology* 75, no. 3: 308–314.

Dubos, René. 1965. "Hippocrates and Modern Dress," *Proceedings of the Institute of Medicine of Chicago* 25, no. 9 (May): 242–251.

———. 1971. "The Diseases of Civilization." In *Mainstreams of Medicine,* ed. L. S. King. Austin: University of Texas Press.

Duda, Richard O., and Shortliffe, Edward H. 1983. "Expert Systems Research." *Science* 220 (April 15).

Edelman, Gerald M. 1977. "Scientific Quests and Political Principles in the Current Crises of Discovery and Government." In *Beyond Tomorrow: Trends and Prospects in Medical Science,* Seventy-fifth Anniversary Conference. New York: Rockefeller University Press.

Edelstyn, G. A., and MacRae, K. D. 1975. "Breast Cancer: Mistaken Concepts, Therapeutic Consequences, and Future Implications." *Journal of the Irish Medical Association* 68 (January 25).

Eisenberg, Leon. 1977. "Psychiatry and Society." *New England Journal of Medicine,* April 21.

"Emotion and Immunity," 1985. *The Lancet* II: 133–134.

Engel, George L. 1960. "A Unified Concept of Health and Disease." In *Perspectives in Biology and Medicine* 3.

———. 1967. "The Concept of Psychosomatic Disorder," *Journal of Psychosomatic Research* 11.

———. 1974. "The Psychosomatic Approach to Individual Susceptibility to Disease." *Gastroenterology* 67: 1085–1093.

———. 1977a. "The Care of the Patient: Art or Science," *Johns Hopkins Medical Journal* 140.

———. 1977b. "The Need for a New Medical Model: A Challenge for Biomedicine," *Science* 196 (April 8).

———. 1978. "The Biopsychosocial Model and the Education of Health Professionals." *Annals of the New York Academy of Sciences.*

———. 1981. "The Clinical Application of the Biopsychosocial Model," *Journal of Medicine and Philosophy,* 6, no. 2 (May).

———. 1985. "Spontaneous Bleeding on Anniversaries: The Biopsychosocial Model Applied to a Personal Illness Experience." AOA Lecture, University of Arizona.

Evans, Alfred S. 1978. "Causation and Disease: A Chronological Journey." *American Journal of Epidemiology* 108, no. 4 (October).

Fields, Howard L. 1978. "Secrets of the Placebo." *Psychology Today,* November.

Fortney, Mary T. 1984. "Cutting the Risk of Heart Attack by Changing Intense Behavior." *Peninsula Times* (California), August 7.

Fox, Bernard. 1978. "Premorbid Psychological Factors as Related to Cancer Incidence." *Journal of Behavioral Medicine* 1: 45–133.

Fox, B. H. 1983. "Current Theory of Psychogenic Effects on Cancer Incidence and Prognosis." *Journal of Psychosoc. Oncol.* 1, no. 1: 17–31.

———. 1984. "Psychosocial Factors in Cancer Risk and Survival: Current State of Information." Presented at the Arthur B. Sutherland Memorial Award Lecture of the Memorial Sloan-Kettering Cancer Center, New York, September 17–19.

Friedman, Meyer, et al. 1984. "Alteration of Type A Behavior and Reduction in Cardiac Recurrence in Postmyocardial Infarction Patients." *American Heart Journal* 108, no. 2 (August).

———. 1986. "Alteration of Type A Behavior and Its Effects on Cardiac Recurrence in Postmyocardial Infarction Patients." *American Heart Journal* 112(4): 653–665.

Friedman, M., and Rosenman, R. H. 1959. "Association of Specific Overt Behavior Pattern with Blood and Cardiovascular Findings." *Journal of the American Medical Association* 169: 1286–1295.

———. 1971. "Type A Behavior Pattern: Its Association with Coronary Heart Disease." *Annals of Clinical Research* 3: 300–312.

———, et al. 1968. "The Relationship of Behavior Pattern A to the State of the Coronary Vasculature: A Study of Fifty-one Autopsy Subjects." *Journal of the American Medical Association* 44: 525–537.

Galimore, R. G., and Turner, J. L. 1977. "Contemporary Studies of Placebo Phenomena." In *Psychopharmacology in the Practice of Medicine*, ed. M. E. Jarvik. New York: Appleton-Century-Crofts.

Gerjudy, Edward. 1981. "Quantum Mechanics," *McGraw-Hill Encyclopedia of Science and Technology*, 4th ed. New York: McGraw-Hill.

Goleman, Daniel. 1980. "Matter over Mind: Interview with Solomon Snyder," *Psychology Today*, June.

———. 1985. "Strong Emotional Response to Disease May Bolster Patient's Immune System." *New York Times*, October 22 and 29.

"Good Attitude Called Aid to Ease Ills, but Not a Cure." 1984. *Evening Bulletin*, (Providence, R.I., United Press International), February 21.

Good, Robert A. 1981. "Foreword: Interactions of the Body's Major Networks." In *Psychoneuroimmunology*, ed. R. Ader and N. Cohen. New York: Academic Press.

Goodfield, June. 1977. "Humanity in Science: A Perspective and a Plea." *Science*. Vol. 198 (Nov. 11): 580–585.

Gordon, James S. 1980. "The Paradigm of Holistic Medicine." In *Health for the Whole Person*. Boulder: Westview Press.

Graham, F. K., and Clifton, R. K. 1966. "Heart Rate Changes as a Component of the Orienting Response." *Psychological Bulletin* 65: 305–320.

Graubard, S. R. 1977. Preface to "Doing Better and Feeling Worse: Health in the United States." *Daedalus* 106, no. 1 (Winter): v–vi.

Greer, S.; Morris, T., and Pettingale, K. W. 1979. "Psychological Response to Breast Cancer: Effect on Outcome." *The Lancet* Vol. II (Oct. 13): 785–787.

Hales, Dianne. 1981. "Psycho-immunity." *Science Digest*, November.

Hamburg, D. A. 1983. "Frontiers of Research in Neurobiology." *Science* 222: 969.

Hannay, Bruce N., and McGinn, Robert E. 1980. "The Anatomy of Modern Technology: Prolegomenon to an Improved Public Policy for the Social Management of Technology." *Daedalus* 109 (Winter).

Harding, Sandra. 1978. "Knowledge, Technology, and Social Relations." *Journal of Medicine and Philosophy* 3, no. 4 (December): 346–358.

Hastings, Arthur C., et al. 1980. "Preface." In *Health for the Whole Person*. Boulder: Westview Press.

Hauser, P. M., et al. 1973. "Health Statistics Today and Tomorrow." *American Journal of Public Health* 63(10): 890–910.

Haynes, S. G.; Feinleib, M; and Kannel, W. B. 1980. "The Relationship of Psychosocial Factors to Coronary Heart Disease in the Framington Study. III. Eight Year Incidence of Coronary Heart Disease." *American Journal of Epidemiology* 111.

Hempel, Carl G. 1959. "The Logic of Functional Analysis." In *Symposium on Sociological Theory*, ed. Llewellyn Gross. New York: Harper and Row.

Hofstadter, Laura. 1985. "Symposium Discusses Strategies for Gene Therapy." Stanford University Medical Center News Bureau, Stanford, Calif. (May).

Holden, Constance. 1980. "Behavioral Medicine: An Emergent Field." *Science* 209 (July 25).

Holmes, H. R. 1976. *Hospital Practice* 11:11.

Holmes, Thomas H. 1980. "Stress: The New Etiology." In *Health for the Whole Person*, ed. A. C. Hastings et al. Boulder: Westview Press.

Holmes, Thomas H., and Masuda, M. 1973. "Life Changes and Illness Susceptibility." In *Symposium on Separation and Depression*, ed. J. P. Scott and E. C. Sanay. Washington, D.C.: AAAS.

Holmes, Thomas H., and Rahe, R. H. 1967. "The Social Readjustment Rating Scale." *Journal of Psychosomatic Research* 11.

Hull, David L. 1981. "Reduction and Genetics." *Journal of Medicine and Philosophy* 6, no. 2 (May).

Hutten, E. H. 1975. *Information, Explanation and Meaning.* (in Italian). Rome: Ermando.

Inglefinger, F. J. 1977. Editorial. *New England Journal of Medicine* 297.

———. 1978. "Medicine: Meritorious or Meretricious?" *Science* 200 (May 26).

Jenkins, C. D. 1976. "Recent Evidence Supporting Psychologic and Social Risk Factors." *New England Journal of Medicine* 294: 987–994, 1033–1038.

Jenkins, C. D.; Rosenman, R. H.; and Zyzanski, S. J. 1974. "Prediction of Clinical Coronary Heart Disease by a Test for the Coronary-Prone Behavior Pattern." *New England Journal of Medicine* 290: 1271–1275.

Kappas, Attallah. 1977. "Considerations on the Future of Medical Research." In *Beyond Tomorrow*. New York: Rockefeller University.

Keller, S. E.; Weiss, J. M.; and Schleifer, S. J.; et al. 1983. "Stress-Induced Suppression of Immunity in Adrenalectomized Rats." *Science* 221: 1301–1304.

Kelman, Sander. 1980. "Social Organization and the Meaning of Health." *Journal of Medicine and Philosophy* 5, no. 2.

King, Lester S. 1983. "Germ Theory and Its Influence." *Journal of the American Medical Association* 249, no. 6 (February 11): 794–798.

Kleinman, Arthur; Eisenberg, Leon; and Good, Byron. 1978. "Culture, Illness, and Care." *Annals of Internal Medicine* 88 (February).

Knowles, John H. 1977. Introduction to "Doing Better and Feeling Worse: Health in the United States." *Daedalus* 106, no. 1 (Winter): 1–9.

Kunz, John C. 1984. "Computer Assisted Decision Making in Medicine." *Journal of Medicine and Philosophy* 9, no. 2 (May).

LaLonde, M. 1975. *A New Perspective on the Health of Canadians.* Ottawa: Minister of National Health and Welfare Information.

Laudenslager, M. L.; Ryan, S. M.; et al. 1983. "Coping and Immunosuppression: Inescapable but Not Escapable Shock Suppresses Lymphocyte Proliferation." *Science* 221: 568–570.

Leach, Edmund. 1973. "Man, the Scientist." In *Peoples of the Earth,* ed. E. Evans-Pritchard. Danbury Press.

LeShan, Lawrence. 1966. "An Emotional Life-History Pattern Associated with Neoplastic Disease." *Annals of New York Academy of Sciences* 125, no. 3.

Levine, J. D. et al. 1978. "The Mechanism of Placebo Analgesia." *The Lancet,* September 23.

Locke, Steven, ed. 1985. *Mind and Immunity.* New York: Praeger: Institute for the Advancement of Health.

Locke, S. E.; Kraus, L.; Lesserman, J.; et al. 1984. "Life Change Stress, Psychiatric Symptoms, and Natural Killer Cell Activity." *Psychosomatic Medicine* 46: 441–453.

Long, J. M. 1982. "The Effect of Status on Blood Pressure during Verbal Communication." *Behavioral Medicine* 5(2): 165–172.

Lown, B.; Temte, J. V.; Reich, P.; et al. 1976. "Basis for Recurring Ventricular Fibrillation in the Absence of Coronary Heart Disease and Its Management." *New England Journal of Medicine* 294: 623–629.

Lynch, James J., et al. 1974. "The Effects of Human Contact on Cardiac Arrhythmia in Coronary Care Patients." *Journal of Nervous and Mental Disease* 158: 88–99.

McKeown, Thomas. 1971. "A Historical Appraisal of the Medical Task." In *Medical History and Medical Care,* ed. G. McLochlan and T. McKeown. London: Oxford University Press.

McWhinney, Ian R. 1978. "Medical Knowledge and the Rise of Technology." *Journal of Medicine and Philosophy* 3, no. 4 (December).

Margulis, L., and Lovelock, J. E. 1974. "Biological Modulation of the Earth's Atmosphere." *Icarus* 21.

Marney, M., and Schmidt, P. F. 1976. "Evolution of Scientific Method." In *Evolution and Consciousness,* ed. E. Jantsch and C. Waddington. Reading, Mass.: Addison-Wesley.

Maruyama, Magorah. 1963. "The Second Cybernetics: Deviation-Amplifying Mutual Causal Processes." *American Scientist* 51 (June).

Maull, Nancy. 1981. "The Practical Science of Medicine," *Journal of Medicine and Philosophy* 6 (May).

May, Jacques. 1968. "The Ecology of Human Disease." In *Environments of Man,* ed. J. Bresler. Reading, Mass.: Addison-Wesley.

Medawar, Peter. 1977. "Biology." In *The Harper Dictionary of Modern Thought*, ed. Alan Bullock and Oliver Stallybrass. New York: Harper and Row.

Miller, Neal E., et al. 1970. "Learned Modifications of Autonomic Functions: A Review and Some New Data." *Circulation Research* 27, supplement 1: 27–32.

Moore, Francis D. 1986. Book Review of *The Healer Within: The New Medicine of Mind and Body. New England Journal of Medicine* 315 (September 18): 772.

Morowitz, Harold J. 1980. "Rediscovering the Mind." *Psychology Today* 14 (August).

———. 1983. "Two Views of Life." *Science 83* (January–February).

Morris, Greer S., and Pettingale, K. W. 1979. "Psychological Response to Breast Cancer: Effect on Outcome." *The Lancet* 2: 785–787.

Morrison, Elting. 1980. "The Uncertain Relation." *Daedalus* 109 (Winter).

Munson, Ronald. 1981. "Why Medicine Cannot Be a Science." *Journal of Medicine and Philosophy* 6 (May).

Murphy, Edmund A. 1978. "Some Epistemological Aspects of the Model in Medicine." *Journal of Medicine and Philosophy* (December).

Odum, Eugene. 1977. "The Emergence of Ecology as a New Integrative Discipline." *Science* 95 (March 24): 4284.

Pepper, G. M., and Krieger, D. T. 1984. "Hypothalamic-Pituitary-Adrenal Abnormalities in Depression: Their Possible Relation to Central Mechanisms Regulating ACTH Release." In *Neurobiology of Mood Disorders*, ed. R. M. Post and J. C. Ballenger. Baltimore: Williams and Wilkins, 245–270.

Pepper, Stephen. 1972. "Systems Philosophy as a World Hypothesis," *Philosophy and Phenomenological Research* (June).

Pettingale, K. W.; Morris, T.; Greer, S.; and Haybittle, J. L. 1985. "Mental Attitudes to Cancer: An Additional Prognostic Factor." *The Lancet* Vol. I (March 30): 750.

Pierce, Charles Sanders. 1960. "The Fixation of Belief" (1931). In *The American Pragmatists*, ed. M. R. Kronovitz et al. Cleveland: World Publishing Co.

Plaut, S. Michael, and Friedman, Stanford B. 1981. "Psychosocial Factors in Infectious Disease." In *Psychoneuroimmunology*, ed. R. Ader and N. Cohen. New York: Academic Press.

Powell, L. H.; Friedman, M.; et al. 1984. "Can the Type A Behavior Pattern Be Altered after Myocardial Infarction? A Second Year Report from the Recurrent Coronary Prevention Project." *Psychosomatic Medicine* 46: 293–298.

Powles, John. 1973. "On the Limitations of Modern Medicine." In *Science, Medicine and Man*, vol. 1. London: Pergamon Press.

Prigogine, Ilya. 1976. "Order through Fluctuation: Self-Organization and Social System." In *Evolution and Consciousness*, ed. E. Jantsch and C. Waddington. Reading, Mass.: Addison-Wesley.

———. 1978. "Time, Structure, and Fluctuation." *Science* 201 (September 1).

———. 1979. "Interview." In *A Question of Physics: Conversations in Physics and Biology*, ed. P. Buckley and F. D. Peat. Toronto: University of Toronto Press.

———. 1984. "Only an Illusion." *The Tanner Lectures on Human Values*, ed. Sterling M. McMurrin. London: Cambridge University Press.

Rahe, R. H. 1973. "Subjects' Recent Life Changes and Their Near-Future Illness Reports." *Annals of Clinical Research* 4.

Rahe, R. H., and Romo, M. 1974. "Recent Life Changes and the Onset of

Myocardial Infarction and Coronary Death in Helsinki." In *Less Stress and Illness*, ed. R. H. Rahe et al. Springfield, Ill.: Charles C. Thomas.

Rapoport, Anatol. 1968. Foreword to *Modern Systems Research for the Behavioral Scientist*, ed. Walter Buckley. Chicago: Aldine.

Reiser, Stanley Joel. 1978*b*. "The Decline of the Clinical Dialogue." *Journal of Medicine and Philosophy* 3, no. 4 (December).

Review Panel on Coronary-Prone Behavior and Coronary Heart Disease. 1981. "Coronary-Prone Behavior and Coronary Heart Disease: A Critical Review." *Circulation* 63: 1199–1215.

Risenberg, Donald E. 1986. "Can Mind Affect Body Defenses against Disease? Nascent Specialty Offers a Host of Tantalizing Clues." *Journal of the American Medical Association* 256 (July 18): 313–317.

Rose, Geoffrey. 1972. "Epidemiology of Ischaemic Heart Disease." *British Journal of Hospital Medicine* 7: 122.

Rosenman, R. H., et al. 1975. "Coronary Heart Disease in the Experience of 8½ Years." *Journal of the American Medical Association* 233, no. 8.

Rosenman, R. H.; Friedman, M.; et al. 1967. "Recurring and Fatal Myocardial Infarction in the Western Collaborative Group Study." *American Journal of Cardiology* 19: 771–782.

Sadegh-Zadeh, Kazem. 1982. "Therapeuticum and Therapy: A Commentary on Lindahl and Lindwall's Skepticism." *Metamedicine* 3.

Schaffner, Kenneth F. 1980. "Theory Structure in the Biomedical Sciences." *Journal of Medicine and Philosophy* (March).

Schleifer, S. J.; Keller, S. E.; et al. 1983. "Suppression of Lymphocyte Stimulation Following Bereavement." *Journal of the American Medical Association* 250: 374–377.

Seldin, Donald W. 1977. "The Medical Model: Biomedical Science as the Basis of Medicine." In *Beyond Tomorrow: Trends and Prospects in Medical Science*. Seventy-fifth Anniversary Conference. New York: Rockefeller University.

Seliger, Susan. 1978. "Loneliness, Stress and Diet Are Killers." *Detroit Free Press*, September 11, pp. 1B–3B.

Shapiro, Arthur K. 1960. "A Contribution to the History of the Placebo Effect." *Behavioral Science* 5.

———. 1964. "Factors Contributing to the Placebo Effect." *American Journal of Psychotherapy*, supplement 1, 18: 73–88.

———. 1968. "The Placebo Response." In *Modern Perspectives in World Psychiatry*, ed. J. G. Howells. Edinburgh: Oliver and Boyd.

Shekelle, R. B.; Gale, M.; Ostfeld, A. M.; and Paul, O. 1983. "Hostility, Risk of Coronary Heart Disease, and Mortality." *Psychosomatic Medicine* 45: 109–114.

Shekelle, R.; Hulley, S.; Neaton, J.; et al. 1983. "Type A Behavior and Risk of Coronary Death in WRFIT." Presented at the 23rd Annual Conference on Cardiovascular Disease Epidemiology. San Diego, Calif., March 3–5.

Shekelle, R. B.; Raynor, W. J. Jr.; Ostfeld, A. M.; et al. 1981. "Psychological Depression and 17-Year Risk of Death from Cancer." *Psychosomatic Medicine* 43: 117–125.

Sinsheimer, Robert L. 1978. "The Presumption of Science." *Daedalus* 107 (Spring).

Spaeth, George L., and Barber, G. Winston. 1980. "Homocystinuria and the Passing of the One Gene–One Enzyme Concept of Disease." *Journal of Medicine and Philosophy* 5, no. 1 (March).

Smith, Adam. 1980. "Mind, Body and Laughter: Can a Change of Attitude Cure Dread Diseases?" *Esquire*, February.

Smith, Richard G., et al. 1985. "Psychologic Modulation of the Human Immune Response to Varicella Zoster." *Archives of Internal Medicine* 145: 2110–2112.

Stark, J. E. 1975. "Therapeutics." *Encyclopaedia Britannica*, vol. 18. Chicago: Encyclopaedia Britannica.

Stone, Peter H. 1982. "The Bomb: The Last Epidemic." *Atlantic*, February.

Temoshok, Lydia. 1983. "Emotion, Adaptation and Disease: A Multidimensional Theory." In *Emotions in Health and Illness: Theoretical and Research Foundations*, ed. L. Temoshok et al. New York: Grune & Stratton.

Temoshok, L.; Sagabiel, R. W.; and Sweet, D. W. 1984. "Psychosocial Factors Associated with Tumor-Host Response in Cutaneous Malignant Melanoma." Presented at the First International Conference on Neuroimmunomodulation. National Institutes of Health, Bethesda, Md., November 30.

Tessler, S. R. 1984. "Doctor's His Own Type A." *Detroit News*, October 11.

Thomas, Lewis. 1977. "Future Directions in Biomedical Research." In *Beyond Tomorrow: Trends and Prospects in Medical Science*. Seventy-fifth Anniversary Conference. New York: Rockefeller University.

Thomas, Susan A. 1986. "Steps in Transactional Psychophysiology Therapy." In *The Healing Heart: Psychological Intervention in Cardiovascular Disease*, ed. A. M. Razin. San Francisco: Jossey-Bass.

Todd, John W. 1974. "Practice of Medicine and Surgery." *Encyclopaedia Brittanica*, 15th ed., vol. 11. Chicago: Encyclopaedia Britannica.

Tolstoy, Leo. 1981. "The Death of Ivan Ilyich." Solotaroff, Lynn trans. New York: Bantam.

Tomkins, Gordon M. 1975. "The Metabolic Code." *Science* 189: 760–763.

Toufexis, Anastasia. 1981. "Taming the No. 1 Killer." *Time*, June 1, pp. 52–59.

Toulmin, Stephen. 1967. "Neuroscience and Human Understanding." In *The Neurosciences*, ed. Gardner C. Quarton et al. New York: Rockefeller University Press.

———. 1975. "Philosophy of Science." *Encyclopaedia Britannica*, vol. 16. Chicago: Encyclopaedia Britannica.

———. 1981. "The Emergence of Post-Modern Science." *Current Developments in the Arts and Sciences: The Great Ideas Today*. Chicago: Encyclopaedia Britannica.

Ulwelling, William. 1978. "The Medical Model of the Future." *Journal of Holistic Health* 3.

U.S. Department of HEW. 1975. *Forward Plan for Health*. FY 1977–1981. Washington, D.C.: GPO, 631–613/489.

Voukydis, P. C., and Forwand, S. A. 1977. "The Effect of Elicitation of the Relaxation Response in Patients with Intractable Ventricular Arrythmias." *Circulation* 56, Supplement 3.

Waldovsky, Aaron. 1977. "Doing Better and Feeling Worse: The Political Pathology of Health Policy." *Daedalus* 106:1 (Winter).

Wartofsky, Marx W. 1978. "Editorial." *Journal of Medicine and Philosophy* 3 (December).

Weiss, Paul. 1967. "1 + 1 ≠ 2." In *The Neurosciences*, ed. G. C. Quarton et al. New York: Rockefeller University Press.

Weissmann, Gerald. 1983. "Proust in Khaki." *Hospital Practice* 18, no. 6 (May).

Williams, R. B.; Lane, J. D.; Kuhn, C. M.; et al. 1982. "Type A Behavior and Elevated Physiological and Neuroendocrine Responses to Cognitive Tasks." *Science* 218.

Winner, Langdon. 1980. "Do Artifacts Have Politics?" *Daedalus* 109 (Winter).

Wolf, Stewart. 1950. "Effects of Suggestion and Conditioning on the Action of Chemical Agents in Human Subjects—The Pharmacology of Placebos." *Journal of Clinical Investigation* 29: 100–109.

———. 1959. "The Pharmacology of Placebos." *Pharmacological Review* 11: 689–704.

Wolff, Harold G. 1953. "Changes in Vulnerability of Tissue: An Aspect of Man's Response to Threat." *The National Institute of Health Annual Lectures*. U.S. Department of Health, Education and Welfare, Publication No. 388, pp. 38–71.

"The Year in Medicine." 1982. *Discover*, January.

Yunis, J. J., et al. 1981. "All Patients with Acute Non-Lymphocytic Leukemia May Have a Chromosomal Defect." *New England Journal of Medicine* 305, no. 3 (July 16): 135–139.

Zarin, Deborah A., and Parker, Stephen G. 1984. "Decision Analysis in Medical Decision Making." *Journal of Medicine and Philosophy* 9, no. 2 (May).

Zieger, D., and Hastings, A. 1980. "Annotated Bibliography." In *Health for the Whole Person*, ed. A. Hastings et al. Boulder, Colo.: Westview Press.

Zucker, Arthur. 1981. "Holism and Reductionism: A View from Genetics." *Journal of Medicine and Philosophy* 6, no. 2 (May).

# Index

Achterberg, J., 285, 286, 287, 289n
Ader, Robert, 115, 119, 121, 125,
    128n, 286, 287, 312
Adler, Rolf, 283, 284
American Rheumatism Association
    Medical Information System
    (ARAMIS), 253
Anderson, Alan, 87, 125, 126
Angell, Marcia, 242, 243, 248, 280,
    281, 283, 284
Aristotle, 185, 188, 291
Ashby, W. Ross, 201
Atherosclerosis, 220, 223, 227–228,
    240, 256–257, 258
Atomism, 44, 185

Bailar, John C., 310n
Bailey, H., 102n
Barber, G. W., 35–36, 56
Bateson, Gregory, 171
Beard, Charles 26
Beckner, Morton, 46
Behavioral conditioning, 125–129
Behavioral medicine, 86–87
Benson, Herbert, 91
Berg, Paul, 268, 290
Bernard, Claude, 37, 38, 171, 245
Bertalanffy, Ludwig von, 110, 160n,
    163n, 201, 203
Bingham, Roger, 171–172
Bio-active messages and programs,
    298–299
Biocultural medicine, 267–275
Biofeedback, 127, 128–130, 131,
    229–230, 231
Biogeochemistry, 169–174
Biomedical model, 29–43
    criticisms of, 137–138

disease in, 7, 29–36, 56–58, 61–62,
    138
first medical revolution and, 29–43
physics and, 144–151, 164–169
Biomedical paradigm, 11–12
Biomedical reductionism. See Reduc-
    tionism
Biomedical scientific method, logic of,
    62
Biomedicine:
    assumptions of, 6–8
    background of, 3–6, 23–28
    critique of, 77–83
    defined, 2
    hard science and, 62–66
    holistic medicine ("cure plus care"),
        and, 89, 104–106
    natural science and, 44–58
    philosophical foundations of, 44–71
    problems of, 4–5, 77–83
    reductionist argument and, 58–62
Biophysics, 26
Biopsychocultural medicine, 269, 291
Biotechnology, 4
Black, D. A. K., 95n
Blake, William, 45, 73, 278
Blum, Robert, 250–252, 253, 254, 263
Blumenthal, J. A., 263n
Blushing analogy, 289–293
Bohr, Niels, 146
Borelli, Giovanni, 178
Boyden, Stephen V., 102n
Brain chemistry, 64–71
Brody, Howard, 133
Bronowski, Jacob, xvii, 61
Brown, Barbara, 129–130, 229
Burnet, Macfarlane, 102n
Bury, J. B., 27